MEMORY AND THE DISSOLUTION OF THE MONASTERIES IN EARLY MODERN ENGLAND

The dissolution of the monasteries was recalled by individuals and communities alike as a seismic rupture in the religious, cultural, and socio-economic fabric of early modern England. It was also profoundly important in shaping contemporary historical consciousness, the topographical imagination, and local tradition. *Memory and the Dissolution* is a book about the dissolution of the monasteries after the dissolution. Harriet Lyon argues that our understanding of this historical moment is enriched by taking a long chronological view of the suppression, by exploring how it was remembered by those who witnessed it and how this memory evolved in subsequent generations. Exposing and repudiating the assumptions of a conventional historiography that has long been coloured by Henrician narratives and sources, this book reveals that the fall of the religious houses was remembered as one of the most profound and controversial transformations of the entire English Reformation.

HARRIET LYON is a Fellow of Christ's College, Cambridge. She has published articles in the *Historical Journal*, the *Sixteenth Century Journal*, and *Reformation*.

T0371249

CAMBRIDGE STUDIES IN EARLY MODERN BRITISH HISTORY

SERIES EDITORS

MICHAEL BRADDICK
Professor of History, University of Sheffield

ETHAN SHAGAN
Professor of History, University of California, Berkeley

ALEXANDRA SHEPARD
Professor of Gender History, University of Glasgow

ALEXANDRA WALSHAM
*Professor of Modern History, University of Cambridge, and Fellow
of Emmanuel College*

This is a series of monographs and studies covering many aspects of the history of
the British Isles between the late fifteenth century and the early eighteenth
century. It includes the work of established scholars and pioneering work by a
new generation of scholars. It includes both reviews and revisions of major topics
and books which open up new historical terrain or which reveal startling new
perspectives on familiar subjects. All the volumes set detailed research within
broader perspectives, and the books are intended for the use of students as well
as of their teachers.

For a list of titles in the series go to
www.cambridge.org/earlymodernbritishhistory

MEMORY AND THE DISSOLUTION OF THE MONASTERIES IN EARLY MODERN ENGLAND

HARRIET LYON

University of Cambridge

Shaftesbury Road, Cambridge CB2 8EA, United Kingdom

One Liberty Plaza, 20th Floor, New York, NY 10006, USA

477 Williamstown Road, Port Melbourne, VIC 3207, Australia

314–321, 3rd Floor, Plot 3, Splendor Forum, Jasola District Centre, New Delhi – 110025, India

103 Penang Road, #05–06/07, Visioncrest Commercial, Singapore 238467

Cambridge University Press is part of Cambridge University Press & Assessment, a department of the University of Cambridge.

We share the University's mission to contribute to society through the pursuit of education, learning and research at the highest international levels of excellence.

www.cambridge.org
Information on this title: www.cambridge.org/9781009014236

DOI: 10.1017/9781009029100

First published 2022
First paperback edition 2023

A catalogue record for this publication is available from the British Library

Library of Congress Cataloging-in-Publication data
NAMES: Lyon, Harriet, author.
TITLE: Memory and the dissolution of the monasteries in early modern England / Harriet Lyon, University of Cambridge.
DESCRIPTION: Cambridge, United Kingdom ; New York, NY, USA : Cambridge University Press, 2021. | Series: Cambridge studies in early modern british history | Includes bibliographical references and index.
IDENTIFIERS: LCCN 2021021811 (print) | LCCN 2021021812 (ebook) | ISBN 9781316516409 (hardback) | ISBN 9781009029100 (ebook)
SUBJECTS: LCSH: England – Church history – 16th century. | Monasteries – England – History – 16th century. | BISAC: HISTORY / Europe / Great Britain / General
CLASSIFICATION: LCC BR756 .L96 2021 (print) | LCC BR756 (ebook) | DDC 274.2–dc23
LC record available at https://lccn.loc.gov/2021021811
LC ebook record available at https://lccn.loc.gov/2021021812

ISBN   978-1-316-51640-9   Hardback
ISBN   978-1-009-01423-6   Paperback

For my parents

Contents

Figures

Acknowledgements

This book began life as a doctoral thesis, which I could not have undertaken without the generous financial support of the Arts and Humanities Research Council. I am delighted that a revised version of that thesis has now found a home with Cambridge University Press. My particular thanks to the series editors, especially Ethan Shagan and Michael Braddick, whose comments have made this a much better book, and to Liz Friend-Smith for guiding me through the publishing process so patiently.

The research process was aided considerably by the rich resources and wonderful staff of Cambridge University Library, especially the Rare Books Room, and Christ's College Library, Cambridge. I was also able to make several trips to other libraries and archives thanks to travel grants from Christ's College; the Faculty of History, University of Cambridge; and the Royal Historical Society. For sharing their expertise on these occasions, I am grateful to the staff of the Archives of the Duke of Northumberland, Alnwick Castle; the Bodleian Library, Oxford; the British Library, London; Cambridgeshire Archives; Canterbury Cathedral Archives; Devon Heritage Centre, Exeter; Durham University Library; and Exeter Cathedral Library.

I am fortunate to be part of a vibrant community of early modernists, both in Cambridge and further afield. I would especially like to thank John Morrill, who has been a constant source of advice and good cheer ever since he supervised me as an undergraduate, and Paul Cavill, who helped to shape the project at a critical early stage. My examiners, Arnold Hunt and Peter Marshall, helped me to think about the shape of the book and to see its central themes with greater clarity. The arguments of several chapters were first tested on conference and seminar audiences in Cambridge and York, at the Institute of Historical Research, London, and at meetings of the Renaissance Society of America in New Orleans and the Sixteenth Century Society in Vancouver and Bruges. I am grateful to all those who asked questions or offered comments on these occasions, as well as to the many friends and colleagues who have shared references or otherwise discussed the project with me. The footnotes testify to the magnitude of many of these debts. In Cambridge, it has been a pleasure to work alongside many brilliant friends: Jens Åklundh, Joe Ashmore, Pippa Carter, Liesbeth Corens, Abigail Gomulkiewicz, Simone Hanebaum, Kirsten Macfarlane, Patrick McGhee, Aislinn Muller, Morgan Ring, Fred Smith, Tom Smith, and Alice Soulieux-Evans. I have also benefitted a great deal from working in close proximity to the 'Remembering the Reformation' project, based at the Universities of Cambridge and York, 2016–19, and I am grateful to Brian Cummings, Ceri Law, Karis Riley, Tom Taylor, Bronwyn Wallace, and Alex Walsham for inviting me to participate in various events connected to their work.

I would probably not have written a book – this one, or any other – were it not for Christ's College, Cambridge. In the ten or more years I have spent at Christ's, first as a student and latterly as a research fellow, I have benefitted enormously from the generosity of its lively community of students, staff, and fellows. My debts in this regard are too numerous to record adequately here, but I should like to offer some particular thanks. David Reynolds is an unfailingly wise and generous mentor. Jane Stapleton welcomed me warmly to the fellowship at a time when, in the final stages of writing up my thesis, my confidence was low. For cheering me on (and up) over lunch and coffee, I am grateful to many friends and colleagues, especially Susan Bayly, Ori Beck, Bob Evans, Maya Feile Tomes, Daniel Field, Nick Gay, Robert Hunt, Sam James, Dai Jones, Geoffrey Martin, Sarah Radcliffe, Jim Secord, Henry Spelman, Emily Tomlinson, Felix Waldmann, and Ed Zychowicz-Coghill. I have often sought advice from Helen Pfeifer and Carrie Vout, who are wonderful friends as well as the very model of academic generosity. Carrie also kindly took a number of the photographs that appear in the pages that follow. My debts to Ned Allen and Natasha Tanna are many and great; I thank them for their friendship and for trying so hard to broaden my cultural horizons. Last, but not least, many of my students have been kind enough to ask about the progress of this book. I hope it does not let them down.

These acknowledgements would be incomplete without mention of the fact that the final phase of writing and editing coincided with the long and difficult months of the COVID-19 pandemic. For raising my spirits, whether over socially distanced dinners, on video calls, or in graveyards, I owe heartfelt additional and renewed thanks to Caroline Egan, Lucy Foster, and Natasha Tanna; and to Nick Gay, Torsten Krude, and Carrie

Vout and Robin Osborne. Those months would have felt much longer and more difficult without them.

Then there are those who have lived with this project the longest. I would neither have started nor finished this book without Alex Walsham, who supervised my doctoral thesis and oversaw its revision into its present form. This book is undoubtedly richer for Alex's considerable generosity with her time and ideas, as well as her extraordinary dedication to her family of students. I am deeply grateful to her for reading multiple drafts so carefully, as well as for her unwavering confidence that I would get there in the end.

My friends and family have shaped this book more than they realise. Carys Brown is the best of friends and read every chapter at least once. Liz Lyon and the Stewarts – June and Arthur; Richard, Sally, and Freya; Hannah, Yussef, Joseph, and Noah – asked brilliant questions and provided brilliant distractions in equal measure. My parents, Carol and John Lyon, have always helped and encouraged me to pursue my interests and ambitions; this book is for them, with love and gratitude.

Note on the Text

Original spelling, punctuation, and capitalisation have been retained in all quotations, except that the use of i and j, u and v has been modernised. In the interests of clarity, standard contractions and abbreviations have been silently expanded and superscript characters silently lowered. For the sake of consistency, signature numbers are rendered in Arabic numerals throughout. Dates are given in Old Style, except that the year is taken to begin on 1 January. Biblical citations are from the Authorised Version of 1611.

Abbreviations

AC	Alnwick Castle, Northumberland
BL	British Library, London
Bodl.	Bodleian Library, Oxford
CUL	Cambridge University Library
CCA	Canterbury Cathedral Archives
CCCC	Corpus Christi College, Cambridge
DHC	Devon Heritage Centre, Exeter
DUL	Durham University Library
HJ	*Historical Journal*
JEH	*Journal of Ecclesiastical History*
L&P	*Letters and Papers, Foreign and Domestic, Henry VIII*, ed. J. S. Brewer, James Gairdner, and R. H. Brodie, 21 vols. and Addenda, 2 vols. (London, 1862–1932)
ODNB	*Oxford Dictionary of National Biography*, www.oxforddnb.com
OED	*Oxford English Dictionary*, http://dictionary.oed.com
P&P	*Past & Present*
SCJ	*Sixteenth Century Journal*
TNA	The National Archives, Kew Gardens, London
TRHS	*Transactions of the Royal Historical Society*

Introduction

England was a different place after the dissolution of the monasteries. Between 1536 and 1540, Henry VIII's government dissolved more than 800 religious houses and, in doing so, disrupted patterns and rhythms of daily life that had existed for centuries. Since the Early Middle Ages, religious orders had performed vital spiritual services for local communities. They were also major landowners, whose vows of chastity, poverty, and obedience went hand-in-hand with a duty to provide charity and hospitality to the laity. Although monasticism was never officially prohibited by the Henrician regime, the dispersal of the religious orders and the partial destruction of monastic buildings amounted to its de facto abolition. Some 12,000 monks, nuns, and friars were pensioned off and absorbed into secular society, whilst their abbeys, convents, and friaries were stripped of anything of use or value by the government's agents and, later, by members of the communities that had grown up around the religious houses. In many places, stone skeletons were all that remained of some of the most magnificent structures in medieval England. For centuries, the monasteries had stood at the heart of local communities; in the space of barely four years, Henry VIII's government had – literally and metaphorically – torn them down. By the spring of 1540, religious houses and religious orders appeared to be little more than emblems of a vanquished past, shadows of a medieval world that was slipping away with the dawning of a new age of Reformation.

The dissolution of the monasteries has conventionally been considered to be the bookend of a story of medieval religion and monastic decline, and an episode with only limited consequences for the decades and centuries that followed. A significant part of this tale, however, remains to be told. This book looks beyond the formal end of the process of dissolution in the early 1540s to its myriad afterlives in early modern England. It is, in other words, a book about the dissolution *after* the dissolution. Taking inspiration from recent studies of early modern memory cultures, it asks new questions about this critical moment in early modern history: how was the dissolution remembered by those who witnessed it and how did this memory evolve in subsequent generations? How did perceptions of the dissolution differ between people from different historical moments, confessional positions, and social backgrounds? And how does this change our understanding of an event typically only studied in light of its origins, course, and immediate consequences? As we shall see, the answers to these questions demand that we rethink our approach to the dissolution of the monasteries and our vision of its evolving significance in the sixteenth and seventeenth centuries and beyond.

This study rests on the premise that historical events are fashioned and crystallised largely in hindsight.[1] The dissolution was no exception: it acquired its status as one of the most critical and controversial episodes in both English history and the Protestant Reformation only in the decades and centuries after the fall of the last religious houses. Through an examination of the various ways in which the dissolution was remembered in the early modern period, this book revises conventional understandings of the Henrician assault on the monasteries. It characterises the dissolution not simply as a highly efficient and relatively painless land grab but as a moment of significant rupture with long-lasting and wide-ranging consequences. Over the course of two centuries, the memory of this episode was continually contested. It was remembered variously (and sometimes simultaneously) as a moment of Henrician triumph; an emblem of Tudor avarice; a cause of social and economic decline; an upswing in the fortunes of the gentry; an act of great sacrilege; and an originary moment in the English Reformation. It was a powerful touchstone for Catholics and religious conservatives who mourned the loss of the religious houses, but also for reformed Protestants, who were increasingly forced to grapple with some of the more problematic consequences of an episode that was also foundational to their understanding of the Reformation. The dissolution played a pivotal role in shaping contemporary senses of time, space, and change – religious, political, social, and economic. The passage of time served, on the one hand, to cement and consolidate the status of the dissolution as an historical watershed and, on the other, to splinter and fragment contemporary opinion as its legacies were repeatedly rewritten in the context of ongoing religious debate and upheaval.

This book engages with all of these themes. It does not pretend to offer a comprehensive account of all the possible ways in which this episode was

---

[1] Philip Abrams, *Historical Sociology* (Shepton Mallet, 1982), p. 191.

remembered in early modern England. Rather, it seeks to show that this was a vitally important episode for different groups and successive generations of early modern people, and ultimately that these different processes of remembering (and selectively forgetting) the dissolution collectively fostered and strengthened the sense in which this episode was experienced and perceived as a moment of profound rupture. If anything, this perception of a break between the medieval past and the Reformation present strengthened with the transition from living memory to inherited recollection. It also underpinned the emergence of the model of medieval/early modern periodisation upon which we continue to rely. This book argues not only that the dissolution of the monasteries is an episode in need of re-evaluation, but that this process of re-evaluation has much to teach us about the relationship between sixteenth- and seventeenth-century memory cultures and the project of writing early modern history. It connects with questions of why some events are transformed into historical watersheds, whilst others are all but forgotten, and how the memory of events is contested in ways that shape our understandings of them. By placing the dissolution in the context of its long afterlives, this book suggests that we can not only expose the distortions that have shaped previous scholarship but also seek to explain them.

The Dissolution of the Monasteries: Points of Departure

The Henrician regime made its first move against the religious houses in January 1535. The Royal Supremacy, which had been enacted the previous year, gave the crown the power to tax the Church. To this end, Thomas Cromwell, Henry VIII's chief minister and vicegerent in spirituals, undertook to investigate the wealth of religious institutions in England and Wales. A detailed survey of their personnel, possessions, and rental incomes – the *Valor ecclesiasticus* – was complete by the end of the summer. This might have been the end of the story, except that the Royal Supremacy had also created a second imperative, to assert the authority of the crown over institutions that owed their allegiance primarily to Rome. Within months, a new round of visitations was underway, intended to establish the loyalty of the religious orders to the new regime and to test standards of piety and behaviour in the religious houses. The commissioners, from whom Cromwell received reports on an almost daily basis, claimed to have uncovered evidence of corruption and impiety in virtually every house in which they set foot. Their missives offered shocking and colourful accounts of the crimes and misdemeanours allegedly committed inside the walls and cloisters of abbeys and convents. By the early months of 1536, with evidence against the religious orders mounting fast, the government was ready to act.

In February 1536, the Henrician regime issued an act of parliament targeting corruption in the smaller religious houses, defined as those worth less than £200 per annum. The preamble to the act ordered their dissolution on the basis of the 'manifest synne, vicious, carnall and abho-mynable lyvyng' that it declared was 'dayly used & commytted amongst the lytell and smale Abbeys, Pryoryes, and other Relygyous Houses'.[2] This initiated a phase of partial – and supposedly voluntary – suppressions. However, as the months wore on, it became clear that this policy was more flexible and deceptive than it had first appeared. Religious houses fell in waves throughout 1537 and 1538, including a number which exceeded the value of the houses brought under scrutiny by the act. Midway into 1539, it finally became clear that the government had the entire monastic institu-tion in its sights. In May, a second act of parliament announced the dissolution of all remaining religious houses, the last of which – Waltham Abbey in Essex – closed its doors in March 1540. The dispersal of ex-monastic lands would keep the Court of Augmentations busy well into the reign of Edward VI, but by the turn of the new decade, at least as far as Henry VIII and his counsellors were concerned, the main work of dissolution was all but over.[3]

As we shall see, the actions of Henry VIII's government during this time were partly the product of a desire to downplay certain aspects of the dissolution. Throughout the 1530s, the regime was engaged in managing the reception of this episode in ways that both shaped how successive generations of early modern people remembered it and have limited and distorted modern scholarship. The major studies of the dissolution remain three foundational interventions of the mid-twentieth century by David Knowles, G. W. O. Woodward, and Joyce Youings.[4] More recently, this

---

[2] 27 Hen. VIII, c. 28, *The Statutes of the Realm*, 11 vols. (London, 1963), iii, p. 575.

[3] On the Court of Augmentations, see W. C. Richardson, *History of the Court of Augmentations, 1536–1554* (Baton Rouge, LA, 1961).

[4] David Knowles, *The Religious Orders in England*, 3 vols. (Cambridge, 1948–59), the third volume republished as *Bare Ruined Choirs: The Dissolution of the English Monasteries* (Cambridge, 1976); G. W. O. Woodward, *The Dissolution of the Monasteries* (London, 1966); Joyce Youings, *The Dissolution of the Monasteries* (London, 1971). For some older perspectives see F. A. Gasquet, *Henry VIII and the Dissolution of the Monasteries*, 2 vols. (London, 1888–9), which approached the dissolution in the context of a narrowly confessional approach to English Catholic history, and Geoffrey Baskerville, *English Monks and the Suppression of the Monasteries* (New Haven, CT, 1937), which attacked the tendency in Catholic historiography to romanticise the dissolution.

literature has been supplemented by a series of local case studies and a few re-examinations of the origins of the dissolution.[5] Nevertheless, it continues to set the agenda for the historiography of the dissolution and to shape our understanding of its significance to Tudor politics and the English Reformation.[6] Quite logically, most of these studies approach the dissolution in terms of its progress in the 1530s and its immediate consequences. The major archives for the dissolution contain the commissioners' correspondence with Cromwell and the various legal and financial records produced by those institutions, including the Court of Augmentations, responsible for managing the transfer of property from Church to state.[7] On the basis of this material, historians including Woodward and Youings, as well as Peter Cunich, have undertaken detailed reconstructions of the transactions that underpinned the dissolution, illuminating how the gift and sale of monastic properties helped to reinforce patronage networks as well as bolstering the flagging finances of the crown.[8] Undoubtedly, the dissolution was a critical watershed in the development of the Tudor state and bureaucracy. Property ownership, and the gains and losses that stood to be made by various parties at the dissolution, is one theme that we will continue to trace beyond 1540. To focus solely on this thread, however, would be to limit our understanding of the long afterlives of the dissolution in early modern England.

A different mode of thinking about the dissolution is offered by Knowles, whose elegiac account of the decline of monasticism embodies another impulse that will be interrogated in this book: nostalgia for the medieval religious houses. In his magisterial three-volume history of the

[5] R. W. Hoyle, 'The origins of the dissolution of the monasteries', *HJ* 28 (1995), pp. 275–305; G. W. Bernard, 'The dissolution of the monasteries', *History* 96 (2011), pp. 390–409. Local studies of the dissolution take different approaches: see, for example, Christopher Haigh, *The Last Days of the Lancashire Monasteries and the Pilgrimage of Grace* (Manchester, 1969); J. H. Bettey, *The Suppression of the Monasteries in the West Country* (Gloucester, 1989); M. Claire Cross, *The End of Medieval Monasticism in the East Riding of Yorkshire* (Beverley, 1993); M. Claire Cross, 'The end of medieval monasticism in the North Riding of Yorkshire', *Yorkshire Archaeological Journal* 78 (2006), pp. 145–57; Patrick J. Greene, 'The impact of the dissolution on monasteries in Cheshire: the case of Norton', in Alan Thacker (ed.), *Medieval Archaeology, Art, and Architecture at Chester* (Leeds, 2000), pp. 152–66.
[6] A new study is forthcoming by James G. Clark.
[7] The commissioners correspondence is held in BL, Cotton MS Cleopatra E IV (Papers relating to the dissolution of the monasteries). A selection of these letters is published in Thomas Wright (ed.), *Three Chapters of Letters Relating to the Dissolution of the Monasteries*, Camden Society, old series, 26 (London, 1843). Other material relating to the dissolution is held in TNA, SP 5 ('Miscellanea relating to the dissolution of the monasteries and to the general surveyors, Henry VIII, 1517–1560').
[8] Peter Cunich, 'The administration and alienation of ex-monastic lands by the crown, 1536–47', unpublished PhD thesis, University of Cambridge (1990).

religious orders in England, Knowles traces the formation and development of the monastic institution before charting its eventual decline.[9] This is an account that situates the dissolution as the culmination of a long, slow process of deterioration in standards and ideals that made the religious orders vulnerable to the charges of the Tudor regime. It is, in other words, an account that posits the eve of the dissolution as a useful end point to the story of medieval monasticism, although it also highlights the resonance of the religious houses and orders in the centuries that followed their suppression. In the epilogue added to the final volume, republished as *Bare Ruined Choirs* (1976), Knowles evokes the splendour and vigour that characterised the monastic institution in its high medieval heyday, the shadows of which skirt the ruins of the monasteries that remain standing today.[10] The significance of monastic remains (of all kinds) is one of the concerns of this book, which treats the dissolution not simply as the final moment of destruction but also as a moment after which conceptions of sacred and monastic space were reimagined.

The supposed decline of monasticism in the fifteenth and early sixteenth centuries has long been used to explain the efficiency of the dissolution and the apparent ease with which it was accepted. Certainly, it has led historians to express scepticism about the extent of its religious ramifications: even for Knowles, the suppression of the monasteries was 'not of itself a great catastrophe', as far as religion was concerned.[11] This speaks to a wider tendency in scholarship on the dissolution to see this episode as largely divorced from other dimensions of the English Reformation.[12] The conservative shift in Henrician religious policy after 1539 has encouraged scholars to see the dissolution less as a harbinger of Protestantism than as a particularly iconoclastic episode in a generally uncertain and erratic period of religious reform.[13] At the same time, there has been a prevailing pessimism about the relevance and popularity of the religious orders in early sixteenth-century England. For this reason, the religious houses and

[9] Knowles, *Religious Orders in England.*   [10] Knowles, *Bare Ruined Choirs,* pp. 304–20.
[11] Ibid., p. 317.
[12] Both Woodward and Youings advance versions of this argument: see Woodward, *Dissolution of the Monasteries,* esp. his discussion of the consequences of the dissolution at pp. 163–73, and Youings, *Dissolution of the Monasteries,* p. 1. See also A. G. Dickens, *The English Reformation,* rev. ed. (London, 1970), esp. chs. 4 and 8; G. R. Elton, *Reform and Reformation: England, 1509–1558* (London, 1977), ch. 1; G. M. Trevelyan, *History of England* (London, 1926).
[13] Opinion differs on whether the dissolution reveals Henry VIII's religion as evangelical or conservative. For two opposing views see G. W. Bernard, *The King's Reformation: Henry VIII and the Remaking of the English Church* (New Haven, CT, and London, 2005), esp. chs. 3, 5, and Richard Rex, 'The religion of Henry VIII', *HJ* 57 (2014), pp. 1–32 at p. 20.

their personnel have largely escaped the attention of revisionists seeking to establish the vitality of what Eamon Duffy described as 'traditional religion'. In Duffy's influential account of the Catholic community on the eve of the Reformation, monasticism is conspicuous only by its absence.[14] His reluctance to engage with this theme is also characteristic of the wider revisionist historiography of late medieval and Reformation Catholicism, which has itself tended to perpetuate the argument that the monasteries were in need of reform, especially compared to the vibrant and dynamic lay Catholic community identified in this literature.[15] More recently, scholars including G. W. Bernard, James G. Clark, and Martin Heale have rehabilitated the reputation of the religious orders, highlighting their spiritual, intellectual, and socio-economic engagement both in local communities and in early Reformation debates.[16] This literature has served productively to call into question the outdated view of late medieval and early modern monasticism as corrupt and irrelevant. The present study is concerned partly with accounting for the prevalence of narratives of monastic corruption, which have coloured both modern scholarship and early modern perceptions of the dissolution.

In order to do so, it is vital that we look beyond 1540. This book treats the dissolution not as an end point but as a beginning. By extending the chronology of the dissolution, it is clear that early modern people remembered this episode neither solely in terms of institutional transformation nor as unconnected with the emergent English Reformation. Nor did they necessarily believe it was complete by 1540: the spectre of domestic monasticism continued to haunt new generations of English Protestants, who

---

[14] Eamon Duffy, *The Stripping of the Altars: Traditional Religion in England, 1400–1580*, 2nd ed. (New Haven, CT, and London, 2005). Duffy acknowledges and justifies his omission of the religious in the preface, pp. xv–xvi.

[15] Monasticism and the dissolution are almost entirely absent from the discussions in Christopher Haigh, 'The continuity of Catholicism in the English Reformation', *P&P* 93 (1981), pp. 37–69; Lucy E. C. Wooding, *Rethinking Catholicism in Reformation England* (Oxford, 2000); Eamon Duffy and David Loades (eds.), *The Church of Mary Tudor* (Aldershot, 2006); Eamon Duffy, *Fires of Faith: Catholic England Under Mary Tudor* (New Haven, CT, and London, 2009). Monasteries are also described as a 'low priority' for post-Reformation Catholics in John Bossy, *The English Catholic Community, 1570–1850* (London, 1975), p. 22.

[16] G. W. Bernard, *The Late Medieval English Church: Vitality and Vulnerability Before the Break with Rome* (New Haven, CT, and London, 2012); James G. Clark, *The Benedictines in the Middle Ages* (Woodbridge, 2011); Martin Heale, *Monasticism in Late Medieval England, c. 1300–1535* (Manchester, 2009). See also Felicity Heal, *Hospitality in Early Modern England* (Oxford, 1990), esp. pp. 231–3; Benjamin Thompson, 'Monasteries, society, and reform in late medieval England', in James G. Clark (ed.), *The Religious Orders in Pre-Reformation England* (Woodbridge, 2002), pp. 165–96; Karen Stöber, 'Bequests and burials: changing attitudes of the laity as patrons of English and Welsh monasteries', in Emilia Jamroziak and Janet Burton (eds.), *Religious and Laity in Western Europe, 1000–1400: Interaction, Negotiation, and Power* (Turnhout, 2006), pp. 131–46.

feared that the work of Reformation remained unfinished, and to inform the debate amongst the English Catholic community about what a restored Catholic Church might look like. As we shall see, whilst the Henrician regime had begun to speak about the monasteries in the past tense as early as 1539, this was an episode that long continued to resonate with the debates of an ongoing Reformation.

Many contemporaries were also forced to grapple with the actions of forebears who had collaborated in the process of dissolution. As Ethan Shagan has demonstrated in his study of Hailes Abbey in Gloucestershire, the work of suppressing the monasteries was not only conducted from the top down or dictated from the centre but actively involved members of the local community.[17] After government agents had stripped the abbey of its most valuable materials, others moved in to reap the spoils: wood, lead, glass, stone, and more. A minority of collaborators was driven to ransack the abbey because of evangelical convictions. At the other end of the spectrum, a small number acted out of a concern to preserve the relics, images, and other material culture of the Cistercian order who lived and worshipped there. For the majority of the collaborators identified by Shagan, however, there was no clear ideological commitment to dissolution. Pragmatism and the potential for personal gain undoubtedly played a role, but so too did the persuasive power of the crown.[18] For all those drawn into the process of suppression in the 1530s, to remember this episode was often to remember their part in it. For their descendants, the knowledge that their parents, grandparents, or great-grandparents had participated in the dissolution could provoke feelings of pride, anxiety, or shame. Moreover, the highly complex picture of the reception of the dissolution in Hailes is suggestive in several respects. It implies that the dissolution can be connected to the wider theological currents of the time, both evangelical and conservative. It also highlights the relationship between religious policy and socio-economic concerns, and the possibility for people at different levels of the social spectrum to profit from the dissolution. Finally, it reveals that this was an episode with important local dimensions, as well as being significant on a national scale.

This book builds on and departs from the existing literature on the dissolution by considering the multiple afterlives of the dissolution over the *longue durée*. It explores the long consequences of the Henrician

---

[17] Ethan H. Shagan, *Popular Politics and the English Reformation* (Cambridge, 2003), ch. 5.
[18] The classic study of the persuasive power of the Crown is G. R. Elton, *Policy and Police: The Enforcement of the Reformation in the Age of Thomas Cromwell* (Cambridge, 1972).

regime's attempts to manage the reception of the dissolution in the 1530s, as well as the different competing but coexisting perspectives that emerged and developed across the generations that followed. In doing so, it exposes the cloistered vision of the dissolution that has characterised previous studies. The result has been a literature that emphasises the short-term consequences and not the long-term afterlives of this profoundly transformative episode. In this light, this book seeks to revise our understanding of both the process of suppression during Henry VIII's reign and its wider significance in early modern England. It does so by asking how the dissolution was selectively remembered and reinvented between the sixteenth and early eighteenth centuries, and beyond.

Remembering the Dissolution: Approach and Sources

There were numerous ways in which people in the sixteenth and seventeenth centuries engaged with the past. Historical knowledge was preserved in libraries, archives, and history books, but it also circulated in the form of sermons, songs, plays, processions, images, objects, rituals, and encounters with the landscape. Memories were recalled in the process of writing diaries, or testifying in court, or telling stories, as well as in many other domains besides. Some, although far from all, of these practices might be considered forms of history.[19] Many also fit the definition of what some disciplines, especially literary scholarship and art history, understand as processes of construction and reconstruction. There is overlap and slippage between these categories and memory, a term that I use in preference because it is a more capacious term than 'history', describing a wider range of forms of engagement with the past, and because I think it better captures the human quality of this engagement than terms such as 'construction'. Most definitions of memory also highlight the important sense in which knowledge about the past is usually recalled in order to serve a purpose in the present. Thus, in her recent study of early modern memory, Judith Pollmann has defined memory as 'a form of individual or collective engagement with the past that meaningfully connects the past to the present'.[20] One of the central aims of this book is to show how the

---

[19] Here my thinking has been shaped by Judith Pollmann, *Memory in Early Modern Europe, 1500–1800* (Oxford, 2017), pp. 2–8 and *passim*.

[20] Ibid., p. 1. This echoes the equally helpful definition of memory offered by Geoffrey Cubitt as 'the study of the means by which a conscious sense of the past, as something meaningfully connected to the present, is sustained and developed within human individuals and human cultures'. See Geoffrey Cubitt, *History and Memory* (Manchester, 2007), p. 9.

dissolution was not a dead issue after 1540; rather, it was repeatedly invoked in light of ongoing processes of religious and social change. This was, as we shall see, an episode that reconfigured how contemporaries viewed their past and present.

In thinking about the dissolution as a memory event, this book draws on, but also departs from, an established theoretical literature. Following the work of the French sociologist and philosopher Maurice Halbwachs in the mid-twentieth century, scholars have long recognised that memory is not a purely personal or psychological process but rather a phenomenon that interacts with and is profoundly shaped by social processes and shared community norms and ideals.[21] It is now widely accepted that memory is practised by both individuals and communities, and is dynamic rather than static, evolving in light of the conditions in which remembering takes place. This scholarship has highlighted how memory practices differ between societies and communities, as well as how they have changed and evolved across time and space.[22] Memory itself therefore has a history. Until recently, this was very much a modern history. The field was pioneered by scholars, including Halbwachs, whose primary interests lay in the period post-1800, in the wake of the age of revolutions and the nationalist crises and colonial atrocities that marked the nineteenth and twentieth centuries. The associ-ation between memory and modernity has been powerful and pervasive. The two World Wars and the Holocaust created a particular incentive to remem-ber the past – a need *not to forget* – and to record the experiences of their

---

[21] Maurice Halbwachs, *Les Cadres Sociaux de la Mémoire* (Paris, 1952), ed. and trans. Lewis A. Coser, *On Collective Memory* (Chicago, 1992).

[22] There is a vast and wide-ranging theoretical literature on memory. For various approaches to this subject, see Pierre Nora, *Les lieux de mémoire*, 3 vols. (Paris, 1984–92), ed. Pierra Nora and Lawrence D. Kritzman, trans. Arthur Goldhammer, *Realms of Memory*, 3 vols. (New York, 1996–8); Pierre Nora, 'Between memory and history: *les lieux de mémoire*', *Representations* 26 (1989), pp. 7–24; Paul Connerton, *How Societies Remember* (Cambridge, 1989); James Fentress and Chris Wickham, *Social Memory* (Oxford and Cambridge, MA, 1992); Jan Assmann, 'Collective memory and cultural identity', trans. John Czaplicka, *New German Critique* 65 (1995), pp. 125–33; Noa Gedi and Yigal Elam, 'Collective memory – what is it?', *History and Memory* 8 (1996), pp. 30–50; Matt K. Matsuda, *The Memory of the Modern* (Oxford, 1996); Jeffrey K. Olick and Joyce Robbins, 'Social memory studies: from "collective memory" to the historical sociology of mnemonic practices', *Annual Review of Sociology* 24 (1998), pp. 105–40; Kerwin Lee Klein, 'On the emergence of "memory" in historical discourse', *Representations* 69 (2000), pp. 127–50; Barbara A. Misztal, *Theories of Social Remembering* (Maidenhead, PA, 2003); Karen E. Till, 'Memory studies', *History Workshop Journal* 62 (2006), pp. 325–41; Astrid Erll and Ansgar Nünning (eds.), *Cultural Memory Studies: An International and Interdisciplinary Handbook* (Berlin, 2008); Joan Tumblety (ed.), *Memory and History: Understanding Memory as Source and Subject* (London, 2013). For two critiques of the field, see Alan Confino, 'Collective memory and cultural history: problems of method', *American Historical Review* 102 (1997), pp. 1366–403; Wulf Kansteiner, 'Finding meaning in memory: a methodological critique of collective memory studies', *History and Theory* 41 (2002), pp. 179–97.

victims.[23] Memory has also been closely linked to the emergence of nation states and the institutions, such as state archives, that embody national memory cultures.[24]

This literature has underlined how modern commemorative practices and institutions helped to foster a sense of collective identity in the wake of traumatic episodes, in ways that are suggestive for thinking about episodes such as the dissolution. At the same time, it is also clear that these communities of memory also functioned to exclude certain groups, especially minority or oppressed populations. In this respect, the field of memory studies owes a significant debt to the emergence of oral history as a methodology and to postcolonial scholarship. The latter especially has made a powerful case against the neutrality of archives and emphasised the need to read sources both along and against the archival grain.[25] In doing so, this literature has encouraged historians to re-examine the links between power, memory, and history, and to recognise the ways in which our scholarship can be shaped and coloured by much earlier processes of remembering and forgetting, preservation and destruction.

Released from confines of the framework of the modern nation state in which they were developed, these insights are now being deployed in ways that undermine the prevailing tendency in the theoretical literature to treat memory and commemoration as hallmarks of modernity. In doing so, recent scholarship from a variety of disciplines is also revealing the potential of pre-modern case studies to extend and revise our understanding of the workings of cultural memory. As Pollmann's definition suggests, the flexibility and capaciousness of memory as a concept is one of its great strengths. Early modern memory is no longer considered simply in terms of mnemonic art and method.[26] Using the insights of memory studies, scholars of the early modern period have addressed a range of subjects,

---

[23] The Second World War and the Holocaust have been especially important case studies in twentieth-century memory: see, for example, Jay Winter, *Sites of Memory, Sites of Mourning* (Cambridge, 1995) and *Remembering War: The Great War and Historical Memory in the Twentieth Century* (New Haven, CT, 2006); Christopher Bigsby, *Remembering and Imagining the Holocaust: The Chain of Memory* (Cambridge, 2006); Mary Fulbrook, *Dissonant Lives: Generations and Violence through the German Dictatorships* (Oxford, 2011).

[24] See, for example, John R. Gillis, 'Memory and identity: the history of a relationship', in John R. Gillis (ed.), *Commemorations: The Politics of National Identity* (Princeton, NJ, 1994), pp. 3–24. See also Eric Hobsbawm and Terence Ranger's comments on 'invented traditions' and modernity in their introduction to *The Invention of Tradition*, 2nd ed. (Cambridge, 1992), pp. 1–14.

[25] See esp. Ann Laura Stoler, *Along the Archival Grain: Epistemic Anxieties and Colonial Common Sense* (Princeton, NJ, 2010).

[26] On the arts of memory see Frances A. Yates, *The Art of Memory* (Chicago, 1966); Jonathan D. Spence, *The Memory Palace of Matteo Ricci* (New York, 1984); Mary Carruthers, *The Book of Memory: Studies of Memory in Medieval Culture*, 2nd ed. (Cambridge, 2008). For a more recent

including the complicated relationships between memory and literature,[27] the material landscape,[28] and contemporary perceptions of the past.[29] *Memory and the Dissolution* is intended to contribute to this wider project of refining and collapsing the association between memory and modernity, and exploring the peculiarities and the universal characteristics of early modern memory cultures.[30]

In particular, the present study is fundamentally concerned with how viewing historical events over the *longue durée* has the potential both to reshape our understanding of these watersheds and to shed fresh light on how such episodes are transformed into turning points. How and why do some events, and not others, acquire the status of historical landmarks? In what ways are the memory of events contested and how does this shape our understanding of them? The dissolution is a particularly valuable case study in this respect. Much of its significance, beyond the important legal and financial dimensions that are clearly visible in the archives of the 1530s, emerged only in hindsight and, crucially, in the context of an ongoing and, in the eyes of some, potentially incomplete Reformation. Scholars of the European Reformations have fruitfully deployed memory as a means of interrogating religious change. In this context, recent studies of both the memory of the French Wars of Religion and the Dutch Revolt have illuminated the varied legacies of religious violence

perspective, see Stephen Clucas, 'Memory in the Renaissance and early modern period', in Dmitri Nikulin (ed.), *Memory: A History* (Oxford, 2015), pp. 131–75.

[27] Philip Schwyzer, *Literature, Nationalism, and Memory in Early Modern England and Wales* (Cambridge, 2004); Andrew Hiscock, *Reading Memory in Early Modern Literature* (Cambridge, 2011); Andrew Gordon, *Writing Early Modern London: Memory, Text, and Community* (Basingstoke, 2013).

[28] Nicola Whyte, *Inhabiting the Landscape: Place, Custom and Memory, 1500–1800* (Oxford, 2009); Alexandra Walsham, *The Reformation of the Landscape: Religion, Identity, and Memory in Early Modern Britain and Ireland* (Oxford, 2011).

[29] In addition to the above, see also Daniel Woolf, *The Social Circulation of the Past: English Historical Culture, 1500–1730* (Oxford, 2003), esp. part IV. For a different approach, see Andy Wood, *The Memory of the People: Custom and Popular Senses of the Past in Early Modern England* (Oxford, 2013); Andy Wood, 'History, time and social memory', in Keith Wrightson (ed.), *A Social History of England 1500–1750* (Cambridge, 2017), pp. 373–91.

[30] For some general studies of early modern memory see Peter Sherlock, 'The reformation of memory in early modern Europe', in Susannah Radstone and Bill Schwarz (eds.), *Memory: Histories, Theories, Debates* (New York, 2010), pp. 30–40; Erika Kuijpers, Judith Pollmann, Johannes Müller, and Jasper van der Steen (eds.), *Memory Before Modernity: Practices of Memory in Early Modern Europe* (Leiden and Boston, MA, 2013); David P. LaGuardia and Cathy Yandell (eds.), *Memory and Community in Sixteenth-Century France* (Farnham, 2015); Matthew Lundin, Hans Medick, Mitchell Merback, Judith Pollmann, and Susanne Rau, 'Forum: memory before modernity: cultures and practices in early modern Germany', *German History* 33 (2015), pp. 100–22; Kate Chedgzoy, Elspeth Graham, Katharine Hodgkin, and Ramona Wray (eds.), 'Memory and the early modern', *Memory Studies* 11 (2018).

and conflict.[31] The experience of rupture and trauma has also been at the heart of studies of the afterlives of significant episodes in British and Irish history, especially the Civil Wars of the 1640s, which have been subject to particularly thorough investigation.[32] Collectively, these interventions have suggested that practices of both commemoration and oblivion were essential to the ways in which contemporaries managed the experience of rupture, as well as alerting early modernists to the role of competing visions of the past in shaping the afterlives of historical events.

By contrast with the Civil Wars, the Reformation has received comparatively little attention as a memory event, although the influential concept of a 'long Reformation' suggests that it could provide fertile ground for such a study.[33] As Alexandra Walsham has argued, the Reformation 'fundamentally reconfigured the mnemonic culture of early modern England in ways that are only just beginning to be more fully explored', including most recently as part of the AHRC-funded 'Remembering the Reformation' project (2016–19).[34] On the level of everyday religious

---

[31] On the French Wars of Religion, see Philip Benedict, 'Divided memories? Historical calendars, commemorative processions and the recollection of the Wars of Religion during the Ancien Régime', *French History* 22 (2008), pp. 381–405; Susan Broomhall, 'Disturbing memories: narrating experiences and emotions of distressing events in the French Wars of Religion', in Kuijpers et al., *Memory Before Modernity*, pp. 253–68; Tom Hamilton, 'The procession of the League: remembering the Wars of Religion in visual and literary satire', *French History* 30 (2016), pp. 1–30. On the Dutch Revolt, see Raingard M. Esser, *The Politics of Memory: The Writing of Partition in the Seventeenth-Century Low Countries* (Leiden and Boston, MA, 2012); Marianne Eekhout, 'Celebrating a Trojan horse: memories of the Dutch Revolt in Breda, 1590–1650', in Kuijpers et al., *Memory Before Modernity*, pp. 129–48; Erika Kuijpers, 'Between storytelling and patriotic scripture: the memory brokers of the Dutch Revolt', in Kuijpers et al. (eds.), *Memory Before Modernity*, pp. 183–202; Jasper van der Steen, *Memory Wars in the Low Countries, 1566–1750* (Leiden and Boston, MA, 2015).

[32] Blair Worden, *Roundhead Reputations: The English Civil Wars and the Passions of Posterity* (London, 2001); Mark Stoyle, 'Remembering the English Civil Wars', in Peter Gray and Kendrick Oliver (eds.), *The Memory of Catastrophe* (Manchester, 2004), pp. 19–30; Fiona McCall, 'Children of Baal: clergy families and their memories of sequestration during the English Civil War', in Matthew Neufeld (ed.), 'Uses of the past in early modern England', *Huntington Library Quarterly* 76 (2013), pp. 617–38; Matthew Neufeld, *The Civil Wars After 1660: Public Remembering in Late Stuart England* (Woodbridge, 2013); Gary Rivett, 'Peacemaking, parliament, and the politics of the recent past in the English Civil Wars', in Neufeld (ed.), 'Uses of the past', pp. 589–615; Micháel Ó Siochrú and Jane Ohlmeyer (eds.), *Ireland, 1641: Contexts and Reactions* (Manchester, 2013); Sarah Covington, '"The odious demon from across the sea": Oliver Cromwell, memory, and the dislocations of Ireland', in Kuijpers et al. (eds.), *Memory Before Modernity*, pp. 149–64; Erin Peters, *Commemoration and Oblivion in Royalist Print Culture, 1658–1667* (Basingstoke, 2017); Edward J. Legon, *Revolution Remembered: Seditious Memories After the British Civil Wars* (Manchester, 2019); Imogen Peck, *Recollection in the Republics: Memories of the British Civil Wars in England, 1649–1660* (Oxford, 2021).

[33] On the concept of the 'long Reformation' see Nicholas Tyacke (ed.), *England's Long Reformation, 1500–1800* (London, 1998).

[34] Alexandra Walsham, 'History, memory, and the English Reformation', *HJ* 55 (2012), pp. 899–938 at p. 936. The English Reformation has been investigated in 'Remembering the Reformation',

practice, the abolition of the doctrine of purgatory, cults of saints, and the practice of intercession challenged traditional practices of commemorating the dead, which had once been a function of the monasteries, amongst other institutions.[35] In this way, the Reformation undermined one of the most important medieval cultures of remembrance: the commemoration of the dead. This was not, however, the only way in which the Reformation changed how early modern people reflected on their past. The project to reform English religion was also, as a wealth of scholarship has highlighted, a project to reform English history.[36] As the sixteenth century wore on, episodes from the more recent past were also subsumed into the Protestant undertaking. As David Cressy has demonstrated, certain events in Elizabethan and Stuart England – the defeat of the Spanish Armada in 1588, the failed Gunpowder Plot of 1605 – helped to transform the Roman Catholic calendar of saints' and holy days into a new calendar that celebrated notable Protestant victories and the glory of Protestant monarchs.[37] The commemoration of such episodes was a powerful weapon in the arsenal of early modern governments.

It is both striking and, in some ways, telling that the constituent events of the Reformation itself have long been neglected in this literature. A recent surge in scholarship stimulated by the 500th anniversary of Martin Luther's (perhaps apocryphal) posting of the ninety-five theses in 1517 has revealed the value of thinking about how the European Reformations were selectively remembered and forgotten, and crucially how the narratives and myths of Reformation were forged through processes of contestation.[38] The English Reformation, of course, had different

University of Cambridge and University of York, https://internal.hist.cam.ac.uk/rememberingth ereformation/index.html. See also Alexandra Walsham, Bronwyn Wallace, Ceri Law, and Brian Cummings (eds.), *Memory and the English Reformation* (Cambridge, 2020) and Brian Cummings, Ceri Law, Karis Riley, and Alexandra Walsham (eds.), *Remembering the Reformation* (London, 2020).

[35] For accounts of this changing commemorative culture, see Bruce Gordon and Peter Marshall (eds.), *The Place of the Dead: Death and Remembrance in Late Medieval and Early Modern Europe* (Cambridge, 2000); Peter Marshall, *Beliefs and the Dead in Reformation England* (Oxford, 2002); Peter Sherlock, *Monuments and Memory in Early Modern England* (Aldershot, 2008); Lucy Wooding, 'Remembrance in the Eucharist', in Andrew Gordon and Thomas Rist (eds.), *The Arts of Remembrance in Early Modern England: Material Cultures of the Post Reformation* (London, 2013), pp. 19–36.

[36] See, for example, Helen L. Parish, *Monks, Miracles and Magic: Reformation Representations of the Medieval Church* (London and New York, 2005) and below, Ch. 2.

[37] David Cressy, *Bonfires and Bells: National Memory and the Protestant Calendar in Elizabethan and Stuart England* (London, 1989).

[38] On the memory of 1517, see esp. C. Scott Dixon, 'Luther's Ninety-Five Theses and the origins of the Reformation narrative', *English Historical Review* 132 (2017), pp. 533–69; Peter Marshall, *1517: Martin Luther and the Invention of the Reformation* (Oxford, 2017); Peter Marshall, 'Nailing the

origins to its German cousin. A fateful combination of a king in need of a divorce and the ascendancy of several notable reformists, including Thomas Cromwell and Thomas Cranmer, set in motion a protracted, piecemeal, and seemingly theologically ambiguous Reformation.[39] Whilst the dissolution of the monasteries was not the originary act of the Henrician Reformation, it was the most visible and tangible manifestation of the idea that the break with Rome was a break with the medieval past. Generations of early modern commentators, as we shall see, therefore came to see this rupture as the defining moment of the Reformation in England and Wales. This status is not unrelated to the fact that the dissolution was also the controversial Reformation episode *par excellence*. As we shall see, it was not calendrical commemoration or ritual celebration that crystallised the dissolution as a key event. Rather, it emerged largely in critical perspective and especially in the increasingly anxious historical imagination of English Protestants, for whom hindsight had soured a moment that ought to have been remembered as one of the greatest triumphs of their movement. In order, then, to understand the true significance of the dissolution in early modern England, we need to interrogate its legacies after 1540. Too controversial to engender a culture of commemoration, it offers a case study of the ways in which memory and reputation are not static but evolve and shift over time and with the passage of the generations.[40]

Taking a view of dissolution beyond the end of Henry VIII's reign requires us to think differently and creatively about sources. The material produced by and for the Henrician government in the 1530s tells a particular story, one of ruthless efficiency and economic transformation. Approximately one-third of all the land in England changed hands during the dissolution, making it the most significant alteration in land ownership since the Norman Conquest. The narrative of monastic corruption and iniquity that underpinned this transformation was powerful and pervasive

---

Reformation: Luther and the Wittenberg door in English historical memory', in Walsham et al. (eds.), *Memory and the English Reformation*, pp. 49–63.

[39] There is a vast literature on the Henrician Reformation. For some different perspectives, see Christopher Haigh, *English Reformations: Religion, Politics, and Society Under the Tudors* (Oxford, 1993), chs. 6–9; Richard Rex, *Henry VIII and the English Reformation*, 2nd ed. (Basingstoke, 2006); Felicity Heal, *Reformation in Britain and Ireland* (Oxford, 2003), part II; Lucy Wooding, *Henry VIII*, 2nd ed. (London, 2015), chs. 5–6.

[40] See also Alec Ryrie, 'The liturgical commemoration of the English Reformation, 1534–1625', in Walsham et al. (eds.), *Memory and the English Reformation*, pp. 422–38. Ryrie makes a similar point that the Henrician regime never sought to celebrate its achievements publicly in the liturgy, p. 430 and *passim*.

in early modern England. This book contends that we stand to benefit from rethinking the tale told across the conventional sources for the dissolution: in the commissioners' correspondence, land grants, and other legal documents. Placing this material in the context of other types of evidence, including contemporary polemic, historical and antiquarian writing, and local and oral tradition, reveals how this vision of efficiency and expediency was perpetuated but also contested over time. It demands that we reassess the records of the dissolution in the light of wider impulses selectively to remember and forget this episode – an episode that, as we shall see, was a great deal more controversial and its legacies much more enduring than has previously been suggested.

In this respect, this book connects with important recent developments resulting from the 'archival turn' in early modern scholarship.[41] In the course of rethinking conventional understandings of the archive as a neutral repository of information, historians and literary scholars have paid more attention to how libraries and archives were collected and compiled in ways that shape and colour the vision of the past preserved therein. As Jennifer Summit has powerfully argued, some of the most important sixteenth- and seventeenth-century collections, including the libraries of Archbishop Matthew Parker and Sir Robert Cotton, were founded on a specific vision of the medieval past that aligned with the ideals and imperatives of the English Reformation.[42] Critically, Summit sees the dissolution itself as the formative moment in this rewriting of the medieval past, as medieval books were (literally and figuratively) released from the chains of the monastic libraries, the contents of which were dispersed and partially destroyed, before what was left was organised anew. In other words, the archival reorganisation engendered by the dissolution of the monasteries was one important way in which this episode served to distinguish the medieval from the early modern.

Many of the conventional sources used by historians to examine the course and immediate aftermath of the dissolution can be found in these collections, especially the Cottonian library, which formed the foundation of what is now the British Library. The commissioners' correspondence

---

[41] See Ann Blair, *Too Much to Know: Managing Scholarly Information Before the Modern Age* (Cambridge, MA, 2010); Liesbeth Corens, Kate Peters, and Alexandra Walsham (eds.), *The Social History of the Archive: Record-Keeping in Early Modern Europe*, P&P Supplement 11 (2016); Jesse Sponholz, *The Convent of Wesel: The Event That Never Was and the Invention of Tradition* (Cambridge, 2017); Liesbeth Corens, Kate Peters, and Alexandra Walsham (eds.), *Archives and Information in the Early Modern World*, Proceedings of the British Academy 212 (Oxford, 2018).
[42] Jennifer Summit, *Memory's Library: Medieval Books in Early Modern England* (Chicago, 2008).

with Thomas Cromwell and other papers relating to the dissolution can be found amongst the Cotton manuscripts, in Cleopatra E IV, a series described by Summit as a 'multivolume chronicle of the Reformation told through original sources'. She sees this material not only as connecting generations of antiquaries and historians (modern and early modern) to the past, but also providing a distinctly Protestant framework within which it could and should be understood. The dissolution occupied a central position in this master narrative of Reformation, connecting centuries of supposedly endemic and fatal Catholic and monastic corruption with the origins of the Church of England. If the Cotton Library played a critical role in 'making the Reformation an archived event', it also served to make the dissolution of the monasteries a cornerstone of this process.[43] The relationship between the dissolution and the nature of the Reformation archive is a theme to which we shall return at the close of this book. Here, it serves to emphasise the sense in which historians have inherited an archive of the dissolution that has itself been coloured and shaped by particular agendas.

The most prominent of those agendas in the material collected from the 1530s and 1540s is, of course, that of the Henrician regime. In suggesting that previous scholarship on the dissolution has been inflected by this agenda, this book does not seek to imply that the regime was itself engaged in managing its archive in a deliberate and calculated way with a view to creating particular afterlives for the dissolution. Rather, it contends that the government was engaged in managing the contemporary reception of the dissolution in ways that have served insidiously to shape the archive available to historians (modern and early modern alike). The work of dissolution, as we have already noted, produced a vast amount of paperwork – visitation articles, reports by the commissioners, pleas for exemption, land grants and leases, and more besides. As we shall see, there is a clear tension in these sources between the desire to celebrate the regime's triumph over monastic corruption and its desire to downplay the wider consequences of the dissolution, including its human cost, its transformative effect in local communities, and its implications for the ongoing English Reformation. In addition to preserving powerful echoes of the government's campaign against the corruption and iniquity it alleged was endemic in the religious houses, this archive has also enabled meticulous reconstruction of the legal and financial aspects of dissolution.[44] Both of these themes are, of course, vital for

---

[43] Ibid., p. 195.
[44] See especially Cunich, 'The administration and alienation of ex-monastic lands'; Richardson, *Court of Augmentations*.

understanding the dissolution of the monasteries. But they have also given this episode a veneer of efficiency and inconsequence, especially as it concerned the Reformation, that has hardly faded in the fifty years or so since Knowles, Woodward, and Youings produced their landmark studies of the dissolution. In order, therefore, fully to capture the significance of the dissolution in the early modern period, we need first to set these more conventional sources more squarely in the context of the religious changes of the 1530s and secondly to explore its long and tangled afterlives.

To this end, this book draws on a diverse body of sources, including chronicles and histories, topographical writing and images, sacrilege narratives and traces of local and oral tradition. These are not, of course, the only sources to preserve contemporary reflections on the dissolution; recent scholarship has encouraged us to see a wide variety of genres as domains for life-writing and memory.[45] Rather, they have been selected because they shed light on particular themes and questions: how did the dissolution become an event that captured the early modern historical imagination? How did contemporaries negotiate the shift in understandings of monastic and sacred space? How was the dissolution remembered in local communities? Within these categories, this book considers examples of texts and images that illuminate particular modes of remembering the dissolution. Some of this material was the product of recent lived experience; much of it deals with inherited rather than personal recollections. It is not my contention that any particular source or body of sources necessarily changed how early modern people remembered the dissolution. Rather, these texts and images are treated (individually and collectively) as indicative of shifting perspectives on the dissolution and evidence of the various modes of selective remembering that shaped its legacies in early modern England.

In turn, these sources helped to perpetuate and propagate particular ideas about the dissolution. Many of them, like the commissioners' correspondence and other legal archives of the dissolution, testify to the reach and pervasiveness of Henrician ideas about the suppression of religious houses. This raises an important question about the power of the government to dictate how the dissolution was received and, therefore, to shape how it was remembered, even inadvertently. On the one hand, this book seeks to account for the ubiquity and longevity of ideas about monastic corruption, and the persistence of the Henrician vision of the dissolution

---

[45] See especially Adam Smyth, *Autobiography in Early Modern England* (Cambridge, 2010).

in its modern historiography. On the other, however, it also strives to show that people did not always remember the dissolution in ways that the Tudor government would have condoned and that they did not erase its religious, cultural, and socio-economic legacies from their memories. To some extent, the model of public commemoration versus seditious remembering employed in recent studies of the memory of the British Civil Wars by Matthew Neufeld and Edward Legon is helpful for thinking about the power relationships that shaped these recollections.[46] However, the usefulness of these categories for thinking about the legacies of the dissolution is limited by the implied dichotomy between public celebration and private subversion. As we shall see, there were multiple different ways of remembering the dissolution in early modern England, both in public and private, that competed and coexisted. It is in this context of contested memory that the full significance of the dissolution must be understood: as a rupture between medieval past and Reformation present.

Modes of Remembering: Framework and Structure

Memory and the Dissolution traces the evolving afterlives of the dissolution across roughly two centuries. The first act of dissolution in 1536 provides a useful starting point, although the discussion that follows will necessarily have an eye to earlier developments in Henrician politics and the condition of monasticism across the medieval period. Finding a logical end point has been a much more difficult task. In deciding to close my story in *c.* 1700, I am conscious that I have chosen largely to exclude the role of the dissolution in the emergence of the picturesque movement in British art and the Gothic trend in English literature, although my discussion prefigures these developments to some extent. Similarly, this book explores the origins, but not the entire evolution, of the enduring fascination with monastic ruins that has been so influential in the modern heritage industry. These are but a few examples of the very long afterlives of the dissolution. I do not, therefore, want to imply that processes of reimagining and rethinking this episode had ended by the turn of the eighteenth century.

Nevertheless, despite its limitations, this terminal date marks a natural cut-off point for the present study in two respects. It is, to a certain extent, dictated by the nature of my sources: printed chronicles, for example, were most popular between the mid-sixteenth and mid-seventeenth centuries, whilst sacrilege narratives reflected anxieties that were especially prevalent

---

[46] Neufeld, *The Civil Wars After 1660*; Legon, *Revolution Remembered*.

and powerful in the mid- and later seventeenth century. Nowhere was the concern about sacrilege more clearly expressed than in Sir Henry Spelman's *History and fate of sacrilege*, written in the 1630s but not published until 1698 – five or so generations after the work of dissolution was concluded in 1540. Crucially, then, the chronological parameters of this book also encompass the transition from a world where individuals could remember the dissolution at first hand, to a world where the memory of the 1530s was inherited from previous generations. The model for this approach derives from the work of Jan Assmann, who has productively distinguished between 'communicative memory', which results from the first-hand experiences of particular individuals, and 'cultural memory', which relates to culturally formed 'reconstructions' of the past and the inherited memory that is shaped by texts and other media, as well as by oral tradition.[47] In other words, memory evolves with the passage of the generations and in response to the changing circumstances in which information about the past is recalled. Recent studies by Norman Jones and Alexandra Walsham have suggested that we might usefully think about the Reformation within such a generational framework; this book adopts a similar approach in its study of the long afterlives of the dissolution.[48]

Memory and the Dissolution begins by rethinking the process of dissolution itself and closes more than a century and a half later, when the distorted vision of the suppression promoted by Henry VIII's government was finally – if only just – beginning to be exposed. Individual chapters trace changing perspectives across at least a century; read in sequence, they also function to effect an overarching forward shift in time. The framework for the discussion that follows is, however, thematic rather than strictly chronological, reflecting the central concern of this study with the multiple tangled afterlives of the dissolution. The first chapter revisits the process of dissolution in the 1530s. With sensitivity to the language employed by the Henrician government, it characterises the dissolution as a long and uncertain process that can be separated into two main phases: the 'reformation of the monasteries' and the 'surrender of the monasteries'. The language of monastic corruption and, subsequently, of the expediency of dissolution are central to understanding the Henrician vision of the dissolution – and it is this triumphalist narrative that the remainder of the book sets out to test, complicate, and unravel. This chapter also notes

[47] Assmann, 'Collective memory and cultural identity'.
[48] Norman Jones, *The English Reformation: Religion and Cultural Adaptation* (Oxford, 2002); Alexandra Walsham, 'The Reformation of the generations: youth, age, and religious change in England, c. 1500–1700', *TRHS* 21 (2011), pp. 93–121.

the emergence of a number of early critiques of the dissolution – Catholic, conservative, and evangelical – which surfaced during the 1530s and 1540s. It is clear that, virtually from the moment it began, the dissolution of the monasteries was controversial amongst reformers and traditionalists alike. However, as we shall see, these critiques did little to dispel – and often simply reinforced – the prevailing and persistent idea that the religious houses were irredeemably corrupt. This is another theme to which subsequent chapters repeatedly return, and which helps to explain the limited vision of the dissolution that has dominated its historiography.

Chapter 2 begins the work of placing the dissolution in the context of its long afterlives. It probes the temporal dimensions of the memory of the dissolution. Questions of how and when the fall of the religious houses came to be considered a rupture with the medieval past and a critical Reformation event are at the heart of this chapter. Recent scholarship has powerfully demonstrated that changing perceptions of the medieval past were also heavily inflected by the project to reform English history. This chapter suggests that the dissolution was central to how commentators across the confessional spectrum perceived the past. Using evidence gleaned principally from chronologically organised sources such as histories and chronicles, it traces the processes through which the dissolution crystallised in the early modern historical imagination. Far from being the relatively insignificant episode described in many modern studies, it was seen by many contemporary commentators as a critical – if not *the* critical – episode in the English Reformation. This chapter also interrogates the emerging tendency exhibited by Catholic and Protestant authors alike to judge Henry VIII's reputation by the dissolution. It is especially striking that, over time, reformed Protestant perspectives on Henry's reign became increasingly anxious and critical. By the mid-seventeenth century, the dissolution had become near synonymous with the reign of the infamous Tudor king, later epitomised in the antiquary Browne Willis's statement that the dissolution was no less than the 'chief blemish of the Reformation'.[49] This chapter therefore posits that the dissolution of the monasteries was in large part the invention of its detractors rather than its supporters.

In Chapter 3 the focus shifts from time to space and the visual and material afterlives of the dissolution. Concentrating on the period between the late sixteenth century and the late seventeenth century, it examines the

---

[49] Browne Willis, *An history of the mitred parliamentary abbies, and conventual cathedral churches*, 2 vols. (London, 1718), i, p. 2.

work of a number of antiquaries who produced topographies and images of former monastic sites. Texts, images, and maps all contributed to processes of both remembering the dissolution and visually erasing and effacing its memory. A fundamental tension can be discerned in many of these sources between a desire to preserve the remnants of the monastic past for posterity and the need to bury that past in oblivion. Taking previous scholarship on the 'nostalgic' element in antiquarian topographies of the dissolution as its main point of engagement and departure, this chapter addresses the role of monastic ruins together with those sites that were converted to new uses, both spiritual and secular, in shaping changing perspectives on this episode. By contrast with earlier work, which has tended to emphasise the role of ruins as *lieux de mémoire*, this chapter argues that we should pay more attention to converted spaces and the ways in which processes of architectural conversion contributed to the forgetting of the monastic past as well as its preservation. The same was true of images made of parish churches and especially domestic properties created out of the remnants of the monasteries. In this respect, the chapter engages with Daniel Woolf's suggestive account of a developing visual culture of 'pastness' in the seventeenth century.[50] In light of the corrosive power of forgetting and oblivion, this chapter hypothesises the emergence of a parallel and equally powerful visual culture of the present.

Building upon the discussion of space in the third chapter, Chapter 4 turns to the legacies of the dissolution in the communities that had been built around monasteries and in the families who later occupied them. In order to access the local and oral dimensions of this memory culture, it further exploits antiquarian writing, using these sources in a different way to previous chapters, to throw a sidelight onto the traditions and stories that circulated orally, and which antiquaries and other travellers encountered as they traversed the country. Important studies of court depositions and testimonies have indicated that the legacies of the dissolution were long-lived in local communities. This chapter explores the residues of tradition preserved in antiquarian writing in light of this literature and, in particular, seeks to connect the socio-economic legacies of the dissolution with the religious dimensions of local memory, which have been underexplored in the historiography. Sacrilege, the chapter argues, provides the key to unlocking this complex memory culture. Antiquaries frequently encountered stories of ghostly hauntings and strange happenings, which preoccupied local people living in or near former monastic places. By exploring sacrilege narratives

---

[50] Woolf, *Social Circulation of the Past*, p. 183.

connected to the dissolution, this chapter also makes a case for the vibrancy and longevity of local memory cultures across the seventeenth century and into the early eighteenth century and beyond. It helps to place well known texts such as Spelman's *History and fate of sacrilege* in context and to erode and collapse the distinctions between 'popular' and 'learned', 'local' and 'national' cultures of history and memory that continue to influence scholarship on early modern historical culture.

Finally, the fourth chapter, together with the conclusion, returns to the archive of the dissolution and the paradox that many of the sources and archives historians have conventionally used to understand the dissolution were themselves products of the rupture it engendered between medieval past and early modern present. If the dissolution has been neglected as a subject of historical study, it is at least partly because of the reconfiguration of the archives set in motion in the 1530s. By dissolving and dispersing the monastic libraries, the Henrician regime also laid the foundations for an archive of Reformation that has helped to underpin the model of periodisation – medieval and early modern, pre- and post-Reformation – upon which scholars continue to rely. The dissolution, which hitherto has tended to slip through the cracks between the medieval and the early modern, ought, then, to be essential to our understanding of this transition, as well as to our understanding of the English Reformation.

A final comment on terminology must be made. Most previous scholarship has referred to this episode as the 'Dissolution of the Monasteries'. This book suggests that this shorthand is not neutral. Rather, it emerged in the context of a particular polemical vision of 1536–40 that began to appear in the late sixteenth and especially the seventeenth century, and which carries with it a set of assumptions and implications. For this reason, lowercase forms have been adopted in most uses of the term and its derivatives – dissolution of the monasteries, rather than Dissolution of the Monasteries. Where this formulation or its synonyms appear with capital letters, these are deliberate usages intended to describe and interrogate the transformation of the long process of dissolution into a major Reformation event. One of the core arguments of this book is that the dissolution shaped contemporary perceptions of the Reformation in ways that continue to have a bearing on the models of periodisation and the analytical vocabulary used by historians to describe this episode. As we shall see, the ubiquity of the name 'Dissolution of the Monasteries' is itself a telling example of how earlier processes of selectively remembering and forgetting the dissolution have left their mark upon modern scholarship.

It is ultimately something of an irony that the dissolution of the monasteries proved to be one of the most significant memory events of the early modern period, since there was no state-sponsored commemorative culture surrounding the dissolution. Perhaps this was because, although it appeared initially to be a triumphant moment for the Henrician regime and the early reformers, this was in fact a deeply contentious and problematic episode. Before exploring the long and contested afterlives of the dissolution, it is to these earliest attempts to shape its reception and legacies that we must first turn.

CHAPTER I

'No News but the Abbeys Shall Be Down'
Reform, Surrender, and Suppression in the 1530s and 1540s

The long process of dissolving the monasteries began with a controversy over monastic corruption. The correspondence passing across Thomas Cromwell's desk in the mid-1530s contained numerous colourful accounts of the iniquitous and depraved behaviour allegedly uncovered in the religious houses during the visitations of 1535–6. From almost every corner of the country, the news was the same: the religious orders were in serious need of reform. In January 1536, it was the turn of William Thirsk, Cistercian abbot of Fountains Abbey in North Yorkshire, to fall under the scrutiny of the Henrician regime. The task was entrusted to Richard Layton and Thomas Legh, two of the most active commissioners for the dissolution. The evidence that they compiled was damning. Writing to Cromwell, Layton and Legh testified that Thirsk had 'gretly dilapidated his howse' through a variety of secular and spiritual crimes, which included 'notoriously keypyng vi. hoorres', 'thefft and sacrilege', and 'one day denyyng thes articles [of religion]' before 'the next daye folowyng the same confessyng' and thus perjuring himself.[1] By denying the Henrician articles of religion, Thirsk had also dirtied his hands with the crime of political disobedience. In response to these allegations, the government's response was immediate and decisive. Thirsk was ejected from his abbacy within days.

Countless similar cases were reported by the king's agents between 1535 and 1540. It was on the basis of this evidence that the first act of suppression was passed in 1536, which targeted the smaller – and supposedly more corrupt – institutions worth less than £200 per annum. Eventually, however, it became clear that the Henrician regime had the entire monastic institution in its sights, and a second act of suppression (1539) initiated the

---

[1] BL, Cotton MS Cleopatra E IV, fol. 114. A selection of the commissioners' correspondence is also published in Thomas Wright (ed.), *Three Chapters of Letters Relating to the Dissolution of the Monasteries*, Camden Society, old series, 26 (London, 1843).

wholesale dissolution of the monasteries. As we shall see, a measure intended to root out corruption and iniquity in the religious houses had been transformed into the de facto abolition of domestic monasticism. With hindsight, it is possible to imagine that this had been the regime's intention all along. Retrospectively, we are also able to recognise the success of the Henrician dissolution in eradicating the religious orders, who returned to England only in the nineteenth century. But hindsight is a blessing and a curse. It obscures, amongst other things, the uncertainty of the years 1536–40 and the different possibilities for the future that were articulated by supporters and critics of the dissolution both before and after 1540.

This chapter explores how contemporaries negotiated these uncertainties and possibilities, as well as the ways in which Henry VIII's government tried to assert a particular vision of the dissolution. Recent studies have demonstrated that the Henrician regime was conscious of its reputation and the need to build a legacy.[2] Setting dissolution polemic, including the correspondence of the commissioners, in this context, this chapter revisits the events of 1536–40 with a view to providing a new perspective on the familiar story of the suppression as an efficient and virtually painless episode in the development of Tudor bureaucracy and the Henrician Reformation.

The discussion that follows is sensitive both to the evolving language of the dissolution and to the problem of agency in early debates about its course and consequences. Interrogating the rhetorical strategies used by the government to justify its assault on the religious houses, it posits a distinct shift in emphasis in Henrician polemic between 1536 and 1540, tracing first the 'reformation' and then the 'surrender' of the monasteries. This dual rhetoric served to underline monastic corruption and the complicity of the religious in their own demise, whilst playing down the wider consequences of this rupture with the medieval past. This vision of the dissolution was contested, however, virtually from the moment of the fall of the first religious houses and from both ends of the confessional spectrum: conservative and evangelical. All of these arguments would influence how early modern people remembered this episode across successive generations, in ways that are not often reflected in conventional historical accounts of the dissolution. This chapter begins to ask how and why this should be the case

---

[2] Mark Rankin, Christopher Highley, and John N. King (eds.), *Henry VIII and His Afterlives: Literature, Politics, and Art* (Cambridge, 2009), esp. chs. 2, 3; Kevin Sharpe, *Selling the Tudor Monarchy: Authority and Image in Sixteenth-Century England* (New Haven, CT, and London, 2009), chs. 2–4.

by raising the question of the relationship between the dissolution of the monasteries and its archive.

The Reformation of the Monasteries, 1536–1538

Layton and Legh's report from Fountains Abbey encapsulates many of the main themes of the wider correspondence collected by Cromwell in the days leading up to the dissolution. Sexual immorality was a particularly common allegation. In November 1535, for instance, John ap Rice reported from Bury St Edmunds in Suffolk that 'it is confessed and proved that there was here suche frequence of women commyng and reassorting to this monastery as to no place more'. Unlike Legh at Fountains, Rice could find no evidence that the abbot of Bury, John Reeve, was sexually deviant, but it was detected that he 'laye moche forth in his granges, and delited moche in playng at dice and cardes, and therein spent moche money, and in buyld-ing for his pleasure'. Worldly living of this sort was another general theme, as was the neglect of spiritual duty. Reeve, it was alleged, 'did not preche openly' and, like Thirsk, he had refused to acknowledge the king's Reformation. He 'semeth to be addict', Rice reported, 'to the mayntenyng of suche superstitious ceremones as hathe ben used heretofor'. He was also accused of being a bad landlord to his lay tenants, having 'converted diverse fermes into copie holdes, wherof poore men doth complayne'.[3] Both the abbot and his house, Rice went on to imply, were deeply unpopular in the local community. A final theme was fraudulence. The religious orders were heavily implicated in the cults of relics and saints that came under fierce attack in the 1530s as part of the Henrician regime's wider project to shatter 'the visual link between past and present'.[4] This was an attempt to erode the material memory culture fostered by traditional religion. Amongst the relics at Bury, Rice reported to Cromwell, 'we founde moche vanitie and superstition', including the coals that had fuelled the flames in which St Laurence had expired, the parings of St Edmund's nails, the penknife and boots of St Thomas of Canterbury, enough fragments of the Holy Cross 'to make a [w]hole crosse', and a number of other objects purported to have therapeutic and thaumaturgic powers.[5]

---

[3] BL, Cotton MS Cleopatra E IV, fol. 120.
[4] Helen L. Parish, *Monks, Miracles and Magic: Reformation Representations of the Medieval Church* (London and New York, 2005), p. 5. On relics and cults of saints in the monasteries, see Martin Heale, 'Training in superstition? Monasteries and popular religion in late medieval and Reformation England', *JEH* 58 (2007), pp. 417–39.
[5] BL, Cotton MS Cleopatra E IV, fol. 120.

In response to reports such as this, Henry VIII's government initiated the first dissolutions of religious houses in March 1536. Despite the fact that the commissioners claimed to have uncovered manifold abuses in large houses like Fountains and Bury, the regime had in its immediate sights only those monasteries, nunneries, and friaries worth less than £200 per annum where, it claimed, standards were particularly poor. So pervasive was the rhetoric of corruption, fraudulence, and iniquity that the preamble to the 'Act for the Suppression of the Lesser Monasteries' (1536) alleged that the religious orders were responsible for the 'utter spoyle & destruccion' of their own houses:

> Manifest synne, vicious, carnall and abhomynable lyvyng, is dayly used & commytted amongst the lytell and smale Abbeys, Pryoryes, and other Relygyous Houses of Monkes, Chanons & Nonnes ... wherby the Governours of suche Relygyous Houses and thir Covent spoyle, destroye, consume & utterly wast, aswell ther Churches, Monasteryes, Pryoryes, pincipall Houses, Farmes, Granges, Londes, Tenementes & Heredytamentes, as the ornamentes of ther Churches & ther goodes and catalles, to the high dyspleasour of Almyghty God, slaunder of good Relygyon & to the greate Infamy of the Kynges Highnes & the Realme.[6]

The act therefore granted these houses to the king so that they might be 'used & converted to better uses' and their inhabitants translated to other communities where they could be 'compellyd to reforme their lyves'. By combating depravity and corruption in the smaller houses, the regime argued, the larger – the 'greate solemyne Monasteryes of this Realme' – might flourish free of this canker.[7]

The idea of monastic reform was not new in 1536. The rhetoric of *reformatio* and *renovatio* originated in the New Testament, and its potency across the medieval period was indicative of a monastic institution, as well as a Roman Catholic Church more generally, which strove vigorously for the restoration of primitive Christianity.[8] The Henrician government's allegations about the corruption of the religious houses had roots in these older discursive strategies. Living memory also furnished several notable precedents for the suppression of monasteries, including the closure of

---

[6] 27 Hen. VIII, c. 28, *The Statutes of the Realm*, 11 vols. (London, 1963), iii, p. 575.   [7] Ibid.

[8] Gerald Strauss, 'Ideas of *Reformatio* and *Renovatio* from the Middle Ages to the Reformation', in Thomas A. Brady, Jr., Heiko A. Oberman, and James D. Tracy (eds.), *Handbook of European History, 1400–1600: Late Middle Ages, Renaissance and Reformation*, 2 vols. (Leiden, New York, and Cologne, 1995), i, p. 6; Julia Barrow, 'Ideas and applications of reform', in Thomas F. X. Noble and Julia M. H. Smith (eds.), *The Cambridge History of Christianity: Early Medieval Christianities, c. 600–c. 1100* (Cambridge, 2014), pp. 345–62.

Creake Abbey in Norfolk in 1506 by Henry VIII's grandmother, Lady Margaret Beaufort, to endow her foundation at Christ's College, Cambridge, and the dissolution of St Frideswide's Priory by the king's former chief advisor, Cardinal Wolsey, to finance Cardinal College, now Christ Church, Oxford in 1522. Wolsey went on to secure a papal bull for the closure of twenty further religious houses in 1524 to support his educational projects in Oxford and Ipswich.[9] Moreover, in the years leading up to the Henrician Reformation, monastic corruption had also been a prominent theme in religious polemic. In 1529, for example, the reformer Simon Fish had published an incendiary pamphlet entitled *A supplicacyon for the beggers* from his exile in Antwerp. The *Supplicacyon* attacked the Catholic Church and accused its monks and ministers of crimes ranging from avarice and idleness to treason, prefiguring many of the main tenets of the commissioners' correspondence in the 1530s.[10] When the 1536 act of suppression highlighted the corruption of the monasteries, it therefore employed a rhetoric that could be traced back across the centuries and that had significant cultural currency in the first decades of the sixteenth century.[11]

This narrative of ongoing reform had the potential to create a powerful continuity with the past. The preamble to the 1536 act declared that 'many contynuall vystytacions hath bene heretofore had by the space of two hundreth yeres and more, for an honest and charytable Reformacion of suche unthrifty, carnall & abhomynable lyvyng', and yet in that time 'vycyous lyvyng' had 'shamelessly encreaseth and augmentith'.[12] The government thus attempted to portray the first and partial dissolution of the monasteries as the consequence of two centuries of failed reform – and thereby to assuage the novelty and gravity of the break with the past engendered by its assault on the religious houses. But the difference in 1536, in the wake of the break with Rome and the creation of the Royal Supremacy, was that the crown had assumed the power to direct against the monasteries the very rhetoric with which the medieval Church had

[9] On dissolutions before Henry VIII, see R. W. Hoyle, 'The origins of the dissolution of the monasteries', *HJ* 38 (1995), pp. 275–305; Lucy E. C. Wooding, *Rethinking Catholicism in Reformation England* (Oxford, 2000), p. 38; Deirdre O'Sullivan, 'The "little dissolution" of the 1520s', *Post-Medieval Archaeology* 40 (2006), pp. 227–58.

[10] Simon Fish, *A supplicacyon for the beggers* (Antwerp?, 1529?).

[11] On anti-monastic satire see also Sophie Murray, 'Dissolving into laughter: anti-monastic satire in the reign of Henry VIII', in Mark Knights and Adam Morton (eds.), *The Power of Laughter and Satire in Early Modern Britain: Political and Religious Culture, 1500–1820* (Woodbridge, 2017), pp. 27–47.

[12] 27 Hen. VIII, c. 28, *Statutes of the Realm*, iii, p. 575.

asserted and framed its own authority.[13] The language of monastic reform thus became a tool for attacking the Catholic Church, rather than an impetus for reform emanating from within it.

As the first suppressions got underway, the rhetoric of monastic corruption and iniquity became increasingly potent. It continued to pervade the commissioners' correspondence in the months following the act. Thomas Bedyll, another of the king's agents, accused the Carthusian prior of the London Charterhouse of 'hypocrisy, vayne glory, confederacy, and obstinacy',[14] whilst Legh went on to report that the abbot of Rievaulx in North Yorkshire was as guilty of 'dissolute lyvyng' as his counterpart at Fountains.[15] This was also the tenor of many unsolicited missives sent to Cromwell, which further attest to the power and reach of the government's campaign against the religious orders. As early as 1535, the London clergyman John Barthlet had reported to Cromwell that he and other 'personez of good conversacion' had 'ffound the prior of the Crossid Fryers in London ... beyng in bedde with his hoore'.[16] Even more damaging was evidence of monastic corruption furnished by those within the religious community itself. A particularly colourful example of this self-incriminating tendency can be found in the evidence of Richard Beerly, a Benedictine monk at Pershore Abbey in Worcestershire. Late in the spring of 1536, he informed Cromwell that his conscience had compelled him to report that 'the relygyon wyche we do obser and keype ys no rull of sentt Benett, nor yt no commandyment of God' but instead 'all fowloys our owne sensyaly and pleser ... all yn vayne glory'.[17] He further claimed – echoing the findings of commissioners elsewhere – that many of his brethren arrived at matins inebriated, whilst others gambled at dice and cards. It is even more striking that those religious who pleaded for exemption from dissolution also inadvertently perpetuated this rhetoric of corruption. Joan Missenden, prioress of Legbourne in Lincolnshire, asked to be spared suppression in 1536, having heard that many other religious houses in the area were to be dissolved 'bicause of theire myslyvng'. 'Ye shall here no compleyntes agaynst us', she wrote to Cromwell, '[neither] in oure lyvyng nor hospitalitie kepyng'.[18] Missenden thus attempted to revert to the rhetoric of piety and charity associated with the monastic vows of

---

[13] See Benjamin Thompson, 'The polemic of reform in the later medieval English church', in Almut Suerbaum, George Southcombe, and Benjamin Thompson (eds.), *Polemic: Language as Violence in Medieval and Early Modern Discourse* (Farnham, 2015), esp. p. 222.
[14] BL, Cotton MS Cleopatra E IV, fol. 252.   [15] Ibid., fol. 137.   [16] Ibid., fol. 134.
[17] Ibid., fol. 161.   [18] Ibid., fol. 270.

poverty, chastity, and obedience that the Henrician regime was attempting so powerfully to invert.

Since the work of G. R. Elton, scholars of the Henrician Reformation have recognised the regime's desire to control propaganda and opinion.[19] More recently, this impulse has also been set in the context of Henry's vision of his own power and concern for reputation and legacy.[20] In particular, Henry was enamoured by the models of the Old Testament kings and sought to fashion his own kingship accordingly.[21] This played out in different ways – in, for example, the visual and material trappings of monarchy, but also in the rhetoric used to announce and justify episodes such as the dissolution of the monasteries. The 1536 act of suppression thus invoked the image of Henry as a godly king battling the corruption, iniquity, and 'slaunder of good Relygyon' that flourished in the monasteries, much to the 'dyspleasour of Almyghty God' and 'greate Infamy of the Kynges Highnes & the Realme'.[22] As we shall see in future chapters, some contemporary polemicists and historians drew on the providential character of the king's intervention in the 1530s and 1540s, although it was left to subsequent generations more explicitly to develop an image of Henry as the divine agent and instrument of the dissolution. Nevertheless, this emphasis on the dissolution as a godly act helps us to make sense of the regime's early emphasis on monastic corruption and the need for reform of the Church. Had it not been for subsequent developments in official policy, history might have remembered this episode as the 'Reformation of the Monasteries'.

It is telling that Henry appears to have invented explanations for those reports that did not conform to this vision of the dissolution. In the spring of 1536, commissioner George Giffard testified in favour of St James's Abbey, a house of Augustinian canons, as well as the female Cistercian priory at Catesby, both in Northamptonshire. However, according to a letter from Giffard to Cromwell of June 1536, news had quickly reached him that the king had been openly displeased with the favourable report, 'seyeng that itt was like that we had received rewardes, whiche caused us to wright as we dyd'. Giffard recounted this information by way of an attempt

[19] G. R. Elton, *Policy and Police: The Enforcement of the Reformation in the Age of Thomas Cromwell* (Cambridge, 1972).
[20] On the afterlives of Henry VIII, see Rankin, Highley, and King (eds.), *Henry VIII and His Afterlives*; Thomas Betteridge and Thomas S. Freeman (eds.), *Henry VIII and History* (Farnham, 2012).
[21] Richard Rex, *Henry VIII and the English Reformation*, 2nd ed. (Basingstoke, 2006), pp. 10, 20–1 and *passim*.
[22] 27 Hen. VIII, c. 28, *Statutes of the Realm*, iii, p. 575.

to persuade Cromwell of his integrity in speaking once again in favour of the religious orders – this time at Wolstrop Priory in Leicestershire, 'the governour wherof is a vere good husband for the howse, and welbeloved of all thenhabitantes thereunto adjoynyng'.[23] He did not succeed in securing a reprieve. Nevertheless, this episode reveals, on the one hand, that evidence was being twisted as early as 1536 in order to conform to the Henrician regime's particular vision of the dissolution. The government and its agents, conscious of the need to manage responses to the suppression, do not appear to have looked favourably upon alternative perspectives. On the other hand, Giffard's continued pleas for the monasteries he visited are also a reminder that, in the early phase of suppression, the government at least paid lip service to the idea of reforming – and not dissolving – the monasteries. This was, after all, a period when wholesale suppression was not only far from inevitable; for many, it was entirely inconceivable.[24]

In the context of parallel developments, however, the position of the monasteries was becoming increasingly precarious. Rather than seeing the dissolution as a discrete episode in the English Reformation, it is helpful here to think about the 'reformation' of monasticism alongside other aspects of religious reform. The wider picture of the Henrician Reformation reveals how the highly persuasive rhetoric of monastic corruption propagated by the government after 1536 was supplemented by a harder-edged language of monastic heresy and treason, and by the exercise of coercive power violently to subvert and repress those who adhered to papal supremacy – including the religious orders. Shortly before the dissolution, in 1534, the Benedictine nun and prophetess Elizabeth Barton, widely known as the Holy Maid of Kent, had been publicly executed with five of her promoters for treason, after speaking against the king's marriage to Anne Boleyn and the break with Rome. Her severed head was displayed prominently at London Bridge as an admonition to those who harboured similar anxieties about the direction of Henrician religious policy.[25] A few years later, in 1538, a similar example was made of the Observant Franciscan John Forest, who was burnt for heresy for his refusal to acknowledge the king as Supreme Head of the Church. Forest's

<hr/>

[23] BL, Cotton MS Cleopatra E IV, fol. 213.
[24] For arguments that the dissolution was not inevitable at this stage, see G. W. Bernard, *The King's Reformation: Henry VIII and the Remaking of the English Church* (New Haven, CT, and London, 2005), pp. 270–4; Richard Rex, 'The religion of Henry VIII', *HJ* 57 (2014), pp. 1–32, esp. pp. 20–5.
[25] On Barton, see Diane Watt, *Secretaries of God: Women Prophets in Late Medieval and Early Modern England* (Cambridge, 1997), ch. 3.

pyre was partially fuelled by a wooden image of the Celtic saint Derfel Gardarn, brought to London from Llanderfel in Merionethshire, Wales, further underlining the blurred boundaries between the regime's campaign against monastic corruption and its assault on idolatry.[26]

Monasteries also provided the settings for some of the set piece acts of iconoclasm of the Henrician Reformation. Two alleged monastic deceptions stand out as particularly infamous and illuminating. First to fall was the Rood of Grace belonging to the Cistercian Abbey of Boxley in Kent – a likeness of Christ that apparently came alive before the faithful who flocked to see it. In February 1538, the rood was denounced by the king's commissioners as a mechanical fraud employed by the monks to extract financial contributions from gullible pilgrims, and publicly condemned in a sermon preached by John Hilsey, bishop of Rochester and himself only a recent convert to evangelical religion from his former vocation as a Dominican prior. The rood was subsequently dismantled and burnt in London before a large audience, witnesses to the disgrace and destruction of one of the most prominent medieval miracles. Then, in November, Hilsey returned to Paul's Cross to condemn another allegedly feigned monastic relic, the Holy Blood of Christ, housed at Hailes Abbey in Gloucestershire. At the time of Hilsey's sermon, the Holy Blood had already been investigated *in situ* by Hugh Latimer, bishop of Worcester, and the gentleman Richard Tracy, and Hailes's own abbot, Stephen Sagar, had pulled down its shrine himself. When the relic was transferred to London, the chronicler Charles Wriothesley, a witness to the exposure of the Holy Blood, recorded that Hilsey 'did let every man behould yt there at Paules Crosse, and all the way as he went to dinneer to the mayres, to loke on yt, so that every person might well perceive the abuse of the sayd thinge'.[27] These episodes powerfully demonstrate the influence and reach of the government's polemical campaign against Catholic relics, idols, and shrines, in ways that would significantly influence popular responses to the legal and political project of dissolving the religious houses.[28]

In his examination of the popular politics of dissolution, Ethan Shagan has argued that iconoclastic episodes such as these help to explain the willingness of so many local people to participate in the spoliation of

[26] On Forest, see Peter Marshall, 'Papist as heretic: the burning of John Forest, 1538', *HJ* 41 (1998), pp. 351–74; Anne Dillon, 'John Forest and Derfel Gadarn: a double execution', *Recusant History* [now *British Catholic History*] 28 (2006), pp. 1–21.

[27] AC, DNP: MS 468A, fol. 86r.

[28] See also Peter Marshall, 'The Rood of Boxley, the Blood of Hailes and the defence of the Henrician church', *JEH* 46 (1995), pp. 689–96.

abbeys and monasteries. After the royal commissioners had done the initial work of destruction at Hailes Abbey, local people plundered the site for wood, lead, glass, iron, and a variety of other more-or-less moveable goods, large and small. Shagan suggests that the locals had not only witnessed but also effectively participated in the denunciation of the Holy Blood; by spreading word of what they had seen and heard they became the 'unwitting vanguard of government propaganda'.[29] The controversy over the Hailes relic brought the local community into contact with the Henrician regime at its most evangelical, and it seems that the plunderers, of whom only a minority were advocates of religious reform, nevertheless 'internalised the reordering of the relationship between Church and state promulgated by the government'.[30] The campaign to correct perceived Catholic abuses thus intersected with the legal process of dissolution, resulting in an apparent shift in attitudes towards monastic space that served to encourage and legitimise popular collaboration in the suppression. Other factors, of course, were also at play: Hailes had been considered an asset of the local community for centuries, and therefore its goods could be absorbed – apparently without much anxiety about the consequences of desacralising the abbey site – into the local economy; there quickly arose an active black market for goods plundered from the abbey in towns and villages for miles around.[31] Perhaps the ease with which these materials were dispersed and recycled is further evidence of the depth and speed with which Henrician arguments for reform of the monasteries had permeated into the local community. The economics of the dissolution are thus difficult to disentangle from its wider resonance and significance in towns and villages across England and Wales.

It is also the case that, by the late 1530s, claims about monastic corruption, fraudulence, and iniquity were functioning to legitimate a process of suppression that had begun to exceed the parameters set out in the 1536 act of dissolution. The exposure of the controversial relics at Hailes and Boxley were exemplary episodes in a wider catalogue of abuses and errors that continued to be reported back to the government, and, as Peter Marshall has demonstrated, forgery and feigning were prominent themes in the polemic produced by the regime and its supporters.[32] Under the weight of the Henrician government's attacks, further monasteries were dissolved throughout 1537 and 1538. As George Rolle reported to Lord Lisle in

---

[29] Ethan H. Shagan, *Popular Politics and the English Reformation* (Cambridge, 2003), p. 172.
[30] Ibid., p. 190. [31] Ibid., p. 181.
[32] See Peter Marshall, 'Forgery and miracles in the reign of Henry VIII', *P&P* 178 (2003), pp. 58–62.

February 1538, 'the abbeys go down as fast as they may and are surrendered to the king'.[33] No longer was it possible to claim that the government was simply undertaking a 'reformation of the monasteries'. Rather, Rolle's comments reveal that a new rhetoric had begun to creep into Henrician polemic. Since 1536, as we have seen, monks like Richard Beerly and Stephen Sagar had offered testimony that implicated the religious orders in the suppression of their own houses. As the dissolution progressed, building on the vision of monastic corruption now embedded in the Henrician Reformation, the notion that monks, nuns, and friars were complicit in their own downfall became increasingly pervasive.

Declarations were drafted for the surrender of religious houses that referred to the crimes of immorality, iniquity, and fraudulence with which they had been so systematically attacked. The inhabitants of these houses were expected to subscribe to these documents in order to receive the pensions granted to them by way of compensation, perpetuating the fiction, to use Norman Jones's term, that the religious were simply exchanging their property for an annuity.[34] In March 1538, Legh wrote to Cromwell from Holme in Cumbria to report that the Cistercian house of Holmcultram had been 'quietly dissolved' and the monks, who 'think themselves in better case than before', dispersed.[35] In September of that year, Richard Greene, abbot of Biddlesden in Buckinghamshire, made a declaration of surrender in which he confessed that he and his brethren did 'profoundly consider that the manner and trade of living which we and others of our pretensed religion have practised and used many days, doth most principally consist in dumb ceremonies', once more deploying the language of forgery and feigning used elsewhere to condemn the religious orders. Greene also acknowledged the dangers of 'submitting ourself principally to forinsical potentates and powers which never came here to reform such discord of living and abuses as now have been found to have reigned among us' by the Henrician commissioners.[36] The religious were thus made complicit in their own dissolution and forced to commit to paper their alleged deceitfulness and depravity.

Monastic corruption was not the total invention of the Henrician regime. But it was central to the government's vision of the suppressions that took place between 1536 and 1538. To think of this period in terms of a 'reformation of the monasteries' is not to buy into Henrician polemic,

---

[33] *L&P*, xiii, part 1, no. 235.
[34] Norman L. Jones, *The English Reformation: Religion and Cultural Adaptation* (Oxford, 2002), p. 70.
[35] *L&P*, xiii, part 1, no. 547.   [36] Ibid., part 11, no. 421.

but rather explicitly to recognise the attempt of the government to limit contemporary discourse on the religious houses and orders to their iniquity and impiety. This continued into 1539, when the rhetoric of monastic corruption and complicity was reconfigured into a rhetoric of surrender, deployed to justify a radical new policy of wholesale dissolution.

The Surrender of the Monasteries, 1539–c. 1540

The suppression of the smaller houses did not signal the end of their 'utter spoyle and destruction' as the Henrician regime had argued in 1536. Rather, the first act of dissolution proved to be the harbinger of the spoil and destruction that was still to come – and of which the Henrician regime was itself the author and the architect. After three years of piecemeal suppression marked by a relentless polemical campaign against the religious, a second act of dissolution was issued in 1539 that retroactively incorporated previously surrendered religious houses into a programme of total suppression. It is a striking feature of Henry VIII's dissolution of the monasteries that, despite the vehemence with which the regime had asserted its rhetoric of iniquity and corruption in 1536, monasticism in principle and as a way of life was never officially abolished. Rather, it was extinguished de facto by the 1539 act, which also marked a profound shift in Henrician rhetoric. Less inflammatory and provocative than its predecessor, the act declared simply that the remaining abbeys, convents, friaries, and all other monastic properties had been granted in perpetuity to the crown. Underpinning the act was the language of complicity and surrender, now vastly amplified, with the effect of portraying the dissolution as a virtually painless transfer of land and wealth from Church to crown:

> Where diverse and sundrie Abbottes, Priours, Abbesses, Prioresses and other Ecclesiasticall Governours ... of their owne free and voluntarie myndes good willes and assentes, without constraynte, coaction or compulsion ... have severally geven granted and by the same their writings severally confirmed all their saide Monasteries, Abbathies, Priories, Nonries, Colleges, Hospitals, Houses of Friers and other religious and ecclesiastical houses & places ... to our saide Soveraigne Lorde [Henry VIII] his heires and successors forever.[37]

For the first time, the word 'dissolution' appeared in the Henrician vocabulary. This was not the 'Dissolution of the Monasteries' that has become the modern shorthand for the events of 1536–40, but rather one

---

[37] 31 Hen. VIII, c. 13, *Statutes of the Realm*, iii, p. 733.

amongst a set of interchangeable terms to describe the transfer of the religious houses to the state: the 'dissolucion, suppression, renouncing, relinquyshinge, forfeyting, [and] gevyng upp' of the remaining monasteries into the king's hands. In doing so, the regime also continued to invoke the collusion of the religious in fall of their own houses. But perhaps most strikingly of all, by repeated reference to 'the said *late* Monasteries, Abbathies, Priories, [and] Nonries' the 1539 act played a memory trick upon its audience, implying that the monastic institution had already collapsed, despite the fact that some religious houses continued to function into the early months of 1540.[38]

Philip Schwyzer has argued that the language of 'lateness' implied recent transformation, which enabled subsequent generations of Reformation polemicists and commentators to capture a keen sense of what had been lost during episodes like the dissolution.[39] However, in this context, in a document drawn up by the Henrician regime before the process of suppression was fully complete, the idea of lateness served a slightly different function. Shifting from the present tense of the first act of suppression to the past tense, the 1539 act fixed the religious houses firmly in the past and described a transformation that might have been recent, but which was also supposedly complete. If the first act of suppression was emblematic of the regime's need to emphasise and memorialise monastic corruption, this second act reflected a new and powerful impulse to downplay the extent of the transformation wrought by the wholesale dissolution of religious houses in England and Wales.

Chief amongst the aspects of the dissolution that the regime sought retrospectively to forget was the fact that it had not actually been achieved 'without constraynte, coaction or compulsion'. Late in 1539, three abbots – heads of houses in Colchester, Glastonbury, and Reading – refused to surrender their abbeys to the crown's commissioners. Resistance was not a feature of the government's vision of the dissolution, which had been pre-emptively laid out in the terms of the 1539 act as an episode of painless surrender. A spate of executions followed. In an especially grisly episode, Richard Whiting, abbot of Glastonbury, and two of his monks, Roger James and John Thorne, were dragged to the top of Glastonbury Tor, where they were hanged, drawn, and quartered. Whiting's head was subsequently placed over the west gate of his abbey and his broken limbs

---

[38] Ibid. My emphasis.
[39] Philip Schwyzer, '"Late" losses and the temporality of early modern nostalgia', *Parergon* 33 (2016), pp. 97–113.

were displayed publicly in Wells, Bath, Ilchester, and Bridgwater. G. R. Elton once described this incident as 'a sudden outburst of violence ... much at variance with the government's previous behaviour' in implementing its religious reforms.[40] Yet the parade of Whiting's remains recalled the set-piece executions of the Holy Maid and Friar Forest earlier in the 1530s, and it also had echoes of the exposure of the corrupt relics at Boxley and Hailes. Whiting's defiance was thus treated like an act of monastic corruption – the dominant narrative of dissolution in 1536–8. If violence of this kind was – as Elton suggests – relatively uncommon during the suppression, it was not entirely at odds with the practices of a regime that was mindful of its reputation and legacies.

However, as the project of dissolution progressed and evolved, and as the regime began to emphasise monastic surrender and to retreat from its earlier argument about the need for the reform of the monasteries, we begin to see a tension emerging in the Henrician government's vision of the suppression. On the one hand, after 1539, it sought to bury the religious houses in oblivion in order to downplay the novelty and gravity of the dissolution and its less palatable aspects. On the other, in order to justify this policy, the government was continually forced to reiterate and remember earlier narratives of monastic corruption. As we shall see in future chapters, successive generations would continue to negotiate precisely this struggle between conflicting impulses to remember and forget.

The very process of dissolution was itself an attack upon the physical and material memory of the medieval past. The dismantling of monastic structures was, like iconoclasm, a powerful mechanism of attempted forgetting.[41] It is clear from the commissioners' correspondence that erasure was a deliberate tactic. In December 1538, a group wrote to Cromwell from 'the late priorye of Christecheurche' at Twynham in Dorset, prefiguring the language that the regime would adopt in the 1539 act of dissolution. They invoked themes of surrender and complicity, writing that the suppression of Christchurch had been a simple and painless affair, since the prior, John Draper, was 'a very honest conformable person'. They had also found the priory 'well furnysschide with juellys [jewels] and plate', plenty of which had been earmarked as 'mete for the kinges majestie is [sic] use'. Other fabrics and fittings received less careful handling. The iconoclasts set about defacing the priory's memorials, including a 'monument curiosly made of Cane [Caen] stone, preparyd by the late mother of [Cardinal]

Raynolde Pole for herre buriall, wiche we causyd to be defacyd and all the armys and badgis clerely to be delete[d]'.[42] Reginald Pole was a notable opponent of the Henrician Reformation; Margaret, his mother, was executed by the Henrician regime in 1541 and buried without the memorial destroyed by the commissioners in 1538. Simultaneously, this kind of material violence represented a profound attack on Catholic commemorative traditions and beliefs about the dead and served to erode the dynastic memory embedded in the very fabric of the religious houses.[43] This was a form of strategic, targeted erasure, and a parallel to campaigns such as the regime's attempts to repress the memory of the murdered Catholic saint Thomas Becket.[44]

Perhaps unsurprisingly, this process of eradication and destruction was entirely absent from official pronouncements made by the Henrician regime. And yet the monasteries had become a critical battleground upon which the government waged its wider campaign both against what Eamon Duffy has called the 'indoor landscape of memory' in churches and religious houses and against the memory rooted in the wider physical landscape.[45] At the same time, the mutilated remnants of images and monuments, and the spaces and voids in which they had once stood, served to commemorate the triumph of the iconoclasts – and, as we shall see in future chapters, this was also true of the ruinous and fragmentary remains of the religious houses themselves.

The last of the abbeys, the Augustinian house at Waltham in Essex, was surrendered to the king's commissioners on 23 March 1540. Although the dissolution was not completely buried in oblivion, in the years that followed, the Henrician regime's attempts to downplay many of its consequences were reinforced by polemic that perpetuated its dual rhetoric of reform and surrender. A brief examination of some of this material reveals that the suppression continued to be invoked by those who retained vested interests in remembering certain aspects and consigning others to oblivion.

---

[42] BL, Cotton MS Cleopatra E IV, fol. 267.
[43] On the Reformation and commemorative practices see Peter Marshall, *Beliefs and the Dead in Reformation England* (Oxford, 2002); Peter Sherlock, *Monuments and Memory in Early Modern England* (Aldershot, 2008); Lucy Wooding, 'Remembrance in the Eucharist', in Andrew Gordon and Thomas Rist (eds.), *The Arts of Remembrance in Early Modern England: Material Cultures of the Post Reformation* (London, 2013), pp. 19–36.
[44] On forgetting Becket, see, for example, Parish, *Monks, Miracles, and Magic*, pp. 93–9.
[45] Eamon Duffy, *Saints, Sacrilege and Sedition: Religion and Conflict in the Tudor Reformations* (London, 2012), p. 110. See also Alexandra Walsham, *The Reformation of the Landscape: Religion, Identity, and Memory in Early Modern Britain and Ireland* (Oxford, 2011), esp. ch. 2.

In particular, monasticism continued to function as an emblem of Catholic corruption in the context of the ongoing Reformation. In 1540, the Cambridgeshire cleric Lancelot Ridley wrote a commentary on St Paul's epistle to the Ephesians in which he urged his reader to 'marke the remissyon of synnes is gyven to us by the bloude of Christe: and not by the popes pardons ... [by] Benedictines habit, cope or cote, by monkes bootes' or by 'fryer observantes shoyes or knotted gyrdles'.[46] By forming a monastic stereotype built on the Henrician vision of corrupt monasticism, evangelical polemicists created what Susan Wabuda has described as 'convenient foil for the new type of solid, bearded *paterfamilias*' used to represent the reformers and which inverted the ideals of chastity, poverty, and obedience with which the religious orders had been founded.[47] This archetype could be invoked retroactively to justify the dissolution of the monasteries in ways that continued to perpetuate the Henrician government's exhortations to monastic reform. In 1546, Simon Fish's 1529 anti-monastic *Supplicacyon* was reprinted in a newly expanded version as *A supplicacyon of the poore commons*. The anonymous author echoed Fish's reforming voice and used the dissolution as an argument for further reform. He praised Henry VIII for 'seking a redresse and reformation of thys greate and intollerable enormitie' of monastic corruption. The regime had, he wrote approvingly, 'with most ernest diligence, supplanted, and as it were, weeded out a greate numbre of valiant and sturdy monckes, fryers, chanons, hermites, and nunnes, which disguised ypocrites, under the name of the contempt of this world, wallowed in the sea in the worldes wealth'.[48] Although the monasteries had fallen, the memory of monastic corruption thus continued to function as a powerful tool in Reformation debates.[49]

In light of the potency of these allegations about standards in the monasteries, others began to develop overtly providentialist accounts of the dissolution. In his 1545 commentary on the Book of Daniel, the evangelical writer George Joye wrote of the 'superfluouse excesse and

---

[46] Lancelot Ridley, *A commentary in Englyshe upon Sayncte Paules Epystle to the Ephesyans, for the instruccyon of them that be unlearned in tonges gathered out of the holy scriptures and of the olde catholyke doctors of the churche* (London, 1540), sig. B2v.

[47] Susan Wabuda, *Preaching during the English Reformation* (Cambridge, 2002), pp. 122, 127.

[48] *A supplicacyon of the poore commons* (London, 1546), p. 268.

[49] See also Harriet Lyon, '"Superstition Remains at this Hour": *The Friers Chronicle* (1623) and England's Long Reformation', *Reformation* 24 (2019), pp. 107–21.

viciouse lyving of ydle bisshops, preistis, and monkis', echoing earlier statements peddled by the Henrician government.[50] He described how:

> So sodenly fyll downe all these abbeis: verely for because their abominable idolatry in M[a]sses, images, pelgrimages, shrynes, and their execrable superstiticiouse rytes and ceremonies, and their chosen holynes in flythye voews and dampnable hypocrisye stode in the place there they ought not to have stonden. And therefore there dropped downe upon them so miserable a perpetuall destruccion even the sign of goddis hevey wrath.[51]

Joye characterised the dissolution as a divine judgement, wrought upon the monks in punishment for the crimes uncovered by the Henrician regime in the mid-1530s, thereby playing up the idea that the monasteries had fallen and surrendered, as opposed to having been torn down purely by human hands. For Joye, it was vital that this memory be kept alive to serve as a warning to future generations of the power of God's wrath. This was especially true in light of new developments in Henrician religious policy: in virtually the same breath as it had announced the wholesale dissolution of the religious houses, Henry's government had also begun to revert to a more doctrinally conservative Reformation, embodied in the Act of Six Articles (1539). In this context, as we shall see, the suppression became a prominent motif in evangelical writing. 'Your prophane popish m[a]sses be abolishyed', Joye admonished, 'as they be well minished and put downe now in many places with the abbeyes.'[52] The memory of the dissolution functioned in this context as a prophylactic against further error, as well as a reminder that, for many, the Reformation remained as yet incomplete.

But there was a tension between this impulse to remember the triumph of the Henrician regime over the monasteries and a different impulse to repress the memory of monastic corruption. This was perhaps most explicit in the writings of John Bale, one of the most prominent and vitriolic of the evangelical polemicists, who had himself once taken vows as a Carmelite friar. Bale's *Actes of Englyshe votaryes* (1546), which was projected as a series of works attacking monasticism but never completed, took a profoundly negative view of monasticism. He described the religious orders as 'whoremongers, bawdes, brybers, Idolaters, hypocrytes, trayters, and most fylthye Gomorreanes' – citizens of the biblical city synonymous with impenitent sin and ultimately destroyed by divine

---

[50] George Joye, *Exposicion of Daniel the prophete gathered oute of Philip Melanchton, Johan Ecolampadius, Chronade Pellicane & out of Johan Draconite &c* (London, 1545), fol. 67v.
[51] Ibid., fol. 168v.   [52] Ibid., fol. 224r.

wrath.[53] Bale recognised that there were many who believed 'that I haye
not herin done wele, in bryngynge so many fylthy exampels of the Popes
unchast masmongers to light, which ought rather to have bene buryed in
oblyvyon'.[54] But for Bale, it was vital that remembrance of this corrupt
tradition be continued so as to prevent backsliding to Catholicism.
Because the *Actes of the Englyshe votaryes* was never completed, its chronology did not extend as far as the Henrician dissolution. But Bale's *Image
of both churches*, first published in Antwerp in the mid-1540s, gives
a flavour of what future parts of the *Actes* might have looked like: 'In
England', he wrote, 'by the Gospell preaching have many of these waters
[stemming from the spring of sin] bene dryed up in the suppression of
monasteries, priories, co[n]vents, & fryers houses.'[55] Bale urged remembrance of this corruption precisely because he, like Joye, feared the
continued threat posed by Catholicism.

For others, the selective memory of the dissolution was underpinned by
a different impulse: the imperative to account for collaboration in the
dissolving and plundering of the religious houses. In 1544, the
Gloucestershire gentleman Richard Tracy published *A supplycacion to our
moste soveraigne lorde Kygne Henry the Eyght*, in which he attacked the
'many popishe monckes which late were Abbottes', describing their 'greate
pensyons' as unworthy and unjust. He also regretted that 'many of their
convent monckes havinge nether lernynge nor other godly qualytes' were
yet 'admytted to have cure of soules' in the reformed Church.[56] This
suggests, perhaps, that there was a continuing interest in keeping alive
the anti-monastic rhetoric of the mid-1530s. Tracy had been heavily
involved in the dissolution of local monasteries and had also acted as the
temporary custodian of the Holy Blood of Hailes after it had been exposed
as a fraud in 1538. He reaped the benefits of his loyalty to the crown and
came into the possession of large tracts of abbey land in the wake of the
suppression, including Clifford Priory in Hertfordshire.[57] His *Supplycacion*

[53] John Bale, *The actes of Englyshe votaryes, comprehendynge their unchast practices and examples by all ages, from the worldes begynnynge to thys present yeare, collected out of their owne legendes and chronycles by Johan Bale* (London, 1546), sig. A2r.
[54] John Bale, *The first two partes of the actes, or unchast examples of the Englysh votaryes, gathered out of their own legends and chronycles by Johan Bale, and dedicated to our most redoubted soveraigne kygne Edward the syxte* (London, 1551), fol. vii.
[55] John Bale, *The image of both churches* (London, 1570), fol. 126v.
[56] Richard Tracy, *A supplycacion to our moste soveraigne lorde Kygne Henry the Eyght* (London, 1544), sig. A6r.
[57] On Tracy's life and career, see Alec Ryrie, 'Tracy, Richard (*b.* before 1501, *d.* 1569)', *ODNB*, www .oxforddnb.com/view/article/27650.

made no reference to this land transfer nor indeed to the dissolution itself or the gains made by the nobility more generally in its aftermath. Here again we find an inherent tension between the desire to repress the memory of the suppression and the need to remember it – in this instance in order to justify the post-dissolution status quo.

The dissolution was, then, widely perceived as an episode with significance for the English Reformation and it continued to exercise a profound influence over debates about the nature and direction of religious reform well into the later years of Henry VIII's reign. But as we have seen in the work of authors like Bale and Joye, this material also deployed the recent memory of the suppression to agitate for further change and thereby to voice a critique of the regime. Henrician attempts to manage the reception of the dissolution therefore involved rebutting and silencing its critics, who were drawn not only from the evangelical camp, but also from amongst those who remained staunchly Catholic or at least conservative in their religion. Recovering these voices requires us to look beyond the conventional sources for the dissolution and to read some of this material against the grain. These critiques denied the Henrician regime a total monopoly over the memory of the suppression and contributed to an emerging and evolving memory culture that was dynamic, polyvocal, and multivalent. It is the earliest of these critiques – the Catholic and conservative critiques – to which we now turn.

Catholic and Conservative Voices

Although the Henrician regime did not commit to wholesale dissolution until 1539, there had always been those who suspected that the government's aspirations to reform the religious houses concealed something more sinister. The State Papers preserve the echoes of a powerful rumour culture that developed in the early, uncertain days of suppression, when the government still purported to be undertaking only a partial dissolution of religious houses. As Thomas Warley wrote to Lady Lisle shortly before the first act of dissolution was announced in early 1536, he had 'no news but the abbeys shall be down'.[58] As the first suppressions got underway, reports continued to travel quickly, both at home and abroad, where they were often received with fear and anger. One of the first openly critical accounts of Henrician policy can be found in the correspondence that passed between Eustace Chapuys, imperial ambassador to the Holy Roman

---

[58] *L&P*, x, no. 573.

Empire, and Charles V. This reveals the development of an early alternative narrative to that propagated by the English government. In April 1536, Chapuys reported angrily that Henry VIII would 'not forbear to throw down the monasteries, and impiously usurp the foundations for the redemption of the dead'.[59] There was no hint of the Henrician rhetoric of reform and corruption in Chapuys's letter. He adopted a violent language of usurpation and of the 'throwing down' of monasteries, and he openly attacked the English government's assault on the medieval memory rooted in the monastic tradition. Before the end of the year – and long before the wholesale dissolution got underway – Chapuys had further lamented to the Habsburg statesman Antoine Perrenot de Granvelle that a 'legion of monks and nuns' had been 'chased from their monasteries' and were 'wandering miserably hither and thither seeking means to live'.[60] Thus Chapuys inverted the key tenets of Henrician rhetoric, which emphasised that the dissolution was an act of reform that had been achieved by the surrender of the religious, and that the whole affair was conducted efficiently and without human cost.

Not only do Chapuys's reports suggest that the dissolution found a cold reception with the Catholic powers of Europe, they also offer a window onto the experiences of the primary victims of the dissolution. Kathleen Cooke estimates that some 8,780 monks and friars and around 1,900 nuns were affected by the dissolution.[61] A number of different fates awaited the religious who had been forced to abandon their homes and vocations. Using wills, pension records, episcopal registers, and ecclesiastical court cases, Claire Cross has traced the post-dissolution movements of religious communities in the East Riding of Yorkshire. As elsewhere in England and Wales, many religious accepted their pensions and were dispersed into secular society. Heads of houses had the most to gain: in December 1538, John Kylwyke, Augustinian prior of Kirkham Priory, was pensioned £50 per annum, and in December 1539, Richard Stopes, Cistercian abbot of Meaux Abbey near Beverley, was granted a yearly pension of £40.[62] Female religious received rather less generous sums, with Christiana Burgh, prioress of the Benedictine house at Nunkeeling, pensioned £8 per annum in September 1539, the same month that Dorothea Knight, Cistercian prioress of Swine Priory, was granted

---

[59] Ibid., x, no. 752.   [60] Ibid., xi, no. 42.

[61] Kathleen Cooke, 'The English nuns and the dissolution', in John Blair and Brian Golding (eds.), *The Cloister and the World: Essays in Medieval History in Honour of Barbara Harvey* (Oxford, 1996), pp. 287–301 at p. 291.

[62] M. Claire Cross, *The End of Medieval Monasticism in the East Riding of Yorkshire* (Beverley, 1993), pp. 48–9.

a yearly sum of £13 6s. 8d.[63] This was still significantly more than the pensions received by more junior members of both male and especially female communities, who were sometimes forced to rely upon relatives or a family inheritance to make ends meet.[64] For most of these dispersed monks, nuns, and friars, pension records provide one of the best means of accessing their lives in the wake of the dissolution. Cross's examination of these documents has revealed that in 1556 Edward VI's government recorded eighty-eight ex-religious still living in the East Riding (thirty-one monks and fifty-seven nuns), and eighteen (two monks and sixteen nuns) were still claiming their pensions well into the 1580s.[65] But although these records testify to the continued existence of the ex-religious in sixteenth-century England, their perspectives and voices are much harder to recover.

We should not assume, like Chapuys, that all ex-religious were miserable about the dissolution or the changing direction of Henrician religious policy. Some friars, especially Observant Friars, were particularly prone to a vision of Church reform that, paradoxically, served to align their ideas with those of the Henrician evangelicals.[66] Many, including the polemicist John Bale as well as John Hilsey, the ex-Dominican prior who denounced the Holy Blood of Hailes in 1538, turned their talent for preaching to the service of the reformers. More generally, for male religious open to reformist ideas, the Reformation afforded new opportunities as secular clergy, sometimes within the very houses in which they had taken their monastic vows. In 1541, brothers Stephen and Nicholas Marley, formerly sub-prior and monk respectively in Durham's Benedictine Abbey, joined many of their brethren as canons of Durham Cathedral, from where they conformed under the reformation reigns of Henry VIII and Edward VI, and the return of Catholicism under Mary I.[67] Perhaps Mary's reign gave them new confidence, as they appear to have opposed the Elizabethan articles of religion; as a result, Nicholas was deprived of his canonry and vicarage at Pittington in 1560.[68] Until the mid-1550s, however, Nicholas and his brother had negotiated their way fairly successfully in the post-dissolution world. The same is true of William Sheppard, once a monk of Faversham in Kent, whose example, as Mark Byford has demonstrated,

---

[63] Ibid., pp. 52–3.   [64] Ibid., pp. 43–4.   [65] Ibid., p. 34.

[66] Richard Rex, 'The friars in the English Reformation', in Peter Marshall and Alec Ryrie (eds.), *The Beginnings of English Protestantism* (Cambridge, 2002), pp. 38–59 at p. 41.

[67] A. I. Doyle, 'The library of Sir Thomas Tempest', in G. A. M. Janssens and F. G. A. M. Aarts (eds.), *Studies in Seventeenth-Century Literature, History, and Bibliography* (Amsterdam, 1984), pp. 83–94 at pp. 85–6.

[68] Ibid., p. 86.

offers a case study of clerical adaptation.[69] A canon at the Augustinian Priory of St Mary and St Nicholas in the village of Leeds in Kent before the dissolution, Sheppard held the rectory at Heydon, Essex, for more than forty years, without apparently compromising the integrity of his religious beliefs.[70] His example testifies to the continuity of vocation that ex-monks could find in the new Church of England, and highlights how the dissolution was not necessarily experienced as a total rupture between an old way of life and a brave new world.

It is also clear, however, that many ex-monks and nuns attempted to maintain something of their former lives. Some fled England in order to practise their religion in safety. There is now a flourishing literature on monks and especially nuns in exile,[71] and the 'Who were the nuns?' and 'Monks in motion' projects have traced the activity of England's female religious and the male Benedictine community respectively in the sixteenth and seventeenth centuries.[72] If monasticism thrived abroad, there is also some evidence of continuing community amongst the ex-religious at home. The Bridgettine Syon household at Denham offers one example of this practice. After the dissolution of Syon Abbey in 1539, the abbess, Agnes Jordan, along with seven sisters, two priests, a chaplain, and a couple of lay brothers became tenants of a house at Southlands, owned by a local Catholic family.[73] Jordan died in 1546 but the rest of the group remained at Southlands for a few years, before they too sought a different way of maintaining their corporate life overseas.[74] Led by Katherine Palmer, a group of nuns left Syon for Antwerp, taking with them their convent seals, relics, vestments, muniments, and part of the extensive Syon library.[75] Indeed, these materials were essential to the continuance of community – and many monks and nuns took a similar approach to the books and goods of their houses, which, as we have seen, were at risk of

---

[69] M. S. Byford, 'The price of Protestantism: assessing the impact of religious change on Elizabethan Essex: the cases of Heydon and Colchester, 1558–1594', unpublished DPhil thesis, University of Oxford (1988), p. 426 and ch. 1 passim.

[70] Ibid., pp. 13, 15–16.

[71] See, for example, Caroline Bowden and James E. Kelly (eds.), *The English Convents in Exile, 1600–1800* (London, 2013); Claire Walker, *Gender and Politics in Early Modern Europe: English Convents in France and the Low Countries* (Basingstoke, 2003).

[72] See 'Who were the nuns?', Queen Mary University of London, https://wwtn.history.qmul.ac.uk/; 'Monks in Motion', Durham University, www.dur.ac.uk/mim/.

[73] Peter Cunich, 'The Syon household at Denham, 1539–1550', in John Doran, Charlotte Methuen, and Alexandra Walsham (eds.), *Religion and the Household* (Woodbridge, 2014), pp. 174–87.

[74] Mary C. Erler, *Reading and Writing During the Dissolution: Monks, Friars, and Nuns, 1530–1558* (Cambridge, 2013), p. 122.

[75] David Knowles, *The Religious Orders in England*, 3 vols. (Cambridge, 1948–59), iii, p. 440.

looting, loss, or destruction. In Durham, the Marley brothers managed to salvage a large number of books from the Benedictine monastery, in which they inscribed their names and which they left in the care of their brother-in-law, Sir Thomas Tempest, whose home became something of a safe haven for monastic books and manuscripts.[76] These efforts to continue community, and to preserve the material remnants of the monasteries, call into question the historiographical tendency to see the ex-religious as merely, to echo Mary Erler's phrase, the 'remnants of a cast-off system'.[77] In her study of the reading and writing practices of monks, nuns, and friars during and after the dissolution, Erler reveals a more complex relationship between attempts at continuity and the acceptance of religious change, in ways that meant the religious were actively engaged in – rather than simply being passive victims of – the struggles of the mid-sixteenth century.[78]

There were also those, of course, who resisted the dissolution vociferously. Richard Hilliard, chaplain to Cuthbert Tunstall, bishop of Durham, left England for Scotland in 1539 and appears to have paused at the monasteries he passed to advise 'houses yet unsuppressed not to surrender till they were violently put therefrom'.[79] This evidence opens a window onto a culture of intrigue and defiance amongst supporters of traditional religion in the 1530s, and, although few heads of houses followed such advice, it is also true that the abbots of Colchester, Reading, and Glastonbury were not the only casualties of the dissolution. Early in the spring of 1535, three Carthusian priors had been put to death for refusing to take the Oath of Supremacy. John Houghton of the London Charterhouse, Robert Laurence of Beauvale Priory, and Augustine Webster of Axholme Priory were hanged, drawn, and quartered at Tyburn, and their mutilated body parts displayed around London as a warning to others considering opposition to the Royal Supremacy. However, it seems that the remaining Carthusians of the London Charterhouse were undeterred, and they continued to reject the encroachment of royal power by opposing the dissolution of their house. With the regime unable to convince or coerce many of the Carthusians into submission, further executions took place at Tyburn and in York in 1535 and 1537. In addition to the three priors, fifteen other Carthusians were either executed or died in prison. After their deaths, as Anne Dillon has

---

[76] Doyle, 'The library of Sir Thomas Tempest', pp. 83–7.   [77] Erler, *Reading and Writing*, p. 13.
[78] Ibid., *passim*.
[79] *L&P*, xiv part 2, no. 723. See also Peter Marshall, *Religious Identities in Henry VIII's England* (Aldershot, 2006), p. 234.

demonstrated, the Carthusian martyrs became the 'talk of Europe and they were celebrated and commemorated by the Catholic community'.[80] Their example also served further to undermine the Henrician government's claim to have conducted the dissolution without resorting to torture, intimidation, or coercion.

In different ways, then, individuals and communities formerly belonging to religious orders kept the memory of the dissolution alive. Given the range of responses to the suppression exhibited amongst the religious orders in the 1530s, it is important and striking that the papers passing through Thomas Cromwell's office (and which now form the principal archive of the dissolution) are largely devoid of religious voices – or, rather, that the religious appear to speak with one voice and on one note through their pleas for exemption. Like Joan Missenden, prioress of Legbourne, who, as we saw previously, avowed the exemplary behaviour of its inhabitants, other heads of house wrote to Cromwell to protest their suppression. In 1536, the abbot of Woburn Abbey, Bedfordshire, insisted that he and his brethren were 'cleane frome any suche crymes and enormites' and requested king and government to 'shewe your pitie and compassion upon us in suche godly wise that we may deserve to contynewe'.[81] The abbess of Godstow near Oxford employed a similar rhetoric of humble piety, combined with exhortations of loyalty to the king, in her own correspondence with Cromwell: 'I truste I have done the beste in my power to the mayntenance of Godes trewe honour, withe all treuthe and obedience to the kynges magestie.'[82] Other heads of house were willing to go further in their desperation to protect their monasteries and nunneries. Early in 1536, Nicholas Austen, the abbot of Rewley, Oxfordshire, offered Cromwell the sum of £100 'so that our house may be sayvd', even if the only way of achieving this was to transform the abbey into a secular college.[83] Unfortunately for Austen, his offer was declined, and the abbey was dissolved in 1539.

Pleas for exemption aside, the religious orders are the most significant archival silence in the documentary record of the dissolution. Perhaps this is due, in part, to self-censorship and dissimulation, the result of traumatic experiences of dissolution or a product of the 'humiliated silence' that followed the defeat of monasticism.[84] But it is also undoubtedly indicative

---

[80] Anne Dillon, *Michelangelo and the English Martyrs* (Farnham, 2012), p. 2 and *passim*.
[81] BL, Cotton MS Cleopatra E IV, fol. 96.   [82] Ibid., fol. 228.   [83] Ibid., fol. 269.
[84] For an intriguing discussion of trauma and the dissolution see Peter Cunich, 'The ex-religious in post-dissolution society: symptoms of Post-Traumatic Stress Disorder?', in James G. Clark (ed.), *The Religious Orders in Pre-Reformation England* (Woodbridge, 2002), pp. 227–38. On forgetting as

of the actions of a regime that had little interest in the perspectives of those who dissented from the 'official' vision of the dissolution.[85] The result is that the religious have largely been written out of the wider history of the suppression or cast in minor roles as the compliant and contrite victims of their own corruption.

Other dissenting voices were harder to suppress, albeit the evidence survives in a mediated form, set down in the hands of court clerks and government agents. The autumn of 1536 witnessed a series of rebellions protesting the regime's religious reforms. The most famous of these risings was the Pilgrimage of Grace, instigated by a group of Yorkshire rebels in October of that year. This rising was perhaps the most significant conservative reaction against the dissolution to emerge in the 1530s and one of the most important popular protests of the Tudor period.[86] The rebels claimed the strength of upwards of 30,000 men; accounting for a degree of overestimation on the part of its leaders, this was nevertheless significant enough to indicate widespread discontent in the region, a stronghold of conservative religious sentiment.[87] Whilst occupying the city of York, the rebels reintroduced Catholic observances and even attempted to restore banished monks and nuns to their religious houses. When they entered negotiations with the leaders of the king's forces, Thomas Howard, duke of Norfolk, and George Talbot, earl of Shrewsbury, they were promised a pardon, as well as a temporary reprieve for the local abbeys and convents. However, Norfolk and Shrewsbury did not keep their promises, and, after the Pilgrimage of Grace was suppressed, its leaders were brought to trial in 1537. When required to account for his actions, local lawyer Robert Aske, the foremost leader of the rising, articulated exactly the vision of the dissolution that the Henrician regime was trying so vigorously to undermine:

> First, to the statute of suppressions, [Aske] did grudge against the same and so did the whole country, because the abbeys in the north parts gave great

'humiliated silence', see Paul Connerton, 'Seven types of forgetting', *Memory Studies* 1 (2008), pp. 59–71, at pp. 67–9.

[85] Although, of course, there was no uniformity of perspective on the dissolution amongst the religious. See Erler, *Reading and Writing*, p. 2 and *passim*.

[86] The memory of the Pilgrimage of Grace merits further investigation. For a suggestive preliminary discussion, see Andy Wood, *The 1549 Rebellions and the Making of Early Modern England* (Cambridge, 2007), p. 6.

[87] R. W. Hoyle, *The Pilgrimage of Grace and the Politics of the 1530s* (Oxford, 2001), p. 293. See also Christopher Haigh, *The Last Days of the Lancashire Monasteries and the Pilgrimage of Grace* (Manchester, 1969), chs. 5–7; M. L. Bush, *The Pilgrimage of Grace: A Study of the Rebel Armies of October 1536* (Manchester and New York, 1996); Andy Wood, *Riot, Rebellion, and Popular Politics in Early Modern England* (Basingstoke, 2001), pp. 49–54; Shagan, *Popular Politics*, ch. 3.

alms to poor men and laudably served God . . . And by occasion of the said
suppression the divine service of almighty God is much diminished, great
number of masses unsaid and the blessed consecration of the sacrament now
not used and showed in these places, to the distress of the faith and spiritual
comfort to man's soul, the temple of God ruffed and pulled down, the
ornaments and relics of the church of God unreverent used, the towns and
sepulchres of honourable and noble men pulled down and sold, no hospitality now in those places kept . . . when the abbeys stood, the said people
not only had worldly refreshing in their bodies but also spiritual refuge both
by ghostly living of them and also by spiritual information and preaching;
and many tenants were their fee'd servants to them and serving men, well
succoured by the abbeys.[88]

Aske and the Pilgrimage rebels perceived the dissolution as an assault on
Catholic piety and a threat to salvation, as well as a shock to the rhythms of
English local life. As Philip Schwyzer has observed, this fed into a vision of
the dissolution as a national calamity.[89] Aske also inverted the Henrician
account of monastic corruption to emphasise the continued piety, charity,
and hospitality of the religious orders – the same virtues that scholars such
as Martin Heale and James G. Clark have sought to recover and rehabilitate from Henrician polemic.[90] But perhaps the most striking aspect of
Aske's statement is his evocative description of the temporal and material
rupture engendered by the dissolution. Wholesale suppression was still two
years from being formally announced when Aske was put to death in
July 1537, and yet his testimony referred poignantly to a time 'when the
abbeys stood' as being a time distinct from his own. Aske's testimony was,
to use R. W. Hoyle's term, a 'eulogy' for the monasteries of the North –
a memorial, in other words, for a past that had already been lost.[91]

Aske's testimony survives because it was recorded in the course of the
defeat of the Pilgrimage of Grace and the punishment of its leaders. The
repercussions for Aske were swift and severe, undermining his message about
the catastrophic consequences of dissolution. At the same time, the regime
was also undertaking various measures – both coercive and persuasive – to
ensure that dissenting voices were silenced. Prior to Aske's execution, in
November 1536, Henry VIII had issued an answer to the petition signed by

---

[88] Quoted in Hoyle, *Pilgrimage of Grace*, p. 47. Also printed in Mary Bateson, 'Aske's examination', *English Historical Review* 5 (1890), pp. 550–74.

[89] Philip Schwyzer, 'The beauties of the land: Bale's books, Aske's abbeys, and the aesthetics of nationhood', *Renaissance Quarterly* 57 (2004), pp. 99–125; Philip Schwyzer, *Literature, Nationalism, and Memory in Early Modern England and Wales* (Cambridge, 2004), ch. 2.

[90] Martin Heale, *Monasticism in Late Medieval England, c. 1300–1535* (Manchester, 2009); James G. Clark, *The Benedictines in the Middle Ages* (Woodbridge, 2011).

[91] Hoyle, *Pilgrimage of Grace*, p. 48.

the Pilgrimage rebels that powerfully underlined the duty of obedience that bound subjects to the crown.[92] Meanwhile, the king also commanded Lord Darcy to 'apprehend as seditious all persons who shall speak of the suppression of the abbeys, taking away of their church goods or of levying new impositions'.[93] Darcy's sympathies, however, lay elsewhere – he had discussed rebellion himself with Chapuys in 1534–5 and ultimately sided with Aske's rebels; as a result, he was executed in June 1537.[94] The king's demand to Darcy reveals that the government was cognisant of alternative perspectives on the dissolution and that an oral culture of sedition was apparently widespread.[95] Suppressing and condemning these dissenting voices was essential to the power and persistence of arguments about the painless and necessary fall of the religious houses.

However, critics of the dissolution could not be silenced completely and in the two decades following the dissolution the Catholic critique continued to find expression in religious debate. The Catholic restoration instigated by Mary I in 1553 offers a particularly illuminating vantage point on the evolving Catholic memory of the suppression. Although it was hoped that domestic monasticism might be re-established during the 1550s, the brevity of Mary's reign served to curtail this endeavour.[96] A handful of institutions were revived, including the monastic presence in Westminster Abbey and the Bridgettine house at Syon Abbey – headed now by Katherine Palmer, who had overseen the exile of the Syon nuns to the Continent – on the banks of the Thames. However, the parliamentary acts announcing the restoration of monasticism reveal some of the barriers faced by Mary's government and are indicative of a programme that never really got going. In 1554, a proclamation was issued that stated that the owners of former monastic properties would 'for the tyme being' be allowed to 'enjoye [their lands] withoute impechmente or trouble'.[97] This time there was no triumphant rhetoric to announce the restoration of the monasteries akin to that which had heralded both their supposed reformation and their eventual surrender under Henry VIII.

---

[92] *Answere made by the kynges hyghnes to the petitions of the rebelles in Yorkeshire* (London, 1536).

[93] *L&P*, xi, no. 611.   [94] On Darcy's career see Hoyle, *Pilgrimage of Grace*, ch. 9.

[95] On seditious speech and the dissolution see David Cressy, *Dangerous Talk: Scandalous, Seditious, and Treasonable Speech in Pre-Modern England* (Oxford, 2010), p. 50.

[96] Mary's limited revival of domestic monasticism is a neglected subject. For one approach see C. S. Knighton, 'Westminster Abbey restored', in Eamon Duffy and David Loades (eds.), *The Church of Mary Tudor* (Aldershot, 2006), pp. 77–123.

[97] *Anno secundo & tertio Philippi & Mariae* (London, 1555), fol. 14r. See also *Anno primo et secundo Philippi & Mariae* (London, 1555), fol. 17r–v.

This reflected the general unwillingness of many amongst the gentry to follow the queen's lead and return their former monastic lands to the Church. In a few cases old monasteries were returned to the crown for the re-establishment of religious communities. In November 1555, for example, the duchess of Richmond was persuaded to hand back Sheen House for the use of those Carthusians who had fled England rather than face execution in 1537.[98] However, in most instances Mary and Reginald Pole, now archbishop of Canterbury, were thwarted in their attempts to regain monastic property. Writing in the late sixteenth century, the Jesuit Robert Persons described how 'many or rather all that had Abby-Lands, the good Queen Mary herself and some very few others excepted, remained with the same, as with a prey well gotten'.[99] Persons's comments reveal another aspect of the selective memory of the dissolution: the beneficiaries of the dissolution – whose number included lay Catholics as well as Protestants – had an interest in retaining their lands and properties and, therefore, a vested interest in forgetting former generations of monastic owners.[100]

The Marian regime's abortive attempts to re-establish a monastic presence in England have usually been considered in terms of Mary and Pole's failure to be more proactive in restoring the religious houses and, more generally, in light of the brevity of her reign.[101] However, we might also see this as symptomatic of a culture in which the Henrician dissolution seemed final. Despite the fact that the ultimate fate of the monasteries had not yet been decided in the 1550s, most Catholic polemicists thought about the suppression in the past tense. In the 1530s, Aske had deployed the language of 'pulling down' the monasteries to communicate something of the violence and finality of the dissolution conducted by Henry VIII, his agents, and collaborators. During Mary's reign, rather than discuss the possibilities for the future of monasticism, Catholic polemicists continued to invert Henrician tropes, developing a language of suppression and subversion that was at odds with the Tudor rhetoric of reform and surrender. Thus the polemicist Richard Smith argued in 1554 that the

---

[98] Dillon, *Michelangelo and the English Martyrs*, p. 35. On exile during the dissolution and in its aftermath, see Frederick E. Smith, 'Religious mobility and the development of English Catholicism, 1534–1558', unpublished PhD thesis, University of Cambridge (2019). I am grateful to Fred Smith for advice on this subject.

[99] Robert Persons, *The Jesuit's memorial for the intended reformation of England under their first popish prince published from the copy that was presented to the late King James II*, trans. Edward Gee (London, 1690), p. 21.

[100] On converted monasteries and forgetting, see below, Chs. 3 and 4.

[101] See Duffy and Loades (eds.), *Church of Mary Tudor*, introduction and ch. 3.

'subversions of abbaies' had been a 'similitude of godlines perswaded by the sayd protestantes, by whose pitifull spoyle procedeth the decay of our common wealth'.[102] Like Aske, Smith also drew upon the pervasive conservative narrative of socio-economic decline to support this argument. 'The abbeys tilled much corne', he continued, 'for the sustenacion of many men, women, and chyldren, but now shepe & beastes fedde there . . . & do cause al thinges to be extreamely deare.'[103] For this catastrophe, Smith believed, the agents of the dissolution in 1530s had been punished. If Henrician polemicists had begun to portray the suppression as a providential victory over Catholic corruption, Marian polemicists took delight in describing how God had reproached the reformers for their actions. In this respect, Thomas Cromwell attracted a great deal of attention, his rise and fall roughly coinciding with the two phases of the dissolution. 'What was the cause of Crumwelles falle [in 1540]', Smith asked, 'but heresie begonne with spoyle of abbeis, & treason against the kyng himselfe?'[104] This was, of course, a strategy carefully designed to avoid laying blame with a king whose heir continued to occupy the throne. But although there was not yet sufficient distance from the events of 1536–40 for an explicit critique of Henry VIII to develop, it is nevertheless striking that Smith appears to have thought of the dissolution as a distinctly Henrician phenomenon.

In one sense, this polemic functioned as a partial remedy against the forgetting of the monastic past. One of the most powerful examples of the capacity of Catholic polemic to sustain and preserve the memory of aspects of the dissolution that were in danger of slipping into oblivion can be found in the Catholic controversialist Miles Huggarde's *The displaying of the Protestantes* (1556). In defiance of Henrician attempts to downplay the violence of the suppression, Huggarde reminded his audience of the execution of the abbots of Reading, Colchester, and Glastonbury, of John Forest, and of a number of other Catholic martyrs, including the martyrs of the Carthusian Charterhouse in London. These men 'and a greate number mo[re]', he wrote, had 'died for the cause of the catholyke fayeth'. He urged that their 'memory shall be magnified tyll the ende of the worlde'.[105] This reflected wider commemorative practices concerning the Reformation martyrs, like those examined by Anne Dillon, which also

[102] Richard Smith, *A bouclier of the catholike fayth of Christes church, conteynyng divers matters now of late called into controversy, by the newe gospellers* (London, 1554), fol. 110r.
[103] Ibid., fol. 19v.   [104] Ibid., fol. 102v.
[105] Miles Huggarde, *The displaying of the Protestantes, & sondry their practises, with a description of divers their abuses of late frequented* (London, 1556), fols. 66v–67r.

compelled Catholics to remember those who had resisted the dissolution and to reflect upon its human cost.[106] One such vehicle for reflection was the martyrological writing of Maurice Chauncy, prior of the re-established Sheen Charterhouse. His retelling of the story of dissolution from the perspective of the persecuted Carthusians appeared in several versions between the 1540s and 1570, and was subsequently printed in further editions in the late sixteenth and seventeenth centuries. Chauncy was reminded that 'it was notorious that [the martyrs] underwent this kind of death and punishment' and sought to commemorate the victims of dissolution rather than the event itself.[107]

Ultimately, however, Henrician polemic continued to set the tone for the memory of the dissolution. Mary's abortive restoration was followed by a new dissolution in 1558 during the reign of her half-sister, Elizabeth. It is striking that neither phase appears to have made much of a mark upon the early modern memory of the dissolution or indeed upon its historiography. Revisionist scholarship has long sought to emphasise the successes of Mary's reign when considered upon its own terms.[108] Perhaps, given more time, things might have been different regarding the monasteries. But as it was, the Marian restoration failed significantly to change the terms of the debate surrounding the dissolution. Catholic polemicists portrayed the suppression as fundamentally an episode in the Henrician Reformation; there is no clear narrative of a Marian 'Restoration of the Monasteries'. The fact that there is no conventional narrative of an Elizabethan 'Dissolution of the Monasteries' also testifies to the perceived totality of the Henrician dissolution in the 1530s. Modern scholarship has also neglected the long process of suppression that took place between 1536 and the accession of Elizabeth. In this respect, modern historians are once again revealed to be the heirs of ideas and traditions of discourse developed during the 1530s and perpetuated and reshaped by successive generations across the sixteenth century.[109]

The accession of Elizabeth serves roughly to demarcate the generational boundary between those who had witnessed and experienced the dissolution and a new generation which had not. Many of the Marian

---

[106] See Anne Dillon, *The Construction of Martyrdom in the English Catholic Community* (Aldershot, 2002); Anne Dillon, *Michelangelo and the English Martyrs*.

[107] Maurice Chauncy, *The history of the sufferings of eighteen Carthusians in England: who refusing to take part in schism, and to separate themselves from the unity of the Catholic Church, were cruelly martyred* (London, 1890), p. 59.

[108] See especially Eamon Duffy, *Fires of Faith: Catholic England Under Mary Tudor* (New Haven, CT, and London, 2009). See also Duffy and Loades (eds.), *Church of Mary Tudor*.

[109] See below, Ch. 2.

polemicists had relied upon their own memories to furnish their accounts of the suppression. Smith, for example, felt a profoundly personal sense of loss for the abbeys that had once 'nouryshed many poore mens chyldren at schole (emongst the which I was one, or els I shoulde never have been learned)'. This experience served to sharpen and augment his more general lament for the 'gret dammage and decay unto the honour and service of God' wrought by the dissolution.[110] Likewise, the former evangelical cleric and 'doctrinal chameleon', John Standish, having reverted (only possibly sincerely) to the Catholic faith in which he had been raised, wrote in 1556 that 'I remember I heard a sermon [given by Thomas Cranmer] at Paules about the time abbeis were suppressed', the content of which he used to critique the Henrician government's failure to fulfil its promise of 1536 that suppressed monasteries would be put to pious uses.[111] But as Elizabeth's reign progressed, the conservative critique was taken up by those who could not remember the dissolution at first hand. This generation was forced to deal with and confront the memories that they had inherited from their ancestors who had been raised in pre-Reformation Catholicism and who had witnessed – and even participated in – the events of the Henrician Reformation.

Around 1591, the Yorkshire cleric Michael Sherbrook penned a manuscript entitled 'The fall of the religious houses'. He viewed the episode partly through the lens of his faint childhood remembrances of the suppression of Roche Abbey, a large Cistercian monastery in Maltby, South Yorkshire, but also principally through the recollections of his father and uncle, who had participated in its spoliation and destruction.[112] In a remarkable passage, Sherbrook wrote that he had once enquired of his father:

> Whether he thought well of the Religious Persons and of the [Roman Catholic] Religion then used? And he told me Yea: For said He, I did see no Cause to the contrary: Well, said I, then how came it to pass you was so ready to distroy and spoil the thing that you thought well of? What should

---

[110] Smith, *Bouclier of the catholike fayth*, fol. 19r–v.

[111] John Standish, *The triall of the supremacy wherein is set forouth the unitie of Christes church militant geven to S. Peter and his successoures by Christe: and that there ought to be one head bishop in earth Christes vicar generall ouer all hys churche militant: wyth answeres to the blasphemous objections made agaynste the same in the late miserable yeres now paste* (London, 1556), sig. R8r. On Standish see Duffy, *Fires of Faith*, pp. 63–4.

[112] This manuscript survives in an eighteenth-century copy: BL, Additional MS 5813, fols. 5–29; published in A. G. Dickens (ed.), *Tudor Treatises*, Yorkshire Archaeological Society Record Series 125 (1959), pp. 89–142.

I do, said He: might I not as well as others have some Profit of the Spoil of the Abbey? For I did see all would away; and therefore I did as others did.[113]

This is a striking example of the transmission of memory from one generation to another, as well as powerful evidence of the complex character of popular collaboration in the dissolution.[114] This was, perhaps, an unwelcome memory and encapsulated the realisation that, for many Henrician Catholics, to remember the dissolution was to remember their part in it.

Sherbrook's comments on the dissolution reveal that, in many ways, he was the heir of his father's memories. Created rector of Wickersley, seven miles from Roche, in 1567, he seems to have upheld the Elizabethan religious settlement and performed his duties diligently.[115] His hazy memory of the 1530s yielded little more than the recollection that he had seen the abbey bells hanging in their timber frames a year or more after Roche fell in 1538.[116] But he also supplied a lengthy history of the suppression, which displayed great sympathy for the religious orders and their houses. Painting a favourable picture of the piety, chastity, and charity of the monks and nuns, Sherbrook reserved his greatest praise for the ways in which they had served the needs of local communities. 'Happy was that Person', he wrote, 'that was Tenant to an Abbey.'[117] He also used a language of pity that remained a consistent feature of conservative critiques of the dissolution and a countermeasure against the rhetoric of Henrician triumph. 'It would have pitied any Heart to see', he lamented, 'what tearing up of the Lead there was.'[118] In his opinion, the lay founders and patrons of monasteries also deserved remembrance for their acts of piety. 'The Commons of England', Sherbrook argued, 'have more Cause to praise the Builders and Founders thereof than the Destroyers and Spoylers thereof; and greatly to lament the overthrow thereof.'[119] The dissolution had thus shaped Sherbrook's sense of the passage of time and, implicitly, the contrast between a childhood of abbey bells and an adulthood lived in a rather less munificent world. 'The estate of the Realm hath come to more Misery since King Henry 8 his time', he wrote, 'than ever it did in all the time before.'[120]

---

[113] Dickens (ed.), *Tudor Treatises*, p. 125.   [114] See Shagan, *Popular Politics*, ch. 5.
[115] Dickens (ed.), *Tudor Treatises*, pp. 28–9; Michael Carter, 'Michael Sherbrook, the fall of Roche Abbey and the provenance of Cambridge University Library MS GG.3.33', *Notes & Queries* 63 (2016), pp. 19–22 at p. 20.
[116] Dickens (ed.), *Tudor Treatises*, p. 125.   [117] Ibid., p. 95.   [118] Ibid., p. 124.   [119] Ibid., p. 89.
[120] Ibid., p. 90.

This manuscript survives only in an eighteenth-century copy and, although the text has been reproduced and, therefore, possibly and unknowably distorted by the pen of the copyist, its preservation is itself indicative of the potent afterlives of the dissolution in historical conscious-ness and cultural memory. Alternative narratives in the form of Catholic and conservative accounts of dissolution began to emerge that ran counter to those promoted by the Henrician regime in the 1530s and which rejected the government's rhetoric of reform and surrender. Catholics perceived the suppression as a moment of severe rupture in the religious and social fabric of early modern England and had also begun to articulate a vision of the dissolution as a break between past and present. The abortive Marian restoration in the 1550s did little to diminish this sense of a breach in the 1530s. Yet, as we have noted, many Catholics were also not immune from the desire to forget certain aspects of the suppression and the memories of those who had collaborated with the regime could be highly ambiguous.

An examination of the conservative critique has already begun to suggest not only that there were vulnerabilities in the Henrician vision of the dissolution, but also that, in its aftermath, contemporary perceptions of the suppression were more complex and ambiguous than has sometimes been suggested. It was not only proponents of traditional religion for whom this was the case. The dissolution also had its detractors at the other end of the confessional spectrum. If there were many in Henrician England who believed that the dissolution had taken the idea of reform much too far, there were also those who thought it had not gone far enough.

The Evangelical Critique

At the heart of the problem with the dissolution in the eyes of many reformers was the government's claim of 1536 that it was seizing monastic property in order that it could be 'used and converted' for 'better uses'.[121] In the early days of the suppression, many of the regime's supporters hoped that this meant that monastic wealth would be transferred into the hands of the Church of England, where it might be used for pious and educa-tional purposes. In this respect, the dissolutions conducted by Margaret Beaufort and Cardinal Wolsey set an important precedent. As we noted previously, both Henry VIII's grandmother and former chief minister had been responsible for small-scale suppressions enacted with explicit intent to found and support new educational establishments. For this reason, these

---

[121] 27 Hen. VIII, c. 28, *Statutes of the Realm*, iii, p. 575.

dissolutions had been wholly uncontroversial. Many hoped that the Henrician dissolution would follow this model. The humanist Thomas Starkey was one prominent proponent of this argument – not least because he believed that the transformation of abbeys into schools and universities might have the added benefit of quelling fears on the Continent, such as those expressed by Chapuys, about the government's move against the monasteries:

> I thynke the troth ys thys, that yf the world might see thes grete monastarys wych yet stond, converted & turned in to lytyl unyversytes, and made therby, as hyt were commyn scholes of lernyng & virtue to the ryght educatyon of youthe, al thes droonys [drones] wych consume the hunnye driven out of the hyvys [hives] as unprofytable to god & to the world, then schold not the supressyon of these lytyl abbays gyve so much occasyon, among blynd pepul ful of foly, of any sklaunderouse infamy.[122]

Starkey thus tapped into the Henrician rhetoric of reform and aligned it with the humanist concern for education, learning, and the good of the commonweal. It was clear that he supported the principle of dissolution, but also that he had specific concerns about its consequences.

At times, it seemed as though Starkey's vision might be realised. It was certainly a vision shared by many reformers. The government received a number of petitions requesting support for particular institutions. In June 1538, for example, Hugh Latimer, bishop of Worcester and a prominent reformer, wrote to Cromwell begging that the king remember Warwick College with 'some piece of some broken abbey'.[123] Often, these requests were granted. A considerable number of monastic buildings were converted into schools and colleges, and many monastic churches were converted into parish churches and secular cathedrals. These included some former religious houses in the Cambridgeshire city of Ely where, as the king informed Thomas Goodrich, bishop of Ely, 'we have lately fownded and erected a catherdral churche in the honour of the holy trynytie in Ely . . . [in] place of the late priory there'. The king wrote that he hoped that further accommodation for the clergy and the master and scholars of the associated grammar school might be found amongst the buildings that remained unoccupied.[124] Not only did conversions of this sort enable the Church of England to retain some of the wealth possessed by the medieval religious houses, it also fostered a degree of continuity in the purpose and function of ex-monastic properties.[125]

---

[122] L&P, xi, no. 73.   [123] Ibid., xiii, part 1, no. 1202.   [124] CCCC, MS 120, 26.
[125] On converted churches, see below, Ch. 3.

Ultimately, however, many of the reformers' hopes for the monasteries were dashed. As much of the commissioners' correspondence in the 1530s reveals, there were other motives at play in the dissolution besides the establishment of new schools and parish churches. 'I desire your favour', Thomas Legh begged Cromwell from Holmcultram in 1538, 'for myself and my brother to have the preferment of the said abbey.'[126] Legh's request belies the gains in material wealth and status that stood to be made by the commissioners and others amongst the Henrician nobility and gentry. Certainly Legh profited from the dissolution, acquiring several leases and rewards from suppressed monasteries.[127] Pleas of this nature far outnumber requests for support for churches and schools in Cromwell's correspondence. It is telling that many of those who wrote to the king's vicegerent for this purpose drew explicitly upon the regime's anti-monastic rhetoric. The diplomat and commissioner for the dissolution Sir Thomas Elyot, for example, was at pains to impress upon Cromwell that 'I have in as moche detestation as any man lyvyng all vayne supersticions, superfluouse ceremonyes, sklaunderouse jouglynges, countrefaite mirakles, [and] arrogant usurpations' of the religious. Having vehemently professed his anti-monastic credentials, he pleaded that 'I therfor moste humbly desyre you my speciall goode lorde, so to brynge me into the kinges most noble remembrance, that of his moste bounteouse liberality it make like highnesse to reward me with some convenyent porcion of his suppressid landis'.[128] If, as Greg Walker and Jennifer Summit have argued, Elyot's confessional colours are difficult to discern, his writings appearing by turn to express sympathy for the religious and to condemn their corruption, this particular petition is nevertheless a striking demonstration of the potency of Henrician rhetoric.[129] It is clear that Elyot knew that the way to secure the king's favour was to echo the government's vision of the dissolution as a measure of reform designed to tackle monastic corruption. This tactic appears, moreover, to have worked: Elyot was permitted to purchase lands formerly belonging to Eynsham Abbey in Oxfordshire at a very favourable rate.[130]

As things turned out, then, the 'better uses' of which the government had spoken in 1536 tended to involve lining the pockets and coffers of the

---

[126] *L&P*, xiii, part 1, no. 547.
[127] Anthony N. Shaw, 'Legh, Sir Thomas (*d.* 1545)', *ODNB*, www.oxforddnb.com/view/article/16363.
[128] BL, Cotton MS Cleopatra E IV, fol. 220.
[129] Greg Walker, *Writing Under Tyranny: English Literature and the Henrician Reformation* (Oxford, 2005), p. 131; Jennifer Summit, *Memory's Library: Medieval Books in Early Modern England* (Chicago and London, 2008), pp. 87–8.
[130] Summit, *Memory's Library*, p. 88.

crown and nobility rather than the church. For many evangelicals, this was a source of profound distress. The ardent Yorkshire evangelical Sir Francis Bigod exemplifies the conflicted position in which many reformers found themselves over the question of monastic land and wealth.[131] Bigod was a strong supporter of Henry VIII's pretended 'reformation' of the monasteries: he was a contributor to the *Valor ecclesiasticus* and, once the dissolution was underway, reported and sought to reform what he perceived to be gross monastic abuses. When the Pilgrimage of Grace broke out in Yorkshire in 1536, Bigod announced his opposition to Aske's conservative rebels and, in doing so, quickly became one of their chief targets. He was captured by the Pilgrims in Hartlepool and carried to York by the rebels, at which point he embarked upon what A. G. Dickens described as a 'fatal course of thinking'.[132] Although he condemned monastic corruption, Bigod was also wary of royal intervention in Church matters. He disliked how the dissolution was unfolding under Cromwell's direction and, after the Pilgrimage rebels were disbanded at the end of 1536, began to agitate for further disruption. This evangelical critic of the suppression thus found his views aligning with its conservative detractors. Bigod, a committed reformer, co-opted the conservative Pilgrimage oath and articles to his own cause and he attempted to revive local opposition to the dissolution. Bigod's Rebellion was thus the improbable sequel to the Pilgrimage of Grace. It was also extremely short-lived: a major confrontation planned for 19 January 1537 in Hull was pre-empted by a dawn raid in which most of Bigod's supporters were captured and, although Bigod himself fled, he was eventually recaptured, imprisoned, and later executed for his opposition to the king. The human cost of the dissolution cannot, therefore, be counted simply in terms of monastic, Catholic, and conservative voices.

Bigod's Rebellion was a unique episode of outright evangelical revolt, but anxiety about the fate of ex-monastic lands and wealth was a more widespread concern. As Alec Ryrie has demonstrated, dissatisfaction with the state of affairs in 1536–40 underpinned a powerful early evangelical critique of the dissolution that fed into the wider 'commonwealth' tradition of political and socio-economic criticism.[133] Unlike the Catholic

---

[131] On Bigod's life and career, see A. G. Dickens, *Lollards and Protestants in the Diocese of York, 1509–1558* (Oxford, 1959), ch. 3; Michael Hicks, 'Bigod, Sir Francis, (1507–1537)', *ODNB*, www.oxforddnb.com/view/article/2375.

[132] Dickens, *Lollards and Protestants*, p. 91.

[133] Alec Ryrie, *The Gospel and Henry VIII: Evangelicals in the Early English Reformation* (Cambridge, 2003), esp. pp. 161–4. On the wider character of evangelical religion under Henry VIII, see also Alec Ryrie, 'Counting sheep, counting shepherds: the problem of allegiance in the English Reformation', in Marshall and Ryrie (eds.), *Beginnings of English Protestantism*, pp. 84–110.

critique, this position was not founded upon an inherent problem with the dissolution in principle, which was part of a wider series of religious changes that evangelicals applauded and commended. Rather, the evangelical critique arose out of concerns about the manner in which monastic wealth and property had been dispersed amongst the nobility rather than channelled back into the Church or into educational institutions that had suffered as a result of the dissolution. At the University of Cambridge, for example, student numbers went into a pronounced decline after the monastic colleges were closed, and the suppression left the university 'significantly impoverished'.[134] 'Hindsight', as Ryrie argues, thus 'soured even the dissolution of the monasteries' in the eyes of many reformers, to whom it seemed that the government was peddling empty rhetoric by pretending that the spoils of the monasteries would be put to pious uses.[135]

One such critic was George Joye, whose commentary on the Book of Daniel we have already encountered as an example of anti-monastic polemic. If Joye was in many respects a loyal Henrician, he was also critical of the government's handling of the dissolution. Drawing upon the biblical account of corruption in the Hebrew temples, Joye condemned the wealth – the 'goods and jewels of oure temples/abbeys' – misused by the Catholic Church. Such idolatry, he argued, 'empowrs kynges and princes may take them awaye and putt them to beter uses'. But the reality of the suppression left Joye wanting. He further argued that the crown had 'translate[d] chirche goodis into prophane uses … suffering the pore chirches, congregacions, and scoles to be cold and hongreye'.[136] He criticised the pensions received by the religious but reserved his strongest criticism for the lay owners of monastic property like Legh and Elyot, mocking 'how fiercely the nobilitie fighteth to reteyne in their handis collegis, abbeis, chauntres, bisshoprykes, benefices &c for their owne profite'.[137] To underline his point, Joye inverted the rhetoric of fraudulence that characterised Henrician attacks upon the monasteries, reapplying it to describe the regime itself. Monarchs, he argued, did not have the power 'to translate to themselves thecclesiastic goodis' if this involved 'the defrauding of the pore chirches and scoles'.[138] Joye thus invoked the covetousness of crown and government as a parallel to the idolatrous practices he detested in the Catholic Church.

---

[134] Ryrie, *Gospel and Henry VIII*, pp. 162–3. On the University of Cambridge during the Reformation, see Ceri Law, *Contested Reformations in the University of Cambridge, 1535–1584* (London, 2018).
[135] Ryrie, *Gospel and Henry VIII*, p. 155.   [136] Joye, *Exposicion of Daniel*, fol. 67r.
[137] Ibid., fol. 141r.   [138] Ibid., fol. 67v.

Like Joye, other evangelical polemicists also attempted to rework the Henrician vocabulary of suppression to suit their own ends. One of the most open and vehement critics of Henry VIII's commitment to reform in the 1540s, Henry Brinkelow, went one step further, adopting the persona of a former Franciscan friar, Roderick Mors, for added rhetorical effect.[139] Mors was a fictional counterpart to real-life figures such as Bale, the ex-Carmelite turned fervent evangelical polemicist. In 1542, writing in *The complaynt of Roderyck Mors*, Brinkelow used this character to attack the government for its pretence that the 'putting downe' of religious houses had served to 'amend that [which] was amisse in them'. Although he condemned corruption in the religious houses, Brinkelow begged his reader to 'see now how it that was amisse [in the monasteries] is amended for al the godly pretense'. He was profoundly concerned by the consequences of the dissolution for the commonwealth and the communities that had relied upon the monasteries. Like Joye, Brinkelow identified a decline in hospitality and charitable giving to the poor; he mourned that in many places there was now 'not one meales meate geven' to travellers and those in need.[140] Socio-economic anxieties of this kind were inherent in the evangelical concern for the misuse of monastic property, feeding into a wider sense that the work of reformation remained incomplete.

Evangelical polemicists thus used the dissolution to advance a profound critique of the wider Henrician Reformation, as well as the suppression itself. It is worth underlining here that this did little to undermine the government's argument that the monasteries had been in severe need of reform. Moreover, by adopting the voice of a former friar, Brinkelow also subtly perpetuated the complicity of the religious in their own suppression. Yet this was not enough to protect polemicists like Brinkelow and Joye from the ire of the Henrician regime. Just as it had sought to silence Catholic critiques of the dissolution, so too the government attempted to repress and discredit its evangelical critics in order to protect its reputation and the legacies of its Reformation. It is no coincidence, for example, that a large proportion of printed polemic of this sort was published on the Continent.[141] *The complaynt of Roderyck Mors* was published from

---

[139] On Brinkelow's exposure as Mors see Alec Ryrie, 'Brinklow [Brinkelow], Henry [*pseud.* Roderyck or Roderigo Mors] (*d.* 1545/6)', *ODNB*, www.oxforddnb.com/view/article/3437.

[140] [Henry Brinkelow], *The complaynt of Roderyck Mors, somtyme a gray fryre, vnto the parliament house of Ingland hys naturall countrey, for the redresse of certain wycked lawes, evell custums and cruell decrees* (Strasbourg, 1542), sigs. D3v–5r.

[141] On the printing practices and persecution of evangelical polemicists see Ryrie, *Gospel and Henry VIII*, ch. 4.

Strasbourg in order to protect Brinkelow's identity. Joye, meanwhile, spent two periods of exile in Antwerp because he felt it was too dangerous to remain in England.[142] He returned from his second flight abroad only after Henry VIII's death in 1547.

Joye's concerns were, perhaps, unsurprising given the changing direction of religious policy in the 1540s. Even before the last monastery had fallen, a conservative reaction was ushered in by the Act of Six Articles (1539), which reaffirmed Catholic doctrines and practices including transubstantiation and clerical celibacy. This only served to heighten evangelical anxiety about the failure of Henry VIII's 'reformation of the monasteries'. In a remarkable manuscript treatise addressed to the king, one anonymous evangelical author launched a vicious attack on the Henrician clergy who, he believed, were in danger of backsliding to popery. Adopting the voice of such a cleric, the author satirised critiques of the dissolution as a moment of rupture and decline. In particular, he mocked the argument that 'suerly suerly good neighbours, we had never mery nor welthie world sithens abbayes were put downe and this new learning browghte in place'. He went on to accuse the conservative Henrician clergy themselves of convincing people that 'the suppression of abbeys is thonely causes of thes their infinite miseryes and so set them for the recoovery of their old welth to wish and desire in their myndes the reedefying of superstitioose howses'.[143] His response to this threat was to recommend not only the mass deprivation of those Henrician clerics deemed unfit, but also their internment.[144] This treatise serves to demonstrate that many reformers believed that the work of reform had not been completed with the dissolution. It is also a powerful reminder that the work of suppression could also be undone. The permanent, wholesale dissolution of the monasteries was not a forgone conclusion in the 1540s – indeed a decade later, Mary I enacted her limited revival of monasticism, partially realising this anonymous evangelical's worst fears.

In his recent study of early Reformation radicalism, Karl Gunther has argued that this piece of vitriolic evangelical polemic was a potent example of the political radicalism that lay at one end of the 'spectrum of voices'

---

[142] H. L. Parish, 'Joye, George (1490×95–1553)', *ODNB*, www.oxforddnb.com/view/article/15153.
[143] BL, Royal MS 17 B XXXV, fol. 9r–v.
[144] See Karl Gunther, *Reformation Unbound: Protestant Visions of Reform in England, 1525–1590* (Cambridge, 2014), pp. 91–2. See also Ryrie, *Gospel and Henry VIII*, p. 44; Shagan, *Popular Politics*, p. 275; Peter Marshall, 'Is the pope Catholic? Henry VIII and the semantics of schism', in Ethan H. Shagan (ed.), *Catholics and the 'Protestant Nation': Religious Politics and Identity in Early Modern England* (Manchester, 2005), pp. 22–48 at pp. 38–9.

competing to be heard in the Henrician Reformation.[145] We might, therefore, expect the dissolution to be a critical episode for the development of radical perspectives on the Reformation – and yet the suppression does not feature anywhere in Gunther's account of Henrician radicalism. It is clear from this treatise, however, that the suppression was a powerful mnemonic for the idea of an incomplete Reformation, as well as a starting point from which evangelicals pressured for further religious change of a more radical nature. Although Gunther is inclined to draw a direct genealogical trajectory between the theology of Henrician radicalism and later species of Protestant radicalism – principally Elizabethan puritanism – the example of the dissolution suggests that we might think about the links between these perspectives in a slightly different way. Rather than necessarily revealing the roots of puritan theology, the anonymous plea to the king provides an illuminating case study of how the memory of the dissolution could be invoked as an impetus to further reform.

Generations of reformers would continue to draw upon the arguments made by evangelical writers in the 1530s and 1540s. Catherine Davies has described how, by the reign of Edward VI, covetousness had become 'the new idolatry', in what was 'a conscious adaptation of the language of anti-popery to the description and criticism of a supposedly reformed commonwealth, so that what was indeed an age-old theme was successfully invested with a fresh contemporary resonance'.[146] This critique also had important implications for the question of agency and motivation in the dissolution. In 1554, the Scottish reformer John Knox argued that the 'suppression of the abbacies did rather smell of avarice, then [sic] of true religion' – a vision further refracted through his hatred of episcopal Church governance and the transformation of 'superstitious freers, ignorant monks, and idle abots' into 'archbishoppes, bishoppes, persons, [and] vicars'.[147] 'For their own bellies sake', Knox wrote, the government had 'wrooted up many weeds' and in the process, church revenues had been 'most wickedly and ungodly spent'.[148] Likewise, the religious controversialist and Marian exile William Turner likened the nobility to suffers of dropsy, having 'swelled so muche'

[145] Gunther, *Reformation Unbound*, pp. 15, 91. See also Karl Gunther and Ethan H. Shagan, 'Protestant radicalism and political thought in the reign of Henry VIII', *P&P* 194 (2007), pp. 35–74.

[146] Catherine Davies, '"Poor persecuted little flock" or "commonwealth of Christians": Edwardian Protestant concepts of the church', in Peter Lake and Maria Dowling (eds.), *Protestantism and the National Church in Sixteenth-Century England* (London, New York, and Sydney, 1987), pp. 78–102 at p. 86.

[147] John Knox, *The appellation of John Knoxe from the cruell and most injust sentence pronounced against him by the false bishoppes and clergie of Scotland* (Geneva, 1558), sig. I4r.

[148] Ibid., sigs. I6r–7r.

with the profits of church lands and the acquisition of former monastic properties. He also directly attacked Henry VIII and his 'covetous counsell'.[149] Henry VIII's avarice also complicated providentialist narratives of the dissolution. The doctrine of providence could cut both ways: if Henry was sometimes portrayed as the divine instrument of dissolution, he was also a figure punished for his greed by posterity. Thus, for Turner, the destruction of the monasteries had soured the idea of Reformation and resulted in the 'spoile of the [w]hole church'. The '[w]hole realme', he argued, 'smarteth for it unto this day'.[150] The dissolution continued to resonate precisely because successive generations continued to believe that they were witnessing and living its effects. This was part of a wider sense amongst English Protestants that they continued to experience punishment for the failures in the Reformation conducted by their forebears.[151]

The evangelical critique identified by Ryrie has been almost entirely ignored in previous studies of the dissolution of the monasteries. Unlike the Catholic critique, which is rendered visible in the sources collected by Cromwell and his agents that pertain to the repression of dissent, the reformist critique is far less apparent in the paperwork of the dissolution. Largely expounded and perpetuated in unofficial forms of polemic and only fully developed in the aftermath of the suppression, it has had little place in an historiography that has been preoccupied with the course and immediate consequences of the events of 1536–40. Yet, as Ryrie has demonstrated, evangelical polemic depicted the dissolution as 'close to catastrophic' in socio-economic and educational terms.[152] As we have seen, this critique also had purchase in wider debates about the nature of Henrician religious policy and the ongoing Reformation. We need, then, to reconcile this account with the vision of the dissolution that has dominated its conventional historiography. The key to unlocking this problem lies in the enduring power and longevity of the dual Henrician rhetoric of reform and surrender, and its preservation in the sources and archives upon which previous accounts of the dissolution of the monasteries have been based.

---

[149] William Turner, *A new booke of spirituall physic for diverse diseases of the nobilitie and gentlemen of Englande* (Rome (i.e. Emden), 1555), fols. 48v–49r and *passim*.

[150] [William Turner], *The hunting of the fox and the wolfe, because they make havocke of the sheepe of Christ Jesus* (London, 1565), sig. D3r.

[151] See Davies, 'Poor persecuted flock'. See also below, Ch. 4.

[152] Ryrie, *Gospel and Henry VIII*, p. 162. See also Christopher Hill, *Economic Problems of the Church from Archbishop Whitgift to the Long Parliament* (Oxford, 1956), p. 3.

A 'Tudor Revolution in the Archives'?

In the 1950s, G. R. Elton developed the idea of a 'Tudor revolution in government'.[153] This highly influential paradigm sought to account for the bureaucratic expansion of the Tudor state in the 1530s and specifically the administrative activities and innovations instigated under Thomas Cromwell. The dissolution was perhaps the pre-eminent episode in this bureaucratic 'revolution'. The sheer scale of the project to dissolve the monasteries necessitated the creation of new institutions, principally the Court of Augmentations, to manage the transfer of monastic property and wealth from the hands of the Church into those of the crown.[154] Precisely because the dissolution entailed various legal and fiscal imperatives, the government amassed a vast collection of paperwork, including the commissioners' correspondence and materials connected to the lease, sale, and grant of ex-monastic lands. Historians of the dissolution have therefore been the beneficiaries of two connected developments: a significant increase in record-keeping during the 1530s and the preservation of much of this material after the confiscation of Thomas Cromwell's papers following his attainder and subsequent execution in 1540.[155] This accident of survival has shaped the historiography of the dissolution in two important ways. First, it has concentrated historians' attention around material created by and for the Henrician regime. Second, and relatedly, it has focussed previous studies on the origins and course of the dissolution, and thereby encouraged a prevailing tendency to see this episode as all but over by the early 1540s. Unlike contemporaries, for whom, as we have seen, the dissolution posed serious questions about the future of religion and society, modern scholarship has tended to see this episode simply as the death knell of the medieval Church and the close of the medieval period.[156]

The commissioners' correspondence, which has formed the backbone of this chapter, offers a case in point of the ways in which the archive of the

---

[153] G. R. Elton, *The Tudor Revolution in Government: Administrative Changes in the Reign of Henry VIII* (Cambridge, 1953).

[154] On the history of the Court of Augmentations, see W. C. Richardson, *History of the Court of Augmentations, 1536–1554* (Baton Rouge, LA, 1961).

[155] On the creation of the archive that is now the State Papers, see Amanda Bevan, 'State Papers of Henry VIII: the Archives and Documents', *State Papers Online, 1509–1714*, Thomson Learning EMEA Ltd, 2007, www.gale.com/intl/essays/amanda-bevan-state-papers-henry-viii-archives-documents.

[156] The key studies are David Knowles, *Bare Ruined Choirs: The Dissolution of the English Monasteries* (Cambridge, 1976); G. W. O. Woodward, *The Dissolution of the Monasteries* (London, 1966); Joyce Youings, *The Dissolution of the Monasteries* (London, 1971). For a full account of this historiography, see above, Introduction.

dissolution has been constructed, both consciously and inadvertently, to support a particular vision of the early Reformation. As we have already noted, the letters that passed between Cromwell and the commissioners tended to amplify certain voices and emphasise the agency of those who enacted the dissolution. Critical voices are few and far between. Postcolonial scholarship and, more recently, scholarship resulting from the 'archival turn', has demonstrated that archives are not neutral repositories.[157] If the survival of the commissioners' correspondence beyond 1540 was at least partly an accident of Cromwell's attainder, its preservation in the seventeenth-century library of Sir Robert Cotton was a more deliberate move. Cotton was one of the most prolific collectors of books and manuscripts of the early modern period.[158] His library, which is now part of the British Library, exemplifies Jennifer Summit's argument that contemporary collecting practices functioned to shape the character of libraries and archives and the ways in which generations of readers and historians have approached their content.[159] She describes the Cotton collection as having been constructed around the 'master narrative' of the Reformation, especially in the chronological ordering of the material compiled in the Cleopatra D and E sequences but also across the library as a whole.[160] The dissolution correspondence is preserved in Cleopatra E. It therefore functions as a critical chapter in the particular story that the Cleopatra series tells about the medieval past and the Reformation. Although neither Cromwell nor the Henrician regime to which he belonged could have foreseen the preservation of these documents in this way, Cotton's narrative of Catholic and monastic corruption overthrown by Henry VIII's Church of England evoked a vision of the dissolution familiar from the legal documents and government polemic of the 1530s.

---

[157] For particularly important interventions in postcolonial scholarship, see Thomas Richards, *The Imperial Archive: Knowledge and Fantasy of Empire* (London, 1993) and Ann Laura Stoler, *Along the Archival Grain: Epistemic Anxieties and Colonial Common Sense* (Princeton, NJ, 2010). On the early modern period, see Ann Blair, *Too Much to Know: Managing Scholarly Information Before the Modern Age* (Cambridge, MA, 2010); Liesbeth Corens, Kate Peters, and Alexandra Walsham (eds.), *The Social History of the Archive: Record-Keeping in Early Modern Europe*, P&P Supplement 11 (2016); Jesse Sponholz, *The Convent of Wesel: The Event That Never Was and the Invention of Tradition* (Cambridge, 2017); Liesbeth Corens, Kate Peters, and Alexandra Walsham (eds.), *Archives and Information in the Early Modern World*, Proceedings of the British Academy 212 (Oxford, 2018).

[158] For an overview of Cotton's life and career, see Kevin Sharpe, *Sir Robert Cotton, 1586–1681: History and Politics in Early Modern England* (Oxford, 1979).

[159] Summit, *Memory's Library*. On the capacity of archives to make memory more generally, see Eric Ketelaar, 'Muniments and monuments: the dawn of archives as cultural patrimony', *Archival Science* 7 (2007), pp. 343–57. See also below, Conclusion.

[160] Summit, *Memory's Library*, p. 195.

In the early modern period, documents preserved in the Cottonian library, including the commissioners' correspondence, were accessible to scholars alongside other records of the Reformation. Also held in the Cotton collection is one of the earliest narrative histories of the dissolution. Entitled 'The manner of dissolving the abbeys by K. H. 8.', this remarkable manuscript illuminates something of the process by which the vision of the dissolution promoted in the commissioners' correspondence was perpetuated in subsequent generations.[161] The anonymous author demonstrated clear knowledge of the visitation correspondence that passed between Cromwell and the commissioners in the 1530s. These letters, he wrote, had revealed:

> Of everie suche [religious] house, the vile lives and abhominable factes, in murders of their bretherne, in sodomyes, in whordomes, in destroying of children, in forging of deedes, and other infinite horrors of life, in so muche as deviding of all the religious persons in England into three partes two of theise partes at the least were sodomites: and this appeared in writting, with the names of the parties and their factes.[162]

Although it is not certain whether the author had seen the writings that he mentions in this passage, it is clear that he was fully aware of the commissioners' findings. He also acknowledged the programme of persuasion instigated by the government, writing that 'Cromwell caused preachers to goe abroade, and maintayned them to instructe the people, and so to perswade the subjectes consciences to stand fast to the king without feare of the popes curse'.[163] The author appears to have bought into the Henrician vision of the suppression wholeheartedly. Not only does 'The manner of dissolving the abbeys' echo the tenor of government exhortations to reform the monasteries in 1536, it also employs the rhetoric of surrender developed in 1539. The success of the government's campaign against the monasteries, the anonymous author argued, had resulted in the conversion of many of the religious themselves to the king's cause, who were then 'readie to make surrender of their houses at the kinges commaundment'.[164] This text thus encapsulates the key themes of the Henrician polemic of which it was at least partly the product: the corruption and iniquity of the religious, the efficiency of the wholesale surrender, and the complicity of the religious in their own downfall.

If this served powerfully to undermine conservative and Catholic critiques of the dissolution, 'The manner of dissolving the abbeys' was also

---

[161] BL, Cotton MS Titus F III, fols. 268v–270r.   [162] Ibid., fol. 269v.   [163] Ibid., fol. 269r.
[164] Ibid., fol. 269v.

a partial riposte to the Henrician regime's evangelical critics. There is some ambiguity in the passage in which the author describes how king and government decided 'to make suche dispersion' of abbey lands and goods 'as it behoved infinite multitudes for their own interest to joyne with the king in hollding them downe'. But he also praised the 'ffownding [of] divers bushoprickes and colleges' and the munificence of the Tudor nobility, whom he characterised as pious in their 'worship and good calling'.[165] It seems reasonable, then, to suggest that 'The manner of dissolving the abbeys' represented a new vehicle for an older brand of Henrician rhetoric. The product of traditions of discourse developed in the 1530s – and possibly of access to the documents produced during this period – this manuscript constitutes an early effort to transform Henrician polemic into an historical narrative of the dissolution. The text ends with the final surrender of the monasteries in 1540. 'Here', wrote the anonymous author, 'is all I can remember.'[166]

'The manner of dissolving the abbeys' is not only anonymous, it is also undated. It is therefore unclear as to whether the author had himself witnessed the dissolution. His claim to 'remember' might, on the one hand, reflect his personal recollections of the fall of the religious houses. The manuscript certainly falls within the date range to make this plausible. It is bound in the Cotton manuscripts with a number of other items gathered during Elizabeth I's reign by William Cecil, Lord Burghley, under the title 'England / Discowrses of the State of England & the Q. majesties proceedings in diverse cases'.[167] If dated to the early part of this period, the author might have been alive to witness the Henrician campaign against the monasteries. On the other hand, his comment might also testify to his inherited memory of the dissolution and the strength of the cultural memory that can be shaped by texts and other media, as well as by oral tradition.[168] In this respect, it is significant that the text of 'The manner of dissolving the abbeys' is almost entirely identical to that set down in a narrative letter dated August 1581, in which the Calvinist lawyer and historian Thomas Norton recounted the fall of the monasteries at the request of Francis Mylles, a servant of Sir Francis Walsingham.[169] An

---

[165] Ibid.   [166] Ibid., fol. 270r.

[167] For the attribution to Cecil, see Colin G. C. Tite, *The Early Records of Sir Robert Cotton's Library: Formation, Cataloguing, Use* (London, 2003), p. 202. I am grateful to Arnold Hunt for advice regarding the attribution of this manuscript.

[168] Jan Assmann, 'Collective memory and cultural identity', trans. John Czaplicka, *New German Critique* 65 (1995), pp. 125–33.

[169] Washington DC, Folger Shakespeare Library, MS X.c.62.

infant in the 1530s, Norton apologised to Mylles that he had no recollections of his own with which to furnish his account, but rather had set down
all that he could remember 'as I have understoode by that which I had red
& heard'. Yet his version too bears the comment that 'here is all that I can
remember'.[170] Norton's remark was thus not a claim to have experienced
the dissolution, but rather a shorthand for information mediated through
cultural memory.

It is difficult to say whether Norton was the author or simply a copyist of
the document preserved in the Cotton manuscripts. He certainly enjoyed
Cecil's patronage, and it is therefore definitely possible either that he had
access to Cecil's material or that he had offered his account for preservation
in his patron's collection.[171] He was also interested in English history,
adopting a providentialist, apocalyptic approach to the past; his most
notable work in this respect, entitled 'Of the v periods of 500 yeares', is
bound next to the anonymous account of the dissolution in the Cotton
volume Titus F III.[172] This evidence is by no means conclusive but,
together with the letter sent from Norton to Mylles in 1581, it does make
Norton a plausible – even the probable – author of 'The manner of
dissolving the abbeys'. Moreover, the question of authorship aside, the
acquisition of this manuscript by Cecil is highly significant because it ties
the dissolution into Elizabethan policy-making and the official and quasi-
official practices of collecting and archiving that served to perpetuate pro-
reform and pro-Tudor narratives. These processes, as Summit reminds us,
continue to shape how we think about the history of the dissolution and
the wider English Reformation.[173]

Another striking example of the power of Tudor archives can be found
in a richly illuminated manuscript, the *Heroica eulogia*, also produced in
the Elizabethan period.[174] The *Heroica* was created by William Bowyer, an
avid collector and Keeper of the Records in the Tower of London, in 1567.
Although the manuscript is unfinished, it was clearly intended for Robert
Dudley, earl of Leicester. Specifically, the *Heroica* was a polemical text,
designed to justify the suppression of monastic properties that had since

---

[170] Ibid., fol. 1v. This manuscript is also discussed below, Ch. 2.
[171] Marie Axton, 'Norton, Thomas (1530×32–1584)', *ODNB*, www.oxforddnb.com/view/article/20359.
[172] BL, Cotton MS Titus F III, fols. 271r–275v. I am grateful to Coral Casey-Stoakes for drawing this to
        my attention and for her advice on Norton.
[173] Summit, *Memory's Library*, p. 2 and *passim*.
[174] San Marino, CA, Huntington Library, HM 160. See also Norman Jones, 'Empowering the earl of
        Leicester', *Verso: The Blog of the Huntington Library, Art Collections, and Botanical Gardens*,
        26 May 2016, www.huntington.org/verso/2018/08/empowering-earl-leicester. I am grateful to
        Arnold Hunt for this reference.

passed into the earl's hands. It includes a series of images of depraved and wicked monks and friars accompanied by biblical exhortations against corruption. Whilst the Henrician religious orders had, as we have seen, been dispersed fairly quietly into secular society, their reputation as corrupt, iniquitous, and immoral continued to live on. In one such image the eponymous 'lecherous monk', *monacho libidinoso*, has his ears boxed by a woman (Figure 1.1). This depiction is sexually suggestive, underlining the depravity and iniquity supposedly uncovered in the monasteries; at the monk's feet, a stray cat plays with a loose thread, reinforcing the message of the Latin verse below about the 'filthiness' of its subject. In another image,

Figure 1.1 'De monacho libidinoso', illustration from William Bowyer, *Heroica eulogia* (1567), Huntington Library, San Marino, California, HM 160, fol. 103r.

the *abbate ingluvioso* – or 'voracious abbot' – sings from a popish hymn-book, a roasted piglet on a platter by his side, the very model of the worldly, avaricious, bloated figures described in the correspondence of the commissioners for the dissolution and other documents compiled by and for Cromwell and the Henrician government (Figure 1.2).

The *Heroica* is a remarkable compilation not only because it demonstrates the longevity and pervasiveness of the Henrician regime's anti-monastic language. Its very existence also reflects how successive generations of the Tudor nobility and gentry continued to perpetuate this rhetoric to justify their occupation of former monastic sites. They continued, in other words,

Figure 1.2 'De abbate ingluvioso', illustration from William Bowyer, *Heroica eulogia* (1567), Huntington Library, San Marino, California, HM 160, fol. 127r.

to have a vested interest in forgetting some of the more problematic and controversial consequences of the dissolution. By invoking ideas about monastic corruption, documents such as this also underline the relationship between the legal, economic, and religious aspects of the dissolution. The *Heroica* was also, of course, a product of Bowyer's particular interest in collecting and of his official duties as the custodian of the largest collection of government records in England in the 1560s.[175] As Keeper of Records, he was the heir of material that passed through the hands of Cromwell and other government officials, and he was responsible for preserving and organising this material. The *Heroica* was thus a product of Henrician polemic, even as it restated and reinterpreted this material for the Elizabethan age.

A growing appreciation of the role of early modern archives in memory formation has begun to cause scholars to refine and reframe the 'Tudor revolution in government'. In light of this insight, Vanessa Harding has recently suggested that we might think instead about a 'Tudor revolution in the archives' – itself in large part a consequence of the paperwork created by the suppression of the religious houses.[176] Harding argues that the explosion in record creation and keeping in the 1530s was both 'a result of the urgent need to manage and remain in control of new areas of activity and responsibility' and the symptom of 'a new interest in creating a permanent and authoritative record'.[177] This chapter has suggested that we might fruitfully extend this interest in an Henrician 'archival revolution' by considering the implications of this growth in record-keeping for modern historical scholarship. It helps us, *inter alia*, to understand the power of the Henrician rhetoric of monastic corruption and iniquity, and the longevity of ideas about the surrender rather than the forcible suppression of the religious houses. The sheer volume of archival material dating from the 1530s and early 1540s connected to the dissolution has been a rich seam for historians – modern and early modern alike – to mine. However, this chapter has suggested that this material offers an inherently narrow vision of the dissolution, heavily inflected by the Henrician regime's desire to downplay many of its consequences. In order fully to understand the significance of the dissolution of the monasteries, we therefore need to turn our attention to different kinds of sources.

---

[175] On Bowyer as Keeper of Records, see J. D. Alsop, 'Bowyer, William (*d.* 1569/70)', *ODNB*, www.oxforddnb.com/view/article/69724.

[176] Vanessa Harding, 'Monastic records and the dissolution: a Tudor revolution in the archives?', *European History Quarterly* 46 (2016), pp. 480–97.

[177] Ibid., p. 481. See also Nicholas Popper, 'From abbey to archive: managing texts and records in early modern England', *Archival Science* 10 (2010), pp. 249–66.

Conclusion: Reformation, Surrender, and Dissolution

The Henrician account of the dissolution has enjoyed a remarkably long afterlife. In the mid-nineteenth century, at a time when the Reformation was again being reinvented and older narratives re-examined in light of new anxieties about the 'myth' of the English Reformation and the emergence of the Anglo-Catholic 'Oxford Movement', Cromwell's visitation correspondence was edited and published under the auspices of the Camden Society.[178] In the preface to the volume, the editor Thomas Wright claimed that these letters 'tell their own story' of monastic corruption – and yet he quickly succumbed to the temptation to tell it himself: 'they throw light on the history of a great event . . . which I regard as the greatest blessing conferred by Providence upon this country since the first introduction of the Christian religion'. Taking the commissioners at their word, Wright argued that 'the great cause of the Reformation has been but ill served by concealing the depravities of the system which it overthrew'.[179] Wright's own vision of the dissolution was thus profoundly shaped by the material produced by and for the Henrician government. It is no small irony that his *Three Chapters of Letters Relating to the Dissolution of the Monasteries* (1843) also continues to provide scholars with an important point of access to the documentary record of the 1530s.

By focussing narrowly upon the years 1536–40, modern historians have therefore been reliant upon archives and collections that amplify certain voices and all but silence others. These libraries and archives – and the source books produced from them – are not neutral but are rather themselves products of the debates and polemical battles of the English Reformation – and, indeed, of the suppression itself. This chapter has suggested that Henry VIII and his government viewed the dissolution in two distinct phases. The first was the 'reformation of the monasteries', during which the government developed a powerful and influential rhetoric of monastic corruption. The second was the 'surrender of the monasteries', during which the regime sought to portray the religious as complicit in their own demise whilst downplaying some of the wider consequences of the suppression. This also functioned to soft-pedal the sense of rupture articulated by its critics – both in terms of a break between past and present

---

[178] On the Reformation in the nineteenth century, see Peter Nockles and Vivienne Westbrook (eds.), 'Reinventing the Reformation in the nineteenth century: a cultural history', *Bulletin of the John Rylands Library* 90 (2014). See also Diarmaid MacCulloch, 'The myth of the English Reformation', *Journal of British Studies* 30 (1991), pp. 1–19.

[179] Wright (ed.), *Three Chapters of Letters*, pp. v–vi.

and a rift in the religious, social, and economic fabric of sixteenth-century England.

Yet history has remembered the 'dissolution' and not the 'reformation' or the 'surrender' of the monasteries. This is something of an anomaly in an historiography that has been so heavily inflected by Henrician polemic. The language of the dissolution is, as we have seen, highly significant for how we understand this episode. Although the Tudor rhetoric of monastic corruption and iniquity has proven remarkably enduring, it is not the only analytical vocabulary that historians have inherited to describe the fall of the monasteries between 1536 and 1540. This language continued to evolve and shift across the early modern period. The very terms that we use to denote this episode are thus part of the problem of its long afterlives, artefacts of particular moments and of the very processes of memory-making itself. With this in mind, the next chapter considers changing perspectives on the suppression across the early modern period and the eventual emergence of the landmark event that we have come to know as the 'Dissolution of the Monasteries'.

CHAPTER 2

'Worthy of Lasting Memory'
The Dissolution in the Early Modern Historical Imagination

Virtually from the moment it began in 1536, the dissolution of the monasteries piqued the interest of chroniclers and historians. Despite the Henrician regime's efforts to downplay the transformation wrought by the dissolution in the 1530s, successive generations of scholars in the sixteenth and seventeenth centuries found themselves forced to confront an episode that had engendered a break with the traditions and institutions that had characterised the world before the Reformation. Given the magnitude of this rupture, it is hardly surprising that the dissolution became the subject of intense historical investigation and debate, both between and within Catholic and Protestant communities. What is surprising and striking, however, is quite how significant a role the suppression played in shaping the early modern historical imagination. Thus for one Jacobean chronicler, the dissolution of the monasteries was not only the most important event in the Protestant Reformation; it was also the most critical 'alteration, or revolution of time' that England had experienced for half a millennium or more.[1]

Recent scholarship has testified powerfully to the ability of a variety of historical genres to serve the purposes of religious controversy, as Protestants and Catholics alike looked to history to justify their respective claims to be the true heirs of the pristine apostolic church.[2] This literature has suggested how Protestant claims that their movement was one of renewal and regeneration, rather than innovation, had profound implications for the vision of medieval Catholicism that became embedded in

---

[1] Edmund Howes, 'An historicall preface' to John Stow, *The annales, or generall chronicle of England* (London, 1615), sig. ¶5v.

[2] For an overview, see Felicity Heal, 'Appropriating history: Catholic and Protestant polemics and the national past', in Paulina Kewes (ed.), *The Uses of History in Early Modern England* (San Marino, CA, 2006), pp. 105–28; Patrick Collinson, 'Truth, lies, and fiction in sixteenth-century Protestant historiography', in Donald R. Kelley and David Harris Sacks (eds.), *The Historical Imagination in Early Modern Britain: History, Rhetoric, and Fiction, 1500–1800* (Cambridge, 1997), pp. 37–68.

contemporary historical consciousness.[3] In the wake of the break with Rome, history was rewritten as part of the exercise to find a 'plausible past for the Reformation'.[4] Ironically, given the desire of sixteenth-century reformers to locate the origins of English Protestantism in antiquity and to highlight the continuity between reformed religion and primitive Christianity, history could also give expression to senses of temporal discontinuity and the idea that the Reformation represented a profound break between past and present. At the same time, Catholic historians and polemicists were also articulating a vision of rupture, which had significant implications for how they understood both the medieval past and the vexed question of the future of Catholicism in England and Europe. The caesura between the Middle Ages and the early modern era upon which more recent models of historical periodisation are predicated is itself partly the product of these earlier processes of writing history and making memory.[5]

This chapter examines the emergence of the dissolution of the monasteries as a critical moment around which early modern perceptions of the medieval past and the English Reformation were crystallised. It is concerned both with changing perceptions of the suppression over time and with how, in turn, this episode functioned to shape contemporary senses of time and chronology. To this end, it draws upon sources which adopt time as an organising principle. Not all of the texts discussed below are 'histories' according to the contemporary understanding of history as a distinct rhetorical mode, but all help to illuminate the evolving memory of the dissolution in historical perspective.[6] After first examining how the suppression was chronicled by those who witnessed it in the 1530s, this chapter traces the constant evolution of the memory of the dissolution across a series of flashpoints: Mary I's Catholic restoration in the mid-1550s and its reversal after 1558, the transition from Tudor to Stuart monarchy in 1603, the advent of Laudian religious policies in the 1630s, the Civil Wars of the 1640s, and the anti-Catholic crises of the late 1670s and early 1680s. Within this framework, it explores how the

---

[3] Donald R. Kelley, *Faces of History: Historical Enquiry from Herodotus to Herder* (New Haven, CT, and London, 1998) ch. 6; Alexandra Walsham, 'History, memory, and the English Reformation', *HJ* 55 (2012), pp. 839–938 at p. 902.

[4] Helen L. Parish, *Monks, Miracles and Magic: Reformation Representations of the Medieval Church* (London and New York, 2005), p. 18.

[5] Walsham, 'History, memory, and the Reformation', p. 901 and *passim*.

[6] On the nature of history in the early modern period, see, for example, D. R. Woolf, *The Idea of History in Early Stuart England: Erudition, Ideology, and the 'Light of Truth' from the Accession of James I to the Civil War* (Toronto, 1990); Paulina Kewes, 'History and its uses', in Kewes (ed.), *Uses of History*, pp. 1–30; Anthony Grafton, *What Was History? The Art of History in Early Modern Europe* (Cambridge, 2007).

Henrician vision of the dissolution was perpetuated and contested by successive generations of historians and antiquaries.

It was through this process of contestation that the protracted and uneven period of suppression we explored in the previous chapter was transformed into a landmark historical event. The sociologist Philip Abrams has contended that events have two related characteristics: temporal specificity and cultural significance. As episodes become fixed in time and in chronological sequence, he argues, they also acquire meaning for a particular community.[7] Inevitably, this transformation is shaped by processes of retrospection and reinvention; events are products of cultural memory as much as, if not more than, of first-hand experiences. As we shall see, the event that we have come to know as the Dissolution of the Monasteries was one such invention of posterity.

Chronicling the Dissolution

Charles Wriothesley, herald and chronicler, witnessed the Henrician campaign against the monasteries from the periphery of the royal court. Born in 1508, he rose to prominence in the service of the Lord Chancellor, Thomas Audley, just as the English Reformation was getting underway.[8] The manuscript chronicle that Wriothesley compiled during these years is testament to the power and reach of Henrician arguments about the expediency of the dissolution. In February 1538, he was present for the public exposure of the alleged monastic fraud known as the Rood of Grace, the miraculous properties of which the government had recently revealed to be a mechanical deception. Wriothesley saw the rood paraded at Westminster, where the authorities 'shewed openlye to the people the craft of moving the eyes and lipps, that the people there might see the illusion that had bene used in the sayde image by the monckes of the saide place of manye yeares tyme out of mynde'. He also heard the sermon preached at Paul's Cross by John Hilsey, bishop of Rochester, condemning 'the abuses of the graces and engines, used in old tyme in the said image' and by which 'the people had bene eluded and caused to doe great adolatrie'.[9] Wriothesley recorded these recollections in his

[7] Philip Abrams, *Historical Sociology* (Shepton Mallet, 1982), p. 191. See also Diana E. Greenway, 'Dates in history: chronology and memory', *Historical Research* 72 (1999), pp. 127–39.
[8] On Wriothesley's life and career, see Gordon Kipling, 'Wriothesley, Charles (1508–1562)', *ODNB*, www.oxforddnb.com/view/article/30071.
[9] AC, DNP: MS 468A, fol. 81r. The manuscript was published as Charles Wriothesley, *A Chronicle of England during the Reigns of the Tudors, from A.D. 1485 to 1559*, ed. William Douglas Hamilton, 2 vols., Camden Society, new series, 2 (London, 1875–7).

chronicle, which thus preserves the echoes of the rhetoric of monastic corruption, fraudulence, and iniquity that saturated contemporary discourse in the 1530s. Wriothesley was not, however, simply an eye- and ear-witness to the revelation of the Boxley fraud. He also played his own small part in its exposure by perpetuating the story of the mechanical rood and committing it to paper.

This entry is also part of a much larger catalogue of monastic errors set down in the chronicle, which delineated the major civic and religious events that occurred in England between the reign of Henry VII and the accession year of Elizabeth I. Wriothesley's chronicle was written very much in the mode of traditional manuscript chronicles: his entries were organised by regnal year and calendar month, and included various constituent episodes in the dissolution of the monasteries, as well as other upheavals of the early Reformation, all of which were recorded contemporaneously with events as they happened. Although he made no attempt to draw causal connections between episodes, each entry was nevertheless located within this overarching temporal framework. The chronicle therefore constitutes one of the earliest extant chronologies of the English Reformation. Wriothesley was not merely a spectator of the dissolution, he was perhaps also its first historian.

The project of chronicling English history, as Patrick Geary has argued, had always entailed deliberate and conscious 'decisions about what should be remembered and how it should be remembered'.[10] The chronicle genre was the primary vehicle for history in the Middle Ages. Modelled on the Books of Chronicles set down in the Old Testament, these texts functioned as cumulative catalogues of political, religious, and providential occurrences, which they fixed in a sequence of times and dates.[11] These were also characteristically laconic forms of historical writing, which refrained from drawing lines of causation between different episodes. The parataxis of chronicles was the product of their function as records of divine intervention in the world, through which God's plan for humanity might be

---

[10] Patrick J. Geary, *Phantoms of Remembrance: Memory and Oblivion at the End of the First Millennium* (Princeton, 1994), p. 9.

[11] On the characteristics of the genre, see, for example, Gabrielle M. Spiegel, 'Genealogy: form and function in medieval historical narrative', *History and Theory* 22 (1983), pp. 43–53; Matthew Innes, 'Using the past, interpreting the present, influencing the future', in Yitzhak Hen and Matthew Innes (eds.), *The Uses of the Past in the Early Middle Ages* (Cambridge, 2000), pp. 1–8; Catherine Cubitt, 'Memory and narrative in the cult of early Anglo-Saxon saints', in Hen and Innes (eds.), *Uses of the Past*, pp. 29–66; Chris Given-Wilson, *Chronicles: The Writing of History in Medieval England* (London and New York, 2004); Rosamond McKitterick, *History and Memory in the Carolingian World* (Cambridge, 2004); Sarah Foot, 'Finding the meaning of form: narrative in annals and chronicles', in Nancy Partner (ed.), *Writing Medieval History*, 2nd ed. (London, 2010), pp. 88–108.

revealed gradually but could not be predicted or second-guessed.[12] For similar reasons, medieval chronicles were also conceived as perpetually ongoing projects, and it was common for chroniclers to engage in parasitic practices of copying, editing, and enlarging earlier compilations. As recent scholarship has suggested, however, it would be wrong to think that the conventions of the genre rendered chronicles devoid of polemic or narrative. Sarah Foot, Chris Given-Wilson, Matthew Innes, and Rosamond McKitterick, amongst others, have all demonstrated that certain narratives were clearly discernible within and between the lines of these laconic texts. By commemorating certain episodes and not others, chronicles conveyed 'cogent stories' not only about the divine plan for human history but also about various royal dynasties and their particular framing of the past.[13] In this context, memory was a mechanism through which the past was made useful to the present.

Early modern chronicles retained this mnemonic function, even as the genre underwent significant transformation in the early sixteenth century. The dissolution was itself partly responsible for changing the conditions in which these texts were produced. In medieval England, the religious orders had been the primary custodians of the genre. Many of the most well-known and significant medieval chroniclers, including Ranulf Higden, William of Malmesbury, and Matthew Paris, were monks. This reflects the role played by the monasteries as centres of learning and record-keeping and their status as the engines of the medieval memory-making machine.[14] It is, then, no small irony that, in the wake of the Reformation, a genre that had once perpetuated an essentially monastic vision of the past quickly became a vehicle for exposing the corruption of the religious orders and preserving their fall for posterity. In the hands of a new generation of semi-professional lay chroniclers, the religious were rendered victims of their own memorialising practices.

Wriothesley was amongst the vanguard of these new post-dissolution chroniclers and historians. In an entry dated 1535, he recorded the visitation of the monasteries by Henry VIII's agents. He was clearly aware of the controversy that was already engulfing the religious houses. The passage

---

[12] On the providential quality of chronicles see Alexandra Walsham, 'Providentialism', in Paulina Kewes, Ian Archer, and Felicity Heal (eds.), *The Oxford Handbook of Holinshed's Chronicles* (Oxford, 2013), pp. 427–42 at p. 429.

[13] Foot, 'Finding the meaning of form', p. 102; Innes, 'Using the past', p. 4. See also Michael Hicks, 'English monasteries as repositories of dynastic memory', in Michael Penman (ed.), *Monuments and Monumentality Across Medieval and Early Modern Europe* (Donington, 2013), pp. 224–38.

[14] See esp. Cubitt, 'Memory and narrative'; Given-Wilson, *Chronicles*, ch. 4.

paraphrases the official injunctions imposed upon the religious by the crown, insinuating their worldliness and hypocrisy, sexual immorality, and duplicity in peddling false relics to the laity:

> Also this year Mr. Thomas Cromwell and Doctor Lee visited all the religious places in England, being ordayned by the Kinges grace for his high visitors, and they tooke out of everie religious house all religious persons from the age of 24 years and under, and shewed them how they shoulde use wilfull povertie, and also he closed up all the residue of the religious persons booth men and woemen that would remaine still, so that they should not come out of their places, nor no men resorte to the places of nonnes, nor weomen to come into the places of religious men, but onlie to heere service and masses in their churches, and also they took out of divers churches of England certaine reliques that the people were wont to worshipp, as Our Ladies girdell at Westminster . . . with other reliques in divers places which [the religious] used for covetousness in deceaphing the people.[15]

This passage suggests not only that the government's rhetoric of monastic corruption and iniquity was well-established long before the dissolution itself got underway in March 1536, but also that the chronicle genre could subtly serve the purposes of Henrician polemic. As with his entry on the Boxley fraud, Wriothesley's comments on the visitations served to perpetuate a distinctly Henrician vision of the condition of the monasteries. His chronicle was thus both an echo of and a mouthpiece for the regime's anti-monastic rhetoric.

The extent to which Wriothesley's manuscript, like other examples of the early modern chronicle genre, was a product of this climate of dissolution and Reformation has long been obscured by a tendency in the history of historiography to prioritise the Continental influences of humanism and jurisprudence at the expense of religion.[16] In this context, the distinction between the chronicle as an old-fashioned form of scholarship and the post-Reformation ecclesiastical histories that employed history in the service of religious controversy has proved highly influential.[17] Writing about Wriothesley's chronicle, F. J. Levy once argued that it was 'simply an

---

[15] AC, DNP: MS 468A, fol. 67v.
[16] See, for example, F. Smith Fussner, *The Historical Revolution: English Historical Writing and Thought, 1580–1640* (New York, 1962); F. J. Levy, *Tudor Historical Thought* (San Marino, CA, 1967); Arthur B. Ferguson, *Clio Unbound: Perception of the Social and Cultural Past in Renaissance England* (Durham, NC, 1979).
[17] Ferguson, *Clio Unbound*, p. 11. For more recent examples of the tendency to read chronicles as secular texts, see D. R. Woolf, 'Genre into artifact: the decline of the English chronicle in the sixteenth century', *SCJ* 19 (1988), pp. 321–45; John O. Ward, '"Chronicle" and "History": the medieval origins of postmodern historiographical practice?', *Parergon* 14 (1997), pp. 101–28.

anachronism' because, like most medieval chronicles, the early portion of the text reproduced passages from previous chronicles, and because it drew no conclusions 'besides the obvious ones of loyalty to the crown and to the city'.[18] Levy underestimated the extent to which these 'obvious' manifestations of Wriothesley's allegiances reflect the Henrician agenda that surfaces repeatedly in his chronicle. This perspective has, nevertheless, proven remarkably enduring. As recently as 2013, it has been argued that Tudor chronicles were devoid of the 'rhetorical flourish and polemic' that characterised other genres of narrative history and sacred biography.[19]

David Womersley has, however, convincingly disputed the notion that the form and content of early modern chronicles represent a 'pre-critical' phase of history writing before the 'steady self-emancipation' of history 'from the bondage of religion'. Rather, he suggests, these texts both contributed to and were shaped by a wider political culture that 'served to saturate English historiography with religious implication', as both reformers and traditionalists looked to history for legitimacy in the wake of the break with Rome.[20] Chronicles were not, therefore, the antithesis of confessional history; rather, they belong to the expansive category of historical genres that were coloured and inflected by Reformation debates. Contemporaries recognised this polemical potential better than have generations of historians. The former Carmelite friar-turned-evangelical polemicist John Bale avowed that monastic chronicles revealed the 'fylthynesse' of their compilers.[21] Having abandoned his earlier vocation, he desired 'some lerned Englyshe mane (as there are now most excellent fresh wyttes) to set forth the Englyshe chronycles in theyr ryght shappe'.[22] Whilst Bale sought to rewrite medieval chronicles,

---

[18] Levy, *Tudor Historical Thought*, p. 24.

[19] Alexandra Gillespie and Oliver Harris, 'Holinshed and the native chronicle tradition', in Kewes et al. (eds.), *Oxford Handbook of Holinshed's* Chronicles, pp. 135–52 at p. 151.

[20] David Womersley, 'Against the teleology of technique' in Kewes (ed.), *Uses of History*, pp. 91–104 at p. 99. For some illuminating case studies of the polemic potential of chronicles, see Sjoerd Levelt, *Jan van Naaldwijk's Chronicles of Holland: Continuity and Transformation in the Historical Tradition of Holland during the Early Sixteenth Century* (Hilversum, 2011); Gerard Kilroy, 'A tangled chronicle: the struggle over the memory of Edmund Campion', in Andrew Gordon and Thomas Rist (eds.), *The Arts of Remembrance in Early Modern England: Memorial Cultures of the Post-Reformation* (Farnham, 2013), pp. 141–59; Alexandra Walsham, 'Chronicles, memory, and autobiography in Reformation England', *Memory Studies* 11 (2018), pp. 36–50.

[21] John Bale, *The actes of Englysh votaryes, comprehendynge their unchast practices and examples by all ages, from the worldes begynnynge to thys present yeare, collected out of their owne legendes and chronicles by Johan Bale* (London, 1546), sig. A4v.

[22] John Bale, *A brefe chronycle concernynge the examinacyon and death of the blessed martyr of Christ, Sir Johan Oldecastell, the lorde Cobham, collected togyther by Johan Bale* ([Antwerp], 1544), sig. A5v. For approaches to Bale's historical writing, see Cathy Shrank, 'John Bale and reconfiguring the

Wriothesley was more concerned with contemporary events. We might, however, view his chronicle as a parallel project with that of reforming medieval history. If, as Womersley suggests, chronicles could function as tools of Reformation, Wriothesley's chronicle was specifically an instrument of the Henrician Reformation.

This is important for understanding Wriothesley's chronology of the dissolution. In 1536, Wriothesley recorded an entry to commemorate the first act of dissolution:

> Also this yeare, at a Parliament holden at Westminster in Februarie last past, and ended the Thursdaie afore Easter, it was granted to the King and his heires, to the augmentation of the crowne, all religious howses in this realme of Englande of the value of tow [*sic*] hundred poundes and under, with all landes and goodes belonging to the said howses, in as ample manner as the said abbottes and priors held theim. The some of the howses amounted to 376, the value of their landes 32 thousand poundes and more, and the moveables of their goodes, as they were sold, amounted above one hundred thousand poundes; and the religious persons that were in the said howses were clearlie putt out, some to [o]their howses, some went abroade in the worlde. Againe it was pitie the great lamentation that the poore people made for theim, for there was great hospitalitie kept amonge theim, and, as it was reported, tenne thousand persons had lost their living by the putting downe of theim, which was great pitie.[23]

Although the tone and tenor of this passage is subtle in comparison with more vitriolic forms of writing about the dissolution, it is nevertheless possible to find clear evidence of the influence of Henrician rhetoric. Wriothesley's support for Henry VIII and his government underpinned his approval of the transfer of former monastic properties 'to the augmentation of the crowne'. There are also hints of a more vituperative antimonastic sentiment in his allusions to the 'ample manner' of living enjoyed by the senior ranks of the religious. Moreover, if he expressed pity for the decline in hospitality and the losses suffered by those who had relied upon the monasteries for their livelihoods – and it is ambiguous here whether Wriothesley was referring primarily to the religious or to their lay servants – there is little evidence of the evangelical critique that we noted in the previous chapter. Indeed, it is telling that Wriothesley's pity was first

---

"medieval" in Reformation England', in Gordon McMullan and David Matthews (eds.), *Reading the Medieval in Early Modern England* (Cambridge, 2007), pp. 179–92; Mark Greengrass and Matthew Phillpott, 'John Bale, John Foxe, and the reformation of the English past', *Archiv für Reformationgeschichte* 101 (2010), pp. 275–88; Susan Royal, 'Historian or prophet? John Bale's perception of the past', *Studies in Church History* 49 (2013), pp. 156–67.
[23] AC, DNP: MS 468A, fol. 71r.

expressed not for the social and economic pressures engendered by the dissolution, but for the fact that the 'poore people' had made such a 'great lamentation' for so endemically corrupt an institution.[24]

Read in sequence with other passages from Wriothesley's chronicle, this entry served to weave his vision of the dissolution into the wider story of the Henrician regime's campaign against Catholic corruption, superstition, and idolatry. Between 1536 and 1538, as we saw previously, the Henrician regime claimed that it was undertaking a reformation of the monasteries. In keeping with this official line, Wriothesley's entries for this period collectively constitute an extended commentary on the necessity of reform. A few months after he saw the Rood of Grace exposed, Wriothesley returned to Paul's Cross to witness the denunciation of the Holy Blood of Hailes.[25] In the same year, he was also a witness to the demise of the heretic friar John Forest, whom he called 'a false traitor to his praynce [prince], an hereticke and a seditious person to the Kinges leighe people'.[26] Episodes such as Forest's execution have not been conventionally considered as elements in the dissolution of the monasteries – and yet, as we noted in the previous chapter, they were clearly part of the concerted campaign against monasticism that profoundly inflected and informed contemporary perceptions of the dissolution.

It is striking that the suppression and spoliation of the religious houses themselves appears to have been of little importance to this narrative of 1536–8, although this is perhaps also unsurprising, since before 1539 the Henrician regime rarely spoke of surrender or suppression. The government had not yet provided a framework for thinking about this episode as anything other than an act of reform. Nevertheless, the physical dissolution of monasteries was unavoidably a part of Wriothesley's experience of the 1530s. Some sixteen entries in his chronicle describe the piecemeal process of suppression, naming specific houses as they fell in waves. By contrast with Wriothesley's extensive commentaries denouncing monastic corruption, passages marking the fall of particular abbeys and convents are remarkably terse and laconic. Shortly after the revelations at Boxley and Hailes, for example, Wriothesley recalled that 'this yere divers religious

---

[24] For a more detailed discussion of this passage, see Harriet Lyon, '"A pitiful thing"? The dissolution of the English monasteries in early modern chronicles, c. 1540–c. 1640', *SCJ* 49 (2018), pp. 1037–56.

[25] AC, DNP: MS 468A, fol. 86r. On the Holy Blood of Hailes, see Peter Marshall, 'The Rood of Boxley, the Blood of Hailes and the defence of the Henrician church', *JEH* 46 (1995), pp. 689–96; Ethan H. Shagan, *Popular Politics and the English Reformation* (Cambridge, 2003), ch. 5. See also above, Ch. 1.

[26] AC, DNP: MS 468A, fol. 83r.

houses of great possessions were suppressed, as the Abbey of Battell in Sussex, Martin Abbey, Stratford Abbey, Lewys, with other more into the Kinges handes'.[27] Devoid of references to monastic corruption and iniquity, this entry is virtually divorced from Wriothesley's previous account of the suppression in 1536. But read in light of earlier entries, Wriothesley's silence becomes pregnant with meaning. The brevity of this passage testifies not to a genre that was blandly unimaginative but rather to the potency and reach of the twin Henrician impulses selectively to remember monastic corruption and strategically to downplay the wider consequences of the dissolution.

When the new policy of wholesale dissolution was announced in 1539, the need to downplay its more controversial aspects began to outweigh the desire to remember the Henrician triumph over monastic corruption. As we saw previously, 1539 marked a profound shift in Henrician rhetoric. Once preoccupied with the language of monastic reform, the government began to emphasise the complicity of the religious orders in their own downfall and quietly attempted to institute a retroactive policy of total suppression and the de facto abolition of English monasticism. Official pronouncements thus played down the transformative effect of the dissolution in local communities and the consequences for the generation of monks, nuns, and friars and their lay servants who were displaced from their homes, vocations, and livelihoods. Wriothesley's chronicle also bears the hallmarks of this desire to forget. Compared with his extensive entry for the suppression of the lesser monasteries, in 1539 he wrote simply that, 'at this parliament, all the religious houses in England, suppressed and not suppressed, were granted to the Kinge to the augmentation of his crowne forever'.[28] Like the act itself, this short passage implied that this transformation amounted to little more than a painless and efficient transfer of land and goods out of the hands of the Church and into those of the state.

Perhaps Wriothesley shared in the vested interests of the crown and its agents. Although he was not a direct beneficiary of this revolution in wealth and property, the gains made by the gentry and nobility would have been only too apparent given the circles in which he moved. His patron, Audley, was a major recipient of monastic land.[29] His cousin Thomas Wriothesley, who succeeded Audley as Lord Chancellor in 1544, acquired former monastic properties in no fewer than eight counties between 1537 and

---

[27] Ibid., fol. 83v.   [28] Ibid., fol. 90r.
[29] L. L. Ford, 'Audley, Thomas, Baron Audley of Walden (1487/8–1544)', *ODNB*, www .oxforddnb.com/view/article/896.

1549.[30] Wriothesley's chronicle also offers some evidence that he may have shared, or at least supported, the interests at the heart of the regime's selective vision of the dissolution. In November 1539, he marked the fall of Barking Abbey in Essex by recording that the building had since passed to the Devonshire lawyer Sir Thomas Denys whom 'hath to wife my ladie Murffen ... sometime [mistress] to Alis my wife that now is'.[31] In this context, it is little surprise that Wriothesley's chronicle was so profoundly inflected by Henrician narratives and arguments.

By 1539, however, it was too late for Wriothesley to rewrite the entire chronology of the dissolution to take account of the government's new impulse to downplay the extent of the transformation wrought by the suppression. The abbeys and convents did not, moreover, disappear overnight, despite the Henrician regime's attempt to make it appear so. Some monasteries continued to function into the spring of 1540, a fact that Wriothesley was ultimately forced to recognise: an entry for March of that year recorded that 'this year also all the religious howses in England were suppressed into the Kinges handes'.[32] It bears repeating that although the brevity of this passage might seem to conform to accounts of the chronicle genre as a laconic and unimaginative mode of historical writing, this appearance is deceptive. Read as part of a larger narrative and alongside the trajectory of the official polemic, Wriothesley's chronicle was no less ideologically inflected for its absences and omissions. To treat this text uncritically is therefore to underestimate the extent to which it was originally a product of and a vehicle for Henrician attempts to manage the reception of this problematic episode of the early Reformation.

The entry for 1540 marks the final appearance of the Henrician dissolution in Wriothesley's chronicle, although he went on to record a number of related and analogous episodes during the reigns of Henry VIII's heirs, all in a similarly laconic fashion to his entry for 1539. These included the dissolution of the chantries under Edward VI, the abortive restoration of monasticism under Mary I, and the eventual re-suppression of the Marian foundations after the accession of Elizabeth I.[33] In this way, Wriothesley's manuscript reminds us that the long process of dissolution was not over by 1540; rather, it continued to be a feature of the English Reformation until at least 1558. Wriothesley's chronology of the suppression therefore far

---

[30] Graves, 'Wriothesley, Thomas'. On Wriothesley's properties and the long memory of the dissolution see also below, Ch. 4.
[31] AC, DNP: MS 468A, fol. 92v.   [32] Ibid., fol. 93v.   [33] Ibid., fols. 124r, 176v, 180r, 184r.

exceeded the parameters of the event that we have come to know as the Dissolution of the Monasteries.

Indeed, for Wriothesley, there was no Dissolution of the Monasteries. Which is to say that, although he witnessed the fall of the monasteries in the 1530s, he would not have recognised the shorthand that modern scholarship habitually employs to denote this episode. Nor would this term have adequately reflected his experience of a piecemeal process that overlapped and coalesced with other facets of Henry VIII's Reformation. Events were the building blocks of the chronicle genre. It is telling, therefore, that Wriothesley's vision of the Henry VIII's dissolution spans some thirty-five entries in his chronicle, which, as we have seen, also mapped clearly onto the rhetorical shifts that characterised official policy. Had the Henrician view on the suppression gone unchallenged, the dissolution might have been the greatest non-event of the English Reformation.

Subsequent generations would develop a vocabulary of 'dissolution' to negotiate the rupture caused by the Henrician suppression that Wriothesley did not possess – and yet, his chronicle is also a source through which we continue to view this episode.[34] We need to recognise, therefore, that Wriothesley's chronicle was a product of the very debates to which it bear witness. It is also worth noting here that the manuscript only survives in the form of a copy produced for the earls of Northumberland in the early seventeenth century.[35] The text that historians have inherited is therefore an artefact of both the 1530s and the early seventeenth century; it is an eyewitness account, but one that has also been refracted through the hand of a later copyist. The shorthand by which historians know this chronicle – Wriothesley's chronicle – has thus served to obscure at least one anonymous agent of remembering and forgetting the dissolution. The preservation of Wriothesley's text also returns us to the question of how the Henrician vision of the dissolution was perpetuated across the early modern period. It is therefore to the long afterlife of Henrician polemic in early modern chronicles and histories to which we now direct our attention.

---

[34] I am grateful to Cathy Shrank, whose comments on a paper given at a workshop in October 2016 and organised by the ARHC-funded 'Remembering the Reformation' project, directed by Alexandra Walsham and Brian Cummings and jointly based at the Universities of Cambridge and York, have shaped my thinking on this point.

[35] On the textual history of Wriothesley's chronicle, see Harriet Lyon, 'Remembering the dissolution of the monasteries: events, chronology, and memory in Charles Wriothesley's chronicle', in Alexandra Walsham, Bronwyn Wallace, Ceri Law, and Brian Cummings (eds.), *Memory and the English Reformation* (Cambridge, 2020), pp. 64–79.

Perpetuating the Henrician Orthodoxy

After Henry VIII's death in 1547, many of the histories and chronicles produced under his Protestant heirs continued to preserve for posterity the Henrician vision of the dissolution. Noteworthy Tudor chronicles include Thomas Lanquet's *Epitome of cronicles* (1549), which stated boldly that during the dissolution 'all friars, monks, canons, [and] nuns ... were rooted out of this realm for their iniquity and naughtiness'.[36] Like Wriothesley, Lanquet also recorded his contempt for the 'dyvers images also havynge inginnes to make theyr eyes open and shutte', a thinly veiled reference to events at Boxley, as well as the 'many other false juglynges, as the bloudd of hayles ... wherewith the people of longe tyme had been deceived', demonstrating the longevity of these infamous deceptions in the public imagination.[37] Likewise *Hall's chronicle* (1548), originally the project of the Henrician lawyer Edward Hall and continued beyond the 1520s by Richard Grafton, King's Printer under Henry VIII and Edward VI, also invoked images of monastic corruption in the form of 'great and fatte abbottes', who 'even at that time' of the first visitations had been considered 'putrified olde okes'.[38] When Grafton, whose press occupied the site of the former house of Franciscan friars near St Paul's Cathedral, published his own *Chronicle at large* in 1568, this passage was repeated verbatim.[39] Like the Henrician polemic of the 1530s, successive Tudor chronicles thus served to emphasise the reformation of monasticism rather than its suppression.

History also continued to serve the purposes of religious controversy and to justify and defend the reformed Church of England. Appearing a decade after Elizabeth I's accession, Grafton's chronicle was published at a time when the dissolution was still within the limits of living memory, but also in the context of a new political imperative to justify the repression of Marian Catholicism. For example, Mary I's abortive Catholic restoration provided an impetus for the re-publication of some older Tudor chronicles and histories after 1558. In 1555, Mary had issued a proclamation calling for

[36] Thomas Lanquet, *Lanquette's chronicle [An epitome of cronicles]* (London, 1559), sig. Bbbb8v. On Lanquet, see Henry Summerson, 'Lanquet, Thomas (1520/21–1545)', *ODNB*, www.oxforddnb.com /view/article/16056.

[37] Lanquet, *Chronicle*, sig. Bbbb8v.

[38] Edward Hall, *The union of the two noble and illustre famelies of Lancastre & Yorke* (London, 1548), fol. 227v.

[39] Richard Grafton, *A chronicle at large and meere history of the affayres of Englande and kinges of the same* (London, 1569), p. 1226. See also Meraud Grant Ferguson, 'Grafton, Richard (1506/7–1573)', *ODNB*, www.oxforddnb.com/view/article/11186.

the destruction of *Hall's chronicle*; in defiance of this order, a new edition appeared in 1560.[40] Lanquet's chronicle was also reprinted in 1559. Meanwhile, new texts reached the presses that continued to perpetuate older narratives of monastic corruption in support of the ongoing Reformation. One of the most notable Elizabethan chronicles was the collaborative project commonly known under the name of one of its compilers, Raphael Holinshed, and first published as *The chronicles of England, Scotlande, and Irelande* in 1577. Like the earlier Tudor chronicles, Holinshed's chronicle transcribed the injunctions against the religious houses made at the time of the 1535 visitations, thereby preserving the direct echoes of Henrician polemic for posterity.[41] It also recorded such exemplary episodes as the execution of Friar Forest and further condemned the 'notable Images' and 'counterfeyte Saintes' peddled by the religious and exposed by the regime in the 1530s. In the same breath, the compilers wrote of the wholesale dissolution of the religious houses that 'all the orders of Friers, and Nunnes, with their cloysters and houses, were suppressed and put downe'.[42] Holinshed's chronicle thus adopted a model for delineating the dissolution that we have seen in countless other sixteenth-century texts: an extensive, overtly polemical account of the Henrician regime's campaign against monastic corruption in 1536–8 and a concise, laconic account of the dissolution itself after 1539.

Precisely because they were accretive, parasitic texts, chronicles had the potential to create powerful continuities of this kind. This was further reinforced by the advent of print, which facilitated the production of chronicles intended for wider consumption than their medieval antecedents.[43] These texts were a different type of chronicle from the manuscript compiled by Wriothesley, which more fully resembled the genre developed in the medieval period. They were commercial products, usually written in the vernacular, and they lacked the organic quality of their manuscript counterparts even as they retained the practices of borrowing and copying from earlier compilations. The result was that these texts themselves became fixed at a particular moment in time. This is a quality that has sometimes been said to have contributed to their eventual

[40] Peter C. Herman, 'Hall, Edward (1497–1547)', *ODNB*, www.oxforddnb.com/view/article/11954.

[41] Raphael Holinshed, *The chronicles of England, Scotlande, and Irelande, with their descriptions*, 2 vols. (London, 1577), ii, p. 1564. On the multivocal nature of Holinshed's *Chronicles*, see Annabel Patterson, *Reading Holinshed's Chronicles* (Chicago and London, 1994); Felicity Heal and Henry Summerson, 'The genesis of the two editions', in Kewes, Archer, and Heal (eds.), *Handbook of Holinshed's* Chronicles, pp. 3–20.

[42] Holinshed, *Chronicles of England, Scotlande, and Irelande*, ii, p. 1571.

[43] D. R. Woolf, *Reading History in Early Modern England* (Cambridge, 2000), ch. 1.

decline. Most notably, Daniel Woolf has argued that chronicles were victims of the changing context in which knowledge of the past was recalled and transmitted: they quickly became outdated, and the expense of reprinting them was much greater than the production costs associated with various parasite genres, which ultimately forced the chronicle into a terminal state of decay.[44] Yet it is precisely this static quality that gives Tudor chronicles particular potential to reveal the processes of remembering and selective forgetting through which the Henrician narrative of the dissolution was perpetuated and contested over time.

These texts also have the capacity to shed light upon the process by which the dissolution was beginning to undergo the transformation from process to event. At the time Holinshed's chronicle was first published, a new generation had reached maturity who had not themselves experienced the Henrician Reformation. With increasing temporal distance on the 1530s, there was a growing tendency to telescope the various waves of suppression into distinct episodes and phases. In other words, although successive Tudor chronicles served to perpetuate Henrician ideas, they also set down increasingly abridged chronologies of the dissolution. By comparison with Wriothesley's thirty-five entries delineating the suppression, Lanquet's chronicle, published a decade after the demise of the last English abbey, contained just eight references to the monasteries and none at all to the fall of specific houses. The entries in both Hall and Grafton's chronicles are clustered around the two parliamentary acts of dissolution in 1536 and 1539. Like Lanquet's chronicle, Hall and Grafton's compilations neglected all mention of individual religious houses in favour of generalised comments about the suppression of the monasteries. Holinshed's Elizabethan chronicle contains just five entries about the Henrician dissolution, including the laconic final statement that described how the religious houses had been 'suppressed and put downe' in 1539. These chronicles suggest, then, that by the mid-sixteenth century, contemporaries were beginning to fix the dissolution to certain specific moments in time.

In this context, the dissolution of the monasteries began to emerge as a distinct episode in the wider Protestant historical imagination. The resonance of the suppression with the anxieties and debates that continued

---

[44] D. R. Woolf, 'Genre into artifact'; D. R. Woolf, *The Social Circulation of the Past: English Historical Culture, 1500–1730* (Oxford, 2003), p. 12 and *passim*. For two recent critiques of this argument, see Judith Pollmann, 'Archiving the present and chronicling for the future in early modern Europe', in Liesbeth Corens, Kate Peters, and Alexandra Walsham (eds.), *The Social History of the Archive: Record-Keeping in Early Modern Europe*, P&P supplement 11, 230 (2016), pp. 231–52; Walsham, 'Chronicles, memory, and autobiography'.

to preoccupy the reformers also served further to crystallise this memory. Thus the historian and controversialist John Foxe, in his famous history and martyrology, the *Actes and monuments* (1563), engaged in a counterfactual discussion of the dissolution that barely concealed a note of anxiety about the future of the Protestant establishment:

> What if it should happen through the mutabilitie of the world, that the kyngdom shuld come into the handes of some wycked prynce of a contrary religion? But what shal we nede to stay long in this matter, when as by the doynges of Quene Mary, every man may consider what she should have done if the monasteries had bene left standing untyll her superstitious daies?[45]

This passage functioned to integrate the dissolution into Foxe's wider narrative of the English Reformation whilst also invoking the threat of monasticism to further the polemical cause of Elizabethan Protestantism. It has been suggested that much of Foxe's writing was intended to establish remembrance amongst his early modern audience. The episodes that Foxe recalled and recounted were designed to illuminate and edify the reader, as well as to involve them in the act of sifting truth from falsehood.[46] In other words, as Peter Sherlock has argued, 'Foxe did not simply create a record of what happened, but found a way in the medium of the printed book to dictate precisely how memory should be interpreted by succeeding generations'.[47] Remembering the Henrician dissolution was an imperative for Foxe in the context of wider attempts to secure the stability of the Elizabethan settlement. In doing so, the *Actes and monuments* served to perpetuate an older vision of the dissolution whilst simultaneously interpreting it for a new generation.

Foxe's 'Book of Martyrs' was highly influential in its time – and has also long continued to inform our understanding of sixteenth-century historical consciousness.[48] It has been argued that the *Actes and monuments* was

---

[45] John Foxe, *Actes and monuments* (London, 1563), p. 593. On the polemic of the *Actes and monuments*, see Patrick Collinson, 'Truth and legend: the veracity of John Foxe's Book of Martyrs', in A. C. Duke and C. A. Tamse (eds.), *Clio's Mirror: Historiography in Britain and the Netherlands* (Zutphen, 1985), pp. 31–54.

[46] Tom Healy, '"Making it true": John Foxe's art of remembrance', in Gordon and Rist (eds.), *Arts of Remembrance*, pp. 125–40. See also Collinson, 'Truth, lies, and fiction', esp. pp. 37–40; Andrew Hiscock, *Reading Memory in Early Modern Literature* (Cambridge, 2011), ch. 3.

[47] Peter Sherlock, 'The reformation of memory in early modern Europe', in Susannah Radstone and Bill Schwarz (eds.), *Memories: Histories, Theories, Debates* (New York, 2011), pp. 30–40 at p. 33.

[48] See, for example, Thomas Page Anderson and Ryan Netzley (eds.), *Acts of Reading: Interpretation, Reading Practices, and the Idea of the Book in John Foxe's* Acts and Monuments (Newark, DE, 2010); Elizabeth Evenden and Thomas S. Freeman, *Religion and the Book in Early Modern England: The Making of John Foxe's 'Book of Martyrs'* (Cambridge, 2011); Jesse M. Lander, 'The monkish Middle

itself born out of a way of thinking about the past shaped by 'the cataclysmic event which began a new phase of historical research in England: the
dissolution of the monasteries'.[49] It was certainly a part of the wider project
engendered by the suppression and the Reformation to establish and
confirm the historical foundations of the Church of England. Perhaps
the most noteworthy of these efforts to 'produce a usable past for
Protestant England' was undertaken by Matthew Parker, the first
Elizabethan archbishop of Canterbury, who assembled a team of scholars
that set about reforming history by annotating, editing, and re-binding
texts, purging them of what they perceived to be Catholic superstition and
corruption.[50] This endeavour was predicated on a sense of regret for losses
sustained during the spoliation and dispersal of monastic libraries. In his
preface to the 1568 bible, Parker mourned the destruction of England's
cultural patrimony, asking 'what other great Libraries have there been
consumed, but of late Dayes? And what libraries of old have throughout
this Realme, almost in every Abby of the same, been destroyed at sundry
Ages . . . it were too long to reherse'.[51] As Jennifer Summit has observed, it
is not clear whether Parker laid the blame for this 'crisis of memory' with
the religious or the Henrician commissioners.[52] Nevertheless, recognising
that the monasteries had been the custodians of the archival memory of
medieval England, the Privy Council gave Parker a commission to survey
what manuscripts survived, often in private collections, from the 'diverse
Abbeys' that were 'as Treasore houses, to keape and leave in memorie,
suche occurrentes as fell in their tymes'.[53] The attempt to restore and
reorder this material was a polemical as well as a practical exercise, intended
not only to expose the superstition of medieval monasticism but also to
erase or rectify it.

Ages: periodisation and polemic in Foxe's *Acts and monuments*', in Sarah A. Kelen (ed.), *Renaissance
Retrospections: Tudor Views of the Middle Ages* (Kalamazoo, MI, 2013), pp. 93–110.
[49] Margaret Aston, *Lollards and Reformers: Images and Literacy in Late Medieval Religion* (London,
1984), p. 234.
[50] Benedict Scott Robinson, '"Darke speech": Matthew Parker and the reforming of history', *SCJ* 29
(1998), pp. 1061–83 at p. 1064. See also Timothy Graham, 'Matthew Parker's manuscripts: an
Elizabethan library and its uses', in Elisabeth Leedham-Green and Teresa Webber (eds.), *The
Cambridge History of Libraries in Britain and Ireland: Volume 1, to 1640* (Cambridge, 2006), pp.
322–42; Jennifer Summit, *Memory's Library: Medieval Books in Early Modern England* (Chicago and
London, 2008), ch. 3; Anthony Grafton, 'Matthew Parker: the book as archive', *History of
Humanities* 2 (2017), pp. 15–50.
[51] Matthew Parker, 'A preface into the Byble', in *The Holie Bible* (London, 1568), sig. 2r, quoted in
Summit, *Memory's Library*, p. 101.
[52] Summit, *Memory's Library*, pp. 102, 104.   [53] CCCC, MS 114A, 12, p. 51.

Medieval chronicles were amongst the targets of this attack on the past: Parker observed, for example, that Matthew Paris's manuscript had been 'foully mutilated in some leaves, and erased in many places by some monks' before it was 'nonetheless restored to integrity through the copy of some honest man'.[54] This gives powerful expression not only to the contention that 'the early modern was constructed through or in negotiation with the medieval', but also to the urgency of the campaign to rewrite English history in the wake of the Reformation.[55] In the library that Parker left to Corpus Christi College, Cambridge, the remnants of monastic collections were kept alongside Protestant visions of the Reformation, including a short Tudor manuscript chronicle written in Latin, which – like so many of the previous chronicles that we have encountered – recorded both the dissolution and related episodes, such as the public exposure of the Boxley Rood and other notable monastic 'fictions'.[56] In this way, Parkerian scholarship, like the efforts of the Tudor chroniclers, functioned to align the overthrow of the religious houses and the revelation of the religious as authors of false miracles and custodians of fraudulent relics with a state-sponsored Protestant national identity.[57] This also goes some way, perhaps, to explaining why historians have tended to be pessimistic about the value of early modern chronicles. As a result of the attempt to reform the past, medieval chronicles became themselves emblems of monkish fraudulence and deceit. The sense of antipathy towards chroniclers from the later sixteenth century onwards identified by Woolf is perhaps a result of their association with the medieval past.[58]

The attempts of reformed Protestants to propagate a vision of English history that, to return to Bale's phrase, reflected the past in its 'ryght shappe' appear to have been reasonably successful. As the dissolution passed out of living memory and into inherited memory, the narratives of the suppression promoted by Grafton and Holinshed, Foxe and Parker continued to have traction. In the previous chapter, we encountered a narrative letter sent from the lawyer Thomas Norton to Francis Mylles in 1581, in which Norton – whose impeccable Protestant credentials included not only the patronage of William Cecil but also his marriage

[54] Quoted in Robinson, 'Darke speech', p. 1081.
[55] Gordon McMullan and David Matthews, 'Introduction: reading the medieval in early modern England', in McMullan and Matthews (eds.), *Reading the Medieval*, p. 6.
[56] CCCC, MS 298, vol. iv, 17, fol. 212r.
[57] Summit, *Memory's Library*. See also Greengrass and Phillpott, 'Reformation of the English past', pp. 282–4.
[58] Woolf, 'Genre into artifact', p. 330. See also Harriet Lyon, '"Superstition remains at this hour": *The friers chronicle* (1623) and England's long Reformation', *Reformation* 24 (2020), pp. 107–21 at p. 121.

to Margaret Cranmer in the year of her father's martyrdom – had promised to set down all that he could remember 'as I have understoode by that which I had red & heard'.[59] He did not name his sources, but his letter contains ample evidence of the Henrician perspective that coloured so many of the Tudor chronicles and histories as well as, evidently, historical consciousness articulated in conversation. Norton thus recounted how the suppression was justified by the 'vile lyves' of the religious and the 'abhominable factes in murders of their brethren in Sodomies, in whordomes, in destroying of children, in forging of deedes & other infinite horrors of lyf'.[60] It is unlikely, as we noted previously, that Norton, who was born in the early 1530s, could claim personally to recall this much of the dissolution. His comment that the letter contained 'all that I can remember' is therefore testament to the longevity of the Henrician vision of the dissolution mediated through cultural memory and in the Protestant historical imagination.

Norton offered a linear narrative of dissolution, but, unlike those set down in contemporary chronicles, it was not definitively fixed to a particular moment in time. Unconstrained by the strict chronological structure of the chronicle genre, Norton made no reference to specific times or dates, including 1536 and 1539. Perhaps this represents the failings of memory, but it also undoubtedly reflects a wider process that was beginning to transform the uneven phases of suppression recorded by Wriothesley into a significant event in the English Reformation. It is striking, in this context, that Norton called this episode the 'dissolution of abbies'. This also recalled the title of the history that Norton may or may not have authored, but of which he was certainly aware, entitled 'The dissolving of the abbeys by K. H. 8'.[61] It is unclear precisely when the term 'dissolution' as it pertained to the fall of the religious houses entered the English lexicon, but it is clear that by the later sixteenth century, perspectives on the suppression had begun to shift in ways that served to collapse and condense the various phases of dissolution into something more coherent and to distinguish it from the wider campaign to discredit the Catholic Church. This was also partly a function of hindsight, which revealed that, despite Henrician claims about the reformation

---

[59] On Norton's career see Marie Axton, 'Norton, Thomas (1530×32–1584)', *ODNB*, www.oxforddnb.com/view/article/20359.
[60] Washington DC, Folger Shakespeare Library, MS X.c.62, fol. 1v.
[61] BL, Cotton MS Titus F III, fols. 268v–270r. See also above, Ch. 1.

and surrender of the monasteries, the actions of the regime in the 1530s had ultimately claimed the entire monastic institution.

Henrician attempts to manage how the dissolution was received in the 1530s continued to shape and colour the histories and chronicles produced during the reigns of his Protestant heirs, even as growing temporal distance functioned increasingly to fix the long process of suppression to particular times and dates. Previously, we noted that neither contemporaries nor historians have paid much attention to the Elizabethan dissolution. It is also striking that the Edwardian suppression of the chantries has been almost completely overshadowed by the Henrician Dissolution of the Monasteries, despite the radical nature of the break engendered by the former with medieval commemorative practices and the doctrine of purgatory.[62] This is relevant, perhaps, to questions of reputation and agency. Edward VI enjoyed a legacy in the early modern period modelled on the young Josiah, biblical iconoclast and child king of Judah, whilst Henry VIII had a rather more ambiguous contemporary afterlife.[63] As we shall see, the dissolution became increasingly central to perceptions of Henry's reign and Reformation, in ways that profoundly influenced how it was remembered across the sixteenth and seventeenth centuries.

The increasing use of the language of 'dissolution' to denote this episode also illuminates something of this growing tendency to collapse and telescope the various phases and episodes experienced by Wriothesley and the generation who had witnessed the suppression in the 1530s. Yet the process by which the dissolution was transformed into a culturally significant event owed at least as much, if not more, to the development of critical perspectives on the Henrician Reformation. In order to explore when and how the dissolution finally acquired the name that was perhaps the clearest hallmark of its cultural significance, we must therefore examine the capacity of historical writing to undermine and contest the vision of this episode expounded in Tudor polemic.

---

[62] On the dissolution of the chantries, see Peter Cunich, 'The dissolution of the chantries', in Patrick Collinson and John Craig (eds.), *The Reformation in English Towns, 1500–1640* (Basingstoke, 1998), pp. 159–74; Peter Marshall, *Beliefs and the Dead in Reformation England* (Oxford, 2002), ch. 2; Phillip G. Lindley, '"Pickpurse" purgatory, the dissolution of the chantries, and the suppression of intercession for the dead', *Journal of the British Archaeological Association* 164 (2011), pp. 277–304.

[63] On Edward VI as Josiah, see Margaret Aston, *The King's Bedpost: Reformation and Iconography in a Tudor Group Portrait* (Cambridge, 1993), pp. 26–37; Diarmaid MacCulloch, *Tudor Church Militant: Edward VI and the Protestant Reformation* (London, 1999), ch. 2.

Contesting the Henrician Orthodoxy

Historical memory, as Bruce Gordon has recently suggested, is profoundly shaped by processes of contestation as well as the ways in which 'hegemonic narratives are crafted to silence or at least subordinate other accounts'.[64] In the previous chapter, we saw how critiques of the dissolution had begun to emerge from both ends of the confessional spectrum as early as 1536. Histories and chronicles could also be vehicles for these alternative narratives of the suppression. At the same time as Wriothesley and Grafton were penning and printing their Tudor chronicles, an anonymous former resident of the London Greyfriars – the same Franciscan friary that had since become Grafton's workshop – continued to work on the institutional chronicle that had once belonged to his house.[65] This is a rare – possibly unique – direct continuation of the monastic tradition into the mid-sixteenth century.[66] The strikingly Henrician outlook exhibited in the chronicler's terse and infrequent references to the closure and spoliation of various religious houses, including the local 'Austynfreeres' and 'Whytfreers', conceals a continued commitment to Catholicism that re-emerged only in his entries for the reign of Mary I.[67] 'So gladde', he wrote after her accession, 'dyd the pepulles harttes rejoyse in hare comyng in', before observing that 'the vii. Day of Aprell [1555] the observanttes ware put in at grenwych agayn'.[68] Divorced from its institutional context, the Grey Friars' chronicle had become something more akin to personal record of the post-Reformation period.[69]

Like Wriothesley's chronicle, this document therefore reveals a particular thread of the personal memory of the dissolution, except that in this case the chronicle reflects the perspective of a victim of the suppression rather than that of a beneficiary. Very few early modern victims wrote down memories that recalled personal trauma or culpability.[70] Nonetheless, the laconic quality of the author's entries is remarkable.

[64] Bruce Gordon, 'History and memory', in Ulinka Rublack (ed.), *The Oxford Handbook of Protestant Reformations* (Oxford, 2016), pp. 765–86 at p. 769.
[65] BL, Cotton MS Vitellius F XII. Published as *The Chronicle of the Grey Friars of London*, ed. John Gough Nichols, Camden Society, old series, 53 (London, 1852).
[66] See Mary C. Erler, *Reading and Writing During the Dissolution: Monks, Friars, and Nuns, 1530–1558* (Cambridge, 2013), ch. 2.
[67] BL, Cotton MS Vitellius F XII, fols. 353v, 355r.   [68] Ibid., fols. 362r, 365r.
[69] On the porous boundaries between historical and institutional genres and forms of life-writing, see esp. Adam Smyth, *Autobiography in Early Modern England* (Cambridge, 2010).
[70] Judith Pollmann and Erika Kuijpers, 'On the early modernity of modern memory', in Erika Kuijpers, Judith Pollmann, Johannes Müller, and Jasper van der Steen (eds.), *Memory Before Modernity: Practices of Memory in Early Modern Europe* (Leiden and Boston, MA, 2013), pp. 1–23 at p. 20.

This is at least partly a product of the conventions of the medieval tradition of which the Grey Friars' chronicle is the residue. But it may also have been shaped by the forces of selective amnesia operating on an account that revisited the traumatic experience of suppression or, possibly, which reflected the guilt of a man whose brotherhood had not followed the model of the Carthusians and resisted the dissolution more vociferously.[71] In other words, the chronicle offers, perhaps, an example of what Paul Connerton has called 'humiliated silence': a specific strategy of deliberate forgetting that functions to distance the individual from a problematic episode in the recent past.[72] It is striking that references to the scribe's own former home are terse and detached, and betray nothing of his feelings about the dissolution. Describing the friary building simply as 'sumtyme the grayfreeres', he noted only that part of the property had since become a kind of warehouse for spoils seized from the French in 1540.[73] Thus the anonymous friar's chronicle may reveal a culture of selective amnesia – or at least an unwillingness to commit difficult memories to paper – which ultimately only served to reinforce Henrician claims that the religious had been complicit in their own demise.

Conservative sentiments also continued to thrive amongst members of the laity. The brief Catholic restoration under Mary I, which caused such anxiety for reformers like Foxe and Parker, offers an opportunity to glimpse the resonance of the memory of the dissolution for the English Catholic community. The civic chronicle of the Marian merchant tailor and London citizen Henry Machyn – misidentified by its nineteenth-century editor as a diary – does not extend as far back in time as the dissolution itself.[74] However, it clearly demonstrates the longevity of the memory of the spoliation of the monasteries into the reign of Mary I, when the queen's limited revival of domestic English monasticism called to mind the Henrician assault on the religious houses.[75] Machyn's chronicle belies

---

[71] On the Carthusian martyrs, see David Knowles, *The Religious Orders in England*, 3 vols. (Cambridge, 1948–59), iii, pp. 229–37; Anne Dillon, *Michelangelo and the English Martyrs* (Farnham, 2012), chs. 1–2.

[72] Paul Connerton, 'Seven types of forgetting', *Memory Studies* 1 (2008), pp. 59–71 at pp. 67–9.

[73] BL, Cotton MS Vitellius F XII, fol. 353v.

[74] In his will, Machyn calls the document 'my cronacle'. See Ian Mortimer, 'Tudor chronicler or sixteenth-century diarist? Henry Machyn and the nature of his manuscript', *SCJ* 33 (2002), pp. 981–98 at p. 986. See also Gary G. Gibbs, 'Marking the days: Henry Machyn's manuscript and the mid-Tudor era', in Eamon Duffy and David Loades (eds.), *The Church of Mary Tudor* (Aldershot, 2006), pp. 281–308; Walsham, 'Chronicles, memory, and autobiography', pp. 45–6.

[75] The implications of the Marian restoration of monasticism are a neglected feature of her reign. See Knowles, *Religious Orders in England*, iii, pp. 421–43; David Loades, 'The personal religion of Mary I', in Duffy and Loades (eds.), *The Church of Mary Tudor*, pp. 1–30 at pp. 23–4; C. S. Knighton,

his anxiety about the religious upheavals he had witnessed in the preceding decades.[76] Machyn mourned the treatment of the shrine of Edward the Confessor 'when that abbay [Westminster] was spowlyed and robyd' and declared its re-establishment 'a godly shyte [sight]', praising also the 'goodly syngyng and senssyng as has bene sene [there]' since the nation had reverted to Catholicism.[77] But if recalling the dissolution served Machyn's purposes in offering thanks for the accession of the new Catholic queen, there are also striking absences that further reflect the subtly partisan quality of his text. In one such example of strategic omission, he offered no comment whatsoever on the execution of the Marian martyrs to whose deaths he surely bore witness. As Machyn's chronicle continued to fulfil something of an institutional function, his practices of inclusion and omission thus also reveal how personal experience and confessional memory could be woven into a document that retained a semi-public status.[78] As with the chronicle of the anonymous Grey Friar, Machyn's silences have the potential to disclose a great deal about the Catholic and conservative experience of the Reformation.

Others were rather more vocal. Robert Parkyn, curate of Adwick-le-Street near Doncaster in Yorkshire, included a chronology of the Reformation in his commonplace book. Recorded in and around the years of Mary's reign, Parkyn displayed what A. G. Dickens called 'violent conservatism' for most of his life, although he conformed to the Elizabethan Church in his later years.[79] The dissolution loomed large in Parkyn's recollections of reform under Henry VIII. His narrative began with the king's divorce from Katherine of Aragon, before noting the break with Rome and the enactment of the Royal Supremacy, 'thrughe authoritie wherof he began to deposse religius howsses'.[80] Adding some local colour, he continued that 'the fyrst wich was dissolvide in Yorke shire was Sawllay [Sawley] and Rwallay [Rievaulx], two notable howsses'.[81] Parkyn's

---

'Westminster Abbey restored', in Duffy and Loades (eds.), *The Church of Mary Tudor*, pp. 77–123; Eamon Duffy, *Fires of Faith: Catholic England Under Mary Tudor* (New Haven, CT, and London, 2009), pp. 26, 44–5.

[76] See also Andrew Gordon, *Writing Early Modern London: Memory, Text, and Community* (Basingstoke, 2013), ch. 1.

[77] John Gough Nichols (ed.), *The Diary of Henry Machyn, Citizen and Merchant-Taylor of London, 1550–1563*, Camden Society, old series, 42 (London, 1848), p. 130.

[78] Walsham, 'Chronicles, memory, and autobiography', p. 46.

[79] A. G. Dickens (ed.), 'Robert Parkyn's narrative of the Reformation', *English Historical Review* 62 (1947), pp. 58–83 at p. 61.

[80] Reproduced in Dickens, 'Parkyn's narrative of the Reformation', p. 65.

[81] Ibid. Interpolations mine. Dickens notes that this statement is inaccurate: Sawley was amongst the early dissolutions, but Rievaulx was not surrendered until 1538.

displeasure at this turn of events was made clearer when he recorded the wholesale suppression of 1539:

> Continewynge the saide tymes, religius howsses was nothinge favoride, but yearely partte dissolvyde, but anno domini 1539 all was suppresside furiusly under footte (evin as tholly temple of Hierusalem was handlyde when the Chaldees had dominion therof) and many abbottes & other vertuus religius persons shamefully was putt to deathe in diversse places of this realme.[82]

Parkyn clearly recognised the violence of the suppression and drew upon a powerful language of shame, entirely absent from Protestant accounts of this episode, to describe the execution of those religious put to death for resisting the dissolution of their houses. Parkyn's narrative was therefore overtly an account of the costs of suppression and, in some sense, it also served to commemorate those who had lost their lives in the 1530s. As he continued into Edward VI's reign, Parkyn continued to deplore the reforms enacted by the new regime. Like the anonymous Grey Friar, he was relieved when Mary succeeded her half-brother and 'all olde cere-monies laudablie usyed before tyme in wholly churche was then revivyde, daly frequentide & uside'.[83]

The reign of Mary I was the earliest flashpoint for the development of what Eamon Duffy has identified as the 'conservative voice', because it marked the 'passing of the initiative – and the weight of rhetorical advantage – to the conservative cause'.[84] Of course, this advantage was not to last beyond Mary's premature death in 1558. The accession of her half-sister, Elizabeth I, forced the 'conservative voice' into an oppositional mode. But even as the terms of religious debate began to shift from 'conservative' and 'evangelical' to 'Catholic' and 'Protestant', regret for some aspects of the dissolution continued to provide common ground for those at the conservative end of the confessional spectrum. If anything, this conservative vision of the dissolution became more pronounced as Elizabeth's reign wore on.

In 1592, more than fifty years after the closure of the last religious houses, the Elizabethan antiquary John Stow published the first edition of his *Annales, or generall chronicle of England*. Stow's antiquarian output was extensive: at the time of its publication, the *Annales* was the most recent in a series of chronicles penned by Stow, both under his own name – *A summarie of English chronicles* (1565; 1587), *The chronicles of England*

---

[82] Ibid.   [83] Ibid., p. 82.
[84] Eamon Duffy, *Saints, Sacrilege, and Sedition: Religion and Conflict in the Tudor Reformations* (London, 2012), p. 222.

(1580) – and as a member of the Holinshed syndicate. But unlike Grafton, with whom Stow sustained a bitter rivalry across their respective publishing careers, and others of the collective involved in producing Holinshed's chronicles, Stow was not possessed of impeccable Protestant credentials. Earlier in his career, he had twice faced controversy for suspected crypto-Catholicism, first over accusations that he had illegally copied and circulated a pamphlet attacking the queen, and then again when Edmund Grindal, then bishop of London, ordered that his property be searched for illegal Catholic books and manuscripts. The investigation revealed thirty-nine objectionable items, and the report that reached William Cecil claimed that Stow's 'bokes declare him to be a great fav[oure]r of papistrye'.[85] Current historiography tends to place Stow somewhere between Church papist and conservative conformist; Ian Archer has suggested that Stow underwent a 'transition to conformity' over the course of his life, much of which he spent engaged in historical and antiquarian activities.[86] This work, as we shall see also in the next chapter, inspired his interest in England's lost religious houses and the changes wrought by the dissolution on the landscape; amongst Stow's surviving manuscripts are several collections relating to monastic history, including a survey notebook listing all the religious houses of medieval England in thirty-four folios.[87]

At first glance, the *Annales* does not appear to reflect Stow's religious or intellectual proclivities in the way that Wriothesley and Grafton's chronicles flaunted their support for the Henrician cause. Most of his entries describing the fall of particular houses echo the concise passages set down by Wriothesley, though Stow's lists are not as extensive as those of his predecessor. Late in 1538, for example, he stated that 'The hospital of S. Thomas Akres in London, the blacke friers, the white friers, the gray friers, and the charter house monks in London, were suppressed, and so all other religious houses immediately after'.[88] There are a few subsequent mentions of dissolved houses, including the conversion of St Mary Overy

<hr/>

[85] Quoted in Janet Wilson, 'A catalogue of the "unlawful" books found in John Stow's study on 21 February 1568/9', *Recusant History* 20 (1990), pp. 1–30 at p. 2.
[86] Ian W. Archer, 'John Stow: citizen and historian', in Ian Gadd and Alexandra Gillespie (eds.), *John Stow (1525–1605) and the Making of the English Past* (London, 2004), pp. 13–26 at pp. 21–2. See also Alexandra Gillespie, 'Introduction', in Gadd and Gillespie (eds.), *John Stow*, p. 2; Patrick Collinson, 'John Stow and nostalgic antiquarianism', in Julia F. Merritt (ed.), *Imagining Early Modern London: Perceptions and Portrayals of the City from Stow to Strype, 1598–1720* (Cambridge, 2001), pp. 27–51.
[87] BL, Additional MS 57945 (John Stow's notebook listing religious houses, *c.* 1600).
[88] John Stow, *The annales of England, faithfully collected out of the most authenticall authors, records, and other monuments of antiquitie* (London, 1592), p. 972.

into a parish church.[89] Yet these entries are not so numerous as in earlier Tudor chronicles, further testifying to how the long process of suppression was being gradually condensed and collapsed into something more akin to an historical event. It is also the case that Stow's chronicle reshaped earlier recollections of the dissolution, subsuming his concise lists of dissolved religious houses into a wider narrative that was polemically and confessionally inflected, if rather more subtly so than some previous chronicles. Thus in an entry dated 1536, Stow offers the following account of the closure of the lesser monasteries. It is an account that is at once both remarkably familiar and profoundly altered from what had gone before:

> In a parliament begun in the moneth of Februarie [1536], was granted to the king and his heires all religious houses in the realme of Englande, of the value of two hundred pound and under, with al lands and goods to them belonging: the number of these houses then suppressed, were 376. the value of their lands then 32000. pound, and more by yeere, the mooveable goodes as they were sold, Robin Hoodes pennywoorthes, amounted to more than one hundred thousand pounds, and the religious persons that were in the saide houses, were clerely put out, some went to other greater houses, some went abroad to the world. It was (sayeth mine author) a pitifull thing to heare the lamentation that the people in the countrie made for them: for there was great hospitalitie kept among them, and as it was thought more than ten thousand persons, masters and servants had lost their livings by the putting downe of those houses at that time.[90]

This passage, which is an expanded version of a previous discussion of the dissolution in Stow's earlier *Chronicles of England* (1580), bears striking resemblance, both structural and linguistic, to its equivalent in Wriothesley's chronicle.[91] Indeed, the internal evidence is sufficient to suggest that the Henrician herald was in fact the anonymous 'author' behind Stow's account of the suppression of the lesser religious houses.[92]

It is unsurprising that Stow, who was a child only about ten years old at the time of the dissolution, borrowed his account from an earlier source, not to say entirely in keeping with the chronicle tradition. Yet the

[89] On processes of conversion see below, Ch. 3.   [90] Stow, *Annales*, p. 966.
[91] The similitude of these entries was underlined by William Douglas Hamilton, who suggested that Stow must have had access either to the original manuscript or to a contemporary copy of Wriothesley's chronicle. See Hamilton, 'Introduction' to Wriothesley, *A Chronicle of England*, p. xx. See also Barrett L. Beer, 'John Stow and the English Reformation, 1547–1559', *SCJ* 16 (1985), pp. 257–71 at p. 258, though Beer does not discuss the passage in question. Note that Wriothesley's chronicle is not listed amongst the chronicles owned by Stow identified in Alexandra Gillespie, 'Stow's "owlde" manuscripts of London chronicles', in Gadd and Gillespie (eds.), *John Stow*, pp. 57–68.
[92] See also Lyon, 'A pitiful thing?'.

implication of the phrase 'sayeth mine author' that what follows is a faithful rendering of its source is profoundly misleading and conceals the notable and important differences between Wriothesley's chronicle and the *Annales*. The latter does not quote verbatim from the Henrician chronicle. Stow erased Wriothesley's polemical comments concerning the 'augmentation of the crowne' and the 'ample' living of the religious. His addition of the contemporary proverb 'Robin Hoodes penny woorthes' to characterise the 'moveable goodes' taken from the religious houses further implies contempt for the king and his commissioners. In early modern parlance, this phrase had a double meaning, referring either to goods sold at half their worth, as Robin Hood had done with those he plundered, or the legendary outlaw's ability to buy goods at any price because 'the owners were glad to get anything of Robin Hood, who otherwise would have taken their goods for nothing'.[93] As evangelical polemicists had noted since the 1530s, Henry VIII could hardly be said to have stolen from the rich to give to the poor. This phrase thus concealed a profound critique of the Henrician government, which found further expression in the final lines of the passage. In a subtle but significant misrepresentation of Wriothesley, Stow conveyed his pity for the communities – no longer limited solely to the 'poore' sorts – robbed of the religious houses around which they had been built and upon which they had relied for employment, charity, and hospitality. Thus where Wriothesley had recorded that:

> it was pitie the great lamentation that the poore people made for theim, for there was great hospitalitie kept amonge theim, and, as it was reported, tenne thousand persons had lost their living by the putting downe of theim, which was great pitie.[94]

Stow wrote that:

> It was (sayeth mine author) a pitifull thing to heare the lamentation that the people in the countrie made for them: for there was great hospitalitie kept among them, and as it was thought more than ten thousand persons, masters and servants had lost their livings by the putting downe of those houses at that time.[95]

Although here Stow focussed wholly upon the lay victims of the dissolution and made no effort to rehabilitate the monks, nuns, and friars who were the Henrician regime's primary targets, this passage nevertheless

---

[93] John Ray, *A compleat collection of English proverbs, also the most celebrated proverbs of the Scotch, Italian, French, Spanish and other languages* (London, 1737), p. 208.
[94] AC, DNP: MS 468A, fol. 71r.   [95] Stow, *Annales*, p. 966.

conceals the irony that a rhetoric intended to assert the expediency of the suppression and the folly of those who had mourned the loss of the monasteries had been transfigured to mould the dissolution itself into the truly 'pitifull thing'.

The ideological inflections apparent in the *Annales* are both a reflection of Stow's religious proclivities and the product of a political culture that policed conformity in matters of religion. Nothing came of the charges to which he was subject in 1569, but the *Annales* evidences amply the ways in which his religious beliefs suffused his sense of history, as well as the necessity of caution in producing a critique of Henry VIII under the second of his Protestant heirs. Other politically charged episodes that have been given a markedly more conservative cast in the *Annales* than in other contemporary histories include the fatal shooting of Robert Packington, one of Foxe's earliest Protestant martyrs, in 1536;[96] the death at the stake of Friar Forest, burned for heresy in 1538;[97] and the accession of Mary I in 1553.[98] In the case of Forest, Stow again paraphrased Wriothesley's chronicle to temper the language of popish error, turning a vituperative condemnation of the 'obstinate' friar into the cautious commemoration of a Catholic martyr.[99]

Stow was not merely a compiler of information, but also an editor, censor, and polemicist of sorts. In this context, it becomes possible to understand his approach to Wriothesley's chronicle and the problem of the latter's anonymity, which, the cumulative and parasitic tendencies of the genre notwithstanding, seems particularly unusual. In a prefatory list, Stow cited the authority of some 300 classical, medieval, and contemporary authorities. These include the works of contemporary and near-contemporary chroniclers such as Thomas Cooper, Edward Hall, Robert Fabyan, and Polydore Vergil, in addition to a variety of other sources that displayed in abundance their evangelical convictions, including the caustic polemic of John Bale and the profoundly anti-Catholic topography of the Kentish antiquary William Lambarde. Although practices of citation were far from standardised in this period, the margins of the *Annales* are littered with references to these and other texts.[100] But there is no explicit reference to Wriothesley anywhere in any of the extant editions of Stow's chronicle. Instead, he has taken the step of parenthetically citing the oblique figure of

---

[96] Peter Marshall, *Religious Identities in Henry VIII's England* (Aldershot, 2006), p. 77.

[97] Lyon, 'A pitiful thing?'.   [98] Kastan, 'Opening gates and stopping hedges', pp. 66–79.

[99] Lyon, 'A pitiful thing?'.

[100] On the history of citation practices, see Anthony Grafton, *The Footnote: A Curious History* (Cambridge, MA, 1997).

'mine author', distancing himself from the very discussion of the dissolution that he had so carefully transfigured. It seems, then, that Wriothesley's obscurity is a product of Stow's intention deliberately to challenge the Henrician orthodoxy and reshape the prevailing vision of the dissolution.

Stow's work, like that of Wriothesley before him, albeit with a very different character and emphasis, was neither an impartial record of the past nor a vehicle for a moribund tradition of historical writing but rather a carefully composed narrative saturated with religious and political significance. The careful piece of textual ventriloquism that is Stow's account of the suppression of the monasteries testifies powerfully to the creative potential of the chronicle genre to contest and reshape historical narratives. It is also undoubtedly, if cautiously, ideological. Thus when Stow's biographer, Barrett L. Beer, claimed that his subject 'did not join the great religious debates of his day and never wrote polemical works to praise or condemn government policy', he mistook the subtle polemic of the *Annales* for the laconic and secular history long associated with the early modern chronicle genre.[101]

Stow's conservative chronicle ought not to be confused with the more unashamedly ideological histories produced by contemporary Catholic historians, mostly written on the Continent. The most significant and powerful example of this genre is the Catholic exile Nicholas Sander's *De origine ac progressu schismatis anglicani* (1585), which was itself indebted to earlier polemics on the schism by authors such as Reginald Pole and Nicholas Harpsfield.[102] As the first printed historical narrative of the English Reformation written from an English Catholic viewpoint, it came to be enormously influential in early modern historiography.[103] In some ways a counterpoint to Foxe's *Actes and monuments*, which had been recently reprinted in a fourth edition in 1583, Sander's history advanced a profoundly negative view of the Reformation, the Elizabethan settlement, and the political and personal machinations of Henry VIII. Although not explicitly conceived as a chronicle, the text bears the main hallmark of this tradition: a series of chronologically ordered chapters, which delineate particular events organised by calendar date and month. These included several episodes commonly absent in Protestant accounts

---

[101] Barrett L. Beer, *Tudor England Observed: The World of John Stow* (Stroud, 1998), p. 85.
[102] Christopher Highley, '"A pestilent and seditious book": Nicholas Sander's *Schismatis anglicani* and Catholic histories of the Reformation', in Kewes (ed.), *Uses of History*, pp. 153–60.
[103] Ibid., p. 147. See also Christopher Highley, *Catholics Writing the Nation in Early Modern Britain and Ireland* (Oxford, 2008), p. 43.

of the sixteenth-century upheavals, notably the martyrdom of the 'most saintly' Carthusians, which, as we saw in the previous chapter, was an important touchstone for the Catholic memory of the Henrician Reformation.[104]

In histories such as *De origine*, the dissolution served as an illuminating episode in a wider Catholic historiography that focussed on finding explanations for the Reformation in Henry VIII's lust and avarice, his divorce from Katherine of Aragon, and the subsequent breach with Rome.[105] Sander thus railed against the 1535 visitation that 'had for its end to enable the king to destroy every monastery the possession of which he coveted' and originated the public campaign against the 'enormities of the religious, partly discovered and partly invented'.[106] On the one hand, this serves as an important reminder that it was not only Protestants who had been preoccupied with the question of reform; Catholics too had long been engaged in attempts to correct and eradicate abuses in the religious houses and the wider Catholic Church. On the other hand, the fact that Sander's acknowledgement that the Henrician commissioners' reports probably contained at least a grain of truth did not excuse the regime's flagrant invention of monastic iniquities – especially when it came to the wholesale dissolution, rather than the supposed reformation of the monasteries initiated in 1536. Sander constructed a narrative that dwelt upon the violence of the Reformation: he lambasted the 'storm' brought down upon the religious orders, as well as the Catholic saints whose shrines and cults they promoted, and which roundly condemned the regime's ultimate project to 'disturb and destroy the remaining monasteries' in England and Wales.[107] For Sander, this was the definitive example of the avarice of the king and his chief ministers, who had so shockingly 'robbed the ... shrines, churches, and monasteries'.[108] It is significant that, in doing so, *De origine* also gave voice to anxieties that Protestants and Catholics shared. In the same way that late Elizabethan Catholic succession tracts, as Peter Lake has demonstrated, were effective precisely because they played on Protestant fears about the uncertain nature of the royal succession in the absence of a biological heir to Elizabeth I, *De origine* tapped into a very real Protestant nervousness about the fervour of the early Reformation iconoclasts.[109] As we

---

[104] Nicholas Sander, *De origine ac progressu schismatis anglicani*, ed. and trans. David Lewis, *The Rise and Growth of the Anglican Schism* (London, 1877), p. 117.

[105] See Highley, 'Pestilent and seditious book', p. 156.   [106] Sander, *De origine*, p. 130.

[107] Ibid., p. 140.   [108] Ibid., p. 143.

[109] See Peter Lake, 'The King (the Queen) and the Jesuit: James Stuart's *True Law of Free Monarchies* in context/s', *TRHS* 14 (2004), pp. 243–60; Peter Lake, *Bad Queen Bess: Libels, Secret Histories, and the Politics of Publicity in the Reign of Queen Elizabeth I* (Oxford, 2016), p. 475 and *passim*.

shall see, this anxiety about the dissolution came increasingly to colour
Protestant accounts of the Reformation as the seventeenth century progressed.

However, some concerns were unique to the Catholic community. In
particular, Catholics were faced with the question of whether monasticism
in the form abolished de facto by Henry VIII might be a part of their future
as well as their past. In 1596, the Jesuit Robert Persons produced
a manuscript outlining plans for a new Catholic restoration. Although
The memorial for the Reformation of England was not a history in the
strictest sense, it was a profoundly historically minded text. Persons viewed
the dissolution itself as 'that infamous Sacriledge and Monstrous Rapine of
King Henry the Eighth, whereby at once he destroyed and pluckt from
God and his Church . . . all the pious Acts and Memories of Religion, that
in more than a Thousand Years before him, his Ancestors had bestowed
that way'.[110] Persons thus lamented the breach created by the Reformation
with Catholic practices for remembering the dead and the endowment of
religious foundations for this purpose, as well as demarcating the dissolution as a significant break with the medieval past. This sense of rupture
was only reinforced by the fact that monasticism was not a particular
priority of Persons's intended Catholic restoration because '(though in it
self most Holy) [monasticism] neither be possible nor necessary in England
presently upon the first Reformation'.[111] He did, however, accept that the
foundation of religious institutions modelled on the Jesuits, as well as other
thoroughly reformed religious orders, might form part of the long-term re-
establishment of English Catholicism. It is significant that Persons did not
view medieval monasticism as a model for a new Catholic Church in
England. Rather, the *Memorial* expressed a sense of rupture between past
and present that, as we saw in the previous chapter, also found clear and
strong expression in other forms of Catholic polemic. This is not to say that
the dissolution was irrelevant in debates about an ongoing Reformation:
Persons resurrected the memory of the suppression simultaneously to
condemn Henry VIII and his government and to rethink the structures
of English Catholicism for a world in which he hoped Catholicism could
yet be successfully restored.

Counter-Reformation polemic of this kind was absent from conservative
conformist accounts of the dissolution, such as that by John Stow. For
although a sense of rupture united Elizabethan Catholic and conservative

---

[110] Robert Persons, *The Jesuit's memorial for the intended reformation of England under their first popish
prince published from the copy that was presented to the late King James II*, trans. Edward Gee
(London, 1690), p. 60.
[111] Ibid., p. 57.

accounts of the dissolution, the tenor and timbre of these reflections were very different. By contrast with the provocative narratives exemplified by Persons's *Memorial* and Sander's *De origine* – both texts disseminated from the relative security of Catholic Europe – conservative works like Stow's *Annales of England* were, as we have seen, born of a different impulse. Stow's chronicle was a product of his particular variety of conservative antiquarianism, often described as a 'nostalgic' expression of a worldview that lamented the decline of charity and hospitality from the medieval period and mourned the disfigurement of the post-Reformation landscape and cityscape.[112] As we shall see in the next chapter, pity for the losses sustained at the dissolution quickly became attached to the physical remnants of monastic sites. Ruins, in particular, became a leitmotif in literary expressions of the conservative voice, including William Shakespeare's lament for the 'bare ruin'd choirs where late the sweet birds sang'.[113] Stow's chronicle was archetypal of this wider conservative tradition, exhibiting an outlook that was predicated on what Patrick Collinson has described as a 'strongly contrasted sense of "then" and "now"' that was to 'persist in the national memory for generations to come'.[114] Early modern perceptions of the dissolution were profoundly shaped by this sense of temporal breach – by the divide between past and present engendered by the Reformation. Precisely because 'conservative voices' tended to articulate and mourn the rupture that the Henrician regime had sought to downplay in the 1530s and 1540s, these historians and commentators were also inclined further to collapse the various phases of the dissolution into a single catastrophic episode and a landmark moment in English history. This tendency became increasingly prevalent, emphatic, and – most importantly – widespread into the early seventeenth century and beyond.

'An Alteration or Revolution of Time'

The primary difference between reflections on the dissolution penned by Catholics and Protestants was that whilst the former saw the sack of the monasteries as part of a larger catalogue of Henrician errors, the latter were

---

[112] Ian Archer, 'The nostalgia of John Stow', in David L. Smith, Richard Strier, and David Bevington (eds.), *The Theatrical City: Culture, Theatre and Politics in London, 1576–1649* (Cambridge, 1995), pp. 17–34 at p. 22; Collinson, 'John Stow and nostalgic antiquarianism'. See also below, Ch. 3.
[113] See Duffy's discussion of this passage from Shakespeare's Sonnet 73 in 'Conservative voice', p. 230. See also Philip Schwyzer, *Archaeologies of English Renaissance Literature* (Oxford, 2007), pp. 102–3.
[114] Patrick Collinson, 'Merry England on the ropes: the contested culture of the early modern English town', in Simon Ditchfield (ed.), *Christianity and Community in the West: Essays for John Bossy* (Aldershot, 2001), pp. 131–47 at p. 137. On the longevity of Stow, see Woolf, *Social Circulation of the Past*, p. 253.

forced to confront the suppression as a difficult episode in an otherwise generally laudable Reformation. As we saw previously, overt Protestant critiques of the dissolution had once been the preserve of a small but committed minority of evangelical polemicists and controversialists. However, in the late sixteenth and early seventeenth centuries, a growing number of Protestants were also beginning to look back upon this episode with a critical eye. The dissolution had become increasingly problematic with the passing of the generation who had witnessed it at first hand and in the context of growing anxiety about the zeal of the early reformers and the avarice of the Henrician regime in the 1530s. Once a defining feature of the conservative voice, many Protestant commentators began to acknowledge the breach that the dissolution had engendered between past and present, as well as the rupture that it had created in the religious, social, and economic fabric of early modern England.

Often this emergent anxiety was characterised by a sense of decline. In 1578, the puritan divine Laurence Chaderton gave a sermon at Paul's Cross, subsequently printed as *An excellent and godly sermon*, which focussed upon the proper preparation of the clergy and was generally intended to promote a more zealous style of piety amongst his audience.[115] It also gave him the opportunity to rail against those 'papists', like Sander and Persons, '[who] always cast in our teeth the great and famous hospitals of their nobility and clergy, [and] the building of abbeys, monasteries, and nunneries, cathedral churches, colleges'.[116] This comment reveals how ongoing religious debate compelled remembrance of the monastic past amongst Protestants, for the simple reason that they had not been allowed to forget about the virtues of charity, hospitality, and lay piety associated with the medieval religious houses. Although Chaderton robustly rejected the Catholic position, he was also ultimately forced to admit that these 'outward works ... indeed are such as do stop our mouths and put us Protestants to silence'.[117] As well as demonstrating the longevity of the Catholic critique of the dissolution,

---

[115] On the *Excellent and godly sermon*, see Peter Lake, *Moderate Puritans and the Elizabethan Church* (Cambridge, 1982), ch. 7; Ellen A. Macek, 'Advice manuals and the formation of English Protestant and Catholic identities, 1560–1660', in Wim Janse and Barbara Pitkin (eds.), *The Formation of Clerical and Confessional Identities in Early Modern Europe* (Leiden and Boston, MA, 2006), pp. 315–31 at pp. 317–18.

[116] Laurence Chaderton, *An excellent and godly sermon, most needefull for this time, wherein we live in all sercuritie and sinne, to the great dishonour of God, and contempt of his holy word. Preached at Paules Crosse the xxvi daye of October, An. 1578* (London, 1578), sig. C5r. On Chaderton, see Lake, *Moderate Puritans*, ch. 3; Arnold Hunt, 'Laurence Chaderton and the Hampton Court Conference', in Susan Wabuda and Caroline Litzenberger (eds.), *Belief and Practice in Reformation England* (Aldershot, 1998), pp. 207–28.

[117] Chaderton, *Excellent and godly sermon*, sig. C5r.

Chaderton's uneasy confession also suggests that earlier evangelical concerns about the misappropriation of monastic property for private uses continued to trouble a new generation of Protestants. His sermon also constituted a form of public remembrance incited by the practices of preaching and hearing that have recently been examined by Arnold Hunt.[118] A sense of anxiety about the dissolution may have been only implicit in Chaderton's remarks, but they are nevertheless indicative of how the mood of the Protestant memory of the dissolution was beginning to shift and change. In particular, Elizabethan Protestants were being forced to grapple with problems of charity, hospitality, and education. As the sixteenth century drew to a close, these concerns were further exacerbated by the sense in which social and economic upheaval combined with the new apparatus for charity enshrined in the Elizabethan Poor Laws (1598) contributed to a decline in the practice of hospitality and philanthropy by the gentry and secular clergy.[119]

By the early seventeenth century, these issues had become prominent in contemporary debate. They therefore helped to keep the memory of the dissolution alive amongst a new generation of Reformation polemicists writing from a variety of religious positions. Versions of the argument that the suppression had engendered a state of interminable decline can be found in the writings of authors including John Cosin, an active member of Richard Neile's circle of anti-Calvinists and later bishop of Durham, Peter Hausted, a notorious critic of puritanism, and William Beale, royalist churchman and Master of Peterhouse, Cambridge.[120] However, it found fullest expression, as Anthony Milton has demonstrated, as a tenet of Laudianism in the 1630s, when political and theological priorities shifted away from the outright condemnation of the Catholic Church as an inveterate evil, a project undertaken by a succession of sixteenth-century polemicists from the Henrician commissioners through to Foxe, towards an appreciation of the piety and ceremonial splendour of a Church that had been corrupted but nevertheless demanded admiration for its generosity and munificence.[121] The implications of this argument for shifting perceptions of the dissolution and its convergence with concerns about the appropriation of monastic lands and church wealth will be more fully

---

[118] See Arnold Hunt, *The Art of Hearing: English Preachers and Their Audiences, 1590–1640* (Cambridge, 2010). Hunt also discusses Chaderton's *Excellent and godly sermon* at pp. 121, 131.
[119] Felicity Heal, *Hospitality in Early Modern England* (Oxford, 1990), pp. 400–3.
[120] See Anthony Milton, *Catholic and Reformed: The Roman and Protestant Churches in English Protestant Thought, 1600–1640* (Cambridge, 1995), pp. 316–18.
[121] Ibid., ch. 6. On Laudianism and the memory of the dissolution, see also below, Ch. 3.

explored in subsequent chapters. Here it informs the context in which Stow's *Annales* became the subject of a new exercise in reshaping the past to suit the concerns and preoccupations of the early Stuart period.

Edmund Howes began work on a continuation of the *Annales* with the encouragement of John Whitgift, archbishop of Canterbury, three years before Stow's death in 1605, although it would be another decade before the new edition went to press.[122] Relatively little is known of Howes's background and career outside of his work as a chronicler and antiquary. Kenneth Fincham and Nicholas Tyacke identify him amongst the breed of Protestants described by Peter Lake as 'avant-garde conformists'.[123] He can also be connected to the endowment of a choir school and salary for an organist at Christ's Hospital and his interest in the Jacobean pro-gramme of restoring ecclesiastical structures further reflected his advo-cacy of the beautification of churches and ritual forms of worship.[124] Although his first continuation of the *Annales* in 1615 narrowly preceded Laudian debates about the 'beauty of holiness', it is plainly apparent from his writing that Howes mourned the charity and the hospitality of the pre-Reformation age. He made no alterations to Stow's original text, except to extend it to cover the early part of the reign of the new Stuart king, James VI and I. But Howes also found ways to bring his proclivities to bear on this new edition of the *Annales* by adding an 'historical preface' that served to colour and reshape Stow's vision of the dissolution. Although he acknowledged the corrupt elements of medieval monasti-cism and the ways in which the religious orders had 'neglected their duty to God and man', Howes nevertheless applauded how medieval monks and nuns upheld their social responsibilities and 'relieved the poore, and raised no rents, nor tooke excessive Fines'. The dissolution when it came thus 'fell sodainley upon [the religious houses]' as swiftly and violently as the 'universal deluge'. Articulating the magnitude of this rupture more clearly than any previous chronicler, Howes wrote that the monasteries had been 'utterly ruinated' by the crown and its agents, 'whereat the

---

[122] Christina DeCoursey, 'Howes, Edmund (*fl.* 1602–1631)', *ODNB*, www.oxforddnb.com/view/art icle/13985.

[123] Kenneth Fincham and Nicholas Tyacke, *Altars Restored: The Changing Face of English Religious Worship, 1547–c. 1700* (Oxford, 2007), pp. 98–100. On the term 'avant-garde conformist', see Peter Lake, 'Lancelot Andrewes, John Buckeridge and avant-garde conformity at the court of James I', in Linda Levy Peck (ed.), *The Mental World of the Jacobean Court* (Cambridge, 1991), pp. 113–33.

[124] On Howes and the Jacobean rebuilding project, see J. F. Merritt, 'Puritans, Laudians, and the phenomenon of church-building in Jacobean London', *HJ* 41 (1998), pp. 935–60 at pp. 937–8, 955.

Clergy, Peeres, and common people were all sore grieved, but could not helpe it'.[125]

Several themes emerge from these comments. The first is the tension between Howes's account of the virtues of medieval monasticism and his unwillingness to name the religious as its primary victims – or even as being amongst its victims at all. 'Flattered and secured' in their accumulated wealth, the dissolution was portrayed as a shock to the religious but not a punishment that was wholly undeserved; it was akin, as Howes alluded, to the providential Flood sent by God to punish the sins of mankind. Secondly, the preface exhibits a profound anxiety about the wanton destruction of the monasteries. Developing the conservative rhetoric of the sixteenth century, the gutted remnants of abbeys and convents scattered across the landscape appear to have been a particular touchstone for this memory, provoking and shaping Howes's sense of the dissolution, for he also wrote that 'many ruins of them remain a testimony of [the medieval monasteries] to this day'.[126] Thirdly, this passage reinforces and augments Stow's account of widespread grief for the loss of the monasteries, which reached beyond the 'common' sorts to those in the higher echelons of English society and those with status in the political establishment.[127]

The significance of this theme of decline becomes apparent when Howes, in the act of recalling the dissolution, was prompted also to ruminate on the social and economic problems of his own time. His pity was not only for the direct victims of the suppression but also for the generations still suffering its consequences. In the 1530s, Howes wrote, the dissolution had provided Henry VIII with the opportunity to free the English people from 'all former services and taxes' and 'neyther ... be any more charged with loans, subsidies, and fifteens'. Here Howes borrowed from much earlier critiques of the failure of the Henrician regime to divert monastic wealth to pious, charitable, and educational uses, which had been prominent amongst justifications for the suppression in the 1530s. But his argument was also heavily inflected by contemporary concerns about taxation. This was not a common feature of either

---

[125] Howes, 'Historicall preface', sig. ¶5v.
[126] Ibid. On monastic ruins, see esp. Margaret Aston, 'English ruins and English history: the dissolution and the sense of the past', *Journal of the Warburg and Courtauld Institutes* 36 (1973), pp. 231–55; Alexandra Walsham, *The Reformation of the Landscape: Religion, Identity, and Memory in Early Modern Britain and Ireland* (Oxford, 2011), pp. 274, 281–3. These issues are explored further below, Ch. 3.
[127] Howes, 'Historicall preface', sig. ¶6r.

Henrician or evangelical rhetoric. It was, however, a closely contested issue
in the early seventeenth century, which witnessed repeated and protracted
conflicts between James VI and I and his parliaments over the state of the
royal finances.[128] It was thus with palpable bitterness that Howes concluded that since the dissolution 'there have been more statute laws,
subsidies and fifteenes then in five hundreth yeares before'.[129]

This claim that the dissolution had been the most problematic rupture
for half a millennium is also of crucial significance to Howes's broader
conception of chronology and historical change. Howes was the chronicler
we met at the outset of this chapter, who characterised the dissolution as so
profound an 'alteration, or revolution of time'. Adopting a cyclical model
of time in which these great 'alterations' or 'revolutions' occurred at 500-
year intervals, Howes used his preface to chart the history of England from
the time of Brutus to his own present day. These 'alterations' in time
tended to take the form of violent wars or conquests, beginning with the
dynastic civil wars sparked by the murder of Porrex, legendary king of the
Britons, by his brother, Ferrex, and the latter's subsequent death at
the hands of his own mother. This was followed at successive half millennia
by the tyrannical rule of Julius Caesar, the Saxon conquest, and the
invasion of the Normans. It is testament to the potency and longevity of
the cultural memory of the dissolution that Howes cited this episode as the
most recent of these temporal ruptures, albeit he characterised it as
a 'milder' sort of revolution than the wars that had preceded it.[130] His
discussion of monastic complacency and worldliness, of the despoliation of
abbeys and convents, and of the consequences visited upon the nation thus
belong to an historical narrative that posits the dissolution as the most
memorable event of the sixteenth century, on a par with some of the most
momentous alterations in English history.

In this respect, it is striking that Howes singled out the dissolution
specifically, as opposed to the break from Rome, the supplanting of papal
power by the Royal Supremacy, or the Protestant Reformation more
generally. One consequence of this decision was to make the suppression
virtually synonymous with the reign of Henry VIII and the religious
upheavals initiated by his government. The accession of James VI and
I in 1603 had created an atmosphere more conducive to critical perspectives

---

[128] On the financial problems of the early Stuart crown, see, for example, Johann Sommerville,
'Ideology, property, and the constitution', in Richard Cust and Ann Hughes (eds.), *Conflict in
Early Stuart England: Studies in Religion and Politics, 1603–1642* (London, 1989), pp. 47–71;
John Cramsie, *Kingship and Crown Finance Under James VI and I, 1603–1625* (Woodbridge, 2002).
[129] Howes, 'Historicall preface', sig. ¶6r.   [130] Ibid.

on both the dissolution of the monasteries and Henry VIII himself.[131] In stark contrast to the Tudor chronicles, Howes explicitly condemned the king for being the principal player in the dissolution: 'because he would goe the next way to worke overthrew [the religious houses] and raced them ... whereat many the Peeres and common people murmured because they expected that the abuses should have bin onely reformed and the rest have still remained'.[132] Discourses of reform designed to combat monastic abuses had been prevalent before the dissolution, but this argument had not been a prominent feature of chronicles produced under Henry's Protestant heirs. For Howes, however, it underpinned an explicit expression of regret for the charity and hospitality of the monasteries that magnified and extended Stow's lament for what had been lost in the early Reformation. Writing that Henry had 'likewise supprest many fayre hospitalles', Howes suggested that 'the commons beganne to think that the king had no intent eyther to relieve the poore, admit maintenance for maimed souldiers, or to ease them of any common charge'. By implicitly praising the value of monastic charity and the hospitality of the religious orders, Howes built up an increasingly critical image of the king, concluding with a description of an aged, obese monarch, who had grown 'very fat and slothfull' and who ruled through 'feare and terror'.[133] For Howes, the dissolution had thus become the chief abuse of a king who had given himself over to greed.

Howes's chronicle is a powerful testament to the transformation of the lengthy and uneven process witnessed by Wriothesley in the 1530s into a landmark moment in the English Reformation, conforming to Abrams's definition of an historical event as an episode to which 'cultural significance has successfully been assigned'.[134] Howes thus made the strongest claim yet about the importance of remembering the dissolution and about its status as a marker of historical time. He was, moreover, self-conscious of his role as a custodian of memory. It had been his duty, he wrote, to recover those episodes in English history worthy of 'lasting memory'. He also recognised more explicitly than previous chroniclers the urgency this project had acquired in the wake of the memory crisis engendered by the Reformation. Demonstrating a clear awareness of the distorting effects of the polemical rhetoric and propagandist tendencies of his peers and

---

[131] Mark Rankin, 'The literary afterlife of Henry VIII, 1558–1625', in Mark Rankin, Christopher Highley, and John N. King (eds.), *Henry VIII and his Afterlives: Literature, Politics, and Art* (Cambridge, 2009), pp. 94–114 at pp. 105–6.
[132] Howes, 'Historicall preface', sig. ¶5v.   [133] Ibid., sig. ¶6v.
[134] Abrams, *Historical Sociology*, p. 191.

predecessors, he claimed not only to preserve the events recorded in the *Annales* for posterity but also to recover them from the 'wilfull forgetful-nesse' of a people negotiating the consequences of almost a century of religious upheaval. Locating the events about which he was writing firmly in the past whilst at the same time emphasising the importance of their memory to the present, his continuation of the *Annales* was to be a 'token and remembrance to after ages' as well as a 'mirrour of the miseries of former tymes'.[135] The result was, of course, itself polemical: a text which attempted to perpetuate a very particular vision of the dissolution.

When the second edition of Howes's *Annales* was published in 1632, this historical preface was reprinted in its entirety. As in 1615, Stow's original entries on the dissolution and Friar Forest remained untouched and the spectre of Wriothesley lingered on in the reproduction of the phrase 'sayeth mine author'. But Howes's editorial practice had transfigured the meaning of these passages by aligning an older, cautiously critical narrative with a much more censorious take on the rupture of 1536–40. Howes's edition of the *Annales* was thus Stow's conservative chronicle translated and reinter-preted for the early Stuart age.

Naming and Commemorating the Dissolution

Howes offered a unique vision of the dissolution in his sweeping cyclical vision of English history. But he was far from alone in his fundamental contention that the fall of the monasteries was a moment of profound temporal rupture and a landmark event in the Protestant Reformation. As we have seen, Protestant chronicles and histories had once been a mechanism for vindicating the Tudor monarchy – or, at least, critiques contained therein had to be extremely subtle and allusive. By the mid-seventeenth century, however, many examples of these genres had become vehicles for attacking Henry VIII and the zeal of the early reformers. This was not a wholesale transformation. Most of these texts, as we saw in the case of Howes, continued to advance an account of the medieval religious orders that was inflected by the earlier rhetoric of monastic corruption. Nevertheless, the histories and chronicles produced in the seventeenth century are also symptomatic of a wider shift in English perspectives on the dissolution itself, as Henrician triumph gave way to a more anxious, ambiguous take on the fall of the monasteries.

---

[135] Howes, 'Historicall preface', sig. ¶8r–v.

The development of critical perspectives on the dissolution can be traced across the seventeenth century. At the same time as Howes was working on his second edition of Stow's *Annales*, Morgan Godwin published an English translation of his father Francis Godwin, bishop of Hereford's *Rerum anglicarum Henrico VIII. Edwardo VI. et Maria regnantibus, annales nunc primum editi* (1616). This chronicle drew heavily upon Stow's chronicles for the early Tudor portion of the text, although it is unclear whether Godwin employed Howes's recently published first edition of the *Annales* or an earlier version overseen by Stow himself.[136] Republished in 1630, also under the title of the *Annales of England*, Godwin's chronicle castigated Henry as an avaricious, violent, and self-interested monarch: a king 'much prone to Reformation (specially if any thing might be gotten by it)'.[137] Godwin thus attributed the dissolution of the larger monastic houses solely to Henry's covetousness:

> Not content with what hee had already corraded [corroded], hee casts his eyes on the wealth of the Abbeys that had escaped the violence of the former tempest: and not expecting (as hee deemed it) a needless Act of Parliament, seizeth on the rest of the Abbeyes and Religious Houses of the Realme.[138]

In doing so, Godwin – like Howes – subsumed the overtly polemical language deployed against Henry by Howes into the main body of his chronicle, tarnishing the king with the 'guilt' of dissolution which plagued him 'like a consuming canker'.[139] By connecting these anxieties with the person of Henry VIII, texts such as Howes's and Godwin's *Annales* thus elevated the dissolution to the status of an event virtually synonymous with the Henrician Reformation itself.

Godwin was not unique in his tendency to read the dissolution as perhaps the most significant episode in the reign and reforms of Henry VIII. In the same year as Godwin's *Annales* was published, John Taylor, the self-styled water poet, produced a collection of memorials of the monarchs of England. His one-page account of the key events of Henry's reign closes with the fall of the religious houses, which he believed exemplified the 'tempest of history' brought on by the schism with the Roman church. For this cause, he wrote, 'the King caused to be suppressed in England and Wales 283 monesteries, 215 Priories, 108 Fryeries, 118 Nunneries, 84 Colledges, 9 Cells, and 103 Hospitals'.[140] There is no mention of subsequent reforms such as the Act of Six Articles (1539), which ushered in

[136] D. R. Woolf, 'Godwin, Francis (1562–1633)', *ODNB*, www.oxforddnb.com/view/article/10890.
[137] Francis Godwin, *Annales of England* (London, 1630), p. 159.   [138] Ibid., p. 161.   [139] Ibid.
[140] John Taylor, *All the works of John Taylor the water poet* (London, 1630), p. 316.

a period of greater conservatism in Henrician religious policy and left behind legacies that were rather less wide-ranging and long-lasting than the earlier rupture of the dissolution. Likewise the Stuart chronicler Sir Richard Baker named the dissolution first amongst 'those great disorders, which have been the blemish of [Henry VIII's] life'. Demonstrating a clear awareness that memory and reputation could be made and erased with pen and ink, he wrote that the dissolution was the principal episode that had caused the king to 'be blotted out of the catalogue of our best princes'.[141] Historical writing thus offers an index of shifting perspectives on Henry VIII, which suggests that the dissolution loomed especially large in increasingly negative perceptions of the king and his Reformation. The suppression was, in other words, the most memorable manifestation of the avarice and covetousness displayed by Henry VIII and his nobles.

This theme was, as we saw in the previous chapter, a characteristic of the polemic produced by the regime's early evangelical critics in the 1530s. By the mid-seventeenth century, however, condemnation of Henry's greed and self-interest had become much more widespread. It is worth noting here that this did not eclipse or even diminish the Henrician narrative of monastic corruption that can be traced – albeit to slightly different degrees – across the trajectory from Wriothesley through Stow to Howes and beyond. If the implication of Godwin's account of the violence of the dissolution is that the religious were victims of the Henrician 'whirle-wind', his chronicle also continued in the manner of the precedent set by government polemic a century earlier by recording various monastic frauds and abuses for posterity. A prominent churchman, Godwin could not condone the 'blinde zeale' of the pre-Reformation age. Amongst the deceptions he identified was the alleged replacement of the real bones of St Thomas Becket with others from a better-preserved corpse. This, he wrote, was an example of the 'superstitious abuse of images' that was the main 'stumbling blocke' to Reformation.[142] Godwin also echoed the long-standing claim about the complicity of the religious in their own suppression, citing their 'guilt of conscience' as the reason many of them 'surrendered their charge even before they were required'.[143] Similarly, Baker's chronicle also exhibits a tension between his negative appraisal of the dissolution and the assertion that the monasteries were the 'forteresses and pillars' of popery, subject to accusations of 'adulteries and murthers' that were 'perhaps no more then [sic] truth'.[144]

---

[141] Sir Richard Baker, *A chronicle of the kings of England* (London, 1643), sig. Fff2v.
[142] Godwin, *Annales*, pp. 159–60.   [143] Ibid., p. 167.   [144] Baker, *Chronicle*, sig. Hhh4r–v.

A comparable vision of the dissolution can be found in the Church of England clergyman Thomas Fuller's *Church history of Britain* (1656), which offered a comprehensive account in eleven books of the history of Christianity in the British Isles.[145] The sixth book, devoted to the 'Originall, Increase, Greatnesse, Decay, and Dissolution' of the religious houses, is characteristic of the rather ambivalent vision of the suppression we have encountered in previous seventeenth-century histories and chronicles. On the one hand, Fuller was critical of the manner in which the Henrician regime had undertaken the dissolution of the religious houses. 'When King Henry the eighth dissolved Monasteries', Fuller continued, 'there was put into his Hand an opportunity and advantage to ingratiate Himself and His memory for ever' by channelling the tithes belonging to the religious houses into the possession of these 'wronged Parish-Priests'.[146] The king's subsequent failure to make restoration was therefore a source of great regret for Fuller. It is worth noting that this constitutes a relatively mild form of the mid-seventeenth-century Protestant critique of Henry VIII. A few years later, shortly after the Restoration of the Stuart monarchy, Fuller's opponent and Laudian churchman, Peter Heylyn, published his *Ecclesia restaurata* (1661), which also served as a partial critique of the *Church history*.[147] In the *Ecclesia restaurata*, Heylyn vigorously condemned the entire Henrician Reformation, which he believed to have hardly been a Reformation at all because of the conservative reaction after 1539. Instead, he located the true origins of the English Reformation in Edward VI's reign – a product of his anti-puritan obsession with the radical nature of Edwardian Protestantism, which also caused him strongly to downplay the significance of the suppression.[148] Indeed, it is striking that Heylyn offered a more sustained discussion of the Edwardian dissolution of the chantries than he did of the Henrician dissolution of the monasteries.[149]

[145] On Fuller's career and religious views, see W. B. Patterson, 'Fuller, Thomas (1607/8–1661)', *ODNB*, www.oxforddnb.com/view/article/10236.
[146] Thomas Fuller, *The church history of Britain from the birth of Jesus Christ until the year M.DC. XLVIII* (London, 1656), book 6, pp. 282–3.
[147] On Heylyn and Fuller's disputes, see John Drabble, 'Thomas Fuller, Peter Heylyn and the English Reformation', *Renaissance and Reformation/Renaissance et Réforme*, new series, 3 (1979), pp. 168–88; Robert Mayer, 'The rhetoric of historical truth: Heylyn *contra* Fuller on *The Church-History of Britain*', *Prose Studies* 20 (1997), pp. 1–20; Anthony Milton, *Laudian and Royalist Polemic in Seventeenth-Century England: The Career and Writings of Peter Heylyn* (Manchester, 2007), p. 174 and *passim*.
[148] For his brief account of the dissolution, see Peter Heylyn, *Ecclesia restaurata, or, the history of the Reformation of the Church of England* (London, 1661), sig. Cv.
[149] See ibid., sigs. Hv–H2r.

Fuller, by contrast, put greater store in the suppression as an important episode in the religious upheavals of the sixteenth century. His criticism of Henry VIII fed into a more general critique of the dissolution itself, returning to the familiar theme of a supposed decline in charity and hospitality in the wake of the fall of the religious houses. For all the faults of the religious orders, he wrote, 'by their hospitality, many an honest and hungry soul had his bowels refreshed, which otherwise would have been starved'.[150] Fuller thus qualified the success of the suppression. Yet, ultimately, none of these arguments served to undermine his decidedly negative view of medieval monasticism. Despite offering a critique of Henry VIII's actions, the *Church history* is also heavily coloured by the Henrician rhetoric of monastic error and corruption. Thus Fuller accused the religious of 'specious pretences of piety' and argued that they were 'notoriously covetous' and a drain on the parish clergy. In his account of the process of dissolution, he also reinforced the Henrician vision of the monasteries by reproducing the preamble to the 1536 act of suppression, which, as we saw in Chapter 1, had so vigorously attacked the 'vi[c]ious, carnall, and abominable living' of the England's monks, nuns, and friars.[151] Conceived as a riposte and a corrective to Catholic histories of the Reformation, such as Nicholas Sander's *De origine*, the *Church history* necessarily sought to balance Fuller's criticism of Henry VIII with the 'infallible truth' of monastic corruption.[152]

With subsequent anti-Catholic crises, these narratives became still more firmly entrenched. Precipitated by the publication of a new French translation of *De origine* in the mid-1670s and against the backdrop of the Exclusion Crisis and Popish Plot (1678–81), Gilbert Burnet produced the first of the three volumes of his monumental *History of the reformation of the Church of England* (1679–1714). Devoted to the evolution of the church under Henry VIII, the first volume of the *History of the reformation* encapsulates the fundamental ambivalence with which Protestants had come to view the dissolution and its chief agent. Portrayed as a king ruled by his passions and appetites, Burnet nevertheless casts Henry as the instrument of divine providence. Making a virtue of necessity, he suggested that only such an imperfect and temperamental monarch could have instigated the destructive work of Reformation.[153] He acknowledged, moreover, that the violence and iconoclasm of the Henrician

---

[150] Fuller, *Church history*, p. 298.   [151] Ibid., p. 310.   [152] Ibid., p. 311.
[153] See Andrew Starkie, 'Henry VIII in history: Gilbert Burnet's *History of the Reformation* (v. 1), 1679', in Thomas Betteridge and Thomas S. Freeman (eds.), *Henry VIII and History* (Farnham, 2012), pp. 151–63 at p. 153.

Reformation had also entailed certain losses – the nunnery of Godstow in Oxfordshire, for example, which had encouraged 'great strictness of life'.[154] Like Wriothesley, writing a century earlier, Burnet was thus willing to admit that not all medieval monks and nuns were irredeemably corrupt. He also characterised the social and economic implications of the dissolution as creating significant disorder in the realm. However, preferring ultimately to address monasticism as a monolithic institution, rather than treating different orders and houses on their own terms, the *History of the reformation* is also inevitably a narrative of monastic decline. Burnet painted a familiar portrait of the Middle Ages when he described how the religious invented 'Relicks without number' to 'feed the devotions of the people', the profits from which enabled them to live 'at ease and in idleness', succumbing to their 'unnatural Lusts' and addicted to idolatry and superstition.[155] He also quoted from the Henrician visitation records to this effect, underlining the power of the Tudor archives to perpetuate a particular vision of the dissolution.[156]

Critically, the *History of the reformation of the Church of England* also suggests that, more than a century after it had taken place, the Dissolution of the Monasteries had finally acquired its name. At the outset of the first volume, Burnet thus announced his intention to 'give an account of the dissolution of the Monasteries'.[157] Like Foxe and Norton before him, Burnet's use of the language of the dissolution appears to have supplanted the need to refer to the key dates of 1536 and 1539; it was, rather, a shorthand in which this chronology was read as given. The name itself was not Burnet's coinage. It is unclear when contemporaries first began to speak of the Dissolution of the Monasteries, although it is evident that this name was the creation of a generation who had not themselves witnessed the suppression in the 1530s. It was, in other words, an invention of posterity, which appears to have been in common parlance by the second half of the seventeenth century. After *c.* 1650, the name is also in evidence in other forms of writing about the past, such as the spatially organised antiquarian studies made by the topographer and chorographer William Dugdale. In the *Antiquities of Warwickshire* (1656), he repeatedly mourned the 'Dissolution of the Monasteries' as 'the greatest blow to Antiquities that ever England had'.[158] For Dugdale, temporal

---

[154] Gilbert Burnet, *The history of the reformation of the Church of England*, 3 vols. (London, 1679–1714), i, p. 238.

[155] Ibid., pp. 188–9.   [156] Ibid., pp. 222–3 and *passim*. See also above, Ch. 1.

[157] Burnet, *History of the reformation*, i, p. 222.

[158] William Dugdale, *The antiquities of Warwickshire illustrated* (London, 1656), preface, p. 22, and *passim*. See also Graham Parry, *The Trophies of Time: English Antiquarians of the Seventeenth Century*

rupture therefore mapped onto a sense of a physical and material break with the past.[159] The name, the Dissolution of the Monasteries, was itself a potent mnemonic for this breach.

Just as the terms 'Protestant' and 'Reformation' were originally pejorative terms, forged by the opponents of religious change, so too were critics of the suppression – or, rather, critics of the way in which Henry VIII had handled the suppression – in large part responsible for its naming.[160] History has remembered not the Reformation or Surrender of the Monasteries, but their Dissolution. This vocabulary of 'dissolution' was not a Henrician invention; rather it emerged over the course of the seventeenth century, as successive generations grappled with the difficult legacies of the fall of the religious houses. The term itself pre-dated the early modern period, with roots in the French *dissolution* and the Latin *dissolutionem*, from *dissolvere*, meaning 'to break up'. Since at least the fourteenth century, 'dissolution' was understood to imply the disintegration of something into its constituent parts, and by the sixteenth century, it was also being used specifically in relation to the termination of parliaments.[161] The Henrician regime itself had used the word in this sense, to describe the 'prorogacion or dissolucion of this present parliament' in 1535.[162] However, as we saw in the previous chapter, in 1539 it was nothing more than an one of a number of interchangeable terms for the transformation of the monastic institution. The second act of suppression thus described the 'dissolucion, suppression, renouncing, relinquyshinge, forfeyting, [and] gevyng upp' of the religious houses.[163] The idea that the government was deliberately breaking up the monasteries did not sit easily alongside its preference for a rhetoric of submission and surrender.[164] A noun of action, 'dissolution' placed greater instrumentality with Henry VIII and his agents. This is not to say that the idea of dissolving any institution was inherently problematic, but rather that the adoption of 'Dissolution of the Monasteries' by the regime's critics is a telling sign that perceptions of the events of 1536–40 were shifting in ways that undermined the Henrician narrative. This was the power of the hindsight possessed by

(Oxford, 1995), ch. 8; Jan Broadway, *William Dugdale: A Life of the Warwickshire Historian and Herald* (Gloucester, 2011).
[159] This is discussed in more detail below, Ch. 3.
[160] On the term 'Protestant', see Peter Marshall, 'The naming of Protestant England', *P&P* 214 (2012), pp. 87–128 at p. 91. On 'Reformation', see Walsham, 'History, memory, and the English Reformation', p. 920.
[161] 'dissolution, n.', *OED*, www.oed.com/view/Entry/55524.
[162] 27 Hen. VIII, c. 26, *The Statutes of the Realm*, 11 vols. (London, 1963), iii, p. 568.
[163] 31 Hen. VIII, c. 13, *Statutes of the Realm*, iii, p. 733.   [164] See above, Ch. 1.

later generations of commentators drawn from across the confessional spectrum, who debated and agonised over the legacies of what was, as we have seen, a highly controversial episode.

The meaning of the dissolution continued to be contested well into the late seventeenth century and beyond. It is for this reason, perhaps, that the suppression was never calendared or celebrated in the sense explored by David Cressy as part of the framework for English national identity and historical consciousness. The vocabulary of dissolution sat uneasily alongside the 'vocabulary of celebration' that underpinned the memorialisation of coronation days and providential deliveries such as the defeat of the Spanish Armada in 1588 or the failure of the Gunpowder Plot in 1605.[165] Indeed, the suppression did not belong to a politically constructed 'public memory' in the same way as these commemorated episodes; it was not invoked as a 'matter of thanksgiving' or a 'stimulus to godliness' and, despite some appeals that Henry VIII had been the divine instrument of the Reformation, it never demanded the same degree of gratitude as these events for the nation's providential deliverance from catastrophe.[166] Rather, it was a morally ambiguous episode, the significance of which the Henrician regime had, in any case, attempted to downplay in the 1530s. Only with the passage of successive generations and the gradual emergence of a widespread critique of Henry VIII did the dissolution acquire the status of an historical event.

This was a critique that found different expressions in conservative and evangelical, Catholic and Protestant writings – and yet the crucial point is that, at a basic level, a critical stance on the dissolution was something that, increasingly, these groups shared. As we have seen, one reason that Catholic polemics on the dissolution were so provocative and effective was that they tapped into genuine Protestant anxieties about the iconoclasm and avarice of the Henrician regime. If, as our definition at the outset of this chapter implies, events are the products of cultural memory, it is significant that this memory also reshapes and interprets the character of these episodes. Thus the event we know as the Dissolution of the Monasteries only emerged in hindsight and largely in critical perspective.

Yet, ironically, the notoriety that rendered the dissolution unsuitable for official commemoration also placed it amongst the most memorable of Henry VIII's religious reforms. The government's attempt to engender

---

[165] See David Cressy, *Bonfires and Bells: National Memory and the Protestant Calendar in Elizabethan and Stuart England* (Berkeley and Los Angeles, CA, 1989), chs. 5, 7, 9.
[166] David Cressy, 'National memory in early modern England', in John R. Gillis (ed.), *Commemorations: The Politics of National Identity* (Princeton, NJ, 1994), pp. 61–73 at pp. 67, 71.

a culture of amnesia around the wholesale suppression had failed. As we have seen, as the dissolution became a critical moment around which early modern perceptions of the past were crystallised, it also became virtually synonymous with the Henrician Reformation. This tendency is obviously apparent, for example, in Howes's account of the suppression as the most significant event of his age. It is also a pervasive theme in the work of Browne Willis, whose two-volume *History of the mitred parliamentary abbies and conventual cathedral churches* (1718) was published a century after Howes's chronicle. Willis's antiquarian interests were prodigiously wide-ranging, but it was his particular fascination with churches and cathedrals, and his concern for their care and preservation, that caused him to reflect upon the suppression of religious houses.[167] He had a clear sense of the dissolution as a watershed moment: in a now famous passage in the *History of the mitred parliamentary abbies*, Willis lamented that it had been nothing less than the 'chief Blemish of the Reformation'.[168] The Dissolution of the Monasteries had thus been transformed from a veritable non-event into one of the most critical and controversial episodes of the entire English Reformation.

Conclusion: Events, Chronology, and Memory

Contemporary perspectives on the suppression shifted constantly with the passage of the generations and in the context of ongoing religious change and upheaval. In this chapter, we have seen how Henrician chroniclers like Wriothesley and Grafton wore their political and confessional colours openly on their sleeves. But it is also clear that conservative commentators like Stow and Parkyn as well as subsequent generations of critics, Catholic and reformed Protestant alike, also found in chronicles and histories an outlet for their censure of the dissolution. Chroniclers like Wriothesley, Stow, Howes, and their successors are also emblematic of the continuities and discontinuities of experience between generations that, as Norman Jones and Alexandra Walsham have argued, have considerable potential to illuminate the nature of religious change.[169] Moreover, the work of these

---

[167] On Willis's career, see Nicholas Doggett, 'Willis, Browne (1682–1760)', *ODNB*, www .oxforddnb.com/view/article/29577.

[168] Browne Willis, *An history of the mitred parliamentary abbies, and conventual cathedral churches*, 2 vols. (London, 1718), i, p. 2.

[169] Norman Jones, 'Living the reformations: generational experience and political perception in early modern England', *Huntington Library Quarterly* 60 (1997), pp. 273–88; Alexandra Walsham, 'The reformation of the generations: youth, age, and religious change in England, *c.* 1500–1700', *TRHS* 21 (2011), pp. 93–121.

contemporary historians and chroniclers offers a glimpse of the larger trajectory of the memory of the dissolution from process to event, and from campaign against monastic corruption, fraud, and iniquity to an episode with rather more complex, not to say wide-reaching and long-lasting, afterlives that were social and economic as well as religious and political.

Cultural discourse on the monasteries was highly complex, polyvalent and multivocal, but it is nevertheless possible to discern some broad themes and shifts in early modern perceptions of the dissolution across the sixteenth and seventeenth centuries. Increasing distance on the 1530s served to telescope and condense the various phases of dissolution and to transform the protracted and uneven process of suppression into a culturally significant event. This transformation was also driven in large part by the emergence of critical perspectives on the Henrician Reformation, which were rooted in a profound and growing anxiety about the covetousness of the king and government. It also suggests, in ways that echo recent work on early modern memory, that there were clear limits to the extent to which monarchs and governments had control over memory in the early modern period.[170] Yet the legacies of the dissolution remained fundamentally ambiguous. Protestant histories and chronicles functioned to perpetuate the vision of the dissolution propagated in Henrician polemic, as well as to challenge and subvert it. The regime's early rhetoric of monastic corruption proved especially potent and enduring, even as other aspects of the dissolution came under sustained attack from new generations of controversialists and historians. It was through this contestation that the Dissolution of the Monasteries came to loom so large in the early modern historical imagination.

The act of writing the history of the dissolution was therefore inherently ideological. As we have seen, there was a clear tendency amongst Catholic and Protestant authors alike to judge Henry VIII's reputation by the dissolution. The chronicles considered here have thoroughly disavowed the historiographical commonplace that the genre was devoid of rhetorical force, even if the partisan quality of early modern chronicles is often more elusive than in the more confrontational and vituperative forms of Reformation apologetic. Although the medieval chronicle genre underwent a series of transformations in the course of the sixteenth and seventeenth centuries, accounts of the death of the chronicle and its transmutation into, to use Daniel Woolf's phrase, a mere 'museum piece'

---

[170] Pollmann and Kuijpers, 'Early modernity of modern memory', p. 21.

have perhaps therefore also been exaggerated.[171] We have seen how the early modern chronicle genre in fact offered vibrant and creative ways of thinking about the past and, more generally, how the expansive category of historical writing to which these texts belonged reflected, and perhaps also helped to shape, changing perceptions of the dissolution over time.

The histories examined in this chapter have also illuminated the process by which the 'Dissolution of the Monasteries' was crystallised into a significant historical event. In this way, early modern commentators have left a lasting legacy for modern scholarship. Contemporary chroniclers like Charles Wriothesley may not have experienced or recognised the 'Dissolution of the Monasteries', but their texts are sources through which historians and literary scholars continue to view this process. Whilst this chapter has sought to expose this label as a seventeenth-century construct, it is also virtually impossible to avoid using the language of dissolution to describe and analyse this episode. In asking how the dissolution was remembered, we are therefore also asking how early modern processes of selective remembering continue to shape modern historiography and our own perceptions of the past.[172] This is not to say that we should abandon the shorthand, but rather that the ubiquity of the name 'Dissolution of the Monasteries' is a powerful reminder that historians have inherited a vocabulary and a temporal framework that were themselves products of the complex, contested, and dynamic memory culture of the English Reformation.

---

[171] Woolf, 'Genre into artifact', p. 352.   [172] Lyon, 'Remembering the dissolution'.

CHAPTER 3

'Raised Out of the Ruins'
Monastic Sites in the Early Modern Topographical Imagination

More than a century after the fall of the last abbey in 1540, the effects wrought by the dissolution upon the physical landscape were still everywhere apparent. Whilst travelling in his home county of Wiltshire in the 1650s and 1660s, the antiquary and natural philosopher John Aubrey was frequently confronted with the crumbling remnants of the medieval monasteries. Pausing to reflect on the evocative power of the monastic ruins that he encountered, Aubrey wrote that the 'eie and mind is no lesse affected with these stately ruines than they would have been when standing and entire'. These mutilated structures aroused in Aubrey a 'kind of pittie' for the lost pre-Reformation world of which they were the damaged likenesses, the shadows and shells. Echoing Francis Bacon, he described them lyrically as *tanquam tabulata naufragii* – like fragments of a shipwreck.[1]

In a seminal essay, Margaret Aston identified this strain of retrospection as a form of nostalgia for the medieval past. According to Aston, the material fragments of the monasteries left behind by the dissolution were particularly significant in shaping the evolution of this memory culture. Ruins, in other words, were mnemonics; they functioned as monuments to and emblems of the state-sponsored effacement of the Catholic past by the Henrician regime. Once primarily a site of conservative and Catholic regret, increasingly, Aston argued, ruins became focal points for developing Protestant anxiety about the actions of the early reformers, and they could evoke visceral feelings of loss and regret, as well as contributing to contemporary senses of social, material, and aesthetic decline. This inspired a number of antiquaries, including Aubrey, to undertake surveys

---

[1] Bodl., MS Aubrey 1–3; published as John Aubrey, *Wiltshire: the topographical collections of John Aubrey, F.R.S., A.D. 1659–70, with illustrations*, ed. John Edward Jackson, Wiltshire Archaeological and Natural History Society (Devizes, 1862), p. 4. See also Francis Bacon, *De augmentis scientiarum* (London, 1623), book 2, ch. 6.

of the landscape with a view to preserving what little remained of the medieval world for posterity. As the remnants of a vanquished past, monastic fragments provided a fillip to historical enquiry and were critical in shaping the early modern topographical imagination. 'Ruins', Aston contended, 'may make historians.'[2]

In Aston's shadow, scholarship on early modern antiquarianism has uniformly emphasised the significance of monastic ruins in the development of the study of the past, elaborating her contention that the dissolution was a critical episode in the emergence of early modern topographical writing.[3] This literature is, then, perhaps the only significant exception in a wider historiography that has tended to take a narrow and chronologically limited view of the dissolution. It has tended to focus on specific authors, such as Aubrey and perhaps most notably the Warwickshire herald William Dugdale, whose monumental three-volume catalogue of religious houses and orders, the *Monasticon Anglicanum* (1655–73) has long been considered emblematic of antiquarian responses to the dissolution in the seventeenth century.[4] More recently, Daniel Woolf has sought to place the 'nostalgic' tradition exemplified by the *Monasticon* in the wider context of contemporary historical consciousness and an emerging culture of 'pastness'.[5] This chapter takes these arguments as its main points of engagement and departure. It reassesses the contribution of antiquaries like Dugdale and also seeks to place the 'nostalgic' antiquarian tradition in the context of the wider early modern topographical imagination.

[2] Margaret Aston, 'English ruins and English history: the dissolution and the sense of the past', *Journal of the Warburg and Courtauld Institutes* 36 (1973), pp. 231–55, at p. 231 and *passim*. For an earlier work that attributed the birth of antiquarianism to the dissolution, see Kenneth Clark, *The Gothic Revival: An Essay in the History of Taste*, 3rd ed. (London, 1962), p. 23. On the evocative power of ruins more generally, see Martin S. Briggs, *Goths and Vandals: A Study of the Destruction, Neglect, and Preservation of the Historical Buildings in England* (London, 1952), ch. 2; Rose Macaulay, *Pleasure of Ruins* (New York, 1953).

[3] For various approaches, see Stan A. E. Mendyk, *'Speculum Britanniae': Regional Study, Antiquarianism, and Science in Britain* (Toronto and London, 1989); Graham Parry, *The Trophies of Time: English Antiquarians of the Seventeenth Century* (Oxford, 1995); Rosemary Sweet, *Antiquaries: The Discovery of the Past in Eighteenth-Century Britain* (London and New York, 2004); Oliver Harris, '"The greatest blow to antiquities that ever England had": the Reformation and the antiquarian resistance', in Jan Frans van Dijkhuizen and Richard Todd (eds.), *The Reformation Unsettled: British Literature and the Question of Religious Identity, 1560–1660* (Turnhout, 2008), pp. 225–42; Angus Vine, *In Defiance of Time: Antiquarian Writing in Early Modern England* (Oxford, 2010).

[4] On Dugdale, see Jan Broadway, *William Dugdale: A Life of the Warwickshire Historian and Herald* (Gloucester, 2011).

[5] Daniel Woolf, *The Social Circulation of the Past: English Historical Culture, 1500–1730* (Oxford, 2003), p. 183.

What follows examines some features of the lament for the past inspired by encounters with monastic ruins, before turning to a category of material remnants that has been almost entirely neglected in the existing literature. In the wake of the suppression, as many as half of all former monastic properties underwent processes of adaptation and conversion for parochial or secular uses.[6] These buildings have been underappreciated as significant products of the material break with the past engendered by the dissolution. Like ruins, monastic conversions had the potential to stimulate historical enquiry, but they also embodied attempts to erase and efface the memory both of medieval monasticism and of the iconoclastic violence of the early Reformation. This chapter interrogates former monastic sites broadly conceived as sites of memory and oblivion and examines the monastic landscape as a palimpsest upon which memories of the dissolution were continuously rewritten and contested. By exploring the place of the suppression in topographical writing and images, it suggests that the historiographical preoccupation with ruins and 'nostalgic' antiquarianism has obscured the complexity of the material and spatial dimensions of the memory of the dissolution, in addition to the capacity of antiquarian writing to promote the forgetting of the monastic past as well as its preservation. This was a genre that not only reflected the development of a wider culture of remembrance but also perpetuated a parallel culture of selective amnesia.

'Ruins and Remains'

Three years before the Henrician commissioners began their destructive tour of England's religious houses, the antiquary John Leland had been awarded his own royal commission to survey the monasteries – or, rather, to survey their libraries. His aim, as he wrote in the 'New Year's Gift' that he prepared for Henry VIII, was to catalogue monastic books and manuscripts to bring them 'out of deadly darkeness to lyvelye lyght'.[7]

---

[6] Maurice Howard, 'Recycling the monastic fabric: beyond the act of dissolution', in David Gaimster and Roberta Gilchrist (eds.), *The Archaeology of the Reformation, 1480–1580* (Leeds, 2003), pp. 221–34 at p. 221.

[7] *The laboryouse journey & serche of Johan Leylande, for Englandes antiquities, geven of hym as a newe yeares gyfte to kynge Henry the viij. in the. xxxvii. yeare of his reygne, with declaracyons by Johan Bale* (London, 1549), sig. B8r. On Leland's bibliographic project, see C. E. Wright, 'The dispersal of the libraries in the sixteenth century', in Francis Wormald and C. E. Wright (eds.), *The English Library before 1700: Studies in Its History* (London, 1958), pp. 148–75; Ronald Harold Fritze, '"Truth hath lacked witnesse, tyme wanted light": the dispersal of the English monastic libraries and Protestant efforts at preservation, ca. 1535–1625', *Journal of Library History* 18 (1983), pp. 274–91; James Simpson, 'Ageism: Leland, Bale, and the laborious start of English literary history, 1350–1550', in Wendy Scase,

A precursor to the reformation of libraries and texts attempted by polemicists and antiquaries like John Bale and Matthew Parker, Leland's bibliographic project was predicated upon an idea that we encountered in the
previous chapter: namely that the religious orders were fraudulent and
inadequate custodians of national memory and history. Its completion,
however, was severely threatened by the 'almost total disregard for books'
displayed by the Henrician regime once the suppression got underway in
1536.[8] Libraries, along with the rest of the monastic fabric, became subjects
of the government's assault on monasticism. The spoliation of the religious
houses was brutal and swift: books and manuscripts were destroyed or
dispersed, at the same time as images and idols were being broken and
defaced. In this way, Leland was robbed of his source material. In the wake
of the destruction, he was obliged to shift to a more topographical mode in
which space was 'called upon to stand in for history' and lost textual
patrimony.[9] The dissolution thus provided the stimulus for his new project
after 1539 to delineate the physical and cultural reality of the Tudor 'worlde
and impery of Englande'.[10] In doing so, it was responsible for the study that
has been called the 'inaugural work of Renaissance geography'.[11] At the
same time, the suppression was also the unacknowledged subject of
Leland's topography, which retold the Reformation as 'a story about
land and buildings'.[12] The *Itinerary of John Leland*, as it became known
after its belated publication in the eighteenth century, was both a product
of and itself reflected Leland's encounter with a landscape upon which the
memory of the medieval past was being reconfigured.[13]

It is striking that the notes that constituted the *Itinerary* – described by
John   Cramsie   as   a   'dynamic   hodgepodge   of   experiences   and

---

Rita Copeland, and David Lawton (eds.), *New Medieval Literatures* 1 (1997), pp. 213–35. See also
below, Conclusion.

[8] James P. Carley, 'Monastic collections and their dispersal', in John Barnard and D. F. McKenzie
(eds.), with the assistance of Maureen Bell, *The Cambridge History of the Book in Britain: Volume IV,
1577–1695* (Cambridge, 2002), pp. 339–47 at p. 340.

[9] Philip Schwyzer, 'John Leland and his heirs: the topography of England', in Mike Pincombe and
Cathy Shrank (eds.), *The Oxford Handbook of Tudor Literature, 1548–1603* (Oxford, 2009), pp. 238–
53 at p. 242.

[10] *Laboryouse journey*, sig. D5v.

[11] Jennifer Summit, 'Leland's "Itinerary" and the remains of the medieval past', in Gordon McMullan
and David Matthews (eds.), *Reading the Medieval in Early Modern England* (Cambridge, 2007),
pp. 159–76 at p. 159.

[12] Ibid., p. 166.

[13] Leland's descent into madness around 1546 prevented his work seeing print within his lifetime. His
notes were published by Thomas Hearne as *The Itinerary of John Leland the Antiquary*, 9 vols.
(London, 1710–12). See also *The Itinerary of John Leland in or about the Years 1535–1543*, ed. Lucy
Toulmin Smith, 5 vols. (London, 1907–10).

remembrances' – are replete with references to monastic ruins, testifying to the rapid nature of the transformation wrought upon the religious houses by the combined forces of iconoclasm, spoliation, and excavation in the 1530s.[14] Leland recorded sights such as the 'ruines of old walles' belonging to a suppressed priory near Kirkby Lonsdale, Cumbria,[15] and the 'defacid' chapel dedicated to St Romwold (d. 662) at Southtowne, now King's Sutton, Northamptonshire.[16] Confronted with these remnants, Leland typically refrained from making overtly polemical or emotional statements about the dissolution, although he was occasionally inspired to deride the Catholic superstition 'of late tymes'.[17] More usually, he employed a laconic formulation that designated sites including Llantarnam Abbey in Cwmbran, south-east Wales, and Warden Abbey, Bedfordshire, as 'lately suppressed'.[18] Yet this terse language of recent transformation also captures the sense of 'then' and 'now' that, even in the late 1530s and early 1540s, pervaded Leland's writing. If the dissolution as we have previously encountered it – as a critical episode of the English Reformation, situated in historical time – is absent from Leland's topography, paradoxically the *Itinerary* offers a greater sense of the suppression as a seismic transformation of the English Reformation than its chronicle cousins, which functioned to pin the dissolution to a series of times and dates. As Cathy Shrank has argued, 'a subtext of devastation lies beyond the understated past tenses' of the *Itinerary*.[19] By eschewing a linear narrative of Reformation and adopting instead a mode of writing structured around space and the damaged fragments of the medieval past, Leland's notes reveal the magnitude and immediacy of the break with that past.

Monastic ruins were, then as now, a powerful emblem of this rupture. An example of *lieux de mémoire*, they exerted a powerful influence over the evolving memory of the dissolution and contemporary perceptions of the past, which, as recent scholarship has underlined, were shaped at least as much, if not more, by spaces and objects than by times and dates.[20] It

---

[14] John Cramsie, *British Travellers and the Encounter with Britain, 1450–1700* (Woodbridge, 2015), p. 70.
[15] *Itinerary of John Leland*, ed. Toulmin Smith, v, p. 45.
[16] Ibid., ii, p. 38. I am grateful to James Clark for information about the dedicatee of this chapel.
[17] See, for example, ibid., v, p. 105.   [18] Ibid., i, p. 101; iii, p. 45.
[19] Cathy Shrank, *Writing the Nation in Reformation England, 1530–1580* (Oxford, 2004), p. 101.
[20] On *lieux de mémoire*, see Pierre Nora, *Les lieux de mémoire*, 3 vols. (Paris, 1984–92), ed. Pierra Nora and Lawrence D. Kritzman, trans. Arthur Goldhammer, *Realms of Memory*, 3 vols. (New York, 1996–8); Pierre Nora, 'Between memory and history: les lieux de mémoire', *Representations* 26 (1989), pp. 7–24. See also David Lowenthal, *The Past Is a Foreign Country* (Cambridge, 1985), p. 238; Simon Schama, *Landscape and Memory* (New York, 1995). For some recent approaches to space and memory in the early modern period, see Nicola Whyte, *Inhabiting the Landscape: Place, Custom and*

might seem something of an irony that an event that the Henrician regime had sought to downplay produced such durable and imposing monuments. Yet many ruins were deliberate creations that stood, as Aston has argued, as 'telling witnesses to the efficiency of Henry VIII's treatment of the religious houses'.[21] In other words, they were not simply by-products of the dissolution, but rather the continuation and the legacy of the government's wider campaign against monasticism and the most visible and tangible symbols of its triumph over Catholic error and corruption. For those who sought to perpetuate the Henrician vision of the dissolution, ruins functioned as sites of memory for the admonition of posterity. Like the images and idols ravaged by Reformation iconoclasm, the sight of ruins was itself admonitory precisely because 'the vanquished past remained *in situ*, a constant reminder to worshippers of the new purified communion, of the idolatrous past from which they had been delivered'.[22]

In the hands of successive generations of polemicists and antiquaries, monastic ruins functioned as powerful polemical weapons. This was certainly the case in the work of the Kentish antiquary and vituperative Protestant apologist William Lambarde, whose major work, the *Perambulation of Kent*, was first published in 1576. The title recalled traditional rituals of walking the boundaries of communities – 'beating the bounds' – that relied upon the mnemonic capacity of the physical landscape to establish the customary geographical limits of villages and parishes.[23] Lambarde's 'perambulation', however, was a rhetorical device that could be used to attack the opponents of Tudor religious reform.[24] Meditating on the religious landscape of medieval Canterbury, he recalled the 'seas of sinne and iniquitie, wherein the worlde (at those dayes) was almost whole drenched' and was compelled to 'prayse God, that hath thus

Memory, 1500–1800 (Oxford, 2009); Alexandra Walsham, *The Reformation of the Landscape: Religion, Identity, and Memory in Early Modern Britain and Ireland* (Oxford, 2011).
[21] Aston, 'English ruins and English history', p. 231; Margaret Aston, *Broken Idols of the English Reformation* (Cambridge, 2015), p. 14.
[22] Margaret Aston, 'Public worship and iconoclasm', in Gaimster and Gilchrist (eds.), *Archaeology of the Reformation*, pp. 9–28 at p. 16.
[23] On this ritual, see Ronald Hutton, *The Rise and Fall of Merry England: The Ritual Year, 1400–1700* (Oxford, 1994), p. 247; Steve Hindle, 'Beating the bounds of the parish: order, memory, and identity in the English local community, c. 1500–1700', in Michael Halvorson and Karen Spierling (eds.), *Defining Community in Early Modern Europe* (Aldershot, 2008), pp. 205–28; Whyte, *Inhabiting the Landscape*, ch. 5; Andy Wood, *The Memory of the People: Custom and Popular Senses of the Past in Early Modern England* (Cambridge, 2013), pp. 200–9.
[24] Alexandra Walsham, 'Matthew Parker, sacred geography, and the British past', unpublished paper, 'Matthew Parker: Archbishop, Scholar, and Collector', Centre for Research in the Arts, Humanities, and Social Sciences and Corpus Christi College, Cambridge, 17 March 2016. I am grateful to Alex Walsham for sharing this piece with me.

mercifully in our age delivered us, disclosed Satan, unmasked these Idoles, dissolved the Synagogues, and raced [razed] to the grounde all Monumentes of building, erected to superstition and ungodlynesse'.[25] Yet, as Lambarde noted, the survival of monastic ruins ensured that these 'monuments of building' had not entirely disappeared into oblivion. As a result, the *Perambulation of Kent* is marked by a tension between conflicting impulses: to erase the memory of corrupt medieval monasticism and to preserve its mutilated remnants as a warning to posterity. Lambarde frequently expressed a desire to forget the monasteries, even as he committed them to paper. Regarding the former Trinitarian priory at Mottenden, for example, he wrote that:

> Neyther would I have afforded it so much as paper, or place here, but only that you understande, with what number of buildings, varietie of sects, and plent of possessions, Poperie was in old time provided for, and furnished. No corner (almoste) without some religious house, or other: Their suites and orders were hardly to be numbred: and as for their lands and revenues, it was a world to beholde them.[26]

Far from being motivated chiefly, as it has sometimes been suggested, by 'the delight he took in collecting and describing ancient things', Lambarde's approach to ruins is indicative of the larger project of the *Perambulation* to reinforce and elaborate a particular strand of Protestant history and memory.[27]

This was a mnemonic culture of which Lambarde was an heir and a product as well as a contributor. Born as the first monasteries fell in 1536, Lambarde could not personally remember the events he described.[28] Rather, his discussion of significant episodes in the Reformation in Kent was drawn from his inherited memory. These included the exposure of the mechanical Rood of Grace from Boxley in 1538, by which 'notable imposture', he wrote, 'fraud, Juggling, and Legierdemain, the sillie lambes of Gods flocke were (not long since) seduced by the false Romishe Foxes'. But although he had no personal memory of this event, Lambarde was nevertheless keenly aware that, at the time of writing in the mid-1570s, these revelations remained 'yet fresh in mynde' for many amongst his readership who had seen first-hand the fraud exposed in the marketplace in Maidstone

---

[25] William Lambarde, *A perambulation of Kent: conteining the description, hystorie, and customes of that shyre* (London, 1576), p. 221.
[26] Ibid., p. 230. [27] Mendyk, 'Early British chorography', p. 470.
[28] On Lambarde's life and career, see Retha M. Warnicke, *William Lambarde: Elizabethan Antiquary, 1536–1601* (London and Chichester, 1973).

or heard it denounced from Paul's Cross. By recording this episode in print, Lambarde helped to perpetuate its memory across the generational divide. Indeed, he was self-conscious of his role as a custodian of memory, judging that the Boxley affair deserved to be 'continued in perpetuall memorie to all posteritie'.[29] For Lambarde, this was also an ongoing project to crystallise the memory of the dissolution around the Henrician rhetoric of monastic corruption and surrender. During the preparation of the second edition (1596), he made a telling correction to his instruction to the reader to 'passe to the Religious houses', changed to 'lett us passe on to the *late* Religious buildings' in an echo of the 1539 act of dissolution.[30] Written in Lambarde's own hand, this amendment represents the minute reworking of the memory of the dissolution, which served to strengthen his vision of monastic ruins as symbols of a vanquished past.

Subsequent generations of Protestant topographers continued to echo and reinforce the triumphalist view of monastic ruins. Richard Carew, in his *Survey of Cornwall* (1602), associated the sites of former religious houses with 'more corrupt ages' than his own.[31] Likewise, in 1630, Joseph Hall, bishop of Exeter, was inspired by ruins to comment that 'every stone hath a tongue to accuse Superstition, Hypocrisie, Idlenesse, Luxury of the late [monastic] owners'.[32] Similar sentiments were also articulated by the historian and topographer Thomas Staveley in the 1670s, for whom the former monasteries of Leicester were emblems of the 'middle & dark Times' and the 'great abuse of Religion' conducted during that period.[33] Individually and collectively, these topographies contributed to the longevity of the Henrician narratives of monastic corruption and the expediency of dissolution. It is little surprise that ruins were inherent to this undertaking: the very purpose of leaving them standing had been to create enduring physical reminders of the suppression of traditional religion. These fragments were, in other words, quite literally monuments to the *ruin* of medieval monasticism.

However, despite the best attempts of Lambarde and his successors, the meaning of ruins could not be fixed. Rather their significance lay in the eye of the beholder. For many Catholics, the fragmentary remains of the religious houses remained hallowed spaces. In 1586, a former employee of

---

[29] Lambarde, *Perambulation of Kent*, p. 182.   [30] Bodl., 4° Rawlinson 263, p. 128. My emphasis.

[31] Richard Carew, *The survey of Cornwall*, ed. John Chynoweth, Nicholas Orme, and Alexandra Walsham, Devon and Cornwall Record Society, new series, 47 (Exeter, 2004), fol. 82r.

[32] Joseph Hall, 'Upon the ruines of an Abby', in *Occasional Meditations*, ed. R[obert] H[all] (London, 1630), p. 191.

[33] BL, Additional MS 15917, fols. 39v, 40v.

Glastonbury Abbey in Somerset told the Jesuit William Weston that he continued to visit its ruins, carrying with him a reliquary that he had rescued from the abbey before its dissolution. The old man had rescued the reliquary, 'a certain cross, venerable and hallowed not so much for its material interest . . . as because it encased the remains of revered saints'.[34] It served as 'protection . . . against the molestation of spirits' as he climbed the hill 'not on his feet, but on his knees' as a mark of devotion and piety.[35] Glastonbury was a popular site of covert pilgrimage, not least for Weston's interlocutor, partly due to its association with the legend of Joseph of Arimathea and the arrival of Christianity in the British Isles. As one Protestant topographer noted in the early seventeenth century, with a disdain that nevertheless reveals the significance of the site for English Catholics, many 'zealous Recusants' had long continued to hold Glastonbury 'in greate veneration'.[36] It seems that the Reformation did not sever the ties between Catholic piety and sacred sites in the landscape, even where those sites lay damaged and destroyed.[37] Indeed, the power of ruins to inspire Catholic devotion endured throughout the early modern period. As late as 1697, the traveller and diarist Celia Fiennes learnt from her landlady in Tadcaster, North Yorkshire, that a local 'papist lady' prayed amongst the abbey ruins there and had created a relic out of the bones disturbed in an old grave.[38] As a focus for recusant piety and devotion, monastic ruins possessed considerable spiritual significance and power.

They were also, however, a monument to Catholic indignation. One of the most evocative expressions of Catholic anger can be found in the form of an anonymous manuscript ballad about Walsingham Priory in Norfolk, which had fallen to the king's commissioners in 1538. Known variously as 'In the wracks of Walsingham' and 'A lament for Our Lady's shrine at Walsingham', the ballad rails against the violent demise of monasticism and its buildings.[39] Several of its verses (lines 13–28) evoke the ruined walls and gates of the priory as testaments to the voraciousness of the Henrician regime and its agents:

[34] William Weston, *The Autobiography of an Elizabethan*, ed. Philip Caraman (London and New York, 1955), p. III.

[35] Ibid., p. 112.

[36] Thomas Gerard, *The Particular Description of the County of Somerset, drawn up by Thomas Gerard of Trent, 1633*, ed. E. H. Bates, Somerset Record Society 15 (London, 1900), p. 98.

[37] Walsham, *Reformation of the Landscape*, pp. 166–89.

[38] Celia Fiennes, *The Journeys of Celia Fiennes*, ed. Christopher Morris (London, 1947), p. 79.

[39] See Gary Waller, *Walsingham and the English Imagination* (Farnham, 2011), esp. pp. 97–101. See also Dominic Janes and Gary Waller (eds.), *Walsingham in Literature and Culture from the Middle Ages to Modernity* (Farnham, 2010).

Bitter was it, O, to view
The sacred vine
(While gardeners played all close)
Rooted up by the swine.

Bitter, bitter, O, to behold
The grass to grow
Where the walls of Walsingham
So stately did show.

Such were the works of Walsingham,
While she did stand;
Such are the wracks as now do show
Of that holy land.

Level, level with the ground
The towers doe lie,
Which with their golden glittering tops
Pierced once to the sky.[40]

Outrage is the dominant mode in this ballad, which is commonly attributed to Philip Howard, earl of Arundel, who infamously converted to Catholicism in 1581 after witnessing the Jesuit Edmund Campion debate a group of Protestant theologians.[41] Specifically, it is the sight of Walsingham's ruins that engendered the bitterness to which the text repeatedly refers, the act of seeing – 'O, to view', 'O, to behold' – prompting the poet to reflect on the dissolution. It is significant that, if 'In the wrackes of Walsingham' was Howard's work, then the priory's ruins functioned as a mnemonic for an event that had occurred some twenty years before the author was born. For the simple reason of their endurance, ruins functioned to sustain Catholic anger and indignation beyond the passing of the generation that remembered the dissolution at first hand.

In its more mournful passages, 'In the wrackes of Walsingham' also epitomises a type of conservative retrospection on the dissolution that has become enshrined in the English literary canon.[42] Walsingham's fallen towers, its 'wracks' that 'now do show', evoke the 'bare ruin'd choirs, where late the

---

[40] 'The ruins of Walsingham', in Emrys Jones (ed.), *The New Oxford Book of Sixteenth-Century Verse* (Oxford, 1992), p. 550.

[41] Waller, *Walsingham and the English Imagination*, pp. 97–8. On Sir Philip Howard, see J. G. Elzinga, 'Howard, Philip [St Philip Howard], thirteenth earl of Arundel', *ODNB*, www.oxforddnb.com/view/article/13929.

[42] See esp. Trevor Ross, 'Dissolution and the making of the English literary canon: the catalogues of Leland and Bale', *Renaissance and Reformation/Renaissance et Réforme*, new series, 15 (1991), pp. 57a–80.

sweet birds sang' (4) famously lamented in William Shakespeare's Sonnet 73.[43] This is, in fact, an image that the two poets share: the Walsingham poet lamented that 'Owls do shriek where the sweetest hymns / Lately were sung' (33–4).[44] The trope of 'bare ruined choirs' has, to quote Philip Schwyzer, become 'a kind of shorthand for the fate of the religious houses',[45] and the potency and prevalence of this imagery has served to forge a connection between ruins and the production of early modern English literature.[46] Although often read as expressions of crypto-Catholicism, recent work has highlighted the polychronic quality of the ruin motif, which was used by authors across the confessional spectrum not only to express regret for past iconoclasm but also to reflect on ongoing religious changes during successive phases of England's long Reformation.[47] At the heart of this critique is a sense that early modern poets and playwrights were not merely nostalgic for a world before the Reformation in the way that Margaret Aston once described.[48] It is my contention that the same is true of the antiquaries with whom 'nostalgia' for the monasteries has been so closely associated.

Protestant antiquarianism in particular has been identified as a product of the 'nostalgic' retrospection identified by Aston. In the previous chapter, we noted the emergence of concerns about the repair and beautification of churches amongst Protestants, as well as Catholics, in the early seventeenth century. Questions of space and ecclesiastical property were at the heart of this shift, which both reflected and engendered changing attitudes towards sacred places and fabrics.[49] As a result, reformed attitudes towards the remnants of the medieval past – and, critically, to the destruction of these sites – began to change. In parallel with what has been described as the 'resurgence of sacred space during the second generation of the Reformation', there emerged a strand of Protestant topography concerned with the preservation of the material past.[50] In light of Aston's argument that

---

[43] *Shakespeare's Sonnets*, ed. and with an analytic commentary by Stephen Booth (New Haven, CT, and London, 1977), p. 64. On Sonnet 73 and the Reformation, see Eamon Duffy, *Saints, Sacrilege, and Sedition: Religion and Conflict in the Tudor Reformations* (London, 2012), ch. 11.
[44] 'The ruins of Walsingham', p. 551.
[45] Philip Schwyzer, *Archaeologies of English Renaissance Literature* (Oxford, 2007), p. 102.
[46] This is an argument advanced by Andrew Hui with reference to ruins of all kinds in *The Poetics of Ruins in Renaissance Literature* (Oxford, 2017), p. 21 and *passim*.
[47] Stewart Mottram, *Ruin and Reformation in Spenser, Shakespeare, and Marvell* (Oxford, 2019), pp. 18–19 and *passim*.
[48] Aston, 'English ruins and English history'.
[49] Anthony Milton, *Catholic and Reformed: The Roman and Protestant Churches in English Protestant Thought, 1600–1640* (Cambridge, 1995), ch. 6.
[50] Sarah Hamilton and Andrew Spicer, 'Defining the holy: the delineation of sacred space', in Sarah Hamilton and Andrew Spicer (eds.), *Defining the Holy: Sacred Space in Medieval and Early Modern Europe* (Aldershot, 2005), pp. 1–24 at p. 21.

this brand of seventeenth-century antiquarianism was essentially 'nostalgic'
for the pre-Reformation world, recent scholarship has continued to place
ruins at the heart of these endeavours. They also continue to serve as
emblems of the emergent Protestant critique of the dissolution and have
been central to what Oliver Harris termed the 'antiquarian resistance' that
sought to undermine the attempts of the reformers to efface the memory of
monasticism.[51] Although Harris acknowledges the fact that this endeavour
was not limited to Protestants, it has been most closely associated with the
regretful, anxious brand of reformed Protestantism that shaped 'nostalgic'
antiquarianism.

It is the paradox of 'nostalgic' antiquarianism that the generation that
mourned monastic ruins had not known a world before the Reformation.
William Camden, researching his monumental national topography, the
Britannia, first published in 1586 and translated into English by Philemon
Holland in 1610, was conscious of the divide that separated his generation
from its iconoclastic forebears. Remembering the dissolution of
Walsingham Abbey, he described how within 'the memory of our fathers,
when King Henry the Eighth had set his minde and eye both, upon the
riches and possessions of Churches, all this vanished quite away'.[52]
Camden thus combined elements of an older critique of the avarice of
the Henrician regime with a new sense of aesthetic outrage and material
loss. In the Suffolk town of Bury St Edmunds, for example, he encountered
the 'carcasse . . . of that auncient monument' of the dissolved Benedictine
abbey 'altogether deformed' having been 'utterly overthrowne' under
'goodlie pretense of reforming religion' in 1539. The sight of this crumbling
edifice inspired in Camden both regret and a strange sense of admiration: 'I
assure you', he wrote to the reader, 'they make a faire and goodlie shew,
which who soever beholdeth, hee may both wonder there at, and withall
take pity thereof.'[53] Likewise, the cartographer John Speed mourned that
ruins 'are become like dead carkases, leaving onely some poore ruines and
remains alive, as reliques to posterity, to shew of what beauty and magnitude they have beene'.[54] John Weever, who devoted his time to sketching
and recording pre-Reformation monuments and their inscriptions, also
appropriated the rhetoric of ruination to describe how 'barbarously'

---

[51] Harris, 'Greatest blow to antiquities'. See also Woolf, *Social Circulation*, pp. 62–4; Susan Guinn-
Chipman, *Religious Space in Reformation England: Contesting the Past* (London, 2013), p. 134 and
passim.

[52] William Camden, *Britain*, trans. Philemon Holland (London, 1610), pp. 243, 479.

[53] Ibid., p. 461.

[54] John Speed, *The theatre of the empire of Great Britaine* (London, 1611), p. 77.

monastic and other church monuments had been '(to the shame of our time) broken downe, and utterly almost all ruinated'.[55] At the former Tonbridge Priory in Kent, he played with the same shipwreck metaphor that would be later employed by Aubrey, writing that 'in the shipwracke of such religious structures' the priory had been 'dasht all a peeces'.[56] The language of the dissolution had thus acquired pronounced spatial and material dimensions. This reflects the potency of the connection between the emergent critique of past iconoclasm and the ruins of the religious houses, which functioned as visible and tangible reminders of this rupture.

It is a striking feature of this particular strand of Protestant antiquarianism that it gave expression to certain ideas and sentiments that had previously been a feature of Catholic discourse on the dissolution. Weever's sense of outrage at the treatment of monastic buildings echoed that of the Walsingham poet, although that anger was tempered by shame. Another illuminating example of this complicated inheritance can be found in the work of the Durham antiquary Robert Hegge. Writing in the 1620s, Hegge was deeply concerned by acts of iconoclasm committed in the early Reformation. 'Some lewd disposed people', he wrote, had 'despised the antiquitie and workthynes of monuments after the subpressinge of Abbeys.'[57] He was particularly alarmed by the story of the desecration of the shrine of St Cuthbert in Durham's monastic cathedral during the dissolution. A local tradition had emerged in Catholic and conservative circles that, despite the commissioners' clumsy violence, the Anglo-Saxon saint's remains had been found intact and undamaged, preserved and protected by divine providence.[58] This narrative was also set down in a remarkable manuscript account of life in the cathedral before and after the Reformation, penned in the late sixteenth century by the Catholic antiquary William Claxton.[59] The 'Rites of Durham' was itself a kind of perambulation of the cathedral and offered a window onto the daily life of the Benedictine monks who had lived within its cloisters before the Reformation. It also railed against the 'subverting of such monuments in the time of Henry. 8th at his Suppression of the Abbeys', advancing a sense of temporal rupture which, as we saw in the previous chapter, was characteristic of Catholic as well as Protestant writing.[60] In the early seventeenth century,

[55] John Weever, *Ancient funerall monuments with in the united monarchie of Great Britaine, Ireland, and the ilands adjacent* (London, 1631), 'Author to the reader'.
[56] Ibid., p. 322. [57] DUL, Cosin MS B.ii.11, fol. 59r.
[58] On local traditions about the dissolution more generally, see below, Ch. 4.
[59] For the attribution to Claxton, see A. I. Doyle, 'Claxton, William (1530–1597)', *ODNB*, www.oxforddnb.com/view/article/69725.
[60] Copy in DUL, Special Collections, MSP 36, p. 64.

the 'Rites of Durham' formed an important part of Hegge's cultural inheritance despite his Protestant convictions. He made a number of copies of the manuscript, which he used to inform his own regretful account of the cathedral as a site of memory for the violent spoliation of Cuthbert's shrine.[61] Such an account would have been virtually unthinkable to earlier Protestant antiquaries like Lambarde. Although the strong sense of pity apparent in the works of Hegge, Camden, and others did not amount to the adoption of Catholic perspectives by Protestants, it is highly telling of how the Protestant memory of the dissolution was evolving over time.

To some contemporary commentators, however, it did indeed appear that this regretful form of antiquarianism concealed a dangerous desire to rehabilitate and even revive certain aspects of medieval Catholicism. In the *Britannia*, for example, Camden was forced to defend himself against those 'who take it impatiently that I have mentioned some of the most famous Monasteries and their founders'. He was careful to differentiate between his pity for the material destruction of buildings erected by the lay founders and patrons of the medieval religious houses and his feelings towards the religious inhabitants of those places. Like other Protestant antiquaries, Camden continued to perpetuate the old rhetoric of monastic corruption in relation to those few 'weeds' which 'in corrupt ages' grew up 'over-ranckly' in the 'seed-gardens from which Christian religion and good learning were propagated over this isle'.[62] But he also railed against his detractors who, he argued, 'would have us forget that our ancestoures were, and we are of the Christian profession when as there are not extant any other more conspicuous, and certaine Monuments, of their piety, and zealous devotion toward God'.[63] Camden thus recognised that the dissolution had been an assault on memory and sought to reverse or at least to curtail its effects. Similarly, Weever embarked upon the preservation of tombs and monuments erected to the lay founders and patrons whose 'honourable memory' had been virtually extinguished by the careless iconoclasm of a previous age.[64] These monuments, to use Peter Sherlock's phrase, 'told posterity what should be known about the past'.[65] Weever therefore believed it his duty to 'continue the

[61] DUL, Special Collections, Cosin MS B.ii.11, fol. 46r. On Hegge's work on St Cuthbert, see Sarah Scutts, '"Truth never needed the protection of forgery": sainthood and miracles in Robert Hegge's "History of St Cuthbert's churches at Lindisfarne, Cuncacestre, and Dunholme" (1625)', in Peter Clarke and Tony Claydon (eds.), *Saints and Sanctity*, Studies in Church History 47 (2011), pp. 270–83.
[62] Camden, *Britain*, 'Author to the reader'.   [63] Ibid., p. 6.
[64] Weever, *Ancient funerall monuments*, 'Author to the reader'.
[65] Peter Sherlock, *Monuments and Memory in Early Modern England* (Aldershot, 2008), p. 3. See also Peter Marshall, *Beliefs and the Dead in Reformation England* (Oxford, 2002); Vanessa Harding,

remembrance of the defunct to future posteritie' by surveying those fragments that remained.[66] This was partially an attempt to undo the efforts of
the Henrician regime to consign the religious houses to oblivion, which had
resulted in the wheat of medieval piety being thrown out with the chaff of
corrupt medieval monasticism. By distinguishing between monastic corruption and lay piety, critics of the dissolution were thus able to use topography
to mourn the medieval past without explicitly grieving the Catholic past.

Fears about the corrosive effects of forgetting underpinned the preservationist impulse in seventeenth-century antiquarianism. In the 1640s and
1650s, these fears were further compounded by the new breach engendered
by the Civil Wars and Interregnum, which raised the spectre of Henrician
iconoclasm and initiated a resurgence of violence against ecclesiastical
property.[67] The puritan campaign against idols sharpened the sense
amongst some antiquaries that the dissolution had been the work of an
earlier 'barbarous generation' who had torn down the 'goodly
structures ... wherewith England was so much adorned' and which were
now once again under threat.[68] The act of puritan iconoclasm was itself
a mnemonic to that of a previous generation. Thomas Philipott, writing
the *Villare Cantianum* (1659), a survey of Kent quite unlike Lambarde's
Perambulation of 1576, conflated the two waves of violence conducted
a century apart: the English landscape, he mourned, had been the victim
of the 'ruinous tempest' and 'whirlwind' of both dissolution in the 1530s
and civil war in the 1640s.[69] Thus the memory of the suppression associated with former monastic spaces was not only shifting over time, it was
also accumulating new layers of meaning and blurring the boundaries
between different episodes and events.

This troubled climate lent a new sense of urgency to antiquarian projects
to preserve the material remnants of the medieval past. The key intervention in this respect was William Dugdale's *Monasticon Anglicanum*. It is

'Choices and changes: death, burial and the English Reformation', in Gaimster and Gilchrist (eds.),
Archaeology of the Reformation, pp. 386–98; Jonathan Finch, 'A reformation of meaning: commemoration and remembering the dead in the parish church, 1450–1640', in Gaimster and Gilchrist
(eds.), *Archaeology of the Reformation*, pp. 437–49; Lucy Wooding, 'Remembrance in the Eucharist',
in Andrew Gordon and Thomas Rist (eds.), *The Arts of Remembrance in Early Modern England:
Memorial Cultures of the Post Reformation* (Farnham, 2013), pp. 16–36.

[66] Weever, *Ancient funerall monuments*, 'Author to the reader'.

[67] See Margaret Aston, *England's Iconoclasts: Volume 1: Laws Against Images* (Oxford, 1988), p. 63;
Julie Spraggon, *Puritan Iconoclasm during the English Civil War* (Woodbridge, 2003).

[68] William Dugdale, *The antiquities of Warwickshire illustrated* (London, 1656), p. 492.

[69] Thomas Philipott, *Villare Cantianum: or, Kent surveyed and illustrated being an exact description of all
the parishes, burroughs, villages and other respective mannors included in the county of Kent* (London,
1659), pp. 168, 283.

this text, perhaps more than any other, that has shaped our understanding of the role and resonance of the dissolution in seventeenth-century Protestant historical culture and the topographical imagination. A labour of more than two decades, the *Monasticon* was begun by the Yorkshire antiquary Roger Dodsworth in the 1630s but acquired its final form and shape thanks to Dugdale's efforts in the 1650s.[70] 'In these our dayes', the *Monasticon* admonished the reader, the 'very memory' of the monasteries 'seems to some people odious and ungrateful ... more useless and insignificant than an Old Almanack'.[71] Like his predecessors, Dugdale believed that the anti-monastic vitriol inspired by the dissolution was in danger of rapidly eclipsing the piety and munificence of previous generations. The *Monasticon* was an attempt not simply to preserve the material remnants of the medieval past but also selectively to resurrect it in ink and paper form. This included ruins and the ruined parts of working buildings, but, as we shall see, the fragments beloved of the 'nostalgic' antiquaries were not the only former monastic sites of interest to Dugdale. They did, however, form part of the material past that he greatly feared was still in danger of slipping into oblivion. This concern underpinned his project to complete the *Monasticon*, and it was also apparent in his interactions with other contemporary antiquaries: for example, he wrote to the Oxfordshire antiquary Anthony Wood, who was also interested in former monastic properties, to recommend that he give his papers to Sir John Cotton, who had inherited the library of the great collector Robert Cotton, and with whom they 'may be more likely to be preserved for posterity', when otherwise he thought them 'in danger to be utterly lost'.[72]

It is this reflective, preservationist impulse in early modern antiquarianism that returns us to Aubrey, with whom we began, and who was perhaps the most nostalgic of the 'nostalgic' antiquaries.[73] Aubrey's full reflection on monastic ruins, set down whilst researching his expansive manuscript survey of Wiltshire in the 1650s and 1660s, attests to the close connection

---

[70] On the *Monasticon*, see Broadway, *William Dugdale*; Christopher Dyer and Catherine Richardson (eds.), *William Dugdale, Historian, 1605–1686: His Life, His Writings and His County* (Woodbridge, 2009).

[71] Roger Dodsworth and William Dugdale, *Monasticon Anglicanum sive Pandectæ Cænobionam, Benedictinorum Cluniacensium, Cisterciensium, Carthusianorum; a primordiis ad eorum usque dissolutionem*, 3 vols. (London, 1655–73); quotation from the abridged English translation, *Monasticon Anglicanum, or the history of the ancient abbies, and other monasteries, hospitals, cathedral and collegiate churches in England and Wales* (London, 1693), sig. A3r.

[72] Bodl., MS Tanner 456a, fol. 10r.

[73] On Aubrey's historical scholarship more generally see Kelsey Jackson Williams, *The Antiquary: John Aubrey's Historical Scholarship* (Oxford, 2016).

between the dissolution and this particular brand of antiquarianism. He was, he wrote:

> Heartily sorry I did not sett down the Antiquities of these parts sooner, for since the time aforesaid many things are irrecoverably lost. In former daies the Churches and great houses hereabout did so abound with monuments and things remarqueable that it would have deterred an Antiquarie from undertaking it. But as Pythagoras did guesse at the vastnesse of Hercules' stature by the length of his foote, so among these Ruines are Remaynes enough left for a man to give a guesse what noble buildings, &c. were made by the Piety, Charity, and Magnanimity of our Forefathers ... the eie and mind is no lesse affected with these stately ruines than they would have been when standing and entire. They breed in generous mindes a kind of pittie; and sett the thoughts a-worke to make out their magnificence as they were when in perfection. These Remaynes are *tanquam tabulata naufragii* [like fragments of a shipwreck] that after the Revolution of so many yeares and governments have escaped the teeth of Time and the hands of mistaken zeale. So that the retrieving of these forgotten things from oblivion in some sort resembles the Art of a Conjuror who makes those walke and appeare that have layen in their graves many hundreds of yeares ... It is said of Antiquaries, they wipe off the mouldinesse they digge, and remove the rubbish.[74]

In this passage, Aubrey encapsulated the essence of what Aston and others have called 'nostalgic' antiquarianism, which was profoundly shaped by the dissolution and the growing sense of loss, pity, and aesthetic outrage provoked by its remnants. Aubrey mourned that the pious benefactions of 'our Forefathers' had been torn down by the 'hands of mistaken zeale', and greatly lamented that so many of England's antiquities had been 'irrecoverably lost'.

Together with Dugdale, Aubrey was at the forefront of a generation of scholars who were similarly self-conscious of their role in resurrecting the past and preserving it from the corrosive forgetting engendered by what Aubrey called 'oblivion'.[75] Reviving these spaces was a form of 'artificial memory', which entailed the imaginative resurrection of lost sites.[76] Aubrey understood this to be the role of the antiquary, whose work consisted in 'retrieving of these forgotten things'. By describing and recording such structures and spaces, these texts acted as remedies against the instability wrought by iconoclasm past, present, and future. On one level, this

[74] Aubrey, *Wiltshire*, p. 4.   [75] Vine, *In Defiance of Time*, pp. 5, 202, and *passim*.
[76] On antiquarianism and 'artificial memory', see William N. West, '"No endlesse moniment": artificial memory and memorial artefact in early modern England', in Susannah Radstone and Katharine Hodgkin (eds.), *Regimes of Memory* (London, 2003), pp. 61–75.

constituted an archival project to rival those of earlier generations, born of and sharpened by the memory of the dissolution.[77] But unlike the bibliographic projects of collectors like John Bale or Matthew Parker that we explored in the previous chapter, the 'nostalgic' antiquaries did not seek to secure a basis for a Protestant national identity. The significance of ruins was, instead, rewritten to form the backbone of an emergent critique of the dissolution, which resisted the partial oblivion engendered by the agents of suppression in the 1530s.

Although the sense of triumph felt by Lambarde, amongst others, persisted in cultural memory long after the first generation of reformers had died out, there is a clear association between the vestigial remnants of the monasteries and the development of critical perspectives on the dissolution. Ruins functioned as tangible and enduring reminders of the Catholic past but also, paradoxically, of Reformation iconoclasm.[78] Modern historians are the heirs of this contemporary preoccupation with the evocative, polemical, and mnemonic power of ruins.[79] This literature has served to give life and strength to an argument that contemporary responses to monastic spaces and places were central to the mnemonic culture of early modern England. Yet to look at the afterlives of the dissolution and the development of early modern antiquarianism solely through this lens is to adopt a form of historiographical tunnel vision. There were multiple material legacies of the suppression in the early modern period. To reduce the memory of the dissolution to ruins and the act of remembrance to an act of resistance is to neglect the wider spatial and material implications of the suppression. Ruins were not the only physical remnants of medieval monasticism. It is to the neglected subject of converted monastic buildings that we now turn.

Converting the Monastic Landscape

The English landscape underwent a profound transformation as a result of the dissolution of the monasteries. This was not, of course, the first time

---

[77] Elizabeth Yale, 'With slips and scraps: how early modern naturalists invented the archive', *Book History* 12 (2009), p. 3. See also Elizabeth Yale, *Sociable Knowledge: Natural History and the Nation in Early Modern Britain* (Philadelphia, 2015), esp. chs. 1, 4, 6.

[78] Aston, 'English ruins and English history'; Eamon Duffy, *The Stripping of the Altars: Traditional Religion in England, 1400–1580*, 2nd ed. (New Haven, CT, and London, 2005), p. 480; Walsham, *Reformation of the Landscape*, esp. ch. 2.

[79] See also Mottram, *Ruin and Reformation*, which criticises the scholarly tendency to view literary responses to ruins as simply backward-looking but also continues to treat the dissolution as a fundamentally destructive episode that produced ruins but little else.

that the sacred landscape had undergone significant change. Like earlier transformations, most notably the spread of Christianity in England in the seventh century, the Reformation was not purely destructive; it was also creative.[80] The conversion of religious houses into parish churches, secular cathedrals, private houses, workshops and warehouses, and public meeting places began as early as 1536. In all, perhaps half of the medieval religious houses experienced this fate.[81] Thus, whilst some contemporaries and many historians have tended to imply that the monastic landscape had, by 1540, been reduced to a landscape of ruins, this was in reality a more varied terrain.

Although the adaptation of monastic architecture has long been over-looked in historical and literary scholarship, it has underpinned a prominent strand of post-Reformation archaeology.[82] In this context, conversions have been envisioned as a tool for perceiving change, as opposed to the fossilised vision of the past embodied in monastic ruins. As Andrew Jones has argued, 'precisely because of the familiarity and apparently unchanging nature of places, change in place offers a stark way of experiencing the passing of time and evoking memory of the past'.[83] This literature has therefore criticised the conventional focus on 'passive and symbolic' ruins.[84] Using the case study of the converted priory at Monk Bretton, South Yorkshire, Hugh Willmott and Alan Bryson have investigated instead how former religious houses enjoyed 'new, active and evolving roles' in the post-Reformation world.[85] Probing the transform-ation of the priory between the dissolution and its excavation in the twentieth century, Willmott and Bryson's work offers a suggestive account of long-term change that raises important questions about the evolving memory of the suppression associated with converted monasteries. At the heart of their analysis is a process of architectural change that testifies to the

---

[80] Walsham, *Reformation of the Landscape*, esp. chs. 1–3. For an overview of the earlier Christianisation of the landscape, see John Blair, *The Church in Anglo-Saxon Society* (Oxford, 2005), ch. 4.

[81] Howard, 'Recycling the monastic fabric', p. 221.

[82] The most comprehensive archaeological study is Hugh Willmott, *The Dissolution of the Monasteries in England and Wales* (Sheffield, 2020). For a sample of archaeological studies of monastic sites, see Helen Sutermeister, 'Excavations on the site of the Tudor manor house at Micheldever, Hampshire', *Post-Medieval Archaeology* 9 (1975), pp. 117–36; Nicholas Doggett, *Patterns of Re-Use: The Transformation of Former Monastic Buildings in Post-Dissolution Herefordshire* (Oxford, 2002); Gaimster and Gilchrist (eds.), *Archaeology of the Reformation*, chs. 14–20; Iain Soden, 'Buildings analysis at Coombe Abbey, Warwickshire, 1993–94', *Post-Medieval Archaeology* 40 (2006), pp. 129–59.

[83] Andrew Jones, *Memory and Material Culture* (Cambridge, 2007), p. 60.

[84] Hugh Willmott and Alan Bryson, 'Changing to suit the times: a post-dissolution history of Monk Bretton Priory, South Yorkshire', *Post-Medieval Archaeology* 47 (2013), pp. 136–63 at p. 136.

[85] Ibid.

gradual effacement of the monastic past achieved by successive phases of conversion, concealment, adaptation, and demolition. This was, effectively, a kind of material forgetting, which engendered a culture of amnesia that became increasingly potent over time.

Early modern topographical writing also has the potential to reveal something about the conversion of monastic buildings and this process of forgetting through erasure. For those who had witnessed the dissolution at first hand, conversions were sites where the past collided with the present. They had the potential to provoke personal memories of the pre-Reformation world but also to engender polemical reflection upon the post-dissolution landscape. During his peregrinations in the early 1540s, Leland did not only encounter ruins. Indeed, the *Itinerary* features a number of properties that had undergone processes of adaptation, and which testify to the extremely rapid pace of conversion after 1539. Leland's account of these places underlines his evangelical priorities and Henrician outlook. At Markyate in Bedfordshire, he witnessed the 'translating of the priorie into a maner place', and during his perambulation of South Yorkshire he noted that Tickhill Friary had been 'translatid to the paroch church'.[86] As Jennifer Summit has argued, the language of 'translation' functioned to downplay the violence of the suppression and its physical and material consequences. In other words, this linguistic device served to minimise the rupture created by the dissolution by assimilating former monastic sites 'into a topography of the newly Protestant nation, a project that involved rethinking, and actively remaking, the relationship between landscape and history, place and time'.[87] Leland's *Itinerary* thus fed into the Henrician project to shape the memory of the dissolution by constructing a vision of the new post-Reformation world in which conversions, like ruins, could stand as monuments to Protestant triumph. At the same time, Leland achieved with topography the same effect accomplished by his contemporaries using bricks and mortar. By recording the conversion rather than the destruction of the landscape, he contributed to the eroding and effacing of the monastic past.

It is a salient feature of topographies of conversion that regret for the monasteries can also be found in the work of those who had personally witnessed the dissolution. Everywhere he went in Elizabethan London, the conservative topographer and chronicler John Stow found former religious houses that had become storehouses, parish churches, secular hospitals, and domestic properties. His monumental *Survey of London*, first published in

---

[86] *Itinerary of John Leland*, ed. Toulmin Smith, i, pp. 104, 36.
[87] Summit, 'Leland's "Itinerary"', p. 161.

1598, testifies to the sheer variety of places that prompted Stow to reflect on the city's monastic past. It blends his observations of these sites with his knowledge of their history and with melancholic retrospection on the world that had been lost. In Aldgate, Stow remembered that there had been 'sometimes an Abby of Nunnes of the order of S. Clare, calld the Minories, founded by Edmund, Earle of Lancaster, Leicester and Darby, brother to King Edward the first, in the yeere 1293'. In recent times, however, he recalled that the nunnery had been transformed and was 'now builded with divers daire [dairy] and large Store-houses for Armour, and habiliments of warre, with divers workhouses serving to the same purpose' as well as 'a small Parish Church ... called Saint Trinity'. For Stow, this process of conversion had wrought the kind of social and economic decline mourned by the later breed of 'nostalgic' antiquaries when faced with monastic ruins. 'Neere adjoyning to this Abby', he wrote, 'was sometime a Farme belonging to the said Nunrie, at the which Farme, I my selfe (in my youth) have fetched many a halfe-penny worthe of milke, and never had lesse than three ale pintes for a half penny in the Summer.'[88] Likewise, Stow's encounter with the former Greyfriars priory of Christ Church, which had since become a parish church, evoked a sense of loss that was profoundly personal: 'As I my selfe have seene', he wrote, 'the Prior kept a most bountifull house of meat and drinke, both for rich and poore, as well within the house, as at the gates, to all comers, according to their estates.'[89] The *Survey* thus demonstrates how geography, like history, could be a quasi-autobiographical undertaking and the vehicle for personal memory as well as a tool with which to record and shape the inherited memory of communities and successive generations.

Confronted with these converted spaces, Stow's *Survey* was in some sense a lament for what he perceived to be a lost golden age of piety and prosperity, further shaped by his own experience of change and ageing.[90] If Stow was one of the first antiquaries to exhibit 'nostalgia' for the medieval past, it was because this was the world of his childhood – a world he had experienced and whose violent passing he lamented.[91] In the previous chapter, we identified similar sentiments in Stow's historical writing,

---

[88] John Stow, *The survey of London: contayning the originall, increase, modern estate, and government of that city, methodically set downe* (London, 1633), p. 118.

[89] Ibid., p. 145.

[90] See Patrick Collinson, 'John Stow and nostalgic antiquarianism', in Julia F. Merritt (ed.), *Imagining Early Modern London: Perceptions and Portrayals of the City from Stow to Strype, 1598–1720* (Cambridge, 2001), pp. 27–51.

[91] Ian Archer, 'The nostalgia of John Stow', in David L. Smith, Richard Strier, and David Bevington (eds.), *The Theatrical City: Culture, Theatre and Politics in London, 1576–1649* (Cambridge, 1995), pp. 17–34 at p. 22; Collinson, 'Stow and nostalgic antiquarianism'.

which was coloured by his conservatism in matters of religion. For Stow, the dissolution of the monasteries was part of an ongoing project to attack the physical and material landscape of his youth, as former monasteries were subsumed into the rapidly changing urban landscape that, in turn, transformed the city's physical and social fabric in the present.[92] He shared with later generations of antiquaries the belief that the past could be excavated from the disfigured landscape and subsequently resurrected using topography.[93] It was also an exercise in selective remembering. Thus Stow informed the lawyer and diarist John Manningham that he had neglected to record a number of Elizabethan monuments in the *Survey* because 'those men have bin the defacers of the monuments of others, and soe [Stow] thinks them worthy to be deprived of that memory whereof they have injuriously robbed others'.[94] But unlike later forms of antiquarianism, it is critically important to understand this melancholic reflection on the past in the context of Stow's experience of the dissolution, precisely because this enabled him to encounter monastic conversions as sites of his personal memory.

For subsequent generations, however, the effacing of the past engendered by conversion produced sites of forgetting rather than *lieux de mémoire*.[95] As we shall see in the case studies that follow, converted buildings helped to erase and sanitise the monastic past. We can also begin to discern something of this shift in relation to monastic place names. Despite the complex etymology of most place names, the longevity of names that recalled former monastic uses is a striking feature of early modern topography.[96] When confronted with converted sites, Stow was frequently able to recall their monastic names. This was as true of 'the late dissolved Priory of St Bartholomew' in the ward of Faringdon and the 'Augustin Friers Church and Churchyard' at Broadstreet as it was of Christ Church.[97] More generally, the persistence of names and associations such as these testifies not only

---

[92] See Lawrence Manley, 'Of sites and rites: ceremony, theatre, and John Stow's *Survey of London*', in Smith, Strier, and Bevington (eds.), *The Theatrical City*, pp. 35–54 at p. 52. See also Archer, 'Nostalgia of John Stow', p. 22.

[93] Vine, *In Defiance of Time*, pp. 43–4.

[94] John Bruce (ed.), *Diary of John Manningham, of the Middle Temple, and of Bradbourne, Kent, barrister-at-law, 1602–1603*, Camden Society, old series, 99 (London, 1868), p. 103. See also Woolf, *Social Circulation*, p. 94.

[95] On the forgetting and the landscape, see Adam Fox, *Oral and Literate Culture in England, 1500–1700* (Oxford, 2000), p. 252; Walsham, *Reformation of the Landscape*, p. 477 and *passim*.

[96] On place names, see P. H. Reaney, *The Origin of English Place-Names* (London, 1969); G. J. Copley, *English Place-Names and Their Origins* (Newton Abbot, 1971); Margaret Gelling, *Signposts to the Past: Place Names and the History of England* (London, 1978); Margaret Gelling and Ann Cole, *The Landscape of Place-Names* (Donington, 2000).

[97] Stow, *Survey of London*, pp. 185, 340.

to a learned, textual memory, such as that preserved by Stow, but also to the development and persistence of other strands of cultural memory in which the past proved difficult fully to erase.

Often monastic names were recorded in legal documents confirming the sale or lease of ex-monastic land to new owners, fostering a kind of legal memory of the dissolution. For instance, the sale of a portion of land in the Barnwell area of Cambridge to St John's College in 1669 recorded the site as 'sometimes belonging to the late dissolved Monastery of Barnwell'.[98] Similarly, a legal case from County Durham in 1631 concerning tithes connected to the former monastery of Newminster in the village of Chapwell made repeated reference to the condition of the property '*ad tempus dissolucionis*'.[99] But these names also had wider resonance. Scrawled on what appears to be the endpapers of a bible, the life-writings of early Stuart London citizen and stationer John Norgate record the deaths in 1624 of two of his children, Elizabeth and Edward, in close succession and their burial 'in St Mary Overies Church yard, close to the Church wall at the heather side of the middle Butteris or arched pillar, that stands against the Church wall to hold it up'.[100] St Mary Overie in Southwark – St Mary 'over the river' – was an Augustinian priory until its suppression in 1539, at which time it received a new dedication to St Saviour. As Stow himself recorded:

> The Church of the said Priory was purchased of the King by the inhabitants of the Borough. Doctor Stephen Gardiner, Bishop of Winchester, putting to his helping hand, they made thereof a Parish Church for the Parish Church of S. Mary Magdalen, on the South side of the said Quire, out of Saint Margaret on the hill, which were made one Parish of S. Saviour.[101]

A century on from the dissolution and a generation after Stow had noted the transformation of St Mary Overie, the evidence of John Norgate suggests that its medieval monastic name was still in use in the local community – even though previous generations of parishioners had themselves been instrumental in the conversion of the priory into the parish church of St Saviour's.

However, it is also true that monastic place names were becoming inextricably associated with their new functions, owners, and edifices. In

---

[98] Cambridge, Cambridgeshire Archives, CB/2/CL/17/2, fol. 240v.
[99] DUL, Special Collections, MSP 52, fol. 67v.
[100] Norfolk, Norfolk Record Office, MC175/1/3–4. I am grateful to Simone Hanebaum for this reference.
[101] Stow, *Survey of London*, p. 451.

the 1590s, within the generation of witnesses to the dissolution, Stow had already witnessed this process at work. In Hart Street, he encountered a building known by many as the 'Crossed Friers' after the brethren of the Holy Cross who had once inhabited it. Since the dissolution, however, Stow recorded that it had become widely known as 'the Lord Lumleyes house'.[102] Likewise, at Christ Church, where Stow had been inspired to reflect on the halcyon days of his childhood, he emerged from his reverie with an eye turned to the present. After 1539, part of the priory had come into the hands of Thomas Audley, then Lord Chancellor, before falling into the inheritance of the dukes of Norfolk. 'The said Thomas Lord Audley builded and dwelt on this Priorie during his life, and dyed there in the yeere 1544', Stow recorded, 'since the which time, the said Priorie came (by marriage of the Lord Audleys daughter and heire) unto Thomas, late Duke of Norfolke.' By this time, Stow noted, the house was commonly known as 'the Dukes Place'.[103] It seems that although Stow could remember its monastic heritage – and preserved it for posterity in his *Survey* – the memory of the pre-Reformation landscape embodied in monastic conversions was already beginning to fade.

The relative absence of converted monasteries in the conventional literature on early modern antiquarianism is partly the inheritance of the antiquarian tradition stretching from Camden to Aubrey and beyond, which preferred ruins to conversions. But it is also a legacy of memory-making processes surrounding conversions that had been set in motion as early as the 1530s. Stow, like Leland, was a witness to a world in transition and could therefore remember the monastic past at first hand. If Leland's rhetoric of 'translation' helped to perpetuate the state-sponsored narrative of the suppression as only a minimal rupture in the material, social, and religious fabric of early modern England, Stow's religious conservatism coloured his regretful memory of the Henrician Reformation. As we have observed, 'nostalgic' reflection of this kind was possible because Stow had experienced the Henrician Reformation and borne witness to the processes of material conversion and adaptation that it engendered. This was as true of sites that retained their spiritual function as churches as it was of domestic and secular conversions. But as the dissolution passed out of living memory and into inherited memory, the cultures of remembrance associated with these various converted spaces diverged. To a greater or lesser extent, each of these categories – the sacred and the domestic – contributed to the erosion of the memory of the medieval past that Stow had sought to keep alive.

[102] Ibid., p. 157.   [103] Ibid., p. 146.

Parish Churches and Secular Cathedrals

It has sometimes been argued that the dissolution of the monasteries ushered in the 'secularisation' of the landscape.[104] This too is an argument born of the historiographical preoccupation with ruins and the fragments left behind by Reformation iconoclasm, and it neglects, *inter alia*, the significant number of monastic cathedrals and churches that retained some of their original functions in new guises as secular cathedrals and parish churches.[105] For the generation that had witnessed the dissolution, as we have seen, monastic sites that had been converted in this way served as mnemonics for the transformation wrought upon the ecclesiastical landscape by the Reformation. Thus in the immediate aftermath of the suppression, the sight of the parish church at Tickhill had prompted Leland to recall how it had been 'translated' and adapted for new purposes, whilst at Christ Church in the mid-sixteenth century, Stow had been inspired to offer a series of melancholy reflections on the nature of religious and social change precisely because its architecture was a relic of the pre-Reformation world of his youth. Even Lambarde, whose polemical cause was best served by those mutilated and decayed sites that attested to the ruin of medieval monasticism, occasionally noted the conversion of a former monastery, including the 'Den of Idolatrie' at Hackington which had 'since … become the Parish Church'.[106] The mnemonic capacity of these sites was predicated on contemporary senses of both change and continuity: these buildings simultaneously recalled something of the medieval past whilst also testifying to the transformative effect wrought by the dissolution upon the ecclesiastical landscape.

The memory of the dissolution associated with these spaces and places also had a pronounced generational dimension. By the late sixteenth century, most people did not possess personal experiences of the transformation of the monasteries that could be brought to bear on their perceptions of the past. In this context, the mnemonic potential of converted churches and cathedrals was complicated by the structural and material continuity they provided with the medieval period.[107] Although

---

[104] See especially C. John Sommerville, *The Secularization of Early Modern England: From Religious Culture to Religious Faith* (Oxford, 1992), p. 18 and ch. 2. *passim*, for whom the dissolution is the pre-eminent episode in the 'secularisation' of early modern England.

[105] We might speak of 'desacralisation' instead of 'secularisation' in this context; see, for example, Alexandra Walsham, 'The Reformation and "the Disenchantment of the World" reassessed', *HJ* 51 (2008), pp. 497–528 at p. 507 and *passim*.

[106] Lambarde, *Perambulation of Kent*, p. 253.

[107] As Lucy Bates has suggested, continuity may therefore have been more perceptible than change. See 'The limits of possibility in England's long Reformation', *HJ* 53 (2010), pp. 1049–70 at pp. 1059–60.

the form and function of ecclesiastical buildings both reflected and contributed to long-term processes of historical change, processes of architectural adaptation and conversion functioned to efface the memory of change rather than preserve it.[108] Converted churches remained sacred places and therefore also inherited many of the spiritual and social functions of the medieval monasteries. They sat uncomfortably in the 'nostalgic' tradition of late sixteenth- and seventeenth-century antiquarianism, which, on the one hand, viewed ruins as mnemonics for the violent profanation of sacred space conducted by the early reformers and, on the other, railed against the alleged misappropriation of ecclesiastical wealth by the Henrician gentry and nobility. If ruins have been seen as the emblems of Protestant 'nostalgia' *par excellence*, the legacy of converted churches and cathedrals was to prove altogether more complicated and ambiguous.

Those antiquaries who found cause to regret the wanton destruction of monastic buildings were less inclined to be alarmed by their conversion into parochial churches or cathedrals because this transformation could be subsumed into the preservationist enterprise. Surveying the parish church in the Wiltshire village of Malmesbury, Camden noted that it might have fared 'no better than the rest, but beene demolished' had it not been for 'T. Stumpes a wealthy clothier', who 'redeemed and bought it for the townsmen his neighbours, by whom it was converted to a Parish-church'. Rescued therefore from both monastic corruption and Reformation iconoclasm, Camden found 'a great part ... yet standing at this day', where it continued to serve the local community.[109] Aesthetic concerns also fed into his appreciation of converted monasteries. At St Albans, he paused at a church 'raised out of the ruins' of the old Benedictine abbey, which he thought deserved 'to be had in admiration' for its 'bigness, beauty and antiquity'.[110] Thus, whereas the sight of monastic ruins had provoked an unfavourable comparison between the mutilated remnants of the monasteries and the golden age of Christian devotion of which they were the shadows and imprints, Camden found in converted churches evidence of a more laudable transformation that created continuity with the past even as it effaced the images and idols that were the residues of Catholic 'superstition'.

The same was true of antiquarian approaches to converted cathedrals. The survival of cathedrals – including the many monastic foundations that

---

[108] See C. Pamela Graves, 'Social space in the English medieval parish church', *Economy and Society* 18 (1989), pp. 297–322 at p. 319.
[109] Camden, *Britain*, p. 243.   [110] Ibid., p. 412.

were converted to secular cathedrals – was itself a remarkable feature of the English Reformation.[111] But although cathedrals of all kinds were rendered vulnerable by the upheavals of religious change, current research suggests that they may have played a greater role in advancing the English Reformation than has hitherto been appreciated.[112] This raises interesting questions about the memory of monasticism attached to these sites. Here there was, perhaps, a vested interest of sorts in erasing the monastic past. It is certainly the case that, in the antiquarian context at least, it does not seem that cathedral buildings with a monastic history were singled out as being particularly problematic, and most reflections tended to focus on the present state of the fabric rather than its past. For example, the Devonshire antiquary and civic official John Hooker, a contemporary of Camden, conducted a survey of Exeter that bears many of the hallmarks of preservationist antiquarianism. But he also applauded the transformation of the Cathedral Priory into the city's secular cathedral. He described the structure he encountered as 'a verie fayre and a sumptuose buyldinge of free stone and with beautifull pyllers of graye marble'.[113] Thus, although antiquaries like Hooker continued to remember the dissolution as a cautionary tale about the fragility of antiquities, they evidently found no reason to lament the transformation of monastic cathedrals and churches into new emblems of Protestant piety.

With the Laudian project to restore the 'beauty of holiness', the memory of the dissolution associated with structures of monastic origin acquired new layers of meaning.[114] At Ely Cathedral in Cambridgeshire, Lieutenant Hammond, a soldier based with a military company in Norwich whose diary also functioned as a topography of the places that he visited, mourned that the structure had been 'rob'd of Princely dignity

---

[111] On cathedrals and the Reformation, see Stanford E. Lehmberg, *The Reformation of Cathedrals: Cathedrals in English Society* (Princeton, NJ, 2014); Diarmaid MacCulloch, 'Worcester: a cathedral city in the Reformation', in Patrick Collinson and John Craig (eds.), *The Reformation in English Towns, 1500–1640* (Basingstoke, 1998), pp. 94–112; Ian Atherton, 'Cathedrals', in Anthony Milton (ed.), *The Oxford Handbook of Anglicanism, Volume I: Reformation and Identity, c. 1520–1662* (Oxford, 2017), pp. 228–42.

[112] See esp. Alice Soulieux-Evans, 'Cathedrals and the Church of England, c.1660–1714', unpublished PhD thesis, University of Cambridge (2018).

[113] John Hooker, *The description of the citie of Excester*, ed. Walter J. Harte, J. W. Schopp, and H. Tapley-Soper, 3 vols. (Exeter, 1919), i, p. 35.

[114] On the 'beauty of holiness', see Milton, *Catholic and Reformed*, ch. 6; Peter Lake, 'The Laudian style: order, uniformity, and the pursuit of the beauty of holiness in the 1630s', in Kenneth Fincham (ed.), *The Early Stuart Church, 1603–1642* (Basingstoke, 1993), pp. 161–85. For two approaches to Laudianism and churches and cathedrals, see J. F. Merritt, 'The cradle of Laudianism? Westminster Abbey, 1558–1630', *JEH* 52 (2001), pp. 623–46; Ian Atherton, 'Cathedrals, Laudianism, and the British churches', *HJ* 53 (2010), pp. 895–918.

and meanes' during the dissolution but also regretted that it continued to stand 'much ruinated and decay'd, and drooping for very Age'.[115] Hammond thus appropriated the rhetoric of ruin to the Laudian cause, subsuming the spoliation wrought during the 1530s into a 'value-ridden' and 'polemically constructed' language of neglect and beautification.[116] By contrast, at Romsey Abbey in Hampshire, Hammond was delighted to find 'a fayre and Cathedrall like church', where he admired the 'loftie, and most stately Ile' and 'hansome monuments' that attested to its Laudian credentials.[117] If the project to repair and beautify ecclesiastical buildings had inspired a generation of antiquaries to lament the physical and material rupture engendered by the dissolution, working sites thus continued principally to provoke rumination on their present state. In both its late sixteenth-century and early seventeenth-century varieties, then, antiquarian writing about ex-monastic cathedrals and churches suggests that it was entirely possible for Protestant topographers to remember the dissolution without recourse to the rhetoric of loss and pity that characterised contemporary writing about monastic ruins. Hammond's comments reflect the complexity of the memory culture attached to former monastic buildings that continued to undergo structural change and repair, as well as how the restoration of church fabrics and fittings functioned to temper and even eclipse the memory of iconoclastic violence.

Churches and cathedrals were also, as recent scholarship on the Reformation in England and Europe has emphasised, sites where memory was challenged and contested.[118] For a more radical breed of Protestant, the degree of structural continuity with the past embodied in converted monasteries was a painful reminder of the incomplete character of the English Reformation. The memory of monasticism was therefore deliberately invoked as a polemical weapon. In this context, ecclesiastical structures had been a bone of contention long before the Laudian impulse started to manifest in debates about sacred space. For the Elizabethan separatist Henry Barrow, the Henrician assault on the monasteries had

---

[115] *A Relation of a Short Survey of the Western Counties Made by a Lieutenant of the Military Company in Norwich in 1635*, ed. L. G. Wickham Legg, Camden Miscellany 16 (London, 1936), pp. 91–2.
[116] I borrow these terms from J. F. Merritt, 'Puritans, Laudians, and the phenomenon of church-building in Jacobean London', *HJ* 41 (1998), pp. 935–60 at p. 960.
[117] *Short Survey of the Western Counties*, p. 59.
[118] See, for example, Duane J. Corpis, 'Losing one's place: memory, history, and space in post-Reformation Germany', in Lynne Tatlock (ed.), *Enduring Loss in Early Modern Germany: Cross Disciplinary Perspectives* (Boston, MA, and Leiden, 2010), pp. 327–67. More generally on the contestation of sacred space, see Spicer and Hamilton (eds.), *Defining the Holy*, esp. chs. 10, 14.

been an exemplary episode of iconoclasm that he hoped to emulate on a larger stage. How, he asked, could churches and cathedrals be permitted to stand 'in their old idolatrous shapes' when superstition was 'so inseperably inherent unto the whole building, as it can never be clensed of this fretting leprosie, until it be desolate, laid on heapes, as their yonger sisters, the abbacies and monasteries are'?[119] In other words, for Barrow, all ecclesiastical structures of medieval origin cradled the memory of the corrupt Catholic past. Barrow's fellow separatist John Smyth, writing in 1609, was likewise persuaded that 'as the goodly buildings of the abbayes, monasteries, and nunries, are already destroyed, and made barnes, stables, swinestyes, jakes, so shal it be done with al the idol temples when the howre of their visitation shal come'.[120] But whilst Smyth's comments testify on one level to the polemical power of remembering the dissolution, they also further underline the extent to which processes of conversion had indeed succeeded in partially effacing the memory of the monastic past. His deliberately polemical and provocative account of the conversion of monasteries in the 1530s praised the Henrician profanation of sacred space and yet failed to acknowledge the fact that some churches and cathedrals had once been abbeys, monasteries, and nunneries. Barrow's critique of churches as the 'younger sisters' of the religious houses likewise carried this implication, whilst maintaining the 'continuous thread of impassioned pleading' that connected iconoclasts across the generations.[121]

Radical Protestant anxiety about the Catholic memory embodied in some churches and cathedrals intensified with political and religious developments in the mid-seventeenth century. The connection between monasteries and post-Reformation churches was not lost on the Church of England clergyman and iconoclast Richard Culmer. Writing half a century after Barrow and Smyth, *Cathedral newes from Canterbury* (1644), published as part of a puritan backlash against the Laudian reforms, accused Canterbury Cathedral of being 'in an abbey-like, corrupt, and rotten condition, which cal[l]s for a speedy Reformation, or Dissolution'.[122] Culmer thus described the memory of the cathedral priory as a canker that riddled the structure.

[119] Henry Barrow, *A briefe discoverie of the false church* ([Dort?], 1590), p. 132.
[120] John Smyth, *Paralleles, censures, observations* ([Middelburg], 1609), repr. in *The works of John Smyth, Fellow of Christ's College, 1594–8*, with notes and biography by W. T. Whitley (Cambridge, 1915), pp. 523–4.
[121] Aston, *Broken Idols*, p. 86.
[122] Richard Culmer, *Cathedrall newes from Canterbury: shewing, the Canterburian cathedrall to bee in an abbey-like, corrupt, and rotten condition, which calls for a speedy Reformation, or dissolution* (London, 1644).

This was a disease, he continued, that had infected generations of Canterbury's clerics:

> The Cathedrall, called Christs-Church, in Canterbury, being a Convent of Monkes at the time of the dissolution of Abbeys, in the reigne of King Henry the eight, it was then (instead of Prior and Convent) turned into Deane, and Chapter . . . these Prelaticall successors of the Idolatrous, proud, lazie, covetous Monkes, as they succeeded them in place, so they followed them in practise, whereby they have a long time caused the godly neare them to groane under their tyranny, superstition, and scandall.[123]

Culmer metaphorically reversed the process of conversion to reveal the original medieval structure from behind its post-Reformation façade in an attempt to instigate a second dissolution of religious places. Selectively remembering the dissolution thus became a deliberate tactic for new generations of iconoclasts, for whom it functioned as a 'destructive precedent' for renewed campaigns against churches and idols.[124] In the event, however, the radical puritan attempt to raze England's cathedrals and churches to the ground was unsuccessful. Lichfield, a cathedral not of monastic origin, was the only such structure to suffer significant demolition at the hands of the image breakers of the 1640s.[125] Moreover, although puritan polemicists might deploy the memory of the dissolution as a rhetorical device, their instinct to destroy was not at all conducive to the topographical modes of expression that preserved the material memory of ex-monastic structures and spaces. As we have already noted, the act of iconoclasm was a mechanism for forgetting the past, or a 'sacrament of forgetfulness'.[126] This was as true of the wave of iconoclasm engendered by the Civil Wars as it was of that initiated by Henry VIII in the 1530s. In 1643–4, the fanatical iconoclast William Dowsing rampaged across Cambridgeshire and Suffolk, vandalising the images, stained glass, and 'popish' fabrics with which he came into contact. Echoing the epistolary itineraries compiled by the Henrician commissioners, Dowsing kept a journal of his iconoclastic peregrinations. At no point, however, did he single out former monastic sites for their origins or associations.[127] Rather,

---

[123] Ibid., sig. A3r.   [124] Aston, *Broken Idols*, p. 80.

[125] On Lichfield Cathedral, see Lehmberg, *Cathedrals Under Siege*, pp. 37–8; Spraggon, *Puritan Iconoclasm*, pp. 197–8.

[126] Duffy, *Stripping of the Altars*, p. 480. See also Aston, *England's Iconoclasts*, p. 256 and *passim*; Aston, *Broken Idols*, esp. part 1.

[127] Trevor Cooper (ed.), *The Journal of William Dowsing: Iconoclasm in East Anglia during the English Civil War* (Woodbridge, 2001). On Dowsing, see Aston, *England's Iconoclasts*, pp. 74–83; John Morrill, 'William Dowsing, the bureaucratic puritan', in John Morrill, Paul Slack, and Daniel Woolf (eds.), *Public Duty and Private Conscience in Seventeenth-Century England* (Oxford,

his actions and those of other mid-century image breakers served to complicate the memories associated with former monastic sites, subsuming the dissolution into a wider narrative of iconoclasm.

It was in this context that churches became a focus of the same anxiety about the vulnerability of antiquities that was characteristic of an earlier brand of preservationist topographical writing about ruins. In 1657, on a perambulation of the Oxfordshire countryside, Anthony Wood paused to record the monastic history of Dorchester Abbey, two miles south-east of Oxford, and its conversion into a parish church, where he mourned its further defacement by 'parliamentary soldiers in the late rebellion'.[128] In an attempt to preserve the memory of the site from further erosion, he also created a plan of the church interior. The preservation of the working structures created out of former religious houses has also been a neglected feature of Dugdale's *Monasticon Anglicanum*. The emphasis placed upon monastic history in this work has encouraged previous scholarship to view the *Monasticon* as the cornerstone of the 'nostalgic' antiquarian tradition inspired by ruins.[129] But although Dugdale listed ruined houses, he did not comment extensively upon their broken state. Indeed, he devoted at least as much space to religious houses that had been converted into churches and cathedrals after 1539 – and, as we shall see, visually this imbalance is even more striking. The dedicatory epistle to the 1693 English edition, written by John Marsham, intended the *Monasticon* as a reminder that 'of all those Cathedral Churches and Episcopal Seats, whose venerable Fabricks we behold at this day, some were formerly Abbies', as well as a means of showing that although 'the very Ruines of many [religious houses] are become invisible ... their Memory still lives in our History and Records'.[130] The act of remembering the pre-dissolution past of churches and cathedrals was therefore an act that defied ongoing attempts to induce amnesia by concealing and adapting, but also by attacking, monastic architecture. To paraphrase Margaret Aston, conversions, as well as ruins, could make historians.

But whilst this preservationist impulse might have been the hallmark of a certain prominent type of topographical writing, it was not characteristic of early modern antiquarianism as a whole. This is more readily apparent in

---

1993), pp. 173–204, revised as 'William Dowsing and the administration of iconoclasm', in Cooper (ed.), *Journal of William Dowsing*, pp. 1–28; Spraggon, *Puritan Iconoclasm*, chs. 4, 7.

[128] Anthony Wood, *The Life and Times of Anthony Wood, Antiquary, of Oxford, 1632–1695, Described by Himself*, ed. Andrew Clark, 5 vols. (Oxford, 1891–1900), i, pp. 223–6.

[129] Dugdale is prominent, for example, in Aston's seminal study, 'English ruins and English history', pp. 241, 251–2.

[130] *Monasticon Anglicanum*, 1693 ed., sigs. A2r, A4r.

the case of converted monasteries than it is in the example of the monastic ruins that inspired 'nostalgic' antiquarianism. In 1657, Dugdale conducted a perambulation of the East Anglian fens with fellow antiquary Elias Ashmole, during which both men kept short journals of the places they encountered. The differences between the two texts are highly suggestive. Dugdale, who was then engaged in researching the second volume of the *Monasticon*, continued to be preoccupied with converted churches. At Crowland in Lincolnshire, he saw 'that part of the Abby Church, which is now standing viz. the west end from the Crosse' and was impressed by its new fabric, recording that it 'hath a costly roofe of timber, most richly gilt, as if it were newly done'.[131] In the Cambridgeshire village of Thorney, he found cause to mourn the 'few scattering ruines' of the Benedictine abbey that had once stood there, but also noted the survival of 'a parte of the Abby Church, and the body thereof from the Crosse to the west end'.[132] By locating converted churches in relation to their ruined elements and using language that acknowledged the fragmentary condition of these structures, Dugdale's diary reveals his preoccupation with the destructive episode of dissolution.

Strikingly, Ashmole's accounts of the same churches that caught Dugdale's attention made no reference to their monastic origins or to the violence of their conversion. Rather he spoke of them in the present tense and with reference only to their present condition: 'At Thorney & Crowland', he wrote, 'there is now only standing the body of the Churches to the Cross Isle, & noe more.' At Crowland, Ashmole also applauded the grandeur of the working church, it being 'very stately & adorned with severall statues'.[133] Likewise, whereas Dugdale recorded that 'when we came to Torksey, we found the ruines of the Priorie about half a Bow shoot Eastwards from the parish church', Ashmole noted simply that 'Neere the Nunry ... is a tumulus'.[134] Ashmole's failure to comment on Torksey's distressed and damaged state belies the different priorities governing the two texts, demonstrating his greater fascination for natural history than the medieval past. Not every observer of the post-Reformation landscape viewed it through the rose-tinted spectacles of nostalgia, pity, and regret.

Indeed, for a number of antiquaries writing in the late sixteenth and seventeenth centuries, converted churches provided an occasion for meditation upon the triumph of Protestant Reformation and the improvement in

---

[131] BL, Lansdowne MS 722/4, fol. 36r.   [132] Ibid., fol. 35v.
[133] Bodl., MS Ashmole 784, fol. 32r.
[134] BL, Lansdowne MS 722/4, fol. 37v; Bodl., MS Ashmole 784, fol. 34r.

piety wrought in parallel with the physical transformation of these structures. This took the form neither of the vitriolic anti-monastic polemic espoused by Lambarde nor of the aesthetic appreciation for parish churches evinced by Hammond and Camden. Rather, it exemplified a brand of antiquarianism that looked forward in time from the dissolution rather than backwards upon it. At the site of a small monastic chapel in Hounslow on the outskirts of London, the Elizabethan cartographer John Norden, born at the end of Henry VIII's reign, remembered how it had passed into the hands of a Henrician auditor, a man called Roane, who had given an annuity 'upon condition that the enhabytantes shall extend a farther contribution to mayntayne a minister ther'.[135] In the 1630s, at the height of the Laudian reforms, Thomas Westcote, a gentry antiquary of Devonshire stock, wrote that 'I remember there is a fair large spacious church, which somtime appertained to the Priory of Plympton' before switching to the present tense to remark that 'since the dissolution of the priory the town hath purchased it, which they bestow upon the vicar, preacher and other pious uses'.[136] Half a century later, the lawyer and antiquary Thomas Denton began a survey of Cumberland at the request of his local MP, Sir John Lowther. Combining his observations of the local landscape with material from the historical collections created by his father, John Denton, Thomas noted at Holmcultram how the abbey church had been 'made ... to serve the inhabitants as a parish church' after the dissolution.[137] The language of service and piety invoked in these works marks a departure from the lament for the pre-dissolution world and the sense of social decline embodied by monastic ruins that has been so profoundly associated with the development of early modern antiquarianism.

Denton and Westcote grappled with a different inheritance than the 'nostalgic' antiquaries. Like Leland, writing more than a century earlier in the context of the Henrician project to manage the memory of the dissolution, topographies in this tradition continued to minimise the material, social, and economic rupture wrought by the dissolution. This type of

---

[135] BL, Additional MS 31853, p. 7. For Norden's topographical collections, see also BL, Harley MS 6252.

[136] Thomas Westcote, *A View of Devonshire in MDCXXX, with a Pedigree of Most of Its Gentry, by Thomas Westcote, gent.*, ed. George Oliver and Pitman Jones (Exeter, 1845), p. 383.

[137] Thomas Denton, *A Perambulation of Cumberland, 1687–1688, including Descriptions of Westmorland, the Isle of Man, and Ireland*, ed. Angus J. L. Winchester in collaboration with Mary Wane, Surtees Society 207 (Durham, 2003), p. 195. See also Angus J. L. Winchester (ed.), *John Denton's History of Cumberland*, Surtees Society 213 (Durham, 2010), pp. 179–80. John Denton attributed the dissolution of the monastic church at Holmcultram to Henry VIII; this attribution does not appear in Thomas Denton's *Perambulation*.

antiquarian writing functioned not to resurrect what had been lost or preserve that in danger of falling into oblivion but rather to establish and consolidate senses of identity and community amongst the local gentry who were its authors and who constituted its primary readership. In other words, it was written by and for the heirs – both literal and metaphorical – of the generation of Henrician nobles who had profited from the dissolution in the 1530s. The dissolution was a critical moment in their heritage. In this context, topography became an important polemical and genealogical tool of the gentry, shaping the memory of the dissolution by promoting the erasure of aspects of the medieval past that their preservationist counterparts fought so hard to conserve. This was vitally important to those who lived as well as prayed in converted monasteries. Indeed, the primary sites of this culture of amnesia were not churches and cathedrals but the domestic properties raised out of the ruins of the religious houses.

'Great Mansions' and 'Stately Houses'

In the greatest land transfer witnessed in England since the Norman Conquest, the dissolution caused around one-third of all the land in the country to pass from the hands of the Church into those of the crown and its agents.[138] Henry VIII retained some of this property, but other sites were sold on to bolster the crown's finances or to reinforce patronage networks. The recipients and purchasers of monastic lands used them to cement or enhance their social and political status. Some amongst the nobility and gentry undertook building projects to transform religious houses into private homes. In the years immediately following the dissolution, some thirty new country houses were constructed with remarkable rapidity out of England's ruins.[139] In addition to noting the creation of monastic ruins and the conversion of some properties into parish churches, Leland also noticed that some religious houses had been converted for secular uses. Titchfield Abbey in Hampshire, for example, had once been a house of Premonstratensian canons. In the wake of the dissolution, however, the incumbent Lord Chancellor, Thomas Wriothesley had 'builded a right stately House embatelid, and having a goodely gate . . . yn the very same Place where the late Monasterie of Premonstratenses stoode'.[140] Wriothesley, who was also the cousin of Charles Wriothesley, whose

---

[138] On the administration of this transfer, see Peter Cunich, 'The administration and alienation of ex-monastic lands by the Crown, 1536–47', unpublished PhD thesis, University of Cambridge (1990).
[139] Howard, 'Recycling the monastic fabric', p. 223.
[140] *Itinerary of John Leland*, ed. Toulmin Smith, i, p. 281.

chronicle we examined in the previous chapter, was one of the most significant beneficiaries of the dissolution after the crown, acquiring former monastic properties in no fewer than eight counties between 1537 and 1547.[141] Like so many domestic conversions of this type, Titchfield became a material expression of the status and wealth accrued by the gentry at the suppression, mirroring the king's own building programme at sites including Dartford Priory and Syon Abbey.[142]

As the archaeology of the dissolution has highlighted, domestic conversions, unlike churches, usually entailed the imposition of an entirely new façade that concealed the original architecture completely.[143] Whilst people still living could remember these transformations, antiquaries continued to commit them to paper. Fifty years after Leland began his peregrinations for what became the *Itinerary*, Camden was similarly struck by the rapid conversion of properties belonging to Thomas Wriothesley, noting at Walden Abbey in Essex that the Lord Chancellor had 'changed the Abbay into his owne dwelling house'.[144] Confronted with the same grand structure, Norden also remarked upon what had become 'now a stately howse of the E. of Sowthampton'.[145] Elsewhere, Stow was prompted at the former nunnery of Holywell in Shoreditch to note that many houses had 'beene builded for the Lodgings of Noblemen, of Strangers borne, and other' since the dissolution.[146] As Stow realised, the process of converting monastic buildings into private houses was an ongoing project, which continued to remodel the monastic landscape so that it reflected new political imperatives and power structures.[147] Insofar as this process was also 'immensely destructive of earlier fabric', these buildings became sites of forgetting the monastic past.[148] By altering, adapting, and appropriating monastic structures, the English gentry created not bleak reminders of what had been lost during the suppression but powerful symbols of what had been gained.

It is worth noting that Catholic as well as Protestant gentry families converted monasteries into secular dwellings – indeed, the preservation of these sites in this way was encouraged by the Catholic Church, albeit with some limitations and conditions. Amongst the cases of conscience heard by

[141] Michael A. R. Graves, 'Wriothesley, Thomas, first earl of Southampton (1505–1550)', *ODNB*, www.oxforddnb.com/view/article/30076.
[142] Howard, 'Recycling the monastic fabric', p. 223. See also Doggett, *Patterns of Re-Use*, pp. 53, 56.
[143] Soden, 'Buildings analysis at Coombe Abbey', p. 154.   [144] Camden, *Britain*, p. 452.
[145] BL, Additional MS 31853, p. 44.   [146] Stow, *Survey of London*, p. 470.
[147] See Christopher Phillpotts, 'The houses of Henry VIII's courtiers in London', in Gaimster and Gilchrist (eds.), *Archaeology of the Reformation*, pp. 299–309.
[148] Iain Soden, 'Buildings analysis at Coombe Abbey', p. 154.

the Church in the Elizabethan and early Stuart periods were a number relating to former monastic property. The 1581 Douai-Rheims cases decided by Robert Persons and William Allen included the question of whether it was lawful for Catholics to buy and sell ex-monastic property. The answer was clear: 'It is lawful to buy stolen property if one intends to restore it to its owner and in the same way it is also lawful to buy monastic property with the intention of restoring it to the monasteries.'[149] In other words, the temporary occupation of monastic buildings was permissible, indeed preferable to their acquisition by Protestants, but in the strict understanding that the owner was 'bound to restore the property to the monastery itself or to the Pope' in the event of a Catholic restoration in England.[150] This judgement was echoed in the Caroline cases of conscience decided by Thomas Southwell, who answered the issue of whether Catholics may buy or sell monastic possessions by declaring that 'both are lawful as things now are in England, as Allen and Persons teach well in their responses'. Although Southwell realised that Persons and Allen's hopes that lay ownership would be only temporary had been dashed, because by the early seventeenth century an imminent Catholic restoration seemed unlikely, he nevertheless concluded that the purchase of 'such property seems to be in the interest of the Church, because Catholics may more easily restore it when the time comes'.[151] It is impossible to say how many English Catholics purchased monastic lands for this purpose – and, as we saw in the previous chapter, the evidence of the Marian restoration suggests that owners of such properties tended to be reluctant to release them.

For centuries before the dissolution, land and property had been 'the means by which a family knew itself in historical perspective'.[152] If ruins were the most tangible manifestation of a vanquished past, monasteries turned manor houses were palpable emblems of the shift in influence from clergy to laity that had accompanied the suppression.[153] As Maurice Howard has demonstrated in the case of post-dissolution Reading, the archaeology of the dissolution reveals how the 'priorities for the use of former monastic spaces changed as the topography of the place and the

[149] Peter Holmes (ed.), *Elizabethan Casuistry* (Thetford, 1981), case G2, p. 43.   [150] Ibid., p. 44.
[151] Peter Holmes (ed.), *Caroline Casuistry: The Cases of Conscience of Fr Thomas Southwell SJ* (Woodbridge, 2012), case 109, pp. 89–90. See also Holmes's introduction, p. xxv.
[152] Patrick J. Geary, 'Land, language, and memory in Europe, 700–1100', *TRHS* 9 (1999), pp. 169–84 at p. 171.
[153] Felicity Heal and Clive Holmes, *The Gentry in England and Wales, 1500–1700* (Basingstoke and London, 1994), p. 326.

interests of its powerful inhabitants developed in the post-Reformation world'.[154] It is unsurprising, therefore, that a particular species of gentry antiquary came to show a far greater interest in the conversion of the monasteries than in their spoliation. Promising the reader an 'hystoricall & chorographicall description' of Norfolk, the Elizabethan cleric Thomas Beckham thus ignored the history of the Reformation in the county and the material remains that antiquaries such as Camden, Aubrey, and Wood would have thought of as its pre-eminent antiquities. Instead, he was compelled to record the 'divers mannours' that had come into the hands of the nobility 'since the dissolucion' of the religious houses.[155] Sir William Pole's 'Survey of Devon', compiled in the late sixteenth and early seventeenth centuries, demonstrated a similar preoccupation with the status and wealth of the local gentry. He noted how Barnstaple Priory had been 'granted to the Lord William Howard of Effingham, & by Charles Earl of Nottingham, it descended unto his son'.[156] At Buckfast Abbey, he was prompted to remark that since the dissolution 'the Manor doth continue still the Kings'.[157] Pole's work was also a foundational source for the topographies of Devon undertaken by Tristram Risdon in the mid-seventeenth century, who repeated Pole's assessment of Buckfast, though he added a piece of information omitted by Pole, recording that the 'skeleton of the vast body' of the old abbey was still to be seen.[158]

These texts are emblematic of a variety of antiquarianism that sits uncomfortably with the 'nostalgic' tradition that has typically been associated with the remnants of medieval monasticism. They belong to the commemorative culture of the sixteenth- and seventeenth-century gentry, in which historical and chorographical writing was deployed as a tool for fostering and fashioning both collective identity and individual reputation.[159] Ironically, many of these endeavours were enabled by the

[154] Howard, 'Recycling the monastic fabric', p. 230.
[155] Bodl., MS Gough Norfolk 26, p. 346. For the attribution to Beckham, see Woolf, *Social Circulation*, pp. 154–5.
[156] DHC, Z 19/18/13b, p. 523.   [157] DHC, Z 19/18/13a, p. 360.
[158] DHC, D.2865, unpaginated. Published as Tristram Risdon, *The chorographical description or survey of the County of Devon, with the City and County of Exeter* (London, 1714). See also Risdon's notebook with historical and topographical observations in Exeter, Exeter Cathedral Archives, MS 3531.
[159] Jan Broadway, *'No Historie so Meete': Gentry Culture and the Development of Local History in Elizabethan and Early Stuart England* (Manchester, 2006); Jan Broadway, 'Symbolic and self-consciously antiquarian: the Elizabethan and early Stuart gentry's use of the past', in Matthew Neufeld (ed.), 'Uses of the past in early modern England', *Huntington Library Quarterly* 76 (2013), pp. 541–58; Claire Bartram, '"Honoured by posteryte by record of wrytinge": memory, reputation and the role of the book within commemorative practices in late Elizabethan Kent', in

release of historic documents out of monastic archives and libraries and their increased accessibility.[160] Many gentry antiquaries were therefore engaged in collecting monastic materials, and some also sought out the remnants of religious houses for precisely this reason. Writing to Camden, the collector and antiquary Henry Savile thus recorded that he had visited Bolton Abbey 'wher I found many Armes of the nobilitie embo[ssed] in stone'.[161] But it was also the case that topography could function as a domain where the early modern gentry remembered – and reshaped – their history. At the site of a former nunnery at Seaton in Cumbria, Denton used the dissolution as an excuse for genealogy, writing that:

> Since the fall of that religious house, it came to the hands of Joseph Pennington, a younger brother of the house of Mulcaster, and is now the inheritance of Miles Pennington Esqr, son of John, son of Miles, son of Joseph, who had it by a match with the daughter and heir to Sir Hugh Askew.[162]

For the Pennington family, the dissolution marked not the end of the medieval world but instead the beginning of its own prosperity. It was this thriving lineage that Denton's topography was intended to commemorate and celebrate. This impulse was strengthened by the fact that antiquaries such as Denton belonged themselves to this gentry community. Adopting a present tense formulation that was common in writing of this kind, the Caroline antiquary Thomas Gerard, when confronted with the site of a thirteenth-century Augustinian nunnery at Ilchester in Somerset, remarked only that 'there stands a new house, the seat of my good friend, Mr Dawe'. Describing the landscape around the property, Gerard continued to refer to the site as 'the Priory', which, he wrote, 'I remember for imitation sake'.[163] Gerard's survey reflected the enduring power of monastic names as markers of place but interpreted their meaning through the lens of a worldview that celebrated the waning of the monastic age.

Implicit in Gerard's description of Ilchester is a sense that the process of conversion had been one of improvement.[164] Likewise, at Wembury in

Michael Penman (ed.), *Monuments and Monumentality Across Medieval and Early Modern Europe* (Donington, 2013), pp. 91–104.
[160] Broadway, *No History so Meete*, p. 121.   [161] BL, Cotton MS Julius F VI, fol. 316r.
[162] Denton, *Perambulation of Cumberland*, p. 74.
[163] Gerard, *Particular Description of Somerset*, pp. 206–7.
[164] This provides a different angle on the theme of improvement explored in Paul Slack, *The Invention of Improvement: Information and Material Progress in Seventeenth-Century England* (Oxford, 2015).

Devon, the antiquary Thomas Westcote admired a house that had once been appropriated to the priory at Plympton but had passed 'at the dissolution' first to the 'illustrious' Lord Chancellor Wriothesley and then to Sir John Hele, 'who added much to the fame and honour of this place' through the conversion of the property into a 'noble mansion'.[165] A little further on at Torre Abbey, Westcote had cause again to remember that 'after the dissolution it came to be the possession of Rudgway' who 're-edified those almost decayed cells to a newer and better form'.[166] The polemical rhetoric of monastic corruption is only implicit in these passages, but the language of re-edification employed by Westcote implies something of the continued resonance of the Henrician narrative of dissolution across the seventeenth century. This type of topographical writing could thus serve subtly to perpetuate older ideas about the dissolution. Gerard also returned more explicitly to this theme in his account of Somerset, delighting in reminding his reader that 'many greate Abbies would not sticke to shew you a nayle' torn from the cross upon which Christ had been crucified, produced 'of the same forge or rather forging'.[167] Like the historical and polemical writing examined in previous chapters, topographical writing thus also employed the memory of monastic corruption as a means of minimising the magnitude of the rupture engendered by the dissolution. It reflected the processes of architectural conversion that had quite literally effaced the material memory of the medieval past.

This tendency to downplay the transformation wrought by the dissolution was augmented by belief that the manor houses of the gentry remained integral to the continuation of the charitable and philanthropic duties undertaken by the medieval religious orders. After the suppression of the monasteries, the onus of hospitality was transferred to the post-Reformation clergy and gentry.[168] Their houses – conversions and new builds alike – were structured around 'public display and openness' as an indication of their occupants' generosity.[169] As we have seen, generations of polemicists and antiquaries argued that the dissolution marked a rupture between past and present that had caused social and economic decline. This argument was also at the root of Stow's nostalgia, which drew an unfavourable comparison between the plenty of the medieval past and the parsimony of his Elizabethan present. Yet for the generation of Protestant antiquaries who could not remember the pre-dissolution world and who

---

[165] Westcote, *View of Devonshire*, p. 387.   [166] Ibid., p. 426.
[167] Gerard, *Particular Description of Somerset*, p. 98.
[168] See Felicity Heal, *Hospitality in Early Modern England* (Oxford, 1990), ch. 7.
[169] Heal and Holmes, *Gentry in England and Wales*, p. 283.

viewed the suppression as critical to the status and reputation of their families and communities, the comparison was reversed.

The Cornish gentleman antiquary Richard Carew completed his *Survey of Cornwall* in 1602. Modelled on Lambarde's *Perambulation of Kent*, although rather less caustic in its polemic than its predecessor, the *Survey* was undertaken with the input of his peers in the local community and was intended largely for their edification and entertainment.[170] A note of criticism crept into his comment that in the immediate aftermath of the suppression 'the golden showre of the dissolved Abbey lands, rayned welnere into every gapers mouth'. This reflected that fact that the Reformation had created a certain amount of instability in the traditional gentry community, whose sense of continuity and cohesion had been tested by the release of Church wealth and property into lay hands, which sponsored the rise of a new elite. It was partly for this reason that the seventeenth century witnessed a vogue for genealogy, heraldry, chorography, and topography.[171] Nevertheless, Carew went on to associate monasticism with 'more corrupt ages' than his own, and this informed his remarks that the owners of a former priory in the parish of St Germans, known to him by its post-Reformation name of Port Eliot, were commendable for their generosity because 'by [their] charity distributeth, *pro virili*, the almes accustomably expected and expended at such places'.[172] Sentiments such as this also gave further expression to the idea that the dissolution had entailed gains as well as losses.

These gains, as we have already noted, were enjoyed not only by Protestants but also by some amongst the Catholic gentry. It is unsurprising, therefore, that Catholic antiquarian writing sometimes adopted a similarly present-centric, genealogical mode. Richard Cust's account of the Catholic antiquary Sir Thomas Shirley characterises Shirley's work partly as an attempt to assert his family's gentle status and 'to ensure that the yardstick used for measuring honour was that of lineage and pedigree'. Cust suggests that this was part of a 'concerted programme' that, strikingly, had begun during the dissolution of the monasteries when Shirley's great-grandfather Francis Shirley purchased the priory church of Breedon in Leicestershire to use as a family sepulchre.[173] Shirley's networks also included other Catholic antiquaries writing in a similar

---

[170] See Alexandra Walsham, 'Richard Carew and English topography' in Richard Carew, *The survey of Cornwall*, ed. John Chynoweth, NicholasOrme, and AlexandraWalsham, Devon and Cornwall Record Society, new series, 47 (Exeter, 2004), pp. 28–9, 33.

[171] Carew, *Survey of Cornwall*, fol. 109r. See also Broadway, *No Historie so Meete*, p. 239.

[172] Carew, *Survey of Cornwall*, fol. 109r.

[173] Richard Cust, 'Catholicism, antiquarianism, and gentry honour: the writings of Sir Thomas Shirley', *Midland History* 23 (1998), pp. 40–70 at p. 52.

vein. Shirley's friend Thomas Habington, a convert to Catholicism whilst a student in Paris around 1580, spent some forty years completing a survey of Worcestershire, finished in the 1640s. In this manuscript, Habington recorded a number of manors that had once belonged to religious houses but which had transferred to lay hands at the dissolution, including the possessions of the Benedictine priory at Little Malvern, which had passed to the noted Catholic family, the Throckmortons.[174] The antiquary Sampson Erdeswicke, who like Habington had spent spells in prison for his Catholic faith, also recorded the conversion of several Staffordshire monasteries in a similar fashion, including the hearsay that a 'Lancashire gentleman' had made 'a parlour of the chancel, a hall of the church, and a kitchen of the steeple' of the old Augustinian priory of Calwich.[175]

There was, perhaps, a note of shock barely concealed in Erdeswicke's comments about the extent of the conversion at Calwich. It is true that writing in the present-centric vein could still be prone to flashes of the outrage typical of wider Catholic discourse on the dissolution. Thus Habington alluded to the 'tumultous tymes' in which Little Malvern had been dissolved,[176] and Shirley was highly critical of 'the unhappie, miserable, and profane subversion of all the religious houses in England'.[177] Later in his writings on Staffordshire, Erdeswicke also found cause to lament monastic ruins, which lay 'broken and defaced' in the landscape and which had come to represent not improvement or the advancement of the gentry but rather the violence of the Protestant Reformation.[178] It should come as little surprise, given the resemblance of these comments to those articulated by Protestant antiquaries, that antiquarian endeavours often formed the basis for the development of cross-confessional networks, although, as Jan Broadway has suggested, relations between individuals of different religious persuasions could often be uneasy.[179] Nevertheless, Shirley's frequent correspondents in the Midlands included both Dugdale and the Calvinist antiquary and magistrate Sir Simon Archer.[180]

---

[174] Thomas Habington, *A Survey of Worcestershire*, ed. J. Amphett, 2 vols. (Oxford, 1895–9), ii, pp. 37–8,

[175] Sampson Erdeswicke, *A Survey of Staffordshire: Containing the Antiquities of that County*, ed. Rev. Thomas Hardwood (London, 1820), p. 362.

[176] Habington, *Survey of Worcestershire*, ii, p. 12.

[177] BL, Harleian MS 4928, fols. 96r, 68v. Quoted in Cust, 'Catholicism, antiquarianism, and gentry honour', p. 62.

[178] Ibid., p. 548.   [179] Broadway, *No Historie So Meete*, p. 95 and ch. 3 *passim*.

[180] See Richard Cust, 'Shirley, Sir Thomas (*c.* 1590–1654)', *ODNB*, www.oxforddnb.com/view/article/47732; Richard Cust, 'Archer, Sir Simon (1581–1662)', *ODNB*, www.oxforddnb.com/view/article/626.

Cust uses Shirley and his network as a case study to suggest that early modern antiquaries of all confessional colours were united by nostalgia and a 'shared antipathy towards recent processes of social, cultural and religious change'.[181] We have seen here how they could also share an interest in the fate of monastic properties which did not fully fit the 'nostalgic' mode.

For Protestants as well as Catholics, it was also the case that the present-centric mode was not necessarily incompatible with melancholic reflection on monastic ruins. Westcote, for example, described how the beholder of the 'skeleton of [the] huge body' of Buckfast Abbey 'may both pity and wonder to see the ruins thereof' because they were the carcasses of medieval lay devotion.[182] Westcote's pity, in an echo of his contemporary, Weever, was directed towards the lay founders of medieval monasteries. At the ruins of the Benedictine nunnery of Polsloe, he was 'put in mind to consider and seriously to meditate upon the fore-intentions of mortal men's purposes in thinking of the first founder of this fabric' and mourned that what had been intended as a lasting memorial to the founder's piety had been ruined and 'is no where (that I can find) remembered'.[183] These vestigial remains were, for Westcote, also further evidence of how 'godly purposes' had been 'abused' by the religious – and were thus the antithesis of conversions, which reflected the restoration of godly piety that had once supported Catholic error and superstition.[184] Likewise, Gerard could not suppress a note of pity that the founders and benefactors of a Carmelite friary supposedly 'now vanished' in Taunton had been 'dubble buryed first in their graves and secondly with the ruines of the Church and priory, for that fatall thunderclapp in Henry the eight's daies . . . overthrew this priory to the ground'.[185] His regret only extended so far, however, because he continued to applaud the 'handsome house' built out of some of the fragments of the Taunton Whitefriars by a prominent local family.[186]

It is striking that these passages find echoes in preservationist antiquarian writing, which – though obsessed with monastic ruins – did not allow converted monasteries to go unnoticed. Sometimes these references were inflected with a muted form of the mournful rhetoric of 'nostalgic' antiquarianism. Hammond, for instance, noted how many of the stones that

[181] Cust, 'Catholicism, antiquarianism, and gentry honour', p. 60.
[182] Westcote, *View of Devonshire*, p. 404.   [183] Ibid., pp. 186–7.   [184] Ibid., p. 145.
[185] Gerard, *Particular Description of Somerset*, pp. 58–9. In fact, this story is apocryphal: although some preparations were made, there never was a Carmelite house in Taunton. See 'Friaries: The Carmelites at Taunton', in *A History of the County of Somerset: Volume 2*, ed. William Page (London, 1911), p. 152, *British History Online*, www.british-history.ac.uk/vch/som/vol2/p152.
[186] Gerard, *Particular Description of Somerset*, p. 59.

had once belonged to St Augustine's Abbey in Canterbury had been 'caryed away and plac'd in great mansions', which themselves now 'fully testify what the pristine beauty and magnificence of this place hath beene'.[187] Others demonstrated that preservationist antiquarianism was capable of having an eye to the present, as well as looking back at the past. Thus in Wiltshire, Aubrey observed a house that had 'belonged to the Abbey of Cainsham, not far off in Somersetshire', which 'after the dissolucion Tho: Earle of Sussex had it'.[188] In some instances, this was framed critically. Norden, for example, appears to have mourned domestic conversions more than the creation of parochial churches. At Daventry in Northamptonshire, he wrote that 'theare was sometime a fayre Monasterye', which had been suppressed by Cardinal Wolsey in the 1520s. 'It is greatly defaced', he wrote, and 'yet so much standeth as giveth entertainment unto a Gentleman of some accompt, named as I take it, Mr. Roper.'[189] Yet others appear to have adopted elements of the rhetoric and function of the present-centric tradition of writing about the dissolution. At a former Carmelite monastery in Aylesford, Kent, Camden remarked that there was 'now seene a faire habitation of Sir William Sidney a learned knight painefully, and expensfully studious of the common good of his countrie as both his endowed house for the poore, and the bridge heere wich the common voice doe plentifully testifie'.[190] Prefiguring later suggestions that lay hospitality and charity exceeded that of the monastic orders, Camden thus clearly demonstrated that the boundaries between retrospective, regretful antiquarianism and its present-centric cousin were far from wholly distinct.

The difference lay in the balance between perceptions of what had been lost at the dissolution and what had been gained – between the instinct to preserve and destroy, remember and forget. During his perambulation of the East Anglian fens, Dugdale also found himself confronted by monasteries that had been converted into country houses. He commented at Swinstead in Lincolnshire that 'there is no appearance of any of the Abby' that had once stood there, 'but all that is left of it, converted into other buildings'.[191] Likewise, travelling through the Cambridgeshire parish of Chatteris, he noted that 'there is no vestigial of the monasterie now lost' because it had since been 'transformed ... into a newe House'.[192] It is striking that Dugdale considered the religious houses at Swinstead and

[187] *Short Survey of the Western Counties*, p. 18.   [188] Bodl., MS Aubrey 3, fol. 98r.
[189] Bodl., MS Top. Northants e 17, p. 38.   [190] Camden, *Britain*, p. 332.
[191] BL, Lansdowne MS 722/4, fol. 36v.   [192] Ibid., fol. 34r.

Chatteris to be wholly 'lost' as a result of their conversion into domestic dwellings. His survey thus testifies to the power of the processes of conversion to erase material memory, as well as the capacity of topography to resurrect it. It is also telling that Dugdale only very rarely mentioned the new owners of former religious houses, betraying his preference for the medieval past. In one such entry towards the end of his journal, Dugdale made an illuminating slip: 'we saw Ramsey Mere', he wrote, 'and Ramsey Abbey. I mean the place where it stood, being now Mr Henry Cromwells seat, on our left hand, somewhat above a mile and half distant'.[193]

By contrast, antiquarian writing in the present-centric, genealogically inspired tradition of many seventeenth-century gentry antiquaries invoked the memory of the dissolution almost uniquely as the transformative moment in the fortunes of prominent local families. It relied upon a vision of the suppression as a creative episode. As a result, this present-centric form of topography fostered and reinforced associations between properties of monastic origin, the buildings in their converted form, and the new owners who inhabited and used them. Andrew Marvell's poem, 'Upon Appleton House', captures the tenor and timbre of this particular memory culture. Written for Thomas Fairfax, commander-in-chief of the parliamentarian forces during the Civil Wars, who retired to the manor house constructed out of the ruins of Nun Appleton Priory in Yorkshire during the Interregnum, it was, in part, an attempt to manage the memory of the dissolution. 'A nunnery first gave it birth', he wrote, '(For virgin buildings oft brought forth), / and all that neighbour-ruin shows / the quarries whence this dwelling rose' (85–8). Invoking the language of sacredness to praise the Fairfax family, Marvell declared that 'surely when the after age / shall hither come in pilgrimage, / these sacred places to adore, / by Vere and Fairfax trod before' (33–6).[194] By converting and occupying former monastic property, men like Fairfax contributed to the

---

[193] Ibid., fol. 34v.
[194] Quotations from Andrew Marvell, 'Upon Appleton House, to my Lord Fairfax', in Nigel Smith (ed.), *The Poems of Andrew Marvell*, revised ed. (Harlow, 2007), pp. 210–41. On 'Nun Appleton House' and the implications of architectural conversion, see Gary D. Hamilton, 'Marvell, sacrilege, and Protestant historiography: contextualizing "Upon Appleton House"', in Donna B. Hamilton and Richard Stier (eds.), *Religion, Literature, and Politics in Post-Reformation England, 1540–1688* (Cambridge, 1996), pp. 161–86; Brian Patton, 'Preserving property: history, genealogy, and inheritance in "Upon Appleton House"', *Renaissance Quarterly* 49 (1996), pp. 824–39; Patsy Griffin, '"Twas no religious house till now": Marvell's "Upon Appleton House"', *Studies in English Literature, 1500–1900* 28 (1998), pp. 61–7; Clinton Allen Brand, '"Upon Appleton House" and the decomposition of Protestant historiography', *English Literary Renaissance* 31 (2001), pp. 477–510; Jane Partner '"The swelling hall": Andrew Marvell and the politics of architecture at Nun Appleton House', *Seventeenth Century* 23 (2008), pp. 225–43.

erosion of the monastic past. This may have been an unconscious process of forgetting, but it may also reflect a deep-seated anxiety about the profanation of sacred space. In the next chapter, we will return to this question and to the critical role of contemporary discourses of sacrilege in shaping this culture of selective amnesia – for it is clear, as we have seen, that the owners of former monastic properties and the antiquaries who wrote for them belonged to a group whose interests in forgetting the dissolution were much greater than in remembering it.

Depicting the Dissolution

The conflicting impulses to remember and forget the dissolution were also encapsulated in the visual depictions of monastic property produced by English antiquaries as part of their surveys of the landscape. Images had the power to resurrect structures that had been lost, to preserve vestigial remains, and subtly to erase the memory of the dissolution; iconoclasm, as we have already noted, had the power both to erode memory and to forge it anew. Aston's argument that encounters with the fragments of the monastic past stimulated practices of historical enquiry has profoundly shaped accounts of the visual culture of the dissolution. Building partly upon Aston's essay, Daniel Woolf has argued that the sixteenth and seventeenth centuries witnessed the development of a 'visual culture of "pastness"'.[195] Indeed, for Woolf, the dissolution functioned as the key temporal marker in the development of this culture, precisely because its residues were 'the most prominent and visible link to a vanishing medieval past'.[196] It is a critical paradox of the dissolution that Henrician attempts to efface the memory of the monastic past inspired a visual culture that sought to preserve it. Yet Woolf also acknowledges the selective vision with which these objects and their pictorial likenesses were viewed. In a highly suggestive discussion of the changing status of material objects, Woolf proposes that the abolition of relic worship helped 'to nurture, rather than to deter, an interest in antiquity', though the boundary between venerated relic and historical artefact remained porous.[197] But, as we shall see, just as antiquarian and topographical writing did not present a uniform account of the dissolution, nor were images of monasteries the preserve of 'nostalgic' antiquarianism.

Before turning to focus on the antiquarian images that accompanied topographical writing, it is worth noting that early modern depictions of

[195] Woolf, *Social Circulation*, p. 183.   [196] Ibid., p. 220.   [197] Ibid., pp. 193–4.

the dissolution itself are rare – and the earliest are allegorical. A remarkable fragment of a manuscript survey of the properties belonging to the Benedictine abbey in Colchester in Essex, conducted at the time of its suppression, incorporates an image that alludes to the trial of Colchester's last abbot, John Beche. A close copy of an engraving of 'The triumph of Mordechai' (1515) by the Dutch artist Lucas van Leyden, depicting the story from the Book of Esther in which Haman is hanged from the gallows he had ordered to be constructed to hang Mordechai, the image was clearly intended to represent Beche's execution on Colchester Abbey's own gallows. The execution scene appears in the distant background of an image that transforms Mordechai's triumph into that of the Henrician regime (Figure 3.1).[198]

Produced as a financial record of the lands and manors once belonging to the abbey, this copy of Leyden's original image also served as a piece of

Figure 3.1 Copy of Lucas van Leyden's 'Triumph of Mordechai', alluding to the execution of John Beche, last abbot of Colchester, and parade of officials through Colchester, c. 1540. London, British Library, Egerton MS 2164. © The British Library Board.

[198] BL, Egerton MS 2164.

Henrician polemic. The story of Haman had powerful allegorical potential: in 1529, the anonymous *Interlude of Godly Queen Hester* had played on parallels between Haman and Cardinal Wolsey, and between the persecuted Jews and the English clergy, especially monks, nuns, and friars.[199] Now inverted, this visual representation of the Henrician regime's triumph over monasticism functioned visually to reinforce the anti-monastic rhetoric that underpinned the Henrician assault on the religious houses. Accordingly, neither the process of suppression nor its material consequences are depicted in this image of the abbot of Colchester's execution, which focusses solely upon the triumph of truth over corruption. This was the crown's vision of the dissolution rendered in visual form, depicting victory over what it proclaimed to be Catholic error and superstition without portraying in significant detail the destructive, violent, and disruptive aspects of the process of suppression.

Of course, the dissolution of the monasteries was violent and destructive. This is apparent in a second image of the dissolution, which was produced a century after the Colchester manuscript. It belongs to the frontispiece of Dugdale's *Monasticon anglicanum* (Figure 3.2). The work of the Bohemian engraver Wenceslaus Hollar and probably completed to Dugdale's own design, the bottom-right panel depicted Henry VIII in classic Holbeinian mode, brandishing a sword in front of a crumbling religious house as the words *sic volo* ('as I will') fall from his lips.[200] Uniquely amongst contemporary images of both the suppression and its physical and material consequences, the title-page of the *Monasticon* thus depicts the act of destruction itself. Surrounding panels portray commitments made by Henry VIII's predecessors to the sanctity of church property.[201] Henry, it implies, has violated their vows. Reflecting Dugdale's preservationist stance on the remnants of medieval monasticism, a cartouche beside the depiction of the dissolution bears the warning from Ovid's *Metamorphoses* that 'a past age has things to offer which we should not despise'.[202] For Dugdale, remarkably, it was also important to preserve something of the religious orders who had inhabited the monasteries.

[199] Greg Walker, '"To speak before the king, it is no child's play": *Godly Queen Hester* in 1529', *Theta* 10 (2013), pp. 69–96 at pp. 69 and *passim*.
[200] See Margery Corbett, 'The title-page and illustrations to the *Monasticon Anglicanum*, 1655–73', *Antiquaries Journal* 67 (1987), pp. 102–10; Marion Roberts, *Dugdale and Hollar: History Illustrated* (Newark, DE, 2002), pp. 55–6; Alexandra Walsham, '"Like fragments of a shipwreck": printed images and religious antiquarianism in early modern England', in Michael Hunter (ed.), *Printed Images in Early Modern Britain: Essays in Interpretation* (Farnham, 2010), pp. 87–109 at p. 93. See also Margery Corbett and David Lightbown (eds.), *The Comely Frontispiece: The Emblematic Title-Page in England, 1550–1650* (London, 1979).
[201] Corbett, 'Title-page to the *Monasticon*', p. 104.   [202] Ibid., p. 109.

Figure 3.2 Wenceslaus Hollar, detail from the title-page of Roger Dodsworth and
William Dugdale, *Monasticon anglicanum*, vol. 1 (London, 1682 ed.), Christ's
College Library, Cambridge, F.16.2. By kind permission of the Master and Fellows
of Christ's College, Cambridge. Photograph courtesy of Caroline Vout.

The *Monasticon* thus depicts a series of monks and friars wearing the habits
characteristic of their various orders (Figure 3.3), prompting remembrance of
the personnel who had inhabited the monasteries as well as the buildings in
which they had lived and worked. When compared with the depiction of
Beche's execution, the various images in the *Monasticon* testify to a profound
shift in emphasis between 1540 and 1655, which further attests to the changing
priorities and proclivities of successive generations. Visual trends thus reflected
those evident in texts in ways that reinforce the idea that increasing temporal
distance on the events of 1536–40 helped to crystallise critical perspectives on
the early Reformation.[203]

However, these examples also beg the question of why there were so few
early modern depictions of the dissolution. This may be partly the product

---

[203] On this theme more generally, see Mark Rankin, 'The literary afterlife of Henry VIII, 1558–1625', in
Mark Rankin, Christopher Highley, and John N. King (eds.), *Henry VIII and his Afterlives:
Literature, Politics, and Art* (Cambridge, 2009), pp. 94–114 at pp. 105–6.

Figure 3.3 Wenceslaus Hollar, 'Ordinis Benedictini Monachus', plate from Roger Dodsworth and William Dugdale, *Monasticon anglicanum*, vol. 1 (London, 1682 ed.), Christ's College Library, Cambridge, F.16.2. By kind permission of the Master and Fellows of Christ's College, Cambridge. Photograph courtesy of Caroline Vout.

of a culture that had a difficult relationship with images. In a highly influential study, Patrick Collison argued that the drive to purge sacred spaces of 'superstitious' idols created societies that suffered from a severe aversion to visual imagery.[204] It is true, for example, that Lambarde's *Perambulation of Kent*, first published in the 1570s, was the product of

---

[204] Patrick Collinson, *The Birthpangs of Protestant England: Religious and Cultural Change in the Sixteenth and Seventeenth Centuries* (London and New York, 1988), p. 119. See also Patrick Collinson, *From Iconoclasm to Iconophobia: The Cultural Impact of the Second English Reformation*, The Stenton Lecture (Reading, 1986).

a moment that was not particularly conducive to the production of images. Depicting ruins pictorially risked undoing the iconoclastic good works of the early reformers, as well as resisting the divine will that sanctioned the dissolution. However, more recent scholarship has critiqued the comprehensiveness of the shift from a medieval culture of affective imagery to one of intense iconophobia in the course of the sixteenth century, suggesting that the historiographical tendency to overlook Protestant imagery is itself a product of early modern debates about images.[205] Tessa Watt has demonstrated the longevity of pre-Reformation imagery in cheap print, and the recent work of Tara Hamling, amongst others, has explored the processes of adaptation and reformation of the image that contributed to the development of a post-Reformation English religious visual culture.[206] As James Knapp has suggested, images also contributed to the formation of historical consciousness, as long as they conformed to the 'Protestant visual scheme' characteristic of works such as John Foxe's *Acts and Monuments*, which combined word and image to narrative effect, thereby undercutting 'any perception of value inherent in the visual'.[207]

Such images could function to commemorate the victories of the reformers. The engraved title-page of Gilbert Burnet's *History of the Reformation of the Church of England* (1681–3), for example, aligned iconoclasm with the establishment of the Church of England and alludes to the dissolution as a key episode in this campaign: beneath Henry VIII's feet and the tattered remains of papal supremacy is depicted a crumbling, dilapidated building reminiscent of other images of ruined abbeys (Figure 3.4).[208] Yet, as we noted in the previous chapter, the dissolution was too controversial to be the subject of a celebratory commemorative

---

[205] Roy Porter, 'Seeing the past', *P&P* 118 (1988), pp. 186–205 at p. 188. For an overview of recent historiographical trends, see Adam Morton, 'Coming of age? The image in early modern England', *Journal of Early Modern History* 15 (2011), pp. 435–57; Alexandra Walsham, 'Idols in the frontispiece? Illustrating religious books in the age of iconoclasm', in Feike Dietz, Adam Morton, Lien Roggen, Els Stronks, and Marc van Vaeck (eds.), *Illustrated Religious Texts in the North of Europe, 1500–1800* (Farnham, 2014), pp. 21–52.

[206] Tessa Watt, *Cheap Print and Popular Piety, 1550–1640* (Cambridge, 1991), ch. 4; Tara Hamling and Richard L. Williams, *Art Re-formed: Re-assessing the Impact of the Reformation on the Visual Arts* (Cambridge, 2007); Malcolm Jones, *The Print in Early Modern England: An Historical Oversight* (New Haven, CT, and London, 2010); David J. Davis, *Seeing Faith, Printing Pictures: Religious Identity during the English Reformation* (Leiden and Boston, MA, 2013). See also the essays in Hunter (ed.), *Printed Images*.

[207] James A. Knapp, *Illustrating the Past in Early Modern England: The Representation of History in Printed Books* (Aldershot, 2003), p. 146.

[208] Although Burnet praised the Henrician regime's assault on monastic corruption, his account of the dissolution more generally was somewhat ambiguous. See above, Ch. 2.

Figure 3.4 Robert White, title-page of Gilbert Burnet, *The History of the Reformation of the Church of England*, vol. 1 (London, 1679), Christ's College Library, Cambridge, F.17.11. By kind permission of the Master and Fellows of Christ's College, Cambridge. Photograph courtesy of Caroline Vout.

culture per se. Although the early reformers frequently conceptualised the suppression as a providential deliverance, its legacies were sufficiently ambiguous and ambivalent to discourage public remembrance. The dissolution may therefore provide a parallel to Judith Pollmann's recent study of the Beeldenstorm of 1566 in the southern Netherlands. Pollmann argues that the memory of iconoclasm tended to be highly selective and its agents anonymised in accordance with hegemonic political agendas, and thus depictions of the image breakers tended to be critical in nature.[209] The highly polemical quality of both Dugdale's image of Henry assaulting the monasteries and Burnet's title-page in which Henry looms above the ruins of Roman Catholicism is therefore a powerful visual manifestation of a mid-seventeenth century reflex to defy the oblivion enacted by previous generations. It was, in other words, a form of what has been called the 'art of iconoclasm'; these depictions 'evoke a past in which they existed intact, and they signal the transform-ations that led to their present altered state'.[210] Images had the potential, therefore, further to underline the temporal rupture with the medieval past, as well as the physical and material consequences of dissolution.

The process of depicting the dissolution was, of course, highly selective: like texts, images preserved a particular vision of the past for posterity. Of those antiquaries who sought to preserve ruins, some favoured depictions that captured their mutilated form, intensifying the textual language of loss and regret. At Eynsham, a former Benedictine monastery in Oxfordshire in 1657, Anthony Wood recorded that he was 'wonderfully strucken' by its crumbling ruins, which served to 'instruct the pensive beholder with an exemplary frailty'.[211] The sketch that he produced to accompany these comments depicts Eynsham in the ruinous state that had inspired such a strong sense of the vulnerability of the material past, compounded by the threat to physical and material antiquities that had been posed by civil war and renewed puritan iconoclasm (Figure 3.5).[212] In a view of all that remained of the west end of the abbey, Wood also attempted to delineate the spaces once occupied by the main body of the church and its north and south aisles, which had long since been razed to the ground.

An attempt to preserve what was left of Eynsham, Wood's image also anticipated later trends in the depiction of ruins: perched precariously atop the right-hand tower of the ruined façade, a figure stares out over the space once occupied by the abbey, prefiguring the picturesque tradition that emerged in the late seventeenth and eighteenth centuries by depicting

---

[209] Judith Pollmann, 'Iconoclasts anonymous: why did it take historians so long to identify the image-breakers of 1566?', *Low Countries Historical Review* 131 (2016), pp. 155–76.

[210] See Alexandra Walsham, 'The art of iconoclasm and the afterlife of the English Reformation', in Antoinina Bevan-Zlatar and Olga Timofeeva (eds.), *What Was an Image in Medieval and Early Modern England?*, Swiss Papers in English Language and Literature 34 (Tübingen, 2017), pp. 478–81. On the relationship between art and iconoclasm, see also Keith Thomas, 'Art and iconoclasm in early modern England', in Kenneth Fincham and Peter Lake (eds.), *Religious Politics in Post-Reformation England: Essays in Honour of Nicholas Tyacke* (Woodbridge, 2006), pp. 16–40; James Simpson, *Under the Hammer: Iconoclasm in the Anglo-American Tradition* (Oxford, 2010); Stacy Boldrick, Leslie Brubaker, and Richard Clay (eds.), *Striking Images, Iconoclasms Past and Present* (Farnham, 2013).

[211] Bodl., MS Wood E1, fol. 44r.   [212] Walsham, 'Fragments of a shipwreck', p. 92.

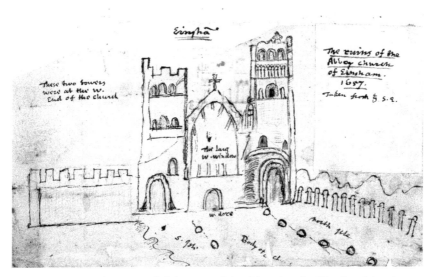

Figure 3.5 Anthony Wood, 'The ruins of the abbey church of Einsham' (1657),
Bodleian Libraries, University of Oxford, MS Wood E 1, fol. 45r.

a kind of dissolution tourism. Amongst these images was the etching made
by Hollar of the crumbling ruins of Newark Abbey in Surrey (Figure 3.6),
shown with two figures standing to the left of the structure, contemplating
its remains. The antiquary and engraver Francis Place made similar images
of ruined religious houses, including the fragments of Byland Abbey in
North Yorkshire, in which can be seen a solitary figure to the right hand of
the frame (Figure 3.7). The prospects of Yorkshire engraved by the
draughtsman William Lodge, depicting the ruins of both Kirkstall Abbey
and Fountains Abbey (Figures 3.8a and 3.8b), also reflect the emergence of
an embryonic cult of ruins, born – paradoxically – of the earlier Protestant
impulse to destroy the monastic past. The material fragments that testified
to the zeal of the early reformers had thus become the objects of a new kind
of Protestant reverence for the past.[213]

Other images took the creative enterprise of preservation one step further
by using the visual as a tool with which to resurrect the architectural glory
of the vanquished past. During his survey of Wiltshire, Aubrey delineated
a 'Prospect of Malmesbury' with, as the caption bears witness, the 'idea of

[213] On this idea see Woolf, *Social Circulation*, pp. 29, 194 and passim.

Figure 3.6 Wenceslaus Hollar, 'Newarcke Abby, in Surry' (?1652–77), British Museum, London, Q,6.91. © The Trustees of the British Museum.

Figure 3.7 Francis Place, 'Part of the Ruines of Byland Abbie' (?1647–1728), British Museum, London, 1850,0223.810. © The Trustees of the British Museum.

Figure 3.8a Detail of Kirkstall Abbey from William Lodge, 'The prospects of the two most remarkable towns in the north of England for the clothing trade, viz. Leeds... and Wakefield' (1680s), British Museum, London, Ii,1.24. © The Trustees of the British Museum.

Figure 3.8b Detail of Fountains Abbey from William Lodge, 'The prospects of the two most remarkable towns in the north of England for the clothing trade, viz. Leeds... and Wakefield' (1680s), British Museum, London, Ii,1.24. © The Trustees of the British Museum.

Figure 3.9 John Aubrey, 'The prospect of Malmesbury', Bodleian Libraries,
University of Oxford, MS Aubrey 3, fol. 35r.

the abbey entire' (Figure 3.9). The medieval structure, the converted
portion of which had captured the topographical imagination of antiquaries
from Camden to Dugdale, was thus revived in pictorial form in its entirety,
towering over the Wiltshire countryside. This, more so than Wood's efforts
at Eynsham, was a creative enterprise that entailed the invention of memory. Aubrey's prospect of Malmesbury was a type of visual fiction, which
compensated for the physical and material losses wrought by the dissolution. He also made a hand-drawn watercolour map of the parish, which
depicted the contemporary topography together with the residues of an
earlier monastic landscape. The map marked the abbey church alongside 'a
religious house ... dedicated to our ladie: for woemen', a hermitage, and
a chapel that had been turned into a 'dwelling house' (Figure 3.10).

    Aubrey claimed to have drawn the map 'by memorie and guesse', which he
justified because of its 'use for the antiquities sake'. He expressed a hope to
commission a proper map of the area but thought his rough sketch 'better than
none at all'.[214] Aubrey's was a rare intervention in a Protestant cartographic
culture that served to erase the memory of the dissolution by obliterating
ruined monasteries from maps.[215] Once again, the desire of some antiquaries to
document the past was drawn into conflict with the impulse to forget. These
new maps of the post-Reformation landscape gave spatial expression to new
post-Reformation community identities, rendered in a 'potent, visual form'.[216]
The famous maps drawn up by John Speed, for example, do not depict the

---

[214] Bodl., MS Aubrey 3, fol. 39r.   [215] Broadway, *No Historie so Meete*, p. 213.   [216] Ibid., p. 207.

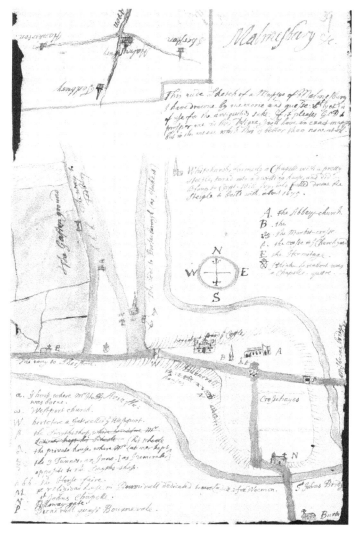

Figure 3.10 John Aubrey, map of Malmesbury, Bodleian Libraries, University of Oxford, MS Aubrey 3, fol. 39r.

monasteries, which he described as 'swallowed up by time', as though they were no longer a feature of the contemporary landscape.[217] In some ways, Aubrey's survey of Malmesbury thus had more in common with Catholic

[217] Quoted in Summit, 'Leland's "Itinerary"', pp. 173–4.

Figure 3.11 Sketch by John Aubrey of Malmesbury Abbey, Oxfordshire, copied 'out of the *Monasticon*', Bodleian Libraries, University of Oxford, MS Aubrey 3, fol. 47r.

cartography, which attempted to document and resurrect the 'rich and still not distant Catholic past', though it was born of a confessionally different species of the preservationist impulse.[218]

 These fictive images of Malmesbury offer a stark contrast with a third sketch of the abbey contained within Aubrey's sprawling manuscript on Wiltshire. Copied 'out of the *Monasticon*', this image depicted only the part of the monastery that had been converted into the parish church, appended to a crumbling wall cast in shadow to the right-hand edge of the page (Figure 3.11).[219] The original had been engraved by Daniel King, who, together with Hollar, produced the plates for the *Monasticon*, most of which depicted the converted churches and cathedrals catalogued in the text. His engraving of Malmesbury was entitled 'The North Prospect of the Conuentuall Church of

[218] Zur Shalev, *Sacred Words and Worlds: Geography, Religion, and Scholarship, 1550–1700* (Leiden and Boston, MA, 2012), p. 214.

[219] Bodl., MS Aubrey 3, fol. 47r.

Figure 3.12 Daniel King, 'The north prospect of the conventuall church of Malmesbury', plate from Roger Dodsworth and William Dugdale, *Monasticon anglicanum*, vol. 2 (London, 1661 ed.), Christ's College Library, Cambridge, F.16.3. By kind permission of the Master and Fellows of Christ's College, Cambridge. Photograph courtesy of Caroline Vout.

Malmesbury, that is to say of that [which] now remaynes' (Figure 3.12). The *Monasticon* is replete with images like that of Malmesbury, centred on conversions rather than ruins, including two renderings by King of the church at Crowland, Lincolnshire – the same structure admired by Dugdale during his and Ashmole's perambulation of the fens – which neglect the ruined elements of the structure in the far corner of the frame (Figure 3.13).[220] If this sits somewhat uneasily with Dugdale's lament for the past, it may be that the huge expense of the *Monasticon* required him to turn to the gentry for commissions. Costing between £3 and £5 per plate, Hollar and King's engravings were financed by individual subscribers, who were usually motivated to donate as a means of commemorating their ancestors or confirming their Laudian religious credentials.[221] One of the plates of Crowland was financed by Sir Thomas Blount; the second was contributed by Sir Wingfield Bodenham and bears the inscription *Pristini aevi Memoriae* ('in memory of

[220] Roberts, *Dugdale and Hollar*, pp. 46, 58; Walsham, 'Fragments of a shipwreck', pp. 99–100.
[221] Walsham, 'Fragments of a shipwreck', p. 94.

Figure 3.13 Daniel King, 'The west prospect of the church of Cro[w]land', plate
from Roger Dodsworth and William Dugdale, *Monasticon anglicanum*, vol. 2
(London, 1661 ed.), Christ's College Library, Cambridge, F.16.3. By kind permission
of the Master and Fellows of Christ's College, Cambridge. Photograph courtesy of
Caroline Vout.

the ancient time').[222] To some extent, these images blurred the boundary
between the preservationist impulse and the present-centric approach to the
physical and material landscape in the context of the ongoing threat to
antiquities and ecclesiastical property. But they served ultimately to play
down the monastic origins of the structures they depicted, promoting the
selective forgetting of the dissolution and the medieval past.

As with texts, this form of visual amnesia was connected to sites of secular
and domestic conversions, which uniformly favoured the reformed aspects

[222] Ibid., p. 99.

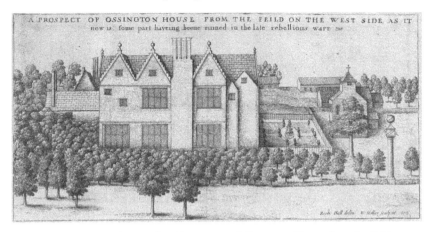

Figure 3.14 Wenceslaus Hollar, 'A prospect of Ossington House from the field on the west side as it now is, some part haveing beene ruined in the late rebellious warr' (1676), British Museum, London, 1862,0614.1434. © The Trustees of the British Museum.

of a building over its monastic heritage. Unlike ruins, these properties did appear on post-Reformation maps, and, although the vogue for country-house sketches and paintings was a development of the eighteenth and nineteenth centuries, the late seventeenth century witnessed the emergence of this trend for pictorial representation.[223] Images of converted properties evince not the visual culture of 'pastness' explored by Woolf but rather a visual culture of the present. Hollar's engraving of Ossington House in Nottinghamshire, once home to monks of the Cluniac order, depicted the hall 'from the feild [*sic*] on the west side as it now is' (Figure 3.14). The caption, printed in Robert Thoroton's *Antiquities of Nottinghamshire* (1676), mourned that 'some part' of the house had been 'ruined in the late rebellious warr' but erased all evidence of its earlier monastic past. Similarly, in the late 1650s, King produced a series of small engravings, etched by Hollar, of more than a hundred English manor houses.[224] These included an image of Nun Appleton House – a commemorative strategy to complement Marvell's

[223] On maps, see Broadway, *No Historie so Meete*, p. 213; Rhonda Lemke Sanford, *Maps and Memory in Early Modern England: A Sense of Place* (London, 2002). On country-house art, see also Heal and Holmes, *Gentry in England and Wales*, p. 303; Kari McBride, *Country House Discourse in Early Modern England: A Cultural Study of Landscape and Legitimacy* (Aldershot, 2001).

[224] These engravings appear to have been intended for a new edition of William Camden's *Britannia*, which never materialised. See Roberts, *Dugdale and Hollar*, p. 114.

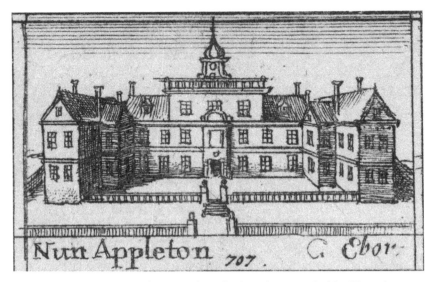

Figure 3.15 Engraving of Nun Appleton by Daniel King, etched by Wenceslaus Hollar (1650s), Bodleian Libraries, University of Oxford, MS Gough Maps 1.

verse – which depicts the country manor in its pristine converted state (Figure 3.15). The name of the property, inscribed beneath the images, is the only reminder of the priory out of which the hall had been constructed. By neglecting the medieval history of sites once occupied by the religious and applauding the virtues of their new lay owners through texts and images, a different breed of early modern antiquary contributed, consciously or otherwise, to the political project set in motion by the Henrician regime to downplay the extent of the rupture wrought by the dissolution.

King's engraving of Nun Appleton preserved a vision of the house at the height of its grandeur. Half a century later, the Leeds antiquary Ralph Thoresby, whose cousin had recently purchased the estate, journeyed 'to see the stately fabric erected by the late Thomas Lord Fairfax, the General, which has been a noble palace'. Yet upon arriving at the hall, he lamented that 'the house is in part ruinous, and being abundantly too large, is shortly to be demolished, and a more convenient one erected out of part of the materials'. Although Thoresby apparently failed to recognise the irony in his words, he expressed hope of seeing another house 'spring out of the ashes' of Nun Appleton, as 'did this [house] out of those of the old nunnery, of which nothing remains, save a few old grave stones'.[225] Thoresby's writing is thus also a reminder that the process of conversion was ongoing across the centuries, shaped by the fashions and fortunes of the English gentry for whom the dissolution was not the end of the life cycle but rather the beginning.

Conclusion: Nostalgia and Amnesia

The material remnants of the dissolution endured long after the passing of the generation that had experienced the suppression at first hand. Consequently, they could function as powerful reminders of the spoliation of the monasteries in the 1530s, but they also carried the potential to be re-inscribed with new memories or eroded of their mnemonic power by processes of conversion and adaptation. The capacity of ruins to act as *lieux de mémoire* has preoccupied scholars of early modern antiquarianism. Potent emblems of the material break with the past initiated by the Henrician regime, ruins became key battlegrounds where the memory of the dissolution was contested, and they inspired the emergence of a brand of antiquarianism marked by a powerful instinct to preserve the past. From this material, modern scholarship has inherited a vision of the dissolution as a moment of 'radical discontinuity' that fostered a sense of regret for a lost past.[226] As Margaret Aston once argued, 'the sight of destruction gives a powerful impulse to preserve and record, [and] is itself conducive to a nostalgia which can merge with concerns for history'.[227]

This chapter has suggested that we might interrogate this 'nostalgic' impulse more closely. The term 'nostalgia' was coined by a Swiss medical student, Johannes Hofer, in 1688 to describe the affliction that would now be called 'homesickness'. With its etymological roots in the Greek *nostos* ('return to native land') and *algos* ('suffering or grief'), it did not acquire its modern meaning of the sentimental or regretful longing for the past until the nineteenth century.[228] The 'nostalgic' antiquaries would not, then, have recognised the label that has been so influential in the historiography of antiquarianism. By use of the term, however, modern scholarship has sought to capture the profound sense of loss articulated by numerous

---

[225] *The Diary of Ralph Thoresby, F.R.S., Author of the Topography of Leeds (1677–1724)*, ed. Rev. Joseph Hunter, 2 vols. (London, 1830), ii, p. 74.
[226] Sweet, *Antiquaries*, p. 241.   [227] Aston, 'English ruins and English history', p. 336.
[228] On the etymology and history of the term 'nostalgia', see Jean Starobinksi, 'The idea of nostalgia', trans. William S. Kemp, *Diogenes* 54 (1966), pp. 84–103; Lowenthal, *Past Is a Foreign Country*, pp. 4–13; 'nostalgia, n.' *OED*, www.oed.com/view/Entry/128472. On early modern nostalgia, see Kristine Johanson (ed.), 'Approaches to early modern nostalgia', special issue of *Parergon* 33 (2016).

historians, antiquaries, and other commentators, which became such a prominent feature in early modern topography. It is indeed a profound irony that this 'nostalgia' for the monasteries was the creation of a generation that could not remember a time before the dissolution.

Nostalgia *avant la lettre* has been identified in various forms in accounts of the dissolution spanning the early modern period. Aston has identified nostalgic features in topographies dating from the Elizabethan period onwards, all of which treated monastic ruins as mnemonics to a profound break between past and present.[229] As Eamon Duffy and others have highlighted, this also found expression in a range of other genres, including the work of the anonymous Walsingham poet and Shakespeare's lament for those 'bare ruin'd choirs'.[230] Indeed, revisionist scholarship on the Reformation has typically borne the imprint of this kind of conservativism. Nostalgia for a lost past is the main theme, for example, of Duffy's exploration of Edwardian church inventories, and Shakespeare's 'bare ruined choirs' have been a powerful motif more generally in this literature.[231] Much of the literature on space, antiquarianism, and cultural memory in the early modern period has also adopted these tropes. R. W. Hoyle has suggested that in the wake of the dissolution there developed a 'nostalgia' for monastic hospitality.[232] Keith Thomas has argued that 'nostalgia for the monasteries' was 'particularly evident in Elizabethan England', contributing to the idea that the Tudor period was a formative moment in the development of the idea of the late medieval golden age. For Thomas, 'nostalgia for the past remained implicit in most social criticism: one attacked an evil by evoking an earlier age when it had not existed'.[233] With Aston, Alexandra Walsham and Susan Guinn-Chipman have also identified nostalgia amongst the distorting filters shaping contemporary perceptions of the landscape and its relationship with cultures of memory and history.[234]

The historiographical preoccupation with the nostalgia evoked by ruins has underpinned the argument that contemporary responses to monastic spaces and materials were central to the mnemonic culture of

[229] Aston, 'English ruins and English history'.   [230] Duffy, *Saints, Sacrilege, and Sedition*, ch. 11.
[231] Ibid., ch. 5. For an earlier example of this tendency see David Knowles, *Bare Ruined Choirs* (Cambridge, 1976), p. 319 and *passim*.
[232] R. W. Hoyle, 'The origins of the dissolution of the monasteries', *HJ* 38 (1995), pp. 275–305 at pp. 227–9.
[233] Keith Thomas, *The Perception of the Past in Early Modern England*, The Creighton Trust Lecture (London, 1983), pp. 14, 17.
[234] Walsham, *Reformation of the Landscape*, pp. 281–2; Guinn-Chipman, *Religious Space*, p. 123.

early modern England and especially to emergent critiques of the dissolution. Architectural survival has, in this context, been viewed as an act of resistance.[235] Yet to reduce the memory of the dissolution to ruins and to remembrance as a challenge to the Henrician orthodoxy is to neglect the wider spatial and material implications of the suppression and the role of other types of former monastic sites in the project to remember – and also the project to forget – the rupture of the 1530s. Few of the so-called 'nostalgic' antiquaries demonstrated the same lament for converted churches that they made for ruined monasteries. More significantly, a number of early modern antiquaries writing within parameters of the genealogical historical culture promoted by the seventeenth-century gentry favoured a present-centric mode that deployed the dissolution as a marker of time in the upswing of their fortunes, whilst simultaneously perpetuating Henrician narratives of monastic corruption and the expediency of the suppression. Neither Carew nor Gerard, Westcote nor Denton fit the model of the antiquary notoriously lambasted by John Earle in his *Micro-cosmographie* (1628) as one afflicted by 'that unnatural disease to be enamored of old age and wrinckles'. Though he 'is of our religion, because we say it is most ancient', Earle continued, 'yet a broken statue would almost make him an Idolator' and he would travel forty miles or more to see a 'ruined Abbey'.[236] Earle, then, identified contemporary antiquarianism with a preoccupation with ruins that has long continued to inflect its modern historiography and therefore of our understanding of the spatial and material dimensions of the afterlives of the dissolution.

The conversion of religious houses into churches, cathedrals, and country houses quite literally involved processes of effacing and adapting the material memory of monasticism, and those topographies that described and depicted these new structures thereby contributed, through silence, absence, and omission, to a post-dissolution culture of amnesia. Seventeenth-century England, like seventeenth-century antiquarianism, was not merely or consistently 'nostalgic' for a world before the Reformation. For Aubrey, Wood, Dugdale, and their peers, the fact that many things had been 'irrecoverably lost' at the dissolution proved

---

[235] This idea underpins Harris, 'Greatest blow to antiquities'; Guinn-Chipman, *Religious Space*. More generally see Sarah Tarlow, 'Reformation and transformation: what happened to Catholic things in a Protestant world?' in Gaimster and Gilchrist (eds.), *Archaeology of the Reformation*, pp. 108–21, who also thinks in terms of resistance and adaptation.

[236] John Earle, *Micro-cosmographie, or, a peece of the world discovered in essayes and characters* (London, 1628), sigs. Cv–C2r.

a source of profound regret, but topography was also a genre in which senses of loss could converge with gain, past with present, and remembering with forgetting. Antiquarian writing has offered a microcosm of the embattled cultures of remembrance and oblivion that shaped the afterlives of the dissolution. However, the memory of the dissolution also had wider resonance for local communities, for whom the preservation and conversion of former monastic property, and the spectre of sacrilege this raised, were profoundly important. It is these local and oral memory cultures to which the final chapter now turns.

CHAPTER 4

'Many Pretty Odd Tales'
Monks, Monasteries, and the Sin of Sacrilege in Local Tradition

For most of those who witnessed the dissolution of the monasteries, the national scale of the destruction would have been almost unimaginable. Unlike the Henrician commissioners, who travelled the length and breadth of the country surveying the religious houses, or the itinerant antiquaries who followed in their wake, the majority of people experienced the dissolution as a distinctly local phenomenon. Not only did this institutional break with the past irrevocably alter local topographies, by creating ruins out of the religious houses or transforming and adapting them for new purposes, it was also profoundly disruptive to patterns of everyday life. Before the suppression, monasticism had been 'at the heart of medieval life and culture'.[1] The religious orders were possessed of more than just spiritual authority; they were landlords and employers and a vital source of social relief, dispensed in the form of both charity and hospitality.[2] Principal amongst the reasons why the dissolution was remembered as a moment of profound rupture, therefore, was its impact on different spheres of everyday life: institutional, religious, social, economic. The experience of this rupture in local communities, as well as the long endurance of many former monastic sites, gave rise to geographically and regionally specific narratives of dissolution. These traditions contributed to the formation of potent local and familial memories of the suppression, which interacted with and evolved alongside the larger memory cultures we have explored in the preceding chapters.

This chapter interrogates the local dimensions of the memory of the dissolution, exploring the diverse variety of traditions about monks and

---

[1] Martin Heale, *Monasticism in Late Medieval England, c. 1300–1535* (Manchester, 2009), p. 1 and *passim*.
[2] See also Benjamin Thompson, 'Monasteries, society, and reform in late medieval England', in James G. Clark (ed.), *The Religious Orders in Pre-Reformation England* (Woodbridge, 2002), pp. 165–96 at p. 189 and, on the wider European context, see Emilia Jamroziak and Janet Burton (eds.), *Religious and Laity in Western Europe, 1000–1400: Interaction, Negotiation, and Power* (Turnhout, 2006).

191

monasteries that emerged in the decades and centuries after 1540. 'Tradition', in this context, is not an entirely unproblematic concept. In the early modern period, the term was religiously inflected and laden with negative associations of backwardness and superstition. 'Unwritten tradition' was frequently invoked by Protestant polemicists as a contrast to the authority of scripture.[3] One corollary of this tendency in Reformation debate was that oral culture came inevitably to be conflated with Catholicism, including traditions passed down through monastic communities.[4] A common formulation in Protestant writing suggested that stories that circulated orally were the inventions and fabrications of the 'mad merry Friers, and lustie Abbey-lubbers' of medieval England.[5] For the same reason that oral culture was so often equated with Catholic traditions, Protestantism has enjoyed an enduring association with the advent of print culture.[6] However, as recent scholarship has revealed, contemporary anti-Catholic polemic has long concealed the ways in which the English Reformation also served to generate and reinvigorate oral and local traditions.[7] This chapter argues that the dissolution was one such episode that inspired a wealth of stories about the past. Broadly conceived as a set of inherited beliefs about the past, tradition provides an illuminating lens through which to explore the varied and complex afterlives of the dissolution in local communities.

These local narratives did not, of course, evolve in a political vacuum. Certain ways of remembering the dissolution were structured by authority. In the previous chapter, we noted that the legal and financial transformation wrought by the dissolution had produced clear winners as well as losers, and that many contemporaries had vested interests in the revolution in land ownership that emerged as one of its critical consequences. In this context, it is unsurprising to see the memory of the dissolution revived in

---

[3] Peter Marshall, 'The debate over "unwritten verities" in early Reformation England', in Bruce Gordon (ed.), *Protestant History and Identity in Sixteenth-Century Europe: Volume 1, The Medieval Inheritance* (Aldershot, 1996), pp. 60–77. For contemporary uses see the definition of 'tradition, n.' in the *OED*, www.oed.com/view/Entry/204302. The older historiography of 'tradition' also inherited some of the problems inherent in these terms: see especially Eric Hobsbawm and Terence Ranger (eds.), *The Invention of Tradition* (Cambridge, 1938).

[4] Alison Shell, *Oral Culture and Catholicism in Early Modern England* (Cambridge, 2007).

[5] J[ohn] H[arvey], *A discoursive probleme concerning prophesies* (London, 1588), p. 69.

[6] See, for example, Elizabeth L. Eisenstein's influential study, *The Printing Press as an Agent of Change*, 2 vols. (Cambridge, 1979).

[7] Ronald Hutton, 'The English Reformation and the evidence of folklore', *P&P* 148 (1995), pp. 89–116; Alexandra Walsham, *The Reformation of the Landscape: Religion, Identity, and Memory in Early Modern Britain and Ireland* (Oxford, 2011), esp. ch. 7; Alexandra Walsham, 'Reformed folklore? Cautionary tales and oral tradition in early modern England', in Adam Fox and Daniel Woolf (eds.), *The Spoken Word: Oral Culture in Britain, 1500–1800* (Manchester, 2002), pp. 173–95.

legal cases connected to former monastic land and property across the early modern period. In other cases, as Andy Wood's important work on popular memory has revealed, legal depositions reveal the subtle ways in which individuals' memories of the dissolution contested the state-sponsored vision of financial gain and growth by drawing upon narratives of socio-economic decline.[8] This chapter begins by examining the depositions used by Wood and others to interrogate the afterlives of the dissolution. It suggests that thinking about the domains where remembering took place and the sources in which recollections were recorded is significant for thinking about the transmission of knowledge about the dissolution. In particular, it suggests that religion is a striking lacuna in these sources. This is testament, in one sense, to the state's success in prioritising the legal and financial dimensions of the dissolution and downplaying many of its wider, more problematic, and controversial consequences. It is also a product of the kinds of testimony that were required in legal settings.

One of the aims of this chapter is to open up the potential of a different type of source, in the form of the traces of local tradition preserved in antiquarian writing. The previous chapter relied upon the evidence of antiquarian texts and images as indicative of the wider relationship between space and memory. Here, we will re-examine this diverse body of material from a different angle and read it against the grain with a view to recovering the local memories encountered by antiquaries, who served as midwives of local and oral tradition. This approach is not without challenges, namely that these memories have been refracted through the world view of their recorders. Nevertheless, it has the potential to shed light on aspects both of the dissolution and of antiquarianism which have hitherto been overlooked. A second goal of this chapter is to place the suppression of the monasteries – and the wider Reformation – at the heart of early modern historical culture. Through the work of Keith Thomas, Adam Fox, and Daniel Woolf, it has become clear that knowledge about the past was articulated and circulated in ways that cut across social divisions and the porous boundaries between interdependent cultures of orality and literacy.[9] However, there has yet to be sustained attention paid to the role of religion and the Reformation in shaping the historical culture and

---

[8] Andy Wood, *The Memory of the People: Custom and Popular Senses of the Past in Early Modern England* (Oxford, 2013), ch. 1.

[9] Keith Thomas, *The Perception of the Past in Early Modern England*, The Creighton Trust Lecture (London, 1983); Adam Fox, *Oral and Literate Culture in England, 1500–1700* (Oxford, 2000), esp. ch. 4; D. R. Woolf, 'The "common voice": history, folklore, and oral tradition in early modern England', *P&P* 120 (1988), pp. 26–52.

consciousness described in this literature. The dissolution offers a powerful case study with which to interrogate these issues. In particular, this chapter suggests that the spectre of sacrilege exerted a critical influence over local memories of the dissolution. As we shall see, anxieties about sacrilege were expressed in various ways and forms, all of which suggest that this concept has the potential to unlock the religious dimensions of the long afterlives of the dissolution in parishes, towns, and villages.

The final aim of this chapter is to underline the vibrancy and longevity of local memory cultures in early modern England. It draws upon a series of case studies that are specific to certain places and communities, but which are also emblematic of wider themes in the long afterlives of the dissolution: financial gain, socio-economic decline, religious rupture, the importance of ex-monastic sites, and the interaction between state authority and the local population. In doing so, it sheds further light on an observation made in Chapter Two, that this was an episode that acquired much of its significance and status as an historical event in critical perspective. As we shall see, this was true at the local level as well as upon the national stage. It was also in light of this evolving critique of the dissolution that, by 1700, the attempts of the Henrician regime to limit and shape discourse on the dissolution in the 1530s and 1540s were finally beginning to be exposed.

Testimonies of Dissolution

Legal testimony, as historians have long recognised, offers a powerful insight into everyday life and the perspectives of ordinary people as recounted in their own words, or at least as recorded in the transcriptions set down by court officials.[10] In an important and suggestive study, Andy Wood has approached these documents as repositories of popular memory, in which deponents recalled information about the past as a means of settling disputes in the present.[11] We have already encountered one striking example of how legal testimony could be used to confront and contest the Henrician regime's vision of the dissolution. In Chapter 1, we examined the deposition of Robert Aske, leader of the Pilgrimage of Grace, a rising

---

[10] On the value of depositions see, for example, Bernard Capp, *When Gossips Meet: Women, Family, and Neighbourhood in Early Modern England* (Oxford, 2004); Malcolm Gaskill, 'Reporting murder: fiction in the archives in early modern England', *Social History* 23 (1998), pp. 1–30; Laura Gowing, 'Gender and the language of insult in early modern London', *History Workshop Journal* 35 (1993), pp. 1–21.

[11] Wood, *The Memory of the People*, pp. 33–5 and *passim*.

predicated upon local concerns about the consequences of the suppression of religious houses in Yorkshire. In his testimony, Aske made the powerful, if somewhat pre-emptive, statement that the world had been a better place 'when the . . . abbeys st[oo]d'. He also argued that in the communities at the centre of the revolt, local people had long been 'well s[uccour]ed by abbeys', which provided them with 'worldly refresshing in their bodies' as well as a source of 'spirituall refuge'.[12] Aske thus testified to what he perceived to be the catastrophic consequences of the dissolution in the localities, even at a time when the long process of suppression and spoliation was far from over. Aske's evidence offers a particularly clear example of how the dissolution was contested in the 1530s.

Depositions have also proven fertile ground for studying different degrees of collaboration in local communities, and they testify to the success of the Henrician regime in making the dissolution primarily an issue of property, wealth, and material gain, as well as the ways in which economic and religious interests could intersect and align. As Ethan Shagan has demonstrated in his study of the spoliation of Hailes Abbey, Gloucestershire, depositions taken in the wake of the looting attest not only to the huge number and variety of goods, large and small, removed from the abbey, but also to the range of motives displayed by participants from across the social spectrum. As we noted in Chapter 1, some had evangelical leanings; others seem to have acted in order to preserve devotional objects in the hope that Henrician religious policy could be reversed. The majority, as Shagan demonstrates, fell into neither category. Rather, having internalised the debates surrounding the early Reformation, they had come to think that it was right and appropriate to confiscate church goods, as materials that belonged not to the religious orders but to the local community.[13] The evidence of those who participated in the spoliation of Hailes is, therefore, highly suggestive of the success of the Henrician project (especially after 1539) to restrict discourse on the dissolution primarily to questions of land ownership and the reuse of monastic wealth, at least in theory, for the support and maintenance of the Church.[14]

As the decades wore on, the transformation in land and property was one aspect of the dissolution that could not be forgotten – although, as we shall see, some of the occupants of former monastic buildings might have

---

[12] Reproduced in Mary Bateson, 'Aske's examination', *English Historical Review* 5 (1890), pp. 550–74 at p. 561. On Aske and the Pilgrimage of Grace, see R. W. Hoyle, *The Pilgrimage of Grace and the Politics of the 1530s* (Oxford, 2001) and above, Ch. 1.
[13] Ethan H. Shagan, *Popular Politics and the English Reformation* (Cambridge, 2003), ch. 5.
[14] See above, Ch. 1.

wished to do so. On a national scale, it was a subject of interest amongst political philosophers and commentators – not least James Harrington, who singled out the dissolution as a critical step on the road to civil war in the 1640s, precisely because it had entailed the translation of so much wealth from church to crown to nobility, tipping the 'ballance of the Common-wealth' too far towards the 'Popular party' and thereby fundamentally weakening the monarchy.[15] As with the histories of the Reformation that we examined in Chapter 2, it is important to note here that as a transformation of property, the dissolution possessed considerable explanatory power. Not only was it an originary moment in the English Reformation, for Harrington it had also engendered a redistribution of power that paved the way for the violent upheavals of the mid-seventeenth century.[16] More generally, on the local level, the memory of the dissolution had rather more mundane, though by no means unimportant, uses. There were certain contexts in which early modern people were compelled to remember the world before the Reformation – in courtrooms, for example, in the course of disputes over boundaries or ownership or the payment of tithes, a form of taxation traditionally levied upon the laity to support the clergy. In this context, monastic history was not necessarily something to be erased or sanitised, but rather something that was recalled in specific ways that served a purpose in the present.

In St Alban's, Hertfordshire, in 1549, a quarrel arose over the ownership of tithes that had formerly belonged to the infirmary of St Alban's Abbey. During the proceedings, evidence was taken from members of the community who could remember the abbey before dissolution. In early modern England, age carried with it the authority of long memory.[17] Many of those who gave depositions were former lay servants of St Alban's. Edmund Pytcheley, aged eighty-three, deposed that he knew the monasteries 'before the dissolution therof' and was 'servant in the same late monastery to th'abbot for the time being viz. the brewer by the space of xv yeres or thereabowtes'.[18] Like another abbey servant, John Stockwell, aged seventy-four, Pytcheley could remember the existence of the

---

[15] James Harrington, *The common-wealth of Oceana* (London, 1656), esp. pp. 40–1.
[16] See also J. G. A. Pocock, 'Machiavelli, Harrington, and English political ideologies in the eighteenth century', *William and Mary Quarterly* 22 (1965), pp. 549–83 at p. 557; Alan Cromartie, 'Harringtonian virtue: Harrington, Machiavelli, and the method of the *Moment*', *HJ* 41 (1998), pp. 987–1009 at p. 987.
[17] Keith Thomas, 'Age and Authority in Early Modern England', The Raleigh Lecture, *Proceedings of the British Academy* 62 (1976), pp. 205–48. See also Fox, *Oral and Literate Culture*, p. 222.
[18] Hertford, Hertfordshire Archives and Local Studies, ASA 8/2, fol. 42v. I am grateful to Arnold Hunt for this reference.

infirmary and confirmed that the tithes went 'towards the fynding and mayntenance of the same office, because the same aged and sick monkes shoulde not be sociate amonge the reste of the monckes'.[19] Legal evidence of this kind attests to how the memories of those who had witnessed the dissolution were recalled to serve the needs of the present in local communities – in this case, to establish the ownership of tithes. It is striking that none of the some forty monks who had resided at St Alban's was called to testify in a case that took place only ten years after the suppression of the abbey. At the same time, it is an important reminder that it was not only the religious orders who lost their livelihoods as a result of the dissolution. If Pytcheley or Stockwell felt they had suffered, however, this was not apparent in their testimony: the evidence they provided was dictated by the remit of the tithes case being heard before the court. Instead, it sheds light on the significance of the financial transformation wrought by the suppression of religious houses and on the long legal afterlives of the dissolution, which stretched across the sixteenth century and beyond.

Whilst the ex-religious did not testify in St Alban's, this was not always true of legal cases in which an intimate knowledge of the religious houses was required. During another dispute over tithes in Canterbury in 1562, several former monks as well as monastic servants of St Augustine's Abbey were obliged to appear before the courts at Westminster. More than twenty-five years had passed since the dissolution of the abbey, but those called to testify could all remember a time before the Reformation. One of the deponents was seventy-five-year-old John Wildbore, alias Dygon, who had once lived as a monk at St Augustine's. Asked to recall the customary ownership of the tithes, Wildbore testified that 'the same parsonage [St Paul's] was evir during his tyme that he was monke there belonging unto the said monasterye of Sainte Awstens'.[20] This example is especially striking because it offers a rare insight into the memory of the ex-religious. We have previously noted the paradox that the religious orders were the group most affected by the dissolution but least represented in the surviving documentary record. Yet legal cases, such as that of the St Augustine's tithes, provided some ex-religious with an outlet for their memories of the dissolution.[21] These were specific recollections, however, prized for their

---

[19] Ibid., fol. 49v.
[20] CCA, DCc ChAnt/C/1059. Further depositions connected to the case can be found in CCA, DCc ChAnt/C/1060.
[21] For some other ways of exploring the experiences of the religious see Mary C. Erler, *Reading and Writing During the Dissolution: Monks, Friars, and Nuns, 1530–1558* (Cambridge, 2013) and above, Ch. 1.

implications for the present – and there is nothing of Wildbore's past life as a monk or his experience (positive or negative) of the religious rupture of the dissolution in his deposition.

As this example suggests, depositions taken in connection with economic disputes or imperatives privileged certain types of response. They were shaped by the questions asked of the deponents and were coloured and inflected by the concerns of the court and refracted through the pens of its clerks. A few years after the tithe dispute at St Augustine's, a similar case arose concerning customary rights of way through the old Canterbury Blackfriars. One witness, George Hovenden, parson of Harrietsham, was called upon to offer the memories he had inherited from his family, long-time residents in the city. Asked whether there was a precedent for a thoroughfare running through the former priory, he simply confirmed that a public path had indeed cut through the site 'in the pryoreys tyme'.[22] Once again, it seems unlikely that this was the extent of the knowledge the Hovenden family possessed about the Blackfriars, but it was the information that mattered as the city continued to manage the practical and logistical consequences of the dissolution. Evidence of this kind therefore testifies to the significance of the economic aspects of dissolution in the decades after 1540. Legal cases constantly revived the memory of the transformation in property ownership engendered by the fall of the monasteries. In doing so, they indirectly but repeatedly lent weight to the Tudor government's argument that the dissolution itself had been little more than a land transfer.

The capacity of state institutions to perpetuate the Henrician vision of the dissolution, even inadvertently, was therefore substantial. However, deponents also had some agency in what they chose to divulge or conceal. Silences and absences in the archival record are difficult to interpret, but it seems unlikely, for example, that John Wildbore's recollections of St Augustine's present the true limits of his memory.[23] Like the anonymous Franciscan chronicler we encountered in Chapter 2, his silence may reflect feelings of trauma or guilt associated with the events of the 1530s. But it might also attest to his desire to avoid incriminating himself by revealing his regret for the passing of the monastic past and the loss of his former vocation in public and before officials of the Elizabethan state. In contrast to Robert Aske, who used his deposition as a platform for the Pilgrimage

[22] CCA, CCA-CC-L/16, fol. 40.
[23] On interpreting archival silence, see Rodney G. S. Carter, 'Of things said and unsaid: power, archival silences, and power in silence', *Archivaria* 61 (2006), pp. 215–33.

rebels, Wildbore would have had little to gain from re-living and lamenting his life in holy orders. Building on Natalie Zemon Davis's highly suggestive and influential study, *Fiction in the Archives* (1987), Arnold Hunt has powerfully argued that we must pay greater attention to 'narratives and story-telling' in legal depositions.[24] The stories told in depositions tend, unsurprisingly, to align more closely with the state-sponsored vision of the dissolution than the understanding of this episode as a moment of profound and traumatic rupture that we have encountered in other sources written by critics of the Henrician regime from across the confessional spectrum. Some things it was perhaps more prudent to forget – or, at least, more prudent not to recollect publicly, in front not only of crown officials but also other members of the local community.

These examples reflect a wider culture in which custom constituted 'a distinct way of remembering, embedding memory in genres of speech and writing and providing it with organisational focus and legal validation'.[25] It was a mechanism through which knowledge of the past was made usable in the present, as a framework for establishing local rights and privileges and as a tool of political and social contestation. In regard to the latter, it is not only the silences in these records that are significant; it is sometimes possible to glean something of a more conservative, nostalgic mode of remembering the dissolution from depositions. Andy Wood's important and exhaustive research into legal sources as repositories of customary memory has suggested not only that the dissolution was a landmark moment in the historical consciousness of many early modern individuals and communities but also that the memory of the dissolution was shaped by a pervasive sense that living standards had declined since the Reformation. For example, Wood explores how, in 1606, at a time when the dissolution was still – just – within the limits of living memory, eighty-two-year-old George Hinton and 104-year-old Thomas Cowper were called to testify to the boundaries of the estates that had formerly belonged to Rievaulx Abbey in North Yorkshire, once one of the largest Cistercian monasteries in the country. Their depositions suggest that the dissolution had profoundly shaped their perceptions of both time and space. Hinton, in a striking echo of his fellow Yorkshireman, Robert Aske, described the suppression as a breach with an indeterminate past which he called 'abb[e]y

---

[24] Natalie Zemon Davies, *Fiction in the Archives: Pardon Tales and Their Tellers in Sixteenth-Century France* (Stanford, CA, 1987); Arnold Hunt, 'Recovering speech acts', in Andrew Hadfield, Matthew Dimmock, and Abigail Shinn (eds.), *The Ashgate Research Companion to Popular Culture in Early Modern England* (Farnham, 2014), pp. 13–30 at p. 22.

[25] Wood, *Memory of the People*, p. 15.

time'.[26] Both men also associated Rievaulx's monastic past principally with a time before enclosure had carved up the landscape.[27] This concern with the topography of Rievaulx suggests that, like aspects of the antiquarian tradition examined in the previous chapter, these local memories had pronounced spatial and material dimensions, which were also reinforced and sustained by traditional rituals and customs such as beating the bounds.[28]

If some of the details recalled by deponents were incidental to the legal cases in question, this only underlines the sense in which the suppression had come to loom large in local memory as a moment of change and decline. In 1605, eighty-year-old Allice Hall remembered before the Court of Exchequer that as a child she 'did allwaies resort to the Abbye & carrye butter & eggs and other thinges thither to sell'.[29] Elsewhere, in the course of recalling how the prior of Tynemouth had perambulated the boundaries of the Northumberland village of Benwell, deponents remembered the benefits of monastic lordship and lamented the economic degradation that had occurred in the decades since the dissolution.[30] This reflects the widespread perception in early modern England that the pre-dissolution past was a 'golden age' of medieval 'merry England'.[31] For Wood, comments such as these are indicative of a wider memory culture in which a 'sense of changing times was strengthened by the Reformation', and the advance of Protestantism and economic decline were inextricably intertwined.[32] He argues that insofar as this evidence 'points towards the long endurance of the local memories of medieval monasticism', it was the 'economic affairs' of the religious houses that loomed especially large in local memory as opposed to 'matters of doctrine'.[33]

Depositions thus render it possible to see how an idea that we have encountered previously in various forms of antiquarian writing, namely that the dissolution was closely associated with a pervasive sense of socio-economic decline, also found wider expression in local and oral cultures. It is in this broader context that we should view perspectives like that of John

[26] Quoted in ibid., p. 91.   [27] Ibid., p. 69.
[28] On this ritual, see Ronald Hutton, *The Rise and Fall of Merry England: The Ritual Year, 1400–1700* (Oxford, 1994), p. 247; Steve Hindle, 'Beating the bounds of the parish: order, memory and identity in the English local community, c. 1500–1700', in Michael J. Halvorson and Karen E. Spierling (eds.), *Defining Community in Early Modern Europe* (Aldershot, 2008), pp. 205–27; Nicola Whyte, *Inhabiting the Landscape: Place, Custom and Memory, 1500–1800* (Oxford, 2009), ch. 5; Wood, *Memory of the People*, pp. 200–9.
[29] Quoted in Wood, *Memory of the People*, p. 83.   [30] Ibid., p. 82.
[31] Thomas, *Perception of the Past*, pp. 13, 18.   [32] Wood, *Memory of the People*, p. 67.
[33] Ibid., p. 81.

Stow, the Elizabethan topographer and chronicler, who also remembered the suppression as a rupture with the plentiful, prosperous world of his childhood. Thus, in the London ward of Aldgate, Stow had been inspired to recall that 'Neere adjoyning to this Abby ... was sometime a Farme belonging to the said Nunrie, at the which Farme, I my selfe (in my youth) have fetched many a halfe-penny worthe of milke, and never had lesse than three ale pintes for a half penny in the Summer'.[34] Some forms of Protestant polemic also help to shed light on the prevalence and potency of this conservative perspective in local communities, suggesting that the testimonies offered by individuals in court cases reflected the wider sentiments of their communities. The Elizabethan pamphleteer and playwright Thomas Nashe, for example, noted a local commonplace in Yarmouth, Norfolk, that the present age was no longer 'as plentifull a world as when Abbies stood', at which time, the people said, they 'should have twentie egges a pennie'.[35] Evidence such as this therefore suggests that the recollections of eyewitnesses found wider purchase in their communities, fostering an inherited memory of the dissolution as a moment of decline.

In these genres, much more so than in depositions, there is sometimes also a hint of something else underpinning this nostalgia for the pre-Reformation world – albeit we often have to read sources creatively to see it. In his *Apologie; or, defence of our dayes* (1589), the Lincolnshire cleric Francis Trigge recorded a commonplace that disturbed him greatly. His parishioners complained that 'these our dayes are worse than the former, that our times are unhappie & miserable: and that the former daies, the dayes of our fathers were happie & verie blessed, verie calme, and prosperous'.[36] The specific grievances that Trigge identified were a blend of socio-economic concerns and, strikingly, religious anxieties. 'Many do lament the pulling downe of Abbayes', he wrote mournfully, 'they say it was never merie world since':[37]

> What shall I repeat or rippe up here, the cutting downe of woods, the spoyling of vestments & coapes, the breaking of Images, the expulsion of Monkes & Nunnes, the ransaking of those rich goodly houses, which things many complaine of, grieve very many to remember at the[ir] hearts.[38]

---

[34] John Stow, *The survey of London: contayning the originall, increase, modern estate, and government of that city, methodically set downe* (London, 1633), p. 118.

[35] R. B. McKerrow (ed.), *The Works of Thomas Nashe*, 5 vols. (Oxford, 1958), iii, p. 171.

[36] Francis Trigge, *An apologie, or defence of our dayes, against the vaine murmurings & complaints of manie wherein is plainly proved, that our dayes are more happie & blessed than the dayes of our forefathers* (London, 1589), sig. A4r.

[37] Ibid., sig. B4v.

[38] Ibid., sig. C2r. On Trigge's comments as a reflection of widespread regret for the lost medieval past, see Thomas, *Perception of the Past*, pp. 17–18.

Trigge himself was deeply critical of this nostalgic tendency, and especially of the suggestion that the Reformation had led to the deterioration of English society. He recorded these complaints in order to dismantle them, but in doing so also preserved in print their strength and ubiquity in his Lincolnshire community.

The echoes of this oral culture represent another form of testimony, taken in a different context to legal depositions, but no less illuminating as a source for local tradition. In particular, looking to the traces of this memory culture in antiquarian or polemical sources reveals the religious dimensions of the afterlives of the dissolution, which are largely absent from reports of legal proceedings. That is not to say that local opinion ran entirely counter to the official vision of the dissolution. Trigge heartily approved of another local commonplace that perpetuated the rhetoric of monastic corruption, profligacy, and iniquity familiar from Henrician polemic. 'The fatnesse and haughtinesse, and idlenesse of Monkes, came into a Proverbe amongst all men', he wrote, 'in so much, that idle persons were called Abbey lubbers: fatt men were saide to have Abbots faces.'[39] This striking passage, which raises the intriguing suggestion that the Reformation had changed how people perceived particular physical features and bodily types, also testifies to the complex religious inheritance of the dissolution in local communities. As Trigge's text suggests, jokes and sayings about monastic corruption were seemingly compatible with regret for the violence and iconoclasm with which the dissolution had been conducted. Whilst pervasive narratives of monastic corruption had thoroughly blackened the reputation of the religious orders, the structures in which they had lived and prayed were often, as we saw in the previous chapter, associated with the piety and munificence of their lay benefactors. Monastic structures therefore occupied a more complex and ambiguous place in local memory than did the monks, nuns, and friars who had once occupied them. This was one way in which contemporaries were able to make sense of an event that they viewed both as central to the successes of the early Reformation and an emblem of the failings and missteps of the first generation of English Protestants.

The remainder of this chapter is devoted to interrogating and exploring the paradox that early modern people remembered the dissolution as both a triumph and a calamity and to connecting the afterlives of ex-monastic property with the underlying religious anxieties and concerns displayed in texts such as Trigge's. Of course, these sources present particular challenges

---

[39] Trigge, *Apologie*, p. 9.

as evidence of oral and local tradition, but they nevertheless help to open up the local memory of the dissolution, and especially its religious dimensions. Like legal records, antiquarian writing can also be used to unearth geographically specific narratives of the dissolution, by contrast with the larger national narratives we have examined in previous chapters. In exploring these traditions, we are able to dig deeper into the relationship between the dissolution and contemporary perceptions of time, space, and the English Reformation.

Local Narratives and Chronologies

Like the learned historical culture that we explored previously, local memories of the dissolution also had pronounced temporal dimensions. We have already seen how people at different levels of the social spectrum thought about the dissolution as a rupture between past and present. It is also the case that individual communities developed regionally specific narratives of dissolution, which reflected the particular experiences of people in these localities. These narratives shared with national histories an overarching concern to account for the transition from a world with monasteries to a world without. However, they were coloured and inflected by anecdotal traditions embedded in local memory and inherited across the generations by means of oral circulation as well as interaction with textual culture, in ways that cut across social and educational boundaries. Our access to these traditions is, of course, possible only via the texts in which they were preserved and perpetuated. This is a problem to which we shall return; however, the examples that follow concern antiquaries who were themselves members of the community they sought to capture in pen and ink. Local tradition was not simply the preserve of the illiterate or semi-literate. The dissolution proved a landmark event in the historical consciousness of early modern people drawn from across the social spectrum. Read carefully between the lines, then, and antiquarian writing conceals a diversity of perspectives.

An illustrative case study from the city of Exeter, Devon, illuminates these processes of remembering the dissolution at the micro level. Traces of oral and local tradition can be found in the chronicles penned by successive generations of Devonshire antiquaries: John Hooker, who was also coroner and later recorder of Exeter; Richard Izacke, sometime the chamberlain and town clerk; and local antiquary Richard Crossing. Although each of these texts is a composite blend of genres, and none is explicitly described or catalogued as a chronicle, they all contain substantial portions that take this form, with events recorded chronologically by calendar or mayoral year. These chronicles do not delineate the national and London-centric narratives of the dissolution that we traced using chronicles in Chapter 2; rather, they attest to its specific afterlives in Exeter. They constitute an example of a form of record-keeping that both reflected and contributed to the vibrancy of local tradition, as well testifying to the porous boundaries between local and national memory cultures.[40]

John Hooker was born in Exeter in or around 1527.[41] A child at the time of the dissolution, he appears to have relied upon various forms of oral, local, and textual tradition to supplement his own memory of the events of 1536–40. This is also an episode which looms large in Hooker's chronicle, but not in the ways we might expect from printed chronicles of the period. A significant entry is made for the first phase of visitation and suppression of the religious houses. Hooker described how the king's commissioners, led by Sir Philip Tregonwell, travelled first to St Nicholas's Priory, a large house of Benedictine monks, and demanded the demolition of the rood loft in the priory church. They employed a local man to undertake the work of destruction and, not seeing any reason to linger, departed for their next target. In their absence, a group of townswomen, named by Hooker as Jone Reve, Agnes Collaton, Alys Mytter, Jone Roode, and others, 'came yn at hast to the sayd Churche, some with spykes ... & some with suche tooles as they could geyte' and broke down the door. Angered by the attack on their priory, the women threatened the workman and 'hurled stones unto hym', causing him to attempt to flee the scene by jumping out of the window, upon which 'very hardely he escaped the breaking of his neck, but yet brake one of his rybbes'. Upon hearing of the disturbance, alderman Philip Blackcaller hastened to St Nicholas's and managed temporarily to restore calm, until another of the women, Elizabeth Glanfold, 'gave hym a blow and sent hym packinge'. The episode was only brought to an end by the arrival of the mayor, who ordered the imprisonment of the women. The resistance subdued, Tregonwell and his fellow commissioners 'pre-vaild to the suppressing of the howse' and, when it was done, they took

---

[40] See Judith Pollmann, 'Archiving the present and chronicling for the future in early modern Europe', in Liesbeth Corens, Kate Peters, and Alexandra Walsham (eds.), *The Social History of the Archive: Record-Keeping in Early Modern Europe*, P&P Supplement 11 (2016), pp. 231–52; Alexandra Walsham, 'Chronicles, memory, and autobiography in Reformation England', *Memory Studies* 11 (2018), pp. 36–50.

[41] S. Mendyk, 'Hooker [Vowell], John (c.1527–1601)', *ODNB*, www.oxforddnb.com/view/article/13695.

mercy on the rebels and 'intreated the mayor for releasynge of the women'.[42]

The story of the townswomen's staunch and impassioned defence of St Nicholas's Priory further underlines the importance of memories of both collaboration (such as that of the local man employed to destroy the rood loft) and resistance (such as that of the women themselves) in local traditions about the dissolution. It is also indicative of the survival of highly specific memories of the dissolution that were attached to certain sites and spaces. It seems unlikely that Hooker, just nine years old in 1536, had remembered all of the details of this incident at first hand. Rather, this tale owed much of its colour to the stories that had been passed down and around the local community. By including this narrative in his chronicle, Hooker preserved the echoes of an oral culture of the dissolution that sat uneasily alongside Henrician narratives of the ease and expediency of suppression. His chronicle thus underlines the potentially subversive quality of local traditions about the dissolution. It also hints at some of the religious dimensions of the dissolution in local cultural memory: although Hooker did not discuss religion explicitly, the story he set to paper reveals the strength and depth of the feeling provoked by the iconoclastic actions of the commissioners and their agents. It is also telling that this is the first vision of the dissolution that we have encountered to prioritise the agency of women, whose names and actions were, unusually, preserved for posterity in Hooker's chronicle as well as local tradition.[43] Via both of these vehicles, the story continued to circulate in Exeter across the generations: in 1681, when Richard Crossing was compiling his own chronicle, his sole 'memorial' for 1536 recorded that 'in Summer 1536 was the Priory of St Nicholas supprest in this Cittie, which was att first withstood by women'.[44]

Local narratives of resistance coexisted with others that perpetuated and validated the Henrician vision of the dissolution. Immediately following his account of the defence of St Nicholas's Priory by the women of Exeter, Hooker set down a second local legend attached to the nearby priory of Polsloe, a female Benedictine house in the east of the city. The crown had made efforts to suppress Polsloe during the dissolution of smaller houses in 1536, but the priory had been granted an exemption, the nuns having 'made by there [*sic*] frendes such meanes' as to secure a reprieve. Of course, this proved temporary, and in 1538 the house finally fell to the king's

---

[42] DHC, ECA Book 51, fol. 343r.
[43] On gender and oral tradition, see Fox, *Oral and Literate Culture*, ch. 3; Woolf, *Social Circulation of the Past*, pp. 306–7.
[44] DHC, ECA Book 54, p. 40.

commissioners. Around that time, a story emerged of the depravity and sexual immorality that had allegedly been uncovered within Polsloe's cloisters. It was said, Hooker recorded, that 'so many of [the nuns] had tasted so m[u]che of the fruit . . . of the garden, that the most parte of them and as some sayde [twelve] or [thirteen] of them were with childe'.[45] If the latter claim seems unlikely – that as many as twelve or thirteen of the nuns were pregnant – this perhaps testifies to the existence of a culture of murmuring and gossiping about the dissolution, possibly prone to exaggeration in light of the pervasive narratives of monastic corruption and iniquity promoted by the Tudor government in the 1530s. In this way, local memory could function as both a product of and a vehicle for these ideas. If, as we have seen, the cultural memory of the dissolution developed in ways that the Henrician regime had neither hoped for nor anticipated, the government's rhetoric was nevertheless a powerful influence on local and oral tradition.

In the printed chronicles we examined in the second chapter, as well as in the Henrician polemic that inflected these and other sources, 1539 was conventionally considered the end point of the dissolution, marked by the retroactive policy of wholesale suppression in the autumn of that year. As a result of the influence of this larger chronology, Hooker denoted this episode using a formulation that was common in other chronicles of the period. 'Thys year', he noted, 'all the Abbeys generally through out all England were suppressed.'[46] But this moment also had different and specific associations in the local community, narratives of which also persisted in the decades and centuries after 1540. Richard Izacke began compiling his manuscript volume of 'Memorials of the City of Exeter' in 1670. Like Hooker and Crossing's chronicles, the 'Memorials' delineated an episode in local history thought worthy of posterity. The sole entry for 1539 makes no mention of the larger dissolution of the monasteries, rather it zeroes in on a local prophetic tradition that had apparently been fulfilled by the fall of St Nicholas's Priory in the previous year:

> In the wynter about the end of November, one of the Myddle Arches of Exebridge fell downe, & was new builded by the Bridgewarden, for which he bought a great store of stone att the Priory of St Nicholas (lately dissolved) & then the prophecy was fulfilled, which was (as twas then reported) that the River of Exe should runne under St Nicholas Church.[47]

---

[45] DHC, ECA Book 51, fol. 343r.   [46] Ibid., fol. 345r.   [47] DHC, ECA Book 53, p. 40.

This passage is indicative of many of the wider themes in the local memory of the dissolution. It reveals one way in which this episode was incorporated into the wider history of cities, towns, and villages, and, in turn, how narratives of dissolution acquired rich local colour and detail. It suggests that the dissolution was an important marker of time in these communities, and not only, in this instance, of historical time but prophetic time as well. Finally, it connects time to space, property, and the reuse and adaptation of sacred sites, which, as we shall see, also powerfully shaped local recollections of the dissolution.

From a brief examination of these local chronicles, we have seen how early modern Exeter possessed a variety of different traditions about the dissolution, which both fed into and were perpetuated by the antiquarian writing of men like Hooker, Crossing, and Izacke. The longevity of local memories of the defence of St Nicholas's Priory and the debauchery of the Polsloe nuns sits somewhat uncomfortably alongside Daniel Woolf's account of historical consciousness in early modern England. Although Woolf offers a sophisticated account of the transmission of knowledge about the past and the reciprocal relationship between oral and literate cultures, he nevertheless posits a narrative of change across the sixteenth and seventeenth centuries predicated on the marginalisation of local and oral memory. He argues that popular tradition was 'at risk of being overwhelmed by a print-based historical culture' and that this 'national historical tradition' was forged in an increasingly text-oriented society.[48] Yet the Exeter chronicles suggest that local beliefs about the past were thriving in the early modern period, perpetuated in and shaped by their interactions with literate culture.

Nor was this textual culture merely the 'graveyard of rural antiquarianism'.[49] The Exeter chroniclers were all native to the city, but, as we shall now see, itinerant antiquaries were also heavily reliant upon oral tradition for information about the places and sites that they visited. Before turning to this theme, however, it is worth underlining that antiquarian writing of this kind is not unproblematic as a source for local tradition. Mediated and refracted through the perspectives and world views of the antiquaries who recorded local stories about the past, these texts are inevitably, at least in part, a reflection of the proclivities and predilections of the recorders of local tradition, as well as that tradition itself. Some antiquaries were openly contemptuous of the traditions they encountered. Like Francis Trigge, who condemned the grievances of his parishioners,

---

[48] Woolf, *Social Circulation*, pp. 320, 351, 390 and *passim*. [49] Woolf, 'Common voice', p. 52.

the early seventeenth-century traveller Fynes Moryson despaired of 'vulgar opinion', which 'preferr[ed] old times to ours'. By contrast, Moryson condemned the age when 'cloisters of monks' had thrived in England and the religious houses had 'spoiled all that they might be beneficial to few'.[50] In other words, he thought that popular pity and regret for the dissolution had been seriously misplaced. There was, then, sometimes an uneasy relationship between antiquaries and their informants, and the latter sometimes expressed perspectives that the former found troubling.

Nevertheless, it is possible to use this material to move beyond what has sometimes been criticised as an 'almost monolithically elite' focus on learned and textual cultures of remembrance, and instead to seek within these genres the residual evidence of oral tradition.[51] Even as antiquaries derided and dismissed popular opinion, the act of committing it to paper reveals something of the reach and power of particular ideas about the dissolution in local communities. In other words, if these onlookers of local tradition were sometimes critical of the beliefs about the past that they encountered, their work nevertheless reveals the longevity of these traditions into the early eighteenth century and beyond. Amongst the perspectives that emerge when antiquarian sources are viewed in this light is a pervasive anxiety about the reuse and misuse of former monastic sites.

'Papish Places' and 'Impious Hands'

Oral culture furnished antiquaries with a variety of inherited traditions that reveal the tangled religious, familial, social, and economic strands of the local memory of the dissolution. These memories, as we have seen, might be elicited under questioning or because of their strong association with particular dates and historical watersheds. In conversation with the itinerant antiquaries who wandered into their towns and villages, people were often prone to recall the dissolution in ways that connected with the local landscape. Contemporary perceptions of the past were, as we have seen, profoundly shaped by interactions with the physical environment. Geographically specific memories of past events were anchored in particular topographical features and sustained through oral circulation and familial and generational patterns of inheritance.[52] Regional topographies thus constitute a rich body of evidence of the local character of the

---

[50] Fynes Moryson, *An itinerary written by Fynes Moryson gent. first in the Latine tongue, and then translated by him into English* (London, 1617), p. 113.

[51] Wood, *Memory of the People*, p. 29.   [52] See also Thomas, *Perception of the Past*, p. 4.

dissolution and its legacies in these communities across the early modern period.

One feature of local tradition that revealed itself when people spoke with antiquaries and topographers was a marked tendency to augment and amplify the significance of particular abbeys or convents to the wider process of dissolution. Thus, the Oxfordshire antiquary Anthony Wood, travelling in Gloucestershire in the 1660s, heard tell of a remarkable narrative. Popular tradition in the town of Winchcombe supposed that after the brutal murder of one of the monks of the Benedictine abbey by a servant of Henry II, the king had granted nearby Sudeley Castle to the abbey by way of recompense. It remained, so the locals believed, in the monks' possession until the reign of Henry VIII, whose generally avaricious appetite extended to a desire to regain the castle for the crown. Supposedly, the king's attempt was thwarted by the monks, causing Henry to fly into a violent rage and declare that 'by the mother of God . . . not only that abbey but all the abbeys in England should be his for this their deniall of Sudely Castle'.[53] The people of Winchcombe had thus developed a (probably apocryphal) narrative of the dissolution that augmented the role of their own locality and community upon the larger stage of the national suppression. It is, of course, difficult to reconstruct the processes of transmission and reinvention that coloured and reshaped local memory across the generations.[54] Wood's account of the dissolution in Winchcombe was the product of several retellings of the story in multiple media, providing ample opportunity for distortion. Nevertheless, the Sudeley Castle narrative is an illuminating example of the transmission of popular tradition in a hybrid oral and literate culture. Wood wrote that he had first encountered the tale at second remove in a manuscript, from which he quoted Henry VIII's declaration.[55] His travels in Gloucestershire appear to have borne out the longevity and potency of this narrative in local memory: the Sudeley Castle episode, as Wood heard tell, was 'as they say, another reason why King Henry VIII desolved the abbeys'.[56] This narrative was kept alive, then, through oral and textual circulation, but also – crucially – by the longevity of the site of the castle itself.

In one sense, the story of the Winchcombe monks defending their right Sudeley Castle offers another example of the narratives of resistance that we have been tracing in local memory. Of course, as with the other sources we have examined here, many of the recollections provoked by sites and spaces

[53] Wood, *Life and Times*, ii, p. 88.   [54] Woolf, *Social Circulation of the Past*, p. 301.
[55] Bodl., MS Twyne 24, p. 553.   [56] Wood, *Life and Times*, ii, p. 88.

also bear the influence of the polemic propagated by the Henrician regime in the 1530s. As we saw in the previous chapter, the crumbling ruins that littered the landscape could function as monuments to the triumph of the reformers.[57] In this context, these sites served as mnemonics for a significant corpus of traditions about depraved and impious monks, nuns, and friars, inspired by the dissolution. Near the Kent coast, for instance, the ruins of Butley Priory helped stories about long-gone 'fat and lazie Abbots and Monasticke Monks', who 'in those their flourishing dayes did take pleasure and delight to cram and stuffe their Paunches with those salacious oysters (gotten there abouts) on their fish-eating dayes', to endure and persist.[58] The conduit for this story was a travelling soldier and diarist, Lieutenant Hammond, for whom the sight of Canterbury cloister also recalled 'dayes of old' when the corrupt religious orders had 'juggled and jumbled' there.[59] The theme of sexual immorality, which was so common in Reformation polemic, also found expression in local tradition. Antiquaries including John Aubrey and Thomas Southouse encountered local stories in communities in Surrey and Kent respectively about subterranean tunnels and passages built under religious houses to facilitate illicit sexual liaisons between monks and nuns.[60] In this sense, sites and spaces in the landscape served to reinforce narratives of monastic depravity that, as Margaret Spufford suggested, had also become prevalent in forms of cheap print, such as ballads.[61] Local tradition thus preserved the echoes of a rhetoric of corruption and iniquity familiar from the 1530s, demonstrating the power and pervasiveness of these ideas as well as the ease with which they could be adapted to suit local topographies.

However, as we saw in the previous chapter, the physical remains of religious houses came to occupy an increasingly ambiguous place in the early modern historical consciousness. Ruins could just as easily function as reminders of the iconoclastic acts committed during the dissolution and the wider Reformation. Their meaning was largely determined in the eye of

---

[57] See esp. Margaret Aston, 'English ruins and English history: the dissolution and the sense of the past', *Journal of the Warburg and Courtauld Institutes*, 36 (1973), pp. 231–55; Walsham, *Reformation the Landscape*, p. 483, and above, Ch. 3.

[58] *A Relation of a Short Survey of the Western Counties Made by a Lieutenant of the Military Company in Norwich in 1635*, ed. L. G. Wickham Legg, Camden Miscellany 16 (London, 1936), p. 3.

[59] Ibid., p. 17.

[60] John Aubrey, *A perambulation of the county of Surrey; begun 1673, ended 1692*, 5 vols. (London, 1718–19), iii, pp. 245–6; Thomas Southouse, *Monasticon Favershamiense in Agro Cantiana: or, a surveigh of the monastry of Faversham in the county of Kent* (London, 1671), p. 117.

[61] Margaret Spufford, *Small Books and Pleasant Histories: Popular Fiction and Its Readership in Seventeenth-Century England* (London, 1981), p. 220.

the beholder – and it seems that the beholders were increasingly anxious about the deeds done in the name of the Henrician campaign against idolatry. Ruins were sometimes unwelcome reminders of the past. In 1692, for example, Thomas Brockbank was travelling from his family home in Witherslack, Cumbria, to Oxford, where he was a student, and fell suddenly into a foul humour upon the 'unexpected sight of a ruin'd Chappel'. 'I could not chuse by make many reflections on it', he mourned, compelled to remember the assault on holy places during the early Reformation.[62] For casual observers like Brockbank, the remnants of religious houses were mnemonics to what had been lost. Upon occasion, however, local tradition could provide a partial remedy for the near-oblivion caused by the destruction of monastic architecture, imaginatively resurrecting it for antiquaries who came calling. At Merton in Surrey, for example, John Aubrey was dismayed to find that there was 'but little of the Building of the Abbey remaining'. However, 'tradition' informed him that 'heretofore here were seven Rings of Bells, and several Chapels', one of which he learnt was 'remaining still, with an old Pulpit, and two old Gates'.[63] Tradition, in other words, could sometimes provide what learning alone could not and acted as a prophylactic against the erasure of material memory engendered by the dissolution.

With the passage of time and the generations, the memory of iconoclasm wrought during the 1530s became muddled and entangled with memories of subsequent waves of destruction and obliteration.[64] This is powerfully illuminated by a common misconception, which arose in the later seventeenth century, in the decades after the Civil Wars and Interregnum. The 1640s and 1650s had witnessed a new assault on sacred spaces, conducted as part of the Cromwellian puritan programme to purge churches and the landscape of 'superstitious' elements. In this context, there evolved a tendency to confuse Thomas Cromwell, destroyer of monasteries, with his kinsman Oliver Cromwell, the Lord Protector. During the conflict, some polemicists had played on the relationship between the two Cromwells. One satirical treatise, *Ad populum: or, a lecture to the people* (1644), had thus castigated 'Archdeacon' Oliver, 'in whose veines doth run th'reforming Bloud and vertues of his Grand Parent, that Man of Iron, [Thomas] whose tough Hand . . . at one Blow made many a stately Abbey lie full low'.[65] But local tradition appears to

---

[62] Preston, Lancashire Record Office, DP 290, p. 68. I am grateful to Carys Brown for this reference.
[63] John Aubrey, *A perambulation of the county of Surrey*, i, p. 226.
[64] For another account of this process see Walsham, *Reformation of the Landscape*, pp. 528–30.
[65] [Peter Hausted], *Ad populum: or, a lecture to the people* (Oxford, 1644), pp. 7–8.

have struggled to maintain this distinction, tending to amalgamate two of the chief agents of early modern iconoclasm into a single quasi-mythical figure.[66] In the late eighteenth century, the diarist and traveller John Byng criticised a misnomer that had been more than a century in the making. 'Whenever I enquire about ruins', he wrote from Eynsham in Oxfordshire, 'I allways get the same answer, that it was some papish place, and destroy'd by Oliver Cromwell, to whose share is laid much more devastation than he really committed'.[67] The memory of iconoclasm was therefore central to popular perceptions of ruins, even if those perceptions did not always accurately reflect past events. Local memory clearly had its limits. Nevertheless, it is also apparent that the dissolution was long-lived in local memory and that it had inspired a wealth of stories and associations between national figures and the local landscape. The dissolution was sometimes misremembered, but it had not been forgotten.

Ruins were not the only remnants that called to mind past iconoclasm. Previously, we examined a culture of present-centric genre of antiquarian writing that reflected and promoted an attempt to erase the monastic past, especially amongst the gentry and nobility who occupied former monastic properties. The transformation of former religious houses into gentlemen's houses was almost as prominent in local memory as the destruction of sacred sites. When Anthony Wood visited the site of Cogges Abbey, Oxfordshire, he found that – like so many other monastic structures – it had since become a private house. 'The priorie did stand where the Lord of Downes house now is, neare to the church', he wrote in his notebook, before continuing, 'the people here think that his [Downes's] Grandfather built the house that now stands there, out of the ruins of the priory houses.'[68] Wood was therefore at least partially reliant on the local community to furnish him with information that books could not. Of course, oral and literate tradition were two intersecting spheres. Journeying on to Great Milton, Wood ventriloquised a local commonplace gleaned at second hand from the Tudor antiquary John Leland, who had 'heard say' of a cell of Abingdon Abbey since converted into a farmhouse. 'The voice goeth there', Leland had written, that a local man, Louch, 'had this priorie land gyven him'.[69] As we have seen, memories of land grants and

---

[66] Alan Smith, 'The image of Cromwell in folklore and tradition', *Folklore* 79 (1968), pp. 17–39 at pp. 23–7.
[67] John Byng, *The Torrington diaries containing the tour through England and Wales of the Hon. John Byng (later fifth Viscount Torrington) between the years 1781 and 1794*, ed. C. Bruyn Andrews, 4 vols. (London, 1970), i, p. 6.
[68] Bodl., MS Wood E 1, fol. 47r.   [69] Ibid., fol. 281r.

changes in ownership served partly to make the past usable in legal cases in the present. But they also echoed and reinforced the dynastic memory embedded in the gentry topographies that we examined in Chapter 3, in which we also noted the emergence of a culture of amnesia amongst those who occupied converted properties. At the root of this culture lay vested financial interests in the dissolution. However, there were others in the local community who did not entirely share these interests. Rather, the sacred past of these sites gave rise to a set of local traditions that underlined the religious rupture engendered by the dissolution.

Many people in early modern England believed that the consequences of the iconoclasm and despoliation that had taken place in the 1530s continued to be felt long after the last of the religious houses had fallen. If Protestant histories and polemics sometimes portrayed the dissolution as a providential deliverance from Romish corruption, there was another strand of providentialism in which the dissolution was a source of anxiety and regret. The Elizabethan cleric Michael Sherbrook, whom we met in the first chapter, exposed some of these anxieties in his account of the spoliation of Roche Abbey in 1538, in which his father and uncle had participated. 'It would have pitied any Heart to see', he wrote:

> What tearing up of the Lead there was, and plucking up of Boards, and throwing down of the Sparres; and when the Lead was torn off and cast down into the Church, and the Tombs in the Church all broken . . . and all things of Price, either spoiled, carped [i.e. plucked] away or defaced to the uttermost.[70]

This passage encapsulates several of the main themes in the long local memory of the dissolution: as well as deploying Roche as a case study of his regret for the material losses sustained in the 1530s and the piety and munificence of the medieval past, it gave local colour and character to Sherbrook's wider account of the dissolution. Sherbrook also evidently remembered this dramatic spoliation as a troubling episode in the history of his own family. His father's act of self-interested desacralisation continued to haunt the younger Sherbrook, who feared that the consequences of the dissolution were still being felt in a community, which had effectively robbed itself of a critical source of spiritual succour, employment, charity, hospitality, and education. 'Such is the Providence of God', he

---

[70] A. G. Dickens (ed.), *Tudor Treatises*, Yorkshire Archaeological Society Record Series 125 (1959), p. 124.

wrote, 'to punish Sinners in making themselves Instruments to punish themselves, and all their Posterity, from Generation to Generation!'[71]

The idea that the dissolution had brought divine wrath crashing down upon both the nation and individual families and communities found powerful expression in local tradition. In 1635, Lieutenant Hammond was travelling in Southampton, where he heard reports that the inhabitants of a house built out of a ruined church 'cannot rest quiet a[t] Nights', because the 'razing downe of churches, to reare up mansions with that stuffe (say they) is not right'. Hammond offered no further detail about these strange happenings, but his comments imply that the locals believed that the occupants of converted properties were being haunted – literally – by their decision to participate in the profanation of sacred space. 'I heard many pretty odd Tales', Hammond wrote of his time in Southampton, and although he had 'neither time nor list' to record them, this in some sense only underlines their popularity and pervasiveness.[72] There was, it seems, a widespread tradition in Southampton that former monasteries and other desacralised places were foci for ghostly activity.

As Alison Shell has demonstrated, there had long been a Catholic ghost culture connected to the memory of the dissolution, which profoundly shaped its emergence as a critical episode in the historical consciousness of the English Catholic community.[73] However, the consequences of the transformation of sacred spaces into domestic properties also informed wider perspectives on the dissolution. In Protestant historical culture, these anxieties about the desacralisation of sacred space were also manifest in the form of the local legends and stories of the supernatural that fed into a 'rich anecdotal tradition' rooted in the monastic landscape.[74] Early modern communities were haunted, quite literally, by the memory of the iconoclasm, violence, and destruction wrought during the 1530s.

Amongst the sites that captured the seventeenth-century historical imagination was Netley Abbey, a ruined Cistercian monastery close to Southampton, where Hammond had heard tell of the many ghosts that wandered former monastic properties. Netley had fallen to the crown in August 1536, when many of its buildings were granted to Sir William Paulet, Lord Treasurer and later marquess of Winchester, who set about converting them for domestic use. In the early seventeenth century, Paulet's descendant, also William Paulet, fourth marquess of Winchester,

---

[71] Ibid., p. 125.   [72] *Short Survey of the Western Counties*, p. 57.
[73] Shell, *Oral Culture and Catholicism*, ch. 1.
[74] Ibid., p. 1 and *passim*. See also Walsham, *Reformation of the Landscape*, ch. 4.

fell into financial difficulties and sold the property to the Seymour family, dukes of Somerset. When William Seymour, third duke of Somerset, died aged nineteen without an heir in 1671, it passed to his sister, Elizabeth Seymour, and her husband, Thomas Bruce, second earl of Ailesbury, before being sold on again in 1676.[75] Around 1700, the property changed hands again, falling into the possession of Sir Berkeley Lucy, who, rather than live in the mansion, sought to dismantle it and sell off its materials for profit. This might seem a simple family saga, but, as Shell argues, the misfortunes of Netley's various owners had all the makings of a classic narrative about the power of providence to punish successive generations for the sins of the father.

When the antiquary Browne Willis visited the site some years later, the locals were only too keen to tell him about the misfortunes that had befallen those connected with the abbey. He learnt that 'some part of this spatious building was desecrated (as Tradition says)' by the conversion of the property into a domestic house, and that the final blow had been dealt by Lucy, who 'sold the whole Fabrick of the Chapel to one [Walter] Taylor a Carpenter of Southampton, who took off the Roof . . . and pulled down great part of the Walls', leaving the 'Chapel and Abbey . . . now quite destroy'd'. For this act of vandalism against the most sacred part of the abbey fabric, the locals believed that Taylor had suffered divine punishment. 'Tis a thing so particular', Willis wrote, 'and so generally known in the Neighbourhood, and may be attested by divers Evidences, and very credible Witnesses' that:

> During the time that this Taylor (who was a Dissenter) was in treaty with Sir [Berkeley] for the Chapel, he was much disturbed in his Sleep with frightful Dreams, (and, as some say, Apparitions, in particular of a Person in the Habit of a Monk) representing to him the Mischief that would befall him in destroying the Chapel, and one Night he dreamt, that a large Stone out of one of the Windows of the Chapel fell upon him and kill'd him. He was so affected with this Dream in particular, that he told what had happen'd to him in his Sleep to a Person of the same Perswasion with himself, viz. one Mr. W a serious man . . . who examining particularly into the Disturbance that had been thus given him, advised him not to proceed in his Contract, there being reason to fear, that some Mischief would befall him if he did; and that the Notice which had been given him was to be looked upon as the kind Admonition of Heaven to prevent his Hurt.[76]

[75] 'Parishes: Hound with Netley', in *A History of the County of Hampshire: Volume 3*, ed. William Page (London, 1908), pp. 472–8, *British History Online*, www.british-history.ac.uk/vch/hants/vol3/p p472-478.
[76] Browne Willis, *An history of the mitred parliamentary abbies, and conventual cathedral churches*, 2 vols. (London, 1718), ii, pp. 205–6.

But Taylor had not heeded his friend's advice. 'Moved by the Gain' that he stood to make from the contract, the carpenter returned to his work demolishing the abbey, at which point providence intervened. 'He was not far advanced into [the work]', Willis noted, 'when endeavouring with a Pickax to get out some Stones at the bottom of the West Wall', Taylor was struck down: 'the whole Body of the Window fell down suddenly upon him, and crushed him in pieces'.[77] In the local community, Taylor's grisly fate was remembered as a punishment meted out for his renewed assault on the old monastic structure at Netley.

The tale of Taylor's misfortune was characteristic of ghost stories connected to former monasteries.[78] Willis recorded the tale without the scepticism that inflected later accounts of the goings on at Netley, which, as the eighteenth century progressed, also became prominent in the new genres of Romantic poetry and Gothic literature, as well as a site for picturesque tourism.[79] But in the late seventeenth and early eighteenth centuries, for antiquaries like Willis as well as for local communities, episodes like the haunting of Netley Abbey remained cautionary tales that testified to the long memory of divine providence, which visited cyclical punishments upon the desecrators of the abbeys and their heirs.[80] The figure of the ghostly monk also suggests that whilst the experiences of the religious orders are something of a lacuna in the archival record of the dissolution, their memory persisted and acquired a new form of agency in ghost stories told long after their demise. In the wake of changing attitudes towards the dead and a reorientation of commemorative practices instigated by episodes such as the dissolution, ghosts had become a post-Reformation tradition in their own right. They were ambivalent figures who operated within the providentialist world view of early modern England and could sometimes be 'directly employed to execute the judgements of God'.[81] They also illuminate the long memory of the dissolution in local communities, underscoring Sasha Handley's contention that 'the history of ghost beliefs ... can be understood as a history of what people remember'.[82]

The supernatural tales told about ghosts who haunted ruined abbeys, convents, and priories provide a new context for thinking about shifts in

---

[77] Ibid., p. 206.   [78] Shell, *Oral Culture and Catholicism*, pp. 39, 48.   [79] Ibid., pp. 40–7.

[80] On the providential world view of early modern England see Alexandra Walsham, *Providence in Early Modern England* (Oxford, 1999).

[81] Peter Marshall, *Beliefs and the Dead in Reformation England* (Oxford, 2002), p. 252.

[82] Sasha Handley, *Visions of an Unseen World: Ghost Beliefs and Ghost Stories in Eighteenth-Century England* (London, 2007), p. 15.

how early modern people remembered the dissolution. Former monastic properties were sites where financial and economic interests collided with religious anxieties, and where debates about whether the gains of the dissolution had outweighed its losses were played out. Ghost stories were a particular species of narrative developed to make sense of this difficult, contested past. Although some antiquaries expressed scepticism about these popular traditions and beliefs, many nevertheless shared the locals' sense that the appropriation of church property for secular purposes was both a crime and a sin. The funnelling of ecclesiastical funds away from the Church and the damage wrought on monastic structures by 'impious hands' were two sides of the same coin.[83] Thus, Lieutenant Hammond, who had scarcely bothered to record the odd tales of ghostly activity he heard in Southampton, considered iconoclastic destruction not only an 'inhumane, sordid' act but also a 'malicious detriment to posterity'.[84] This he knew from both local tradition and learned culture to be the sin of sacrilege – and it is this concept that holds the key to unlocking the religious dimensions of the long afterlives of the dissolution.

The Spoils of Sacrilege

Sacrilege was a widespread concept in seventeenth-century England.[85] It was also a highly subjective concept, which eluded precise definition, and its application was often contentious.[86] Anxiety about the reuse and misuse of sacred space was fuelled by general concerns about the appropriation of church property and wealth by the state, especially lay impropriations and the withholding of tithes.[87] As we saw previously, post-Reformation debates over the ownership of tithes once possessed by religious houses compelled a kind of legal memory of the dissolution. But there were also specific concerns stemming from the memory of Reformation iconoclasm

---

[83] Quotation from *Short Survey of the Western Counties*, p. 92.   [84] Ibid., p. 34.
[85] On early modern concepts of sacrilege see Keith Thomas, *Religion and the Decline of Magic: Studies in Popular Beliefs in Sixteenth- and Seventeenth-Century England*, 4th ed. (London, 1997), pp. 113–21; Martin Dzelzainis, '"Undouted realities": Clarendon on sacrilege', *HJ* 33 (1990), pp. 515–40; Anthony Milton, *Catholic and Reformed: The Roman and Protestant Churches in English Protestant Thought, 1600–1640* (Cambridge, 2002), pp. 196–8, 331–4, and *passim*; Michael Butler Kelly, 'The invasion of things sacred: church, property, and sacrilege in early modern England', unpublished PhD thesis, University of Notre Dame (2013).
[86] Kelly, 'Invasion of things sacred', p. 5 and *passim*.
[87] See Peter David Yorke, 'Iconoclasm, ecclesiology, and the "beauty of holiness": concepts of sacrilege and the peril of idolatry in early modern England', unpublished PhD thesis, University of Kent (1997).

and destruction.[88] Whilst anxiety about sacrilege is most closely associated with the Laudian movement in the early seventeenth century, there were many besides the Laudians who felt nervous about the appropriation of ecclesiastical property during the Reformation. The ghost stories relayed to Hammond and Willis were a particular type of sacrilege narrative, but this anxiety also took other forms and was expounded and elaborated in a variety of genres. It also cut across the social hierarchy, finding different expression in learned and popular tradition but also collapsing and eroding this artificial dichotomy. What follows traces some different sacrilege narratives about the dissolution, adopting a broad definition of sacrilege as the profanation of sacred space or holy objects. In this way, this concept has the potential further to illuminate how people across the social spectrum remembered the rupture of dissolution, as well as the wider context in which some of the more prominent seventeenth-century sacrilege narratives emerged.

There is some evidence that, as early as the 1530s, some of the purchasers and recipients of monastic lands had grappled with the question of what it meant to transform and occupy sacred spaces. Uncovering these early anxieties about sacrilege, however, requires us to read our sources against the grain. In January 1538, Thomas Wriothesley, first earl of Southampton, was undertaking renovations at Titchfield Abbey in Hampshire, which he had recently acquired from the king. The work was overseen by John Crayford, who was also a commissioner for the dissolution. It is in Crayford's correspondence with the Wriothesley family that the question of sacrilege emerges, albeit indirectly. Indeed, Crayford encouraged the earl to dismantle the abbey church, urging that 'Mrs. Wriothesley nor you neither be not meticulous ne scrupulous to make sale of such holly [holy] thinges' as altars and other consecrated objects. 'As for plukyng down the church', he continued, '[it] is but a smale matter, mynding (as we dowbt not that you will) to buylde a chaple' in its place.[89] From these comments, however, we might infer an underlying fear about the spoliation of sacred space and the sin of sacrilege on the part of the Wriothesleys and, perhaps, in the wider gentry community – fears that Crayford took pains to allay, in part with encouragement and in part by suggesting that a new ecclesiastical structure be erected on old consecrated ground.

---

[88] Walsham, *Reformation of the Landscape*, p. 283.

[89] *L&P*, xiii, part 1, no. 19. See also Felicity Heal and Clive Holmes, *The Gentry in England and Wales, 1500–1700* (Basingstoke and London, 1994), p. 327; Nicholas Doggett, *Patterns of Re-Use: The Transformation of Former Monastic Buildings in Post-Dissolution Herefordshire* (Oxford, 2002), p. 56.

This was no mere 'superstition' on the part of the Wriothesley family, but rather it reflected the widespread belief, drawn from the Old Testament, that it was a sin to profane the holy.[90] Biblical precedents furnished contemporaries with numerous examples of the divine punishments enacted upon those who committed sacrilege. One of the most prominent examples was Achan, who pillaged Jericho of sacred objects, bringing divine wrath down upon the Israelites. This story was a key influence on early modern providentialism.[91] As a result of his transgression, Achan was stoned to death, together with his family and household (Joshua 7:20–6). Indeed, it was widely believed that punishment for sacrilege was not only meted out upon the culprit but also upon their family line. The Bible taught that sacrilege was a curse, which was passed down through the generations. When the Babylonian king Nebuchadnezzar bequeathed stolen objects from the Jewish Temple in Jerusalem to his heir, Belshazzar, he brought the curse of sacrilege upon his own posterity (Jeremiah 52:17–19). After using the sacred items at a great banquet, Belshazzar died the same evening, heralding the extinction of the family line (Daniel 5:1–4).[92] Sacrilege was a serious business.

Perhaps for this reason, few amongst the gentry were as quick as the Wriothesleys to undertake such drastic alterations to monastic churches.[93] The paucity of this kind of evidence is, perhaps, at least partly a consequence of its ephemeral nature. But it undoubtedly also reflects the circumstances surrounding the dissolution in the 1530s. There was a delicate balance between sacrilege and idolatry. Both of these concepts were determined largely in the eye of the beholder.[94] During the suppression, the Henrician regime had publicly and prominently denounced images and idols, the 'superstition' embedded in the very fabric of the monasteries.[95] As we have seen, the campaign against idolatry shaped contemporary perceptions of the dissolution and underpinned the attempts of crown and government to erase certain aspects of the medieval

---

[90] Described as a 'superstition' in Doggett, *Patterns of Re-Use*, p. 56.
[91] The classic exploration of the story of Achan is Blair Worden, 'Oliver Cromwell and the sin of Achan' in Derek Beales and Geoffrey Best (eds.), *History, Society, and the Churches: Essays in Honour of Owen Chadwick* (Cambridge, 1985), pp. 125–46. See also Alexandra Walsham, *Providence in Early Modern England* (Oxford, 1999), pp. 141, 293.
[92] On these and other biblical examples of sacrilege see Kelly, 'Invasion of things sacred', pp. 69–71, 299–300, and *passim*.
[93] See Heal and Holmes, *Gentry in England and Wales*, p. 327.
[94] Here, I echo Kelly, 'Invasion of things sacred', pp. 5, 10, and *passim*.
[95] See G. R. Elton, *Policy and Police: The Enforcement of the Reformation in the Age of Thomas Cromwell* (Cambridge, 1972), ch. 4; Peter Marshall, The Rood of Boxley, the Blood of Hailes and the defence of the Henrician church', *JEH* 46 (1995), pp. 689–96. See also above, Ch. 1.

past. This is not necessarily to say that anxieties about the reuse of sacred space were not prevalent in the sixteenth century, but rather that they were not a part of the public discourse developed by the Henrician reformers or, indeed, that of its evangelical critics, who placed greater emphasis upon the confiscation of Church wealth.[96] It took the best part of a century for the balance to start to shift. As late as 1597, the cleric Thomas Beard, in his catalogue of the punishments that divine providence had visited upon England, *The theatre of Gods judgements*, felt able to castigate Cardinal Wolsey's acquisition of religious houses in the early 1520s as 'irreligious sacrilege' but remained conspicuously silent on the matter of the wholesale Henrician dissolution of the monasteries.[97]

By the early seventeenth century, however, many people had come to see the attempts of the Tudor reformers to correct 'superstition' as sacrilegious acts. They grappled with the precept set down in Romans 2:22: 'Thou that detest idols, doest though commit Sacrilege?' In this context, anxieties that had typically been expressed privately within families and communities began to find expression in a different form. Polemicists and theologians began to connect the debate over tithes and wealth more explicitly to the question of sacrilege. In 1613, the Church of England minister Foulke Robartes published *The revenue of the gospel is tythes*, which attacked the post-Reformation practice of lay tithe-holding as sacrilegious.[98] We saw previously how legal cases about tithes could provide a forum in which contemporaries recalled the monastic past and the dissolution. But tithes were also at the centre of a heated polemical debate. In this context, the dissolution was an exemplary – and admonitory – episode. Robartes was compelled to revisit the memory of the dissolution as an especially damaging act of sacrilege. 'Self-love and covetousnesse', he wrote, had made 'overblind and entangle[d] the men of [the Henrician] age' and encouraged them to steal from the Church.[99] This was an extension of earlier critiques of the avarice of the Henrician regime, interpreted in light of the emerging early seventeenth-century discourse of sacrilege, which drew together economic and religious concerns and anxieties. In this way, the memory

[96] On the evangelical position, see Alec Ryrie, *The Gospel and Henry VIII: Evangelicals in the Early English Reformation* (Cambridge, 2003), esp. pp. 161–4, and above, Ch. 1.
[97] Thomas Beard, *The theatre of Gods judgements where is represented the admirable justice of God against all notorious sinners* (London, 1642), p. 293. See also Kelly, 'Invasion of things sacred', pp. 315–16.
[98] On these practices, see Lucy M. Kaufman, 'Ecclesiastical improvements, lay impropriations, and the building of a post-Reformation church in England, 1560–1600', *HJ* 58 (2015), pp. 1–23.
[99] Foulke Robartes, *The revenue of the gospel is tythes, due to the ministerie of the word, by that word* (Cambridge, 1613).

of the dissolution was highly pertinent to ongoing debates about the nature of sacred space and the balance of power between church and state.

Robartes belonged to a network engaged in legal research that stridently attacked lay ownership of tithes. This position was, however, not uncontroversial. In response to emergent critiques of lay tithe holding, the lawyer and scholar John Selden published his provocative polemic *The historie of tithes* in 1618. Selden attacked the idea that the clergy were entitled to tithes under either natural or divine law. Thus, although Selden wished that the wealth and lands of the monasteries had 'been bestowed rather for the advancement of the Church to a better maintenance of the labouring and deserving Ministerie, to the fostering of good Arts, reliefe of the Poore, and other such good uses', he nevertheless concluded that practices concerning tithes had evolved and changed over the course of history, and that the Church was not unequivocally entitled to those tithes.[100] Amongst the critical responses to the *Historie of tithes* was a text by the cleric and controversialist Richard Montagu, who held a rather different interpretation of the seizures of property and wealth made at the dissolution. Montagu described how Henry VIII and his agents, 'finding Monasteries possessed of Tithes, then when he seised on, chopped and changed Church and Religion, as he pleased, and turned all things upside downe, took them as Lay [tithes]'. These 'Lay men', he argued, 'had, nor have, nor can have right unto them, by any authority under heaven'.[101] Those in possession of such tithes, or who built on Church property 'calling the lands after their owne names', were doomed to catastrophe and the failure of the family line 'most . . . before the third succession [generation], without all question, are broken, blowne up, and gone far away from thence'.[102] This was a powerful expression of a common idea: those who destroyed, desacralised, or otherwise damaged sacred spaces brought providential punishment down upon themselves, their families, and their communities.

Anxiety about the reuse of sacred space was widespread in early modern England.[103] It is no coincidence, however, that critiques of the dissolution as a sacrilegious act proliferated in the 1630s during the Laudian campaign to restore the 'beauty of holiness', nor that Laud was a strong supporter of Montagu and others who attacked the lay ownership of tithes. An early but

---

[100] John Selden, *The historie of tithes, that is, the practice of payment of them, the positive laws made for them, the opinions touching the right of them, a review of it* (London, 1618), p. 486. On Selden's *Historie of tithes* see also Kelly, 'Invasion of things sacred', esp. pp. 388–92; Paul Christianson, 'Selden, John (1584–1654), *ODNB*, www.oxforddnb.com/view/article/25052.

[101] Richard Montagu, *Diatribae upon the first part of the late History of Tithes* (London, 1621), p. 76.

[102] Ibid., pp. 388–9.   [103] Milton, *Catholic and Reformed*, pp. 332–4.

characteristic example of the Laudian critique of the dissolution was the sermon preached by Edward Brouncker and published as *The curse of sacriledge* (1630). Like the antiquarian texts produced at this time, theologians and polemicists like Brouncker were forced to traverse the fine line between criticism of the dissolution and criticism of the Henrician break with Roman Catholicism. Brouncker was therefore careful to criticise the monks as well as their suppressers. In an argument that recalled aspects of the early evangelical critique of the dissolution, he argued that 'when the superstitious & idolatrous use' of monastic property and wealth was 'abolished', that capital 'ought to have been returned to their primitive and lawfull use' in the reformed Church.[104] 'Who needs spectacles to see', he asked:

> How it was only filthy avarice which made this state [the Henrician regime] to doe otherwise at that great day of dissolution of religious houses? For if it had been sanctified zeale, why did they not at the same time pull downe an[d] dispose of the very stones and timber of their Churches, whenas they had been as fully dedicated and more abused to superstition than ever the tithes which belonged unto them?[105]

In other words, it was the sin of sacrilege that Brouncker believed to be the most objectionable aspect of the dissolution. The curse of sacrilege, he argued, had also stained the very memory and reputation of the Henrician reformers, and he further suggested that their crimes continued to have profound consequences for their heirs and successors. 'Though Sacriledge be sweet and pleasant in the mouth', he wrote, 'that is at the beginning, yet it will be bitter in the belly, that is at the latter end.'[106]

Indeed, for the authors of treatises on sacrilege, it was precisely the question of the providential punishments for sacrilege meted out across the generations – as identified by authors like Montagu and Brouncker – that kept the dissolution fresh in memory. In the 1640s, the polemicist John Blaxton compiled a manuscript catalogue of commentaries on sacrilege under the title 'The English Appropriator', in order to relate many 'memorable examples of gods fearefull judgements upon sacrilegious persons' across the ages.[107] This included the opinion of the philosopher and theologian Ralph Cudworth, who wrote that 'even the stones in the ruinated Abbeys and other religious houses shall rise up in judgement against us' for the crime of sacrilege, despite the otherwise righteous act of

---

[104] E[dward] B[rouncker], *The curse of sacriledge, preached in a private parish church, the Sunday before Michaelmas last* (Oxford, 1630), p. 31.
[105] Ibid., p. 30.   [106] Ibid., p. 17.   [107] Bodl., MS Add A 40, fol. 131r.

Henry VIII in banishing Catholic corruption and 'superstitious idolatry' from the realm.[108] Implicitly, many authors also hinted at the wider popular tradition concerning gentry families who suffered as a result of their associations with monastic property. 'What if we should make a catalogue of all those courtiers, & others', wrote Robartes, 'who in the dissolution of the Abbyes were much enriched by the spoile of the Church, how fewe of so great estates are not alreadie ruinated?'[109] Likewise the Church of England clergyman Ephraim Udall deployed the dissolution as a cautionary tale, writing that:

> It is a thing to be thought on, That many ancient Families (as some intelligent men have observed) who inherited the Lands of their Ancestours . . . when they took in some of the spoiles made in Tithes and Glebe, by the Statute of Dissolution; their possession quickly spued out of the old possessor of them as a loathsome thinge; the Bread of God providing as the Bread of deceit, gravell in their Teeth . . . I could therefore wish, That all our Gentry that would preserve their Inheritances, without ruine to their posterity: would beware that they bring not any spoiles of the Churche into their Houses, lest they be spoyled by them.[110]

Inverting the rhetoric of ruin to chastise the purchasers of monastic properties and their heirs, the authors of sacrilege narratives gave expression to a vision of the dissolution that further elaborated the changing relationship between the suppression and contemporary senses of time as well as place. A rupture with traditional religion, the dissolution had also become the source from which sprang new Protestant anxieties about their lineage and posterity.

When Udall alluded to 'some intelligent men', he likely referred primarily to the most prominent author of sacrilege narratives in early modern England: the antiquary Sir Henry Spelman.[111] Spelman's major exploration of this subject, *The history and fate of sacrilege*, was deemed too provocative for the presses upon its completion in 1632, and it remained unpublished within his lifetime.[112] Attempts were made to print the work in the 1660s, but the project was hampered by delays and later by the loss of the manuscript in the Great Fire of London.[113] Nevertheless, the manuscript

---

[108] Ibid., fol. 60r.   [109] Robartes, *Revenue of the gospel*, p. 79.

[110] Ephraim Udall, *Noli me tangere, is a thinge to be thought on, or vox carnis sacrae clamantis ab Altari ad Aquilam sacrilegam, noli me tangere ne te perdam* (London, 1642), p. 32.

[111] On Spelman's life and career see esp. Kelly, 'Invasion of things sacred', chs. 2, 6.

[112] An earlier work on the question of tithes and church property, *De non temerandis ecclesiis*, was published in 1613.

[113] Stuart Handley, 'Spelman, Sir Henry (1563/4–1641)', *ODNB*, www.oxforddnb.com/view/article/26104.

appears to have circulated in the antiquarian community as early as the
1630s, providing readers with a series of definitions and a history of
sacrilege, before launching into an exhaustive account of the various evils
that had befallen both the agents of the dissolution and the subsequent
occupiers of monastic property in Spelman's home county of Norfolk. The
memory of the suppression touched Spelman's own life and family: his
paternal grandfather was William Saunder, Receiver for the Court of
Augmentations; his wife, Eleanor L'Estrange, was the great-
granddaughter of one of Henry VIII's commissioners for the dissolution;
and his uncle, Francis Saunder, was involved in several disputes over land
appropriated from the Church.[114] It is not hard to imagine that Spelman
feared the consequences of the actions of his ancestors. We noted in the
previous chapter that gentry antiquaries and their audiences appear to have
preferred to forget England's medieval monastic topography and the role
played by the gentry in the conversion of religious houses into family seats.
But, according to Spelman, like the ghosts who visited the popular historical imagination, the occupiers of monastic property were also visited by
the consequences of past actions. Indeed, Spelman's work is no less
important for helping us to understand the local dimensions of the
memory of the dissolution than the echoes of seventeenth-century oral
culture.

Spelman found a wealth of evidence in Norfolk – much of it gleaned
from conversations with local people – that purchasers and occupiers were
targets for divine wrath: family lines failed, financial decline forced the sale
of property, or else they were struck 'very often by grievous accidents and
Misfortunes'.[115] As had been the case at Netley Abbey, these punishments
were visited not only upon those directly guilty of spoiling sacred space but
also upon successive generations of their heirs. Recent experience furnished
Spelman with numerous examples of grave misfortune that mirrored and
echoed those set down in the Old Testament. These included the tale of
Mr Jenner, the architect of a seventeenth-century house built in the ruins
of the famous medieval pilgrimage site at Walsingham Abbey. In *The
history and fate of sacrilege*, Spelman confirmed the local commonplace
that the family had suffered as a result of this sacrilegious act. Jenner's
eldest son and heir, Thomas, died within his father's lifetime; his second
son, Francis, was drowned in a boating accident. After Thomas's death, his

---

[114] Kelly, 'Invasion of things sacred', pp. 35–6, 44, 51.
[115] Sir Henry Spelman, *The history and fate of sacrilege, discover'd by examples of scripture, of heathens, and of Christians; from the beginning of the world continually to this day* (London, 1698), pp. 243–4.

children suffered financial ruin and were forced to go 'up and down abegging'. The family line died out.[116] According to Spelman, other families in the area had also suffered similar fates. For example, he traced the trials and tribulations of the owners of Hempton Abbey through five generations of occupants, describing a family plagued by the inability to produce male heirs. Instead they conceived a series of daughters, many of whom were also driven 'out of [their] wits' by the strange curse placed upon them.[117] This range of misfortunes – boating accidents, lack of male heirs, financial difficulty, premature death – might seem so wide and diverse as to be coincidental. It is significant, therefore, that in seeking to explain these tragedies so many contemporaries returned to the dissolution as the root cause. This was not simply an entry in the chronicle of English history for many in early modern England; it was part of their present.

Some families were so concerned by these tales of misfortune that they returned some of their property and wealth to the Church. In the early 1630s, Viscount Scudamore, fearful of the consequences of his ancestors' sacrilege, converted part of the ruined abbey of Dore in Herefordshire, which had been in his family's possession for a century, into a new parish church.[118] Spelman also cited instances of the occupants of monastic property attempting to make recompense. Towards the end of Elizabeth I's reign, Norfolk gentleman Sir Roger Townshend had bought Coxford Priory from Edward de Vere, earl of Oxford, who had himself only been granted the property by the crown after its original owner, Thomas Howard, duke of Norfolk, was executed in 1572 for his part in the Ridolfi Plot against Elizabeth I. After acquiring the old priory, Townshend undertook the demolition of the church, hoping to use the stone to build a new house at Rainham. During the building work, however, the steeple fell down upon a neighbouring house, killing its occupant, Mr Seller. Believing this to be the wrath of God, Townshend felt compelled to return to the Church 'three or four impropriations'.[119] By committing the example of Roger Townshend, as well as the numerous stories that dwelt upon the misfortunes of the gentry, to paper, Spelman drew together learned sacrilege narratives and local traditions engendered by the dissolution. Many of these cautionary tales were also indicative of the problematic memory of the dissolution amongst local gentry families, many of whom might have preferred to bury the past in oblivion.

---

[116] Ibid., pp. 260–1.   [117] Ibid., pp. 262–3.
[118] Ian Atherton, 'Viscount Scudamore's "Laudianism": the religious practices of the first viscount Scudamore', *HJ* 34 (1991), pp. 569–73.
[119] Spelman, *History and fate of sacrilege*, p. 269.

The most notable family to suffer for their part in the dissolution was, of course, the Tudors. In his wider history of the dissolution, Spelman found cause to lay blame upon all Henrician nobles, temporal and spiritual, for their role in the suppression. Amongst the courtiers who had suffered for the dissolution was Thomas Audley, the Lord Chancellor in whose service the chronicler Charles Wriothesley had worked, as we saw in Chapter 2, and who was punished by being denied an heir for his title. He 'died without Issue-male'.[120] Early Protestant martyrs of the Reformation, including Bishops Latimer and Ridley, also had their grisly fates attributed to their supporting roles in the dissolution – an account entirely at odds with the Protestant impulse to glorify their memory, as epitomised in texts such as John Foxe's *Actes and monuments* (1563 and subsequent editions).[121] But, for Spelman, Henry VIII was the true agent and architect of sacrilege, and his heirs were the primary victims of divine wrath. By instigating the dissolution, Spelman argued, Henry had flooded the nation in an:

> Ocean of Iniquity and Sacrilege, where whole thousands of Churches and Chapels dedicated to the Service of God in the same manner that the rest are which remain to us at this day, together with the Monasteries and other Houses of Religion and intended Piety, were by King Henry VIII. In a temper of indignation at the Clergy of that time mingled with insatiable Avarice, sacked and rased as by an Enemy.[122]

This was a crime for which the whole Tudor line had subsequently been punished. 'Touching on [Henry's] Children and Posterity', Spelman wrote, 'after the time that he entered into these Courses, he had two Sons and three Daughters, whereof one of each kind died Infants: the other three succeeding in the Crown without Posterity'.[123] By breaking with the medieval past, Spelman thus believed Henry VIII to have tarnished his own afterlife.

Spelman died in 1641, but his second son, Clement, continued his work well into the 1660s. Writing to John Cosin, bishop of Durham, Clement Spelman reiterated the catalogue of the 'more than ordinary misfortunes' that had befallen the house of Tudor since the dissolution. He laid the blame for Henry's insecure succession, Edward VI's untimely death, Lady Jane Grey's swift removal, Mary I's barrenness, and the end of the Tudor line with Elizabeth I all with the dissolution of the monasteries. He also argued that the curse had passed with the crown to James VI, whose first son Prince Henry had died prematurely, and then to Charles I, whose

---

[120] Ibid., p. 203.   [121] Ibid., p. 199. On Foxe and the dissolution, see above, Ch. 2.
[122] Spelman, *History and fate of sacrilege*, pp. 182–3.   [123] Ibid., p. 191.

misfortune Henry Spelman had not lived to witness, but who Clement believed to be the ultimate victim of providence. According to Clement, the Civil Wars that cost Charles his life were not, moreover, merely a punishment upon the crown. The nation too was suffering the long consequences of the dissolution: 'since the punishment was nationall, I must beleeue the sinne soe too', Clement wrote, 'and I know noe nationall sinne in England but that of Sacrilidge Committed as a Law by act of parliament' in 1539.[124] The dissolution had thus become a powerful explanatory mechanism for more recent calamities.

Clement Spelman's account of the parallel between the original crime – the sacrilegious suppression of the monasteries – and the punishment – civil war and unstable government – is highly illuminating: 'The Kinge [Henry VIII] makes use of a Crumwell [Thomas] to Dissolve the Monastryes, and [G]od of a Crumwell [Oliver] borne in a dissolved Monastreye to punish the Kinge [Charles I]'.[125] If supporters of the dissolution had sometimes attempted to portray Henry VIII as a divine instrument, Spelman thus inverted this trope, making Oliver Cromwell – whose family did indeed possess large estates in Hinchingbrooke and Ramsey, Cambridgeshire, that had once been religious houses for monks and nuns of the Benedictine order – the divine instrument of the crown's downfall.[126] 'Thus our punishment sprang from our sinnes', Spelman argued, since 'King Henry 8 had taken all the Challices from the Altars of the Dissolved Monastryes and the Parliament and [Oliver] Crumwell seise all the Kings [Charles I's] plate', whilst Charles had himself languished in a 'dissolved hospital his prison'. Spelman begged Cosin to encourage the new Stuart king Charles II to make restoration of the crown's remaining ex-monastic and ex-ecclesiastical properties to the Church. For, as he believed he had demonstrated, the dissolution was not simply an event that belonged to the past. Rather the memory of the suppression continued to haunt successive generations, not only of Tudors and Stuarts, but of the entire English people, who had shared in Henry VIII's crimes. Arguing that 'Parents, my Lord, live in their Children', Clement Spelman's was thus a story of cyclical judgements in which the sins of the father continued to be visited upon the present.[127]

Treatises against sacrilege continued to be printed and sermons continued to be preached into the late seventeenth century. Towards the end

[124] DUL, Special Collections, Cosin Letter Book 1, 1B, 94.   [125] Ibid.
[126] On Cromwell's early life and family property, see John Morrill, 'Cromwell, Oliver (1599–1658)', *ODNB*, www.oxforddnb.com/view/article/6765.
[127] DUL, Special Collections, Cosin Letter Book 1, 1B, 94.

of the 1660s, Sir Simon Degge compiled a catalogue of the punishments
that had befallen the occupants of monastic properties in Staffordshire, as
a means of demonstrating that 'our ancient gentry were so guilty of Henry
the 8th sacrilegious robbing the Church'.[128] Like Henry Spelman, Degge
described how 'tis my Observations that the Owners become Bankrupts
and Sell, or else die without issue Male, whereby their Memories perish'.[129]
In other words, in expiation for erasing the memory of the monasteries, the
gentry families of England found themselves slipping into oblivion. 'To
show that all prophanation, and invasion of things Sacred, is an offence
against the eternal Law of nature', admonished the theologian Robert
South, 'we need not go many Nations off, nor many Ages back, to see
the Vengeance of God upon some Families, raised upon the Ruines of
Churches, and enriched with the spoils of Sacrilege, gilded with the name
of Reformation.'[130] There is little doubt that he was referring to the
dissolution of the monasteries. Then, shortly before the turn of the
eighteenth century, Spelman's *History and fate of sacrilege* finally reached
print. Considered too provocative for publication in the 1630s, its appearance in 1698 remained controversial, but it is nevertheless indicative of
a memory culture in which the dissolution had become increasingly
contentious. The title-page of the new print edition of the *History and
fate of sacrilege* bore the warning: 'A treatise omitted in the late edition of
[Spelman's] *Posthumous Works*, and now published for the terror of evil
doers'.[131]

One of Spelman's readers was the Catholic antiquary Charles Eyston.
Despite their religious differences, Eyston recognised the account of sacrilege and the tales of dreadful punishments meted out by providence that he
encountered. For he too had heard tell of the awful fates suffered by those
who committed acts of sacrilege. Writing in the *History and antiquities of
Glastonbury*, published by Thomas Hearne in 1722, Eyston recounted
a conversation with a 'man of Credit' who had informed him that the
local market house, which had been 'built with Materials that belonged to
the [abbey] Church', had been 'lost, in a great measure'. Both Eyston's
acquaintance and the author himself interpreted this as a punishment for
the spoil of monastic property. 'Whoever reads Sir Henry Spelman's

[128] Sir Simon Degge, 'Observations upon the possessors of monastery-lands in Staffordshire' (1669),
    appendixed to Sampson Erdeswicke, *A survey of Staffordshire* (London, 1717), p. 2.
[129] Ibid., p. 4.
[130] Robert South, *Twelve sermons preached upon several occasions* (London, 1692), pp. 338–9.
[131] Spelman, *History and fate of sacrilege*, title-page.

History of Sacrilege', Eyston wrote, 'will not wonder, that such a Fate should attend it.'[132]

Learned treatises such as the widely influential *History and fate of sacrilege* gave powerful expression to the idea that Henry VIII's assault on sacred space had repercussions that resonated across the generations. But, as we have seen, these concerns were widespread, articulated in different ways and in different contexts: in the ghost stories and other 'pretty odd tales' about monastic property sustained by local tradition, in the anxiety of gentry families about the consequences of converting former religious houses, and in writings that sought to account for the problematic dynastic memory of England's most infamous Tudor king. If these concerns were articulated in different ways – by learned authors in the course of debates over tithes, or in local traditions about hauntings or the failure of family lines – they were nevertheless all expressions of a belief that was widespread in seventeenth-century England: namely, that the dissolution of the monasteries in the 1530s continued adversely to affect individuals, families, and society as a whole. The memory of the dissolution was also critical to attempts to make sense of the more recent past, and especially of the tumultuous and turbulent decades between the onset of civil war and the accession of Charles II. All of these aspects of the memory of the dissolution play up the religious rupture engendered by the dissolution, not by rehabilitating monasticism but rather by questioning the transformation of sacred spaces into secular and domestic properties. They reflect the multifaceted nature of the early modern memory of the dissolution and the reciprocal nature of local and learned traditions. It is in this wider context that we must view interventions such as Spelman's famous discourse on sacrilege and in which we can finally make sense of contemporary attempts to remember and forget the dissolution of the monasteries.

The 'Plot' Against the Monasteries

Abraham de la Pryme was born in Hatfield in the East Riding of Yorkshire in 1671, almost a century and a half after the dissolution of the monasteries had taken place. The descendant of Huguenot immigrants from Ypres, who had arrived in England to take part in the great drainage projects led by Dutch engineers in the early part of the seventeenth century, he did not possess a family memory of the dissolution. Yet the long consequences of this episode touched his life: upon learning that some of the property he

---

[132] *The history and antiquities of Glastonbury* (Oxford, 1722), p. 104.

possessed in Hatfield had once belonged to a religious house, such was de la Pryme's distress that he made over the land to the parish.[133] Haunted by the spectre of sacrilege and anxiety about the misappropriation of ecclesiastical wealth, he returned repeatedly in his writings to the suppression and its long afterlives. The travel diary that he kept throughout the 1690s and the historical and topographical manuscripts that were products of his detailed research into the history of Hatfield and Kingston upon Hull, where he was appointed curate and reader at Holy Trinity Church in 1698, encapsulate many of the themes explored in this and previous chapters. His work was also a conduit of the local traditions that he had inherited from previous generations, and which shaped and coloured the narrative of dissolution contained therein. His writing reveals not only the limits of the endurance of the Henrician vision of the dissolution; it also offers a striking example of how the regime's attempts to manage its reception in the 1530s were finally beginning to be exposed.

De la Pryme was keenly conscious of the long consequences of the misuse of sacred space. 'Considering the havock that was made of all sacred things in the days of the Reformation', he wrote, 'it is a mercy and a particular and great providence of God that we have what we have.'[134] Providence, as de la Pryme knew only too well, could punish as well as preserve. For the sin of sacrilege, he believed, 'the Curse of God [had] eaten out & Ruin'd almost all the Receivers & possessors' of the monasteries 'long before this day'.[135] His diary is also a text that draws on different aspects of the sacrilege debate. Part of de la Pryme's anxiety stemmed from his belief that the 'Tythes & Goodes of the Church' belonging to the 'Religious Houses, before the Reformation' had been given 'most sacrilegiously to Irreligious Laietes since, contrary to the known Lawes of God & Man'.[136] Writing in the tradition of the Laudian clerics of the early seventeenth century, he thus captured the wider anxiety about the appropriation of ecclesiastical property that shaped perceptions of the dissolution. This was 'plain Sacrilege', which he knew as 'one of the most Horriblest Crimes that is under the Sun'.[137]

During his travels, de la Pryme had also uncovered numerous examples of misfortune, bequeathed to him by local memory and tradition. At Low Melwood, Lincolnshire, in 1698, he viewed a house fashioned out of the

---

[133] C. E. A. Cheesman, 'Pryme, Abraham (1671–1704)', *ODNB*, www.oxforddnb.com/view/article/22852.

[134] Abraham de la Pryme, *The diary of Abraham de la Pryme, the Yorkshire antiquary*, ed. Charles Jackson, Surtees Society 54 (Durham, 1870), p. 226.

[135] BL, Lansdowne MS 890, fol. 40v.   [136] Ibid., fol. 90r.   [137] Ibid., fol. 91r.

fabric of what had once been a 'most fine and stately priory'. 'It is a very
unfortunate place', he lamented, 'as common all religious places have been
to the sacrilegious and wicked devourers and raptors of the same.' For this
reason, 'no family [had] as yet possessed [Low Melwood] one hundred
years together'.[138] De la Pryme's notes contain many other tales of this
kind, including another of a catastrophic fire that had consumed the
'abbey-house, as they called it' at Holderness in the East Riding of
Yorkshire, killing its inhabitants and destroying 'all the corn stacks and
buildings about it'.[139] Most of these stories he learnt from local people; he
was, to use Adam Fox's phrase, a 'great collector of local traditions'.[140] But
the limits of popular memory were also readily apparent to de la Pryme: 'I
went to see Kettelby', he wrote in April 1694, 'but I found that it had never
been a religious house, as I had been informed, but only a gentleman's
hall.'[141] Such was the prevalence of cautionary tales about the conversion of
monastic properties, perhaps, that the popular historical imagination saw
ruins in the skeletons of country houses whether or not there was strong
evidence of monastic origins.

It is also clear that the dissolution had profoundly shaped de la Pryme's
sense of time and his perception of the English Reformation. The history
that he penned of his hometown of Hatfield digressed into a lengthy
treatise about the suppression, which he viewed as the harbinger of the
entire Reformation. English Protestantism had 'fortuitously layd its Chief
foundations', he wrote, 'while the King & his Papists were carrying on the
most Sacrilegous Business that the world ever beheld'. If he remembered
the dissolution as Henry VIII's principal legacy, he also regretted that the
suppression had become near-synonymous with Henry's Reformation. It
was an irony, he thought, that God had 'Wrought and Establish'd
a Reformation by & through the Means of the very Papists
themselves'.[142] He wished that the king had only reformed monastic
abuses – as he had claimed to be doing in 1536 – and allowed the Church
to retain the wealth of the monasteries:

> If he had but done these or such like Lawfull things which are no commit-
> ting of Sacriledge, nor no destruction of Holy things, then would every
> thing have been done honourably, then would his Praises have been sung in
> all the Congregations of the Saints, & his memory would have smelld like
> pretious Ointment unto the world's End.[143]

---

[138] De la Pryme, *Diary*, p. 174.   [139] Ibid., p. 154.   [140] Fox, *Oral and Literate Culture*, p. 222.
[141] De la Pryme, *Diary*, p. 90.   [142] BL, Lansdowne MS 897, fol. 122r.   [143] Ibid., fol. 123r.

But this was not to be Henry VIII's afterlife, at least for de la Pryme. Not only had the king committed the heinous crime of sacrilege, he had done so under false pretences. De la Pryme described the dissolution as a 'plot' that was 'so strongly layd against all Religious Places, Monastryes, Prioryes, Nunnerys, Colledges, Hospitals, &c, that in a little time they were all most barbarously & Wickedly destroyd'.[144] In other words, by accusing the religious orders of being fraudulent and corrupt, crown and government had themselves been guilty of fraud and corruption. The ongoing conspiracy theory of the dissolution had been uncovered.

De la Pryme's chronicle of the dissolution, contained within the history of Kingston upon Hull, unpicked the polemical campaign against the monasteries – the campaign of which so many earlier texts and traditions had been the products:

> In [1536] . . . came on the great and wonderfull Dissolution of All the Lesser Monastrys, Nunnerys, and Priorys, which was not Occasioned by . . . the Superstitions that they held, nor for the Evill lives that they led, for most of that which was laid to their chargers upon the last head was all Lyes, fictions, & Inventions of the Inquisitors to Ruin them, itt being Notoriously Known that them villains where Ever they came hired people to swear any thing against them, even the most horrid Crimes that ever were . . . The Real truth of the Matter and the real cause of their Ruin was their being Rich & the King poor, they frugall and the Monstrous prodigall in every Respect who disappearing of any Loans, Subsidys or Taxes took this way of Robbing of God & the whole Nation to enrich himself by.
>   To bring all this the better about care was taken to Invent Storys of the Monks & Nunns of their being the most wicked, Atheistical, & Loudest creatures that ever were . . . Preachers were sent out all over the Nation to preach up the pretended Abominable lives of the Religious and to sett the vulgar as much against them as ever they could.[145]

The rhetoric of fraudulence and corruption once employed by the Henrician regime to condemn the religious orders was thus turned against the regime itself. De la Pryme accused the king of inventing a fiction of monastic corruption to conceal the true motives behind the dissolution: private gain and personal power. His account of the employment of preachers to denounce the religious orders recalls the activities of those such as John Hilsey, bishop of Rochester, whom we met in Chapter 1 denouncing monastic relics at the abbeys of Hailes and Boxley. Together with the commissioners for the dissolution, whom de la Pryme accused not

---

[144] Ibid., fol. 115r.   [145] BL, Lansdowne MS 890, fol. 39r–v.

simply of fabricating monastic errors but carefully considering how best to incriminate the religious orders, these agents helped to embed the Henrician rhetoric of fraudulence and iniquity in the cultural memory of early modern England. This is not to say that de la Pryme was correct to reduce all reports of monastic misdemeanours to 'Lyes, fictions, & Inventions', but rather to recognise that the Henrician vision of the dissolution was beginning to falter and fail.

Nor was de la Pryme the only antiquary to uncover the long memory of this deceit. His near contemporary, John Aubrey, encountered a curious narrative in the Surrey village of Ockham, in connection with an apparently spurious tradition of a local nunnery:

> What propagated the current Opinion here, was, that (as the Clerk told me) his Father remember'd, to have gone into a Vault at Newarke Abbey, which, say the people, went under the River to a Nunnery here, by which the poor deluded people would insinuate Male Practices between the Monks and Nunes, a common Slander, thrown upon the Religious at the Time of the Reformation, when it was necessary for the Promoters of the Monastick Destruction, to alledge some specious Pretence to stop the Clamours of Mankind against their proceedings.[146]

Like de la Pryme, Aubrey thus inverted Henrician rhetoric with a view to exposing the dubious practices employed by crown and government in the 1530s. This passage also further underlines the generational process of remembering and forgetting the dissolution in local communities and the centrality of the local landscape to particular narratives of the suppression and its long afterlives. Most importantly, it reveals the limits of some powerful ideas: namely, that the medieval and early sixteenth-century religious orders had been endemically corrupt, that the dissolution of the monasteries was characterised by efficiency and expediency, and that the Henrician regime had acted only out of an altruistic desire to reform the Church.

De la Pryme's investigations into the dissolution had convinced him of quite the opposite: that the religious orders had been corrupted by agents of the Tudor government and numerous allegations of their iniquity falsified for financial and material gain. By way of a final comment on local memory, it is worth noting that – in a way that is striking, but not especially surprising – the voices of the gentry and nobility whose families had been involved in the dissolution and who continued to occupy monastic properties were largely absent from the public debate about

[146] Aubrey, *Perambulation of Surrey*, iii, pp. 245–6.

sacrilege. Local communities and authors of sacrilege narratives alike told stories about the occupiers of monastic property, but few such occupiers told these stories about themselves. When they did, it was with a tone of shame and regret that further underlines the desirability of forgetting the dissolution for many amongst the gentry, whose ancestors had participated in that 'plot' against the religious houses.

A short but highly unusual narrative, possibly uncovered by William Dugdale in the course of his antiquarian research into the monasteries, suggests that some gentry families had failed fully to bury the uncomfortable memory of their actions in the 1530s. A short note dated July 1652 relates an exchange between Lord Brudenell, probably Thomas Brudenell, first earl of Cardigan, and Sir William Stanley, which had taken place some thirty years before the earl revealed it to the anonymous author of the note. Brudenell recalled that the conversation began with Stanley's enquiry about Sir Henry Cromwell, father of Oliver Cromwell and owner of the former nunnery at Hinchingbrooke in Huntingdonshire. Upon hearing that the elder Cromwell was dead, Stanley related a tale he had heard some years previously from Sir William Dorver, a courtier to Henry VIII, who described how Sir Richard Cromwell, nephew of Thomas Cromwell, 'much thirsted after' the 'most pleasant seate' at Hinchingbrooke. Richard Cromwell together with Dorver and 'divers young gentlemen' went 'to visit the Nunnes with a purpose to debauch them, and soe render them odious to the intent [that] he might accomplish his ends' of himself gaining the property. When the men were 'repulsed in their enterpryse with much scorne' by the nuns, who 'behav[ed] themselves with exceeding modesty and gravity', Cromwell and his friends 'gave it out that [the nuns] lived viciously, and were whores'. As a result of this fiction, Cromwell finally seized possession of the nunnery. Dorver told this tale 'with great reluctancye and sorrow, apprehending his part to the very soule, which he much repented of'.[147] Dorver's reluctance in divulging this information is not surprising, but his example suggests that many other families may have been wracked by a similar guilt.

Perhaps more significantly, this remarkable story also returns us to the idea that some families were eventually forced to confront their part in enacting and perpetuating the lies that had been told about the dissolution in the 1530s. Like the itinerant antiquaries who sought out the local traditions that made sense of local landscapes, families and communities

---

[147] Bodl., MS Eng. Hist. c 485, fol. 100. The note is pasted into the back of a copy of John Speed's 'Catalogue of Religious Houses', thought to be from William Dugdale's personal collection.

were also starting to unpick the Henrician narrative of the suppression of the monasteries, especially as it pertained to their own towns, villages, and households. For Dorver and de la Pryme, like Spelman, and all those who told ghost stories about former religious houses, these inherited memories were often difficult and shameful. They reflected badly upon individuals and communities, as well as, of course, upon the Tudor regime itself. We began in Chapter 1 by exploring how Henry VIII and his agents managed the process of dissolution in ways that have long continued to shape how it was remembered. We close here with the exposure and denunciation of the Henrician regime.

Conclusion: The Limits of Memory

Local tradition, in its various forms, testifies to the many tangled afterlives of the dissolution of the monasteries in early modern England. Some of these strands reveal the longevity of the Tudor government's rhetoric of monastic corruption and the success of its vision of the dissolution as primarily a transformation of land and property. Others emerged in the form of alternative narratives of dissolution and as forms of resistance and critique. This proved especially complex over the *longue durée*, as communities and families grappled with the actions not only of past governments, but also their own ancestors and predecessors. This book has suggested that archival silence can be both meaningful and textured, revealing something about the problematic nature of the memory of the suppression for certain groups. Yet, as we have seen, on both the local and the national stage, successive generations also contested and reshaped the legacies that the Henrician regime had attempted to consolidate in the 1530s. This chapter has argued that the dissolution of the monasteries engendered a diverse range of local traditions that kept alive memories of both medieval monasticism and Reformation iconoclasm. The local memory of the dissolution offers a case study of Alexandra Walsham's contention that this amorphous body of tradition was 'not a fossil so much as a living tissue' that evolved across early modern period and beyond.[148]

A few examples, in addition to the evidence discussed above, must suffice to suggest that the afterlives of the dissolution endured well beyond 1700. In 1717, John Thomlinson, curate of Rothbury, Northumberland, recorded in his diary a conversation with his uncle where they discussed how fire had swept through the neighbourhood, where 'most of the houses

---

[148] Walsham, *Reformation of the Landscape*, p. 554.

[were] built out of an abbey' and which 'some think a judgement'. His own family, he lamented, had once owned property believed to be constructed with 'many stones' originally from the abbey.[149] Whilst in Glastonbury, the eighteenth-century antiquary William Stukeley witnessed a presbyterian attempting to sell stone from the old abbey. Stukeley recorded that few were willing to buy from him, 'thinking an unlucky fate attends the family where these materials are used', as proven by 'many stories and particular instances' of such punishment in local tradition. Even those who were 'but half religious', according to Stukeley, were willing only to build 'stables and out-houses' from the abbey stone and 'by no means any part of the dwelling house'.[150] In the 1750s, Richard Pococke, bishop of Ossory, had also visited Glastonbury, where he wrote that 'the people here seem to have learnt by tradition to lament the loss of support they had from this abbey, and affirm no one ever prospered who took the stones of it away, out of disrespect, to build, or for any other uses'.[151] Pococke thus confirmed that the legacies of the dissolution were many and multifaceted, incorporating both a sense of socio-economic decline and profound religious anxieties about sacrilege and iconoclasm.

Many of these traditions fed into a folklore of the dissolution, fostered through the long endurance of oral and local memory cultures *and* in the texts that, as we have seen, preserved many of them for posterity. If these tales sometimes appeared to contradict each other, they were not necessarily incompatible in the minds of most seventeenth-century Protestants. Stories about secret passages built by nuns and monks for illicit liaisons co-existed with those about the providential punishments meted out to those who engaged in sacrilege.[152] It took a long time for doubts about the extent of monastic corruption in the 1530s to surface openly – far longer than it took for contemporaries to exhibit anxiety about the destruction of sacred space and the assault on medieval piety – although, as we have seen, the Henrician vision of the dissolution did not survive the seventeenth century entirely intact. Local tradition had a significant role to play in this respect;

---

[149] John Crawford Hodgson (ed.), *Six North Country Diaries*, Surtees Society 118 (Durham, 1910), p. 76.

[150] William Stukeley, *Itinerarium curiosum* (London, 1776), p. 152.

[151] James Joel Cartwright (ed.), *The Travels Through England of Dr Richard Pococke, successively bishop of Meath and of Ossory during 1750, 1751, and later years*, Camden Society, new series, 42 (London, 1888), pp. 148–9.

[152] On the folklore of the dissolution, see esp. Theo Brown, 'Some examples of post-Reformation folklore in Devon', *Folklore* 72 (1961), pp. 392–4; Theo Brown, *The Fate of the Dead: A Study in Folk-Eschatology in the West Country after the Reformation* (Cambridge, 1979), pp. 19, 41. On the character of folklore more generally, see esp. Walsham, 'Reformed folklore?'; Woolf, 'Common voice'.

it was as important to the wider critique of the dissolution as was learned historical culture or religious polemic. If this has not always been recognised, and if historians once tended to neglect the evidence of folklore, it may be partly because the idea of 'tradition' continued to become increasingly entangled in the later eighteenth and nineteenth centuries with 'the superstitions and monkery of olden time'.[153] The Reformation forged and cemented links between Catholicism, oral culture, and the 'dark' medieval period.[154] The religious orders, having been all but eradicated in reality by Henry VIII's government in the 1530s, came to function as emblems of this 'backward' pre-Reformation age. In doing so, they became associated with the stories and tales that formed the basis of medieval folklore. The historiographical tendency to overlook this evidence may, then, be yet another long-term consequence of the dissolution itself.[155]

This examination of evidence that has often been dismissed as 'folklore', however, has revealed clearly that national narratives did not displace or eclipse local narratives. Thinking in terms of 'local tradition' has helped us to avoid resorting to the dichotomies and polarities that have long coloured the historiography of early modern historical culture. Although much of this literature has emphasised the mutually reinforcing relationship between oral and literate forms of communication, it has also, perhaps inevitably, perpetuated distinctions between popular and learned, local and national historical consciousness.[156] This chapter has drawn upon a wide-ranging body of material to suggest that local traditions about the dissolution were enduring and vibrant. Local memory also fed into the wider memory cultures that shaped learned sacrilege narratives, including Spelman's *History and fate of sacrilege*, and antiquarian histories, including de la Pryme's work on the towns of Hatfield and Kingston upon Hull. Indeed, as members of the communities about which they wrote, Spelman and de la Pryme are no less significant for thinking about local memory than the testimony of their informants. It is unhelpful, then, to draw sharp distinctions between local and national, popular and learned cultures of memory.

---

[153] William Hone (1780–1842), quoted in Richard M. Dorson, *The British Folklorists: A History* (London, 1968), p. 39.

[154] Shell, *Oral Culture and Catholicism*, pp. 1–2 and *passim*.

[155] On this tendency, see Hutton, 'Evidence of folklore', esp. pp. 91–3.

[156] In different ways, this is true of Wood, *Memory of the People*, whose use of the term 'popular memory' implies such a dichotomy, and Woolf, *Social Circulation of the Past*, p. 351, who argues that national historical narratives eventually displaced local narratives over the course of the early modern period.

By bringing together a variety of genres, including legal, local historical, and topographical antiquarian writing, it has been possible to gain a clearer picture of how knowledge about medieval monasticism, the dissolution, and the Reformation was communicated and circulated in the sixteenth and seventeenth centuries. As we have seen, these concerns were kept alive into the early eighteenth century and beyond by pressing questions about the reuse of sacred space and the implications of owning ex-monastic property. For many people, the dissolution was a tale of rising and declining fortunes, which left a clear mark upon both historical consciousness and family memory. In many ways, it was on the micro level that the long consequences of the dissolution were felt most acutely, not least because it was perceived as an episode that continued to have power over people's lives long after the formal process of suppression had concluded. By *c.* 1700, an event that the Henrician regime had sought to downplay in the 1530s and 1540s was therefore remembered in many circles as one of the most important and controversial moments – if not *the* most important and controversial moment – of the entire English Reformation.

Conclusion

The dissolution of the monasteries proved difficult to forget. Long after the last religious houses fell in 1540, contemporaries continued to grapple with its consequences for religion, property, and everyday life in local communities. This was an episode that shaped early modern historical consciousness and perceptions of the landscape, and which loomed large in contemporary understandings of – and anxieties about – the origins of the English Reformation. The story of the dissolution, as we have seen, could be told in many ways, including as part of a national history or in any number of local variants. The Henrician vision of the reform and surrender of the monasteries was only one possible narrative. Successive generations perpetuated, refined, and contested aspects of this view. In doing so, they revealed the true extent of the seismic transformation wrought by the dissolution in the 1530s. In the foregoing chapters, we have also seen how the domains in which contemporaries remembered the dissolution were as varied and diverse as those memories themselves: polemic, histories, chronicles, topographies, popular print, depositions, poetry, sacrilege narratives, local traditions, and the residues of oral culture have all informed our understanding of the significance of the dissolution in early modern England. There remains, however, one final avenue that we have yet to explore, one version of this tale that we have yet to tell.

When the religious houses were dissolved, their rich and substantial libraries and archives were either dispersed or destroyed. These acts of careless biblioclasm have received a great deal of attention from historians and literary scholars, who have tended to characterise the suppression as a cataclysmic assault on the cultural patrimony of medieval and early sixteenth-century England.[1] This is a concern that modern scholarship

---

[1] There is a vast literature on this theme. See C. E. Wright, 'The dispersal of the libraries in the sixteenth century', in Francis Wormald and C. E. Wright (eds.), *The English Library before 1700: Studies in its History* (London, 1958), pp. 148–75; Ronald Harold Fritze, '"Truth hath lacked witnesse,

has inherited from previous generations of early modern antiquaries and scholars, whose responses to the dissolution of monastic libraries encapsulate many of the themes examined in the foregoing chapters. Retelling the story of the dissolution as a story about books and libraries emphasises, *inter alia*, the prevalence and endurance of the powerful rhetoric of reformation and monastic corruption, the conflicting impulses to remember and forget the dissolution, and its potential to be creative as well as destructive. Finally, it also returns us to the question posed at the very outset of this book: why has the Henrician vision of the dissolution been so influential in modern scholarship when an investigation into its long afterlives reveals that it was remembered as a highly significant, controversial, and contested episode in the early modern period?

In the early 1530s, some years before the Henrician government embarked on the dissolution of the monasteries, the antiquary John Leland had envisaged his own reformation of the religious houses – or, more specifically, of their libraries. Leland, as we saw in Chapter 3, had travelled the length and breadth of the country with the intent to bring monastic collections 'out of deadly darkeness to lyvelye light'.[2] He viewed this process of illumination as one of revelation, which served to expose 'all maner of superstycyon, and crafty coloured doctryne of a rowte of Romayne Byshoppes' in the documents he surveyed.[3] He sought, in other words, to reform English history. Leland's efforts were, of course, thwarted by Henry VIII's more violent approach to reforming the monasteries. Most of the commissioners and their agents were, at best, careless with monastic books and, at worst, treated them with the same outrage with which they approached idols like the Rood of Boxley. Mirroring the wider Henrician policy of dissolving rather than reforming the religious houses, the act of destroying medieval documents amounted to the erasure of the monastic past rather than its reformation.

---

tyme wanted light": the dispersal of the English monastic libraries and Protestant efforts at preservation, ca. 1535–1625', *Journal of Library History* 18 (1983), pp. 274–91; James P. Carley, 'Monastic collections and their dispersal', in John Barnard and D. F. McKenzie (eds.), with the assistance of Maureen Bell, *The Cambridge History of the Book in Britain: Volume IV, 1577–1695* (Cambridge, 2002), pp. 339–47; Nigel Ramsay, '"The manuscripts flew about like butterflies": the break-up of English libraries in the sixteenth century', in James Raven (ed.), *Lost Libraries: The Destruction of Great Book Collections since Antiquity* (London, 2004), pp. 125–44. For perhaps still the best attempt to survey those books and manuscripts that survive, see Neil R. Ker, *Medieval Libraries of Great Britain: A List of Surviving Books* (London, 1941).

[2] *The laboryouse journey & serche of Johan Leylande, for Englandes antiquities, geven of hym as a newe yeares gyfte to kynge Henry the viij. in the. xxxvii. yeare of his reygne, with declaracyons by Johan Bale* (London, 1549), sig. B8r.

[3] Ibid., sig. Cr.

The wanton destruction of libraries left antiquaries like Leland in a difficult position. In the published version of the 'New Year's Gift' that he had prepared for Henry VIII, approval for the eradication of monastic corruption fought horror at the fate of the monastic collections:

> To destroye all [books and manuscripts] without consyderacyon, is and wyll be unto Englande for ever, a most horryble infamy . . . A great nombre of them whych purchased those superstycyouse mansyons, reserved of those lybrarye bokes, some to serve theyr inkes, some to scour theyr candelstyckes, & some to rubbe their bootes. Some they sold to the grossers and sope sellers, & some they sent over see to the bokebynders, not in small nombre, but at tymes whole shyppes full, to the wonderynge of the foren nacyons.[4]

Appearing in 1549, these are not the words of Leland himself, but those of his friend and self-appointed successor John Bale, who has also made frequent appearances throughout this book. In Bale's hands, Leland's original commission was fully subsumed into the project of dissolution: he claimed that Leland had been entrusted with a mission to 'serche and peruse the Libraries of [the] realme in monasteries, conventes, and colleges, before their utter destruccyon, whyche God then appoynted for their wyckednesse sake'.[5] But not all of the consequences of this policy were palatable to Bale. 'I must confess [the monasteries] most justly suppressed', he wrote, and yet he could 'scarsely utter . . . wythout teares' how the 'worthy workes of men godly mynded, and lyvelye memoryalles of our nacyon' had perished 'wyth those laysy lubbers and popyshe bellygoddes'.[6]

Before the emergence of the generation of preservationist antiquaries who lamented monastic ruins, there was thus a type of preservationist bibliophile who sought to recover books and manuscripts that were at risk of slipping entirely into oblivion. In this context, there also developed a strand of memory that recalled the dissolution as little more than a sack of libraries. Corresponding with Archbishop Matthew Parker in 1560, Bale thus remembered the 1530s as a 'tyme of the lamentable spoyle of the lybraryes of Englande' when 'there was no quyckar merchaundyce than lybrary bokes'.[7] Parker himself mourned the libraries destroyed 'of late Dayes'.[8] He also recognised the suppression as an assault on memory, recalling how the medieval monasteries had functioned as 'treasure houses, to kepe and leave in memorie such occurentes as fell in their times'.[9] In the

---

[4] Ibid., sig. Br.   [5] Ibid, sig. B8v.   [6] Ibid., sigs. A7v–A8r.   [7] CUL, Additional MS 7489.
[8] Matthew Parker, 'A preface into the Byble', in *The Holie Bible* (London, 1568), sig. *iir.
[9] CCCC, MS 114A, 12, p. 49. See also Anthony Grafton, 'Matthew Parker: the book as archive', *History of Humanities* 2 (2017), pp. 15–50, esp. pp. 41–2.

wake of this break with the past, post-Reformation collectors began to compile new libraries and archives to replace those that had been so carelessly destroyed by the Henrician regime. Bale and Parker were both part of a wider network of antiquaries who sought to preserve what they could of the nation's textual patrimony, and their contacts also included those undertaking similar projects on the Continent, including Matthias Flacius Illyricus, principal amongst the Magdeburg Centuriators.[10] Other prominent advocates of a national library in England included the antiquary and alchemist John Dee, who had made supplication to Mary I in 1556 for the creation of a new royal library. Dee too lamented the disastrous consequences of the dissolution for books and manuscripts, and he begged the queen to:

> Have in remembrance, how that, among the exceeding many most lamentable displeasures, that have of late happened unto this realm, through the subverting of religious houses ... it hath been, and for ever, among all learned students, shall be judged, not for the least calamity, the spoile and destruction of so many and so notable libraries.[11]

No such national collection was established under Mary, although Dee did amass a substantial personal library of medieval books.[12] So too did Parker, who bequeathed his own extensive collection of books and manuscripts to his Cambridge college, Corpus Christi, in 1574.[13]

These efforts also coincided and coalesced with the continuing efforts of the reformers to write monastic corruption out of English history. Preservation was an act of reformation. The Parker circle edited, annotated, and reorganised the material it gathered; Bale desired that the old medieval chronicles be rewritten for the post-Reformation age and 'set forth ... in theyr right shappe'.[14] As Jennifer Summit has so powerfully argued, their libraries and collections were, therefore, products of the Reformation. They were designed and arranged with an eye to the formation of a state-sponsored national identity, and they endorsed and

---

[10] Norman L. Jones, 'Matthew Parker, John Bale, and the Magdeburg Centuriators', *SCJ* 12 (1981), pp. 35–49.
[11] John Dee, 'A supplication to Q. Mary, by John Dee, for the recovery and preservation of ancient writers and monuments', in *Autobiographical Tracts of Dr John Dee*, ed. James Crossley (London, 1851), p. 46. The original, which was damaged in the Ashburnham House fire of 1731, is preserved in BL, Cotton MS Vitellius C VII, fol. 310r.
[12] On Dee, see William H. Sherman, *John Dee: The Politics of Reading and Writing in the English Renaissance* (Amherst, MA, 1995).
[13] See also R. I. Page, *Matthew Parker and His Books* (Kalamazoo, MI, 1993).
[14] John Bale, *A brefe chronycle concernynge the examinacyon and death of the blessed martyr of Christ, Sir Johan Oldecastell, the lorde Cobham, collected togyther by Johan Bale* ([Antwerp], 1544), sig. A5v.

reinforced the legitimacy of the Royal Supremacy and religious reform. In this way, collectors 'actively processed, shaped, and imposed meaning on the very materials they contained'.[15] The dissolution of the monasteries was at the root of this transformation.

In the same way that the wider afterlives of the dissolution continued to evolve across the early modern period, this reconfiguration of archival memory also spanned the sixteenth and seventeenth centuries. The project to reshape the past was sustained into the seventeenth century by the collector Sir Robert Cotton, whom we met in Chapter 1.[16] As a second-generation Reformation collector, Cotton acquired his books not directly from the monastic libraries but rather from other collectors; practices of organisation more than selection determined how his library was read and used – including by many of the figures we have encountered in the course of this book.[17] The Cottonian library preserved medieval and monastic manuscripts alongside the records of Reformation. Cotton thus created the archival equivalent of 'a multipart chronicle of English Reformation history, told through original sources'.[18] Amongst those sources was a substantial number of papers relating to the suppression of religious houses, including the correspondence that passed between Thomas Cromwell and the commissioners for the dissolution.[19] As was saw in the first chapter, the nineteenth-century edition of this correspondence compiled from the Cotton collection was said to 'tell [its] own story' of monastic corruption and the providential delivery of the English nation via a divine instrument in the form of Henry VIII.[20] And yet, as we have seen, this was a story authored by Henry VIII, by Cromwell and the commissioners, and by those religious who resorted to, or were forced to ventriloquise, the Henrician regime's rhetoric of corruption and iniquity in order to secure their pensions and their futures. The well-worn story of the dissolution with which this book began has been many centuries in the making.

We are confronted, then, with the paradox that the very archives and collections that we conventionally use to illuminate the process of dissolution in the 1530s were also themselves products of the dissolution of

---

[15] Jennifer Summit, *Memory's Library: Medieval Books in Early Modern England* (Chicago and London, 2008), p. 15.

[16] On Cotton, see Kevin Sharpe, *Sir Robert Cotton, 1586–1681: History and Politics in Early Modern England* (Oxford, 1979); Colin G. C. Tite, *The Manuscript Library of Sir Robert Cotton* (London, 1994); Colin G. C. Tite, *The Early Records of Sir Robert Cotton's Library: Formation, Cataloguing, Use* (London, 2003).

[17] Summit, *Memory's Library*, p. 137.   [18] Ibid., p. 149.   [19] BL, Cotton MS Cleopatra E IV.

[20] Ibid., p. v.

monastic libraries and practices of collecting engendered by the
Reformation. These libraries and archives were – and are – sites of memory. In constructing their libraries in a particular way, early modern
collectors and archivists like Parker and Cotton also taught readers –
contemporaries and modern historians alike – how to approach
evidence.[21] In other words, the crisis of material and textual memory
engendered by the dissolution not only helped to transform post-
Reformation archival practices; it has also served to shape and inflect
modern scholarship on the early modern period.

Understanding the long consequences of the fall of the religious houses
and the loss of their libraries helps us to expose and explain the distortions
that have shaped previous accounts of the dissolution. When
G. W. O. Woodward, Joyce Youings, and David Knowles set the agenda
for studies of the dissolution some fifty years ago or more, they painted
a largely pessimistic picture of its significance for early modern people.[22] In
this respect, they were the heirs of Henrician attempts to manage how the
dissolution was received in the 1530s. Only by looking beyond 1540 have we
been able to see the various ways in which successive generations started to
unpick the strands of the Henrician story, and to contest and rethink the
significance of the dissolution in light of their own religious, political, and
social preoccupations. We have seen, over the course of the preceding
chapters, the ways in which this episode shaped movements including
Protestant historiography, Laudianism, and antiquarianism. In this way,
the dissolution was not simply a moment consigned to the past, but a tool
with which to interrogate the future, whether in the form of debates about
the direction of the Church of England or anxieties over the legitimacy of
occupying ex-monastic property.

This book has encouraged us to rethink the dissolution of the monasteries in several important ways. One the one hand, it has sought to
complicate our understanding of the process of dissolution in the 1530s
and early 1540s. For those who lived through it, as we saw in Chapter 1, the
long process of dissolution was closely entangled with other facets of the
Reformation, including policies against images and cults of saints and
debates over the oath of supremacy and the nature of heresy. It is vital
that we recognise this overlap between the different elements of Henrician

---

[21] Summit, *Memory's Library.*, p. 15.
[22] David Knowles, *The Religious Orders in England*, 3 vols. (Cambridge, 1948–59), iii, abridged as *Bare
Ruined Choirs: The Dissolution of the English Monasteries* (Cambridge, 1976); G. W. O. Woodward,
The Dissolution of the Monasteries (London, 1966); Joyce Youings, *The Dissolution of the Monasteries*
(London, 1971).

religious policies, not least because it helps us to integrate the dissolution more fully into our vision of the early English Reformation, from which it has so long been divorced. No longer is it possible to argue, with A. G. Dickens, that the dissolution had only 'indirect connections' with the emergence of Protestantism in England.[23] For many early modern people, the dissolution of the monasteries was near synonymous with the English Reformation.

On the other hand, I have argued that we can only really make sense of this process in light of its long afterlives. In particular, I have sought to demonstrate that the dissolution continued to resonate with the debates of the ongoing Reformation across the sixteenth and seventeenth centuries and assumed much of its significance in hindsight, long after the dust had settled upon the ruins and remains of the religious houses. In Chapter 2, we saw how the uncertain and uneven process of suppression in the 1530s was ultimately transformed into a critical Reformation event, shaped by the passage of the generations and the emergence of critical perspectives on the reign and reforms of Henry VIII. The third chapter explored the material dimensions of this process, highlighting how selective nostalgia for the monastic past coexisted with a present-centric approach to the dissolution. Historians, then as now, have been captivated by ruins, but monastic conversions functioned to erode the architectural memory of the monasteries and implicitly to perpetuate older narratives about the triumph of the Henrician regime. And yet it also seems that the memory of iconoclastic and sacrilegious acts committed by the early reformers continued – sometimes quite literally – to haunt the communities that had been built around the medieval religious houses. Chapter 4 argued that the dissolution gave rise to potent sacrilege narratives that connected the Henrician past with the present and linked the religious and economic dimensions of the transformation wrought in the 1530s. These narratives also testify both to the religious dimensions of the local memory of the suppression and the vibrancy and longevity of these local memory cultures into the early eighteenth century and beyond. These are themes in the long memory of the dissolution that have been neglected in previous studies, in part because the transformation of record-keeping practices wrought by the suppression has served for so long to conceal them. Only by viewing the dissolution of the monasteries in the context of its long and varied afterlives has it been possible to recover its significance as one of the most controversial and contested episodes of the sixteenth century.

---

[23] A. G. Dickens, *The English Reformation*, rev. ed. (London, 1970), p. 199.

To a certain extent, contemporary debate about the dissolution was drawn along confessional lines. The earliest critiques of the suppression, as we saw in the first chapter, emerged at both the conservative and evangelical ends of the spectrum. Whilst the former was predicated upon a desire to resist and reverse the dissolution, the latter applauded the project in principle but condemned the uses to which the proceeds of the suppression had been put. These divisions were never entirely collapsed, but it is a striking feature of this memory culture that time and retrospection fostered some shared convictions amongst Catholics and Protestants. As we saw in Chapter 2, the dissolution became a bone of contention for polemicists, church historians, and antiquaries as diverse in their beliefs as John Stow, Edmund Howes, Thomas Fuller, Peter Heylyn, Nicholas Sander, Robert Persons, and Gilbert Burnet. Each of these authors, however, shared the conviction that the dissolution was a, if not *the*, critical moment in the English Reformation. Increasingly, Protestants began to exhibit anxiety about the iconoclastic zeal of the early reformers – a concern that bore some traces of arguments previously voiced only in Catholic and conservative circles, albeit in an adapted form that stopped far short of criticising the wider project of the Reformation. Ongoing Catholic attacks on the dissolution, such as Sander's characterisation of the suppression as an emblem of Henrician covetousness and greed, were powerful, in part, because they tapped into the unease and ambivalence with which many Protestants had started to view this episode. Responding to Catholic critics and to each other, Protestant historians including Fuller, Heylyn, and Burnet articulated a negative vision of the dissolution, epitomised in Browne Willis's famous claim in 1718 that the dissolution had been nothing less than the 'chief blemish of the Reformation'.[24]

But although there were salient continuities and connections between Protestant and Catholic memories of the dissolution, this book has also exposed some of the fault lines between and within these groups. For most Catholics, the dissolution was a particularly catastrophic episode in a wider Reformation that they sought to reverse. A more contentious issue was the role of monasticism in the desired future Catholic restoration. We have seen how Mary I's efforts to re-found English religious houses were largely thwarted by those who had little desire to return their newly acquired property to the Church. By the later sixteenth century, Persons's vision of Catholic England required only the participation of the Jesuit order; he

---

[24] Browne Willis, *An history of the mitred parliamentary abbies, and conventual cathedral churches*, 2 vols. (London, 1718), i, p. 2.

saw no immediate need to revisit the Marian project to re-establish domestic monasticism. The dissolution was thus a part of Catholic debates about their future as well as the past. Protestants, by contrast, almost always treated the suppression as an irreversible event. Although they tended to view it as a deeply problematic episode, it belonged to a Reformation that they otherwise generally applauded and, in some cases, sought to extend. But Protestant opinion could also be divided: as we saw in Chapter 3, the strand of Protestant antiquarianism that historians have tended to characterise as 'nostalgic' for the medieval past coexisted with a present-centric mode of writing that saw the dissolution as marking an upswing in gentry fortunes rather than an assault on the piety and architectural magnificence of the monastic world. Far from diminishing the cultural significance of the dissolution for either the Protestant or Catholic community, these debates between and within the different confessions served to keep the memory of the suppression alive into the late seventeenth century and beyond.

Setting the dissolution in the *longue durée* has been essential to the arguments advanced in this book. The value of such an approach lies not only in its capacity to illuminate how perceptions of the dissolution shifted over time but also its potential to shed light on the workings of early modern memory. The suppression has offered a case study of a Reformation event that reconfigured contemporary perceptions of the past. We saw in Chapter 2 how the suppression was critical in shaping contemporary senses of time and chronology. In Chapter 4, we explored how the fall of the monasteries also served to foster local traditions about the past that were closely connected to anxieties about sacrilege and the sacredness of former monastic sites. This book has therefore questioned previous accounts of the 'social circulation of the past' in which religion has tended to be overlooked.[25] Rather it has argued that the dissolution – and by extension the Reformation – was central to the changing historical culture of early modern England. The dissolution, in other words, offers us a powerful example of how wider processes of religious change in the sixteenth and seventeenth centuries 'precipitated significant shifts in the mental and cultural environment within which people perceived, investigated, and interpreted the past'.[26] It demands that we take seriously the

---

[25] See especially D. R. Woolf, *The Social Circulation of the Past: English Historical Culture, 1500–1730* (Oxford, 2003).

[26] Alexandra Walsham, 'History, memory, and the English Reformation', *HJ* 55 (2012), pp. 899–938 at p. 936.

impact of the Reformation on how contemporaries perceived the past, as well as its role in shaping how that past was recorded and archived.

Although it has been impossible comprehensively to catalogue contemporary responses to the dissolution, I have sought to interrogate a series of case studies that reflect the different ways in which early modern people remembered the dissolution and invested it with the significance of a critical historical event. In different ways, this was also an event that served increasingly to demarcate the boundary between past and present, between a world of monks, monasteries, and traditional religion, and a dawning age of Reformation. The dissolution represented an important institutional break with the past. The religious houses had once been powerful emblems of the Catholic Church. The Henrician Reformation reduced them to ruins or encouraged their conversion – in both respects, this represents their adaptation for a new Protestant world. In this way, the dissolution was a highly tangible manifestation of what iconoclasm could achieve: it had brought low a national institution, and its effects could be witnessed in almost every community across England and Wales. It is, then, little surprise that so many early modern historians singled out this moment as a critical watershed or that local communities developed a sense that 'abbey time' was a time distinct from their own. This boundary, of course, was partially porous. The ghosts, literal and figurative, of the monastic past continued to inform debates and anxieties about the future across the early modern period. But the dissolution itself remained a turning point in contemporary historical conscious – a profoundly important 'alteration' or 'revolution' of time, to return to the words of the seventeenth-century chronicler Edmund Howes.[27]

We might, then, propose a model of periodisation in which the 'early modern period' begins not with the accession of the first Tudor king, Henry VII, in 1485 or at the turn of the sixteenth century, but with the dissolution of the monasteries. Or, rather, we might recognise that of the many possible models of periodisation, the dissolution marked a dividing line that was invoked with striking frequency in the sixteenth and seventeenth centuries, as contemporaries tried to make sense of their past, present, and future.[28] By thinking along the same lines, we have been able to recover the role of the Reformation in shaping early modern

---

[27] Edmund Howes, 'An historicall preface' to John Stow, *The annales, or generall chronicle of England* (London, 1615), sig. ¶5v.
[28] Different possibilities for periodising the medieval/(early) modern divide are explored in Jennifer Summit and David Wallace (eds.), 'Medieval/Renaissance: after periodisation', special issue of the *Journal of Medieval and Early Modern Studies* 37 (2007).

historical consciousness and, more importantly, the specific power and significance of the dissolution in this process. This was an episode that engendered a physical, institutional, and symbolic break with the medieval past, and which had wide-ranging and far-reaching consequences for religion and society in early modern England. It was also at the root of a reorganisation of archives that has left lasting legacies for modern scholarship. In all of these ways, the dissolution was so much more than the efficient and painless land transfer of Henrician propaganda. It was a critical moment in which the memory of the medieval past was destroyed and forged anew. In this book, I have told the story of the dissolution of the monasteries in several different ways, all of which have underlined the magnitude of this rupture. We ought, then, to see this episode not only as central to the tumultuous history of the English Reformation, but also as foundational to our understanding of the divide between the medieval and the early modern.

Bibliography

Manuscript Sources

Cambridge, Cambridge University Library
Additional MS 7489 (John Bale to Matthew Parker, 1560).

Cambridge, Cambridgeshire Archives
CB/2/CL/17/2 (Lease Book B).

Cambridge, Corpus Christi College
MS 114A, 12 (Letter from the Lords of the privy council, July 1568).
MS 120, 26 (Letter of Henry VIII to Thomas Goodrich, bishop of Ely, and others, 1542).
MS 298, vol. iv, 17 (Brief annals of English affairs, 1530–40).

Canterbury, Canterbury Cathedral Archives
CCA-CC-L/16 (Commission, the Blackfriars case, 1593–97).
DCc ChAnt/C/1059 (Exemplification of depositions, 4 September 1560).
DCc ChAnt/C/1060 (Exemplification of depositions, 28 January 1566).

Durham, Durham University Special Collections
Cosin Letter Book 1, 1B, 94 (Clement Spelman? to Bishop Cosin?, c. 1660–62).
Special Collections, MSP 36 (Transcripts and notes of documents relating to Durham, early eighteenth century).

Exeter, Devon Heritage Centre
D.2865 (Tristram Risdon, 'Geographical description of the county of Devon').
ECA Book 51 (John Hooker's chronicle).
ECA Book 53 (Memorials of the city of Exeter).
ECA Book 54 (Richard Crossing, 'Particular or catalogue of the antiquities of Exeter', 1681).
Z 19/18/13 a–b (Richard Izacke's transcript of Sir William Pole's 'Survey of Devon').

Exeter, Exeter Cathedral Library
MS 3531 (*Liber Tristram Risdon*).

London, British Library

Additional MS 5813 (Michael Sherbrook, 'Falle of religious howses, colleges, chantreys, hospitalls &c').

Additional MS 15917 (Thomas Staveley, 'The history and antiquitys of the ancient town and once citty of Leicester', 1679).

Additional MS 31853 (John Norden, 'A chorographicall discription of the severall shires and islands of Middlesex, Essex, Surrey, Sussex, Hamshire, Weighte, Garnesey & Jarsey performed by the traveyle and view of John Norden', 1595).

Additional MS 57945 (John Stow's notebook listing religious houses, *c.* 1600).

Cotton MS Cleopatra E IV (Papers relating to the dissolution of the monasteries).

Cotton MS Julius F VI (Historical and topographical papers of William Camden).

Cotton MS Titus F III (Miscellaneous papers, including 'The manner of dissolving the abbeys by K. H. 8.').

Cotton MS Vitellius C VII (Works of John Dee).

Cotton MS Vitellius F XII (Greyfriars' chronicle).

Egerton MS 2164 (Survey of lands of Colchester Abbey, *c.* 1540).

Harley MS 6252 (John Norden, 'Speculi Britanniae Pars. A topographicall and historical description of Cornwall', presentation copy for James I).

Lansdowne MS 722/4 (William Dugdale, 'Things observable in our Itinerarie begun from London', 19 May 1657).

Lansdowne MS 890 (Collections relating to the history and antiquities of the town of Kingston-upon-Hull).

Lansdowne MS 897 (Collections including Abraham de la Pryme's 'The history and antiquities of the town and parish of Hatfield').

Royal MS 17 B XXXV (Treatise addressed to the king on 'such pestilent evylls and pernitioose mischefes as I see … within this realm').

London, Kew Gardens, The National Archives

SP 5 (Miscellanea relating to the dissolution of the monasteries and to the general surveyors, Henry VIII, 1517–60).

Norfolk, Norfolk Record Office

MC175/1/3–4 (Endpapers, apparently from a bible, containing notes by John Norgate senior, 1615–32).

Northumberland, Alnwick Castle

Archives Filing No. 135 (D. P. Graham's files, *c.* 1960s: 'Books and manuscripts from the collection of the 9th earl of Northumberland (1585–1632)').

DNP: MS 468A (Charles Wriothesley's chronicle).

Oxford, Bodleian Library

4° Rawlinson 263 (Printed copy of William Lambarde's *Perambulation of Kent* with his corrections and additions, *c.* 1596).

MS Add A 40 (John Blaxton, 'The English appropriator, or, sacriledge condemned', 1640s).

MS Ashmole 784 (Ashmole's 'Journey into the fens', 1657).

MS Aubrey 1–2 ('The naturall history of Wiltshire', 1685).

MS Aubrey 3 ('An essay towards the description of the north division of Wiltshire').

MS Eng. Hist. c 485 (Copy of Speed's catalogue of religious houses in England and Wales from the collection of William Dugdale, *c.* 1650).

MS Gough Maps 1 (101 views drawn by Daniel King, etched by Wenceslaus Hollar, for William Camden's *Britannia*).

MS Gough Norfolk 26 ('An hystoricall & chorographicall description of Norffolk').

MS Tanner 456a (Correspondence of Anthony Wood).

MS Top. Northants e 17 (John Norden, 'Account of Northants (copy) and survey of Berks, Dorset and Sussex').

MS Twyne 24 (Miscellaneous transcripts, including extracts from the lost Sudeley cartulary).

MS Wood E1 (Anthony Wood's topographical notes on Oxford villages).

Preston, Lancashire Record Office

DP 290 (Diary and letter-book of the Revd. Thomas Brockbank, vicar of Cartmel, 10 April 1671–26 December 1709).

San Marino, CA, Huntington Library

HM 160 (William Bowyer, 'Heroica Eulogia', 1657).

Washington DC, Folger Shakespeare Library

MS X.c.62 (Copy of letter from Thomas Norton, Sharpenhoe, Bedfordshire, to Francis Mylles, 31 August 1581).

Printed Primary Sources

Anno primo et secundo Philippi & Mariae (London, 1555).

Anno secundo & tertio Philippi & Mariae (London, 1555).

Answere made by the kynges hyghnes to the petitions of the rebelles in Yorkeshire (London, 1536).

Aubrey, John, *A perambulation of the county of Surrey; begun 1673, ended 1692*, 5 vols. (London, 1718–19).

　Wiltshire: the topographical collections of John Aubrey, F.R.S., A.D. 1659–60, with illustrations, ed. John Edward Jackson, Wiltshire Archaeological and Natural History Society (Devizes, 1862).

Bacon, Francis, *De augmentis scientiarum* (London, 1623).

Baker, Sir Richard, *A chronicle of the kings of England* (London, 1643).

Bale, John, *A brefe chronycle concernynge the examinacyon and death of the blessed martyr of Christ, Sir Johan Oldecastell, the lorde Cobham, collected togyther by Johan Bale* ([Antwerp], 1544).

The actes of Englyshe votaryes, comprehendynge their unchast practices and examples by all ages, from the worldes begynnynge to thys present yeare, collected out of their owne legendes and chronycles by Johan Bale (London, 1546).

The first two partes of the actes, or unchast examples of the Englysh votaryes, gathered out of their own legends and chronycles by Johan Bale, and dedicated to our most redoubted soveraigne kygne Edward the syxte (London, 1551).

The image of both churches (London, 1570).

Barrow, Henry, *A briefe discoverie of the false church* ([Dort?], 1590).

Bateson, Mary, 'Aske's examination', *English Historical Review* 5 (1890), pp. 550–74.

Beard, Thomas, *The theatre of Gods judgements where is represented the admirable justice of God against all notorious sinners* (London, 1642).

Bevan, Amanda, 'State Papers of Henry VIII: the Archives and Documents', *State Papers Online, 1509–1714*, Thomson Learning EMEA Ltd, 2007, www.gale.com/intl/essays/amanda-bevan-state-papers-henry-viii-archives-documents.

Brewer, J. S., Gairdner, James, and Brodie, R. H. (eds.), *Letters and Papers, Foreign and Domestic, Henry VIII*, 21 vols. and Addenda, 2 vols. (London, 1862–1932).

[Brinkelow, Henry], *The complaynt of Roderyck Mors, somtyme a gray fryre, vnto the parliament house of Ingland hys naturall countrey, for the redresse of certain wycked lawes, evell custums and cruell decrees* (Strasbourg, 1542).

B[rouncker], E[dward], *The curse of sacriledge, preached in a private parish church, the Sunday before Michaelmas last* (Oxford, 1630).

Bruce, John (ed.), *Diary of John Manningham, of the Middle Temple, and of Bradbourne, Kent, barrister-at-law, 1602–1603*, Camden Society, old series, 99 (London, 1868).

Burnet, Gilbert, *The history of the reformation of the Church of England*, 3 vols. (London, 1679–1714).

Byng, John, *The Torrington diaries containing the tour through England and Wales of the Hon. John Byng (later fifth Viscount Torrington) between the years 1781 and 1794*, ed. C. Bruyn Andrews, 4 vols. (London, 1970).

Camden, William, *Britain*, trans. Philemon Holland (London, 1610).

Carew, Richard, *The survey of Cornwall*, ed. John Chynoweth, Nicholas Orme, and Alexandra Walsham, Devon and Cornwall Record Society, new series, 47 (Exeter, 2004).

Cartwright, James Joel (ed.), *The Travels Through England of Dr Richard Pocoke, successively bishop of Meath and of Ossory during 1750, 1751, and later years*, Camden Society, new series, 42 (London, 1888).

Chaderton, Laurence, *An excellent and godly sermon, most needefull for this time, wherein we live in all sercuritie and sinne, to the great dishonour of God, and contempt of his holy word. Preached at Paules Crosse the xxvi daye of October, An. 1578* (London, 1578).

Chauncy, Maurice, *The history of the sufferings of eighteen Carthusians in England: who refusing to take part in schism, and to separate themselves from the unity of the Catholic Church, were cruelly martyred* (London, 1890).

Cooper, Trevor (ed.), *The Journal of William Dowsing: Iconoclasm in East Anglia during the English Civil War* (Woodbridge, 2001).

Culmer, Richard, *Cathedrall newes from Canterbury: shewing, the Canterburian cathedrall to bee in an abbey-like, corrupt, and rotten condition, which calls for a speedy Reformation, or dissolution* (London, 1644).

de la Pryme, Abraham, *The diary of Abraham de la Pryme, the Yorkshire antiquary*, ed. Charles Jackson, Surtees Society 54 (Durham, 1870).

Dee, John, 'A supplication to Q. Mary, by John Dee, for the recovery and preservation of ancient writers and monuments', in *Autobiographical Tracts of Dr John Dee*, ed. James Crossley (London, 1851).

Degge, Sir Simon, 'Observations upon the possessors of monastery-lands in Staffordshire' (1669), appendix to Sampson Erdeswicke, *A survey of Staffordshire* (London, 1717).

Denton, Thomas, *A Perambulation of Cumberland, 1687–1688, including Descriptions of Westmorland, the Isle of Man, and Ireland*, ed. Angus J. L. Winchester in collaboration with Mary Wane, Surtees Society 207 (Durham, 2003).

Dickens, A. G. (ed.), 'Robert Parkyn's narrative of the Reformation', *English Historical Review* 62 (1947), pp. 58–83.

Tudor Treatises, Yorkshire Archaeological Society Record Series 125 (1959), pp. 89–142.

Dodsworth, Roger and William Dugdale, *Monasticon Anglicanum sive Pandectæ Cænobionam, Benedictinorum Cluniacensium, Cisterciensium, Carthusianorum; a primordiis ad eorum usque dissolutionem* 3 vols. (London, 1655–73); abridged and translated as *Monasticon Anglicanum, or the history of the ancient abbies, and other monasteries, hospitals, cathedral and collegiate churches in England and Wales* (London, 1693).

Dugdale, William, *The antiquities of Warwickshire illustrated* (London, 1656).

Earle, John, *Micro-cosmographie, or, a peece of the world discovered in essayes and characters* (London, 1628).

Erdeswicke, Sampson, *A Survey of Staffordshire: Containing the Antiquities of that County*, ed. Rev. Thomas Hardwood (London, 1820).

Fiennes, Celia, *The Journeys of Celia Fiennes*, ed. Christopher Morris (London, 1947).

Fish, Simon, *A supplicacyon for the beggers* (Antwerp?, 1529?).

Foxe, John, *Actes and monuments* (London, 1563).

Fuller, Thomas, *The church history of Britain from the birth of Jesus Christ until the year M.DC.XLVIII* (London, 1656).

Gerard, Thomas, *The Particular Description of the County of Somerset, drawn up by Thomas Gerard of Trent, 1633*, ed. E. H. Bates, Somerset Record Society 15 (London, 1900).

Godwin, Francis, *Annales of England* (London, 1630).

Grafton, Richard, *A chronicle at large and meere history of the affayres of Englande and kinges of the same* (London, 1569).

Habington, Thomas, *A Survey of Worcestershire*, ed. J. Amphett, 2 vols. (Oxford, 1895–9).

Hall, Edward, *The union of the two noble and illustre famelies of Lancastre & Yorke* (London, 1548).

H[all], R[obert] (ed.), *Occasional meditations* (London, 1630).

Harrington, James, *The common-wealth of Oceana* (London, 1656).

H[arvey], J [ohn], *A discoursive probleme concerning prophesies* (London, 1588).

[Hausted, Peter], *Ad populum: or, a lecture to the people* (Oxford, 1644).

Hearne, Thomas, *The history and antiquaries of Glastonbury* (Oxford, 1722).

Hearne, Thomas (ed.), *The itinerary of John Leland the antiquary*, 9 vols. (London, 1710–12).

Heylyn, Peter, *Ecclesia restaurata, or, the history of the Reformation of the Church of England* (London, 1661).

Hodgson, John Crawford (ed.), *Six North Country Diaries*, Surtees Society 118 (Durham, 1910).

The Holie Bible (London, 1568).

Holinshed, Raphael, *The chronicles of England, Scotlande, and Irelande, with their descriptions*, 2 vols. (London, 1577).

Holmes, Peter (ed.), *Caroline Casuistry: The Cases of Conscience of Fr Thomas Southwell SJ* (Woodbridge, 2012).

   Elizabethan Casuistry (Thetford, 1981).

Hooker, John, *The description of the citie of Excester*, ed. Walter J. Harte, J. W. Schopp, and H. Tapley-Soper, 3 vols. (Exeter, 1919).

Huggarde, Miles *The displaying of the Protestantes, & sondry their practises, with a description of divers their abuses of late frequented* (London, 1556).

Hunter, Rev. Joseph (ed.), *The Diary of Ralph Thoresby, F.R.S., Author of the Topography of Leeds (1677–1724)*, 2 vols. (London, 1830).

Jones, Emrys (ed.), *The New Oxford Book of Sixteenth-Century Verse* (Oxford, 1992).

Joye, George, *Exposicion of Daniel the prophete gathered oute of Philip Melanchton, Johan Ecolampadius, Chronade Pellicane & out of Johan Draconite &c* (London, 1545).

Knox, John, *The appellation of John Knoxe from the cruell and most injust sentence pronounced against him by the false bishoppes and clergie of Scotland* (Geneva, 1558).

The laboryouse journey & serche of Johan Leylande, for Englandes antiquities, geven of hym as a newe yeares gyfte to kynge Henry the viij. in the. xxxvii. yeare of his reygne, with declaracyons by Johan Bale (London, 1549).

Lambarde, William, *A perambulation of Kent: conteining the description, hystorie, and customes of that shyre* (London, 1576).

Lanquet, Thomas, *Lanquette's chronicle [An epitome of cronicles]* (London, 1559).

Legg, L. G. Wickham (ed.), *A Relation of a Short Survey of the Western Counties Made by a Lieutenant of the Military Company in Norwich in 1635*, Camden Miscellany 16 (London, 1936).

McKerrow, R. B. (ed.), *The Works of Thomas Nashe*, 5 vols. (Oxford, 1958).

Montagu, Richard, *Diatribae upon the first part of the late History of Tithes* (London, 1621).

Moryson, Fynes, *An itinerary written by Fynes Moryson gent. first in the Latine tongue, and then translated by him into English* (London, 1617).

Nichols, John Gough (ed.), *The Chronicle of the Grey Friars of London*, Camden Society, old series, 53 (London, 1852).

    The Diary of Henry Machyn, Citizen and Merchant-Taylor of London, 1550–1563, Camden Society, old series, 42 (London, 1848).

Persons, Robert, *The Jesuit's memorial for the intended reformation of England under their first popish prince published from the copy that was presented to the late King James II*, trans. Edward Gee (London, 1690).

Philipott, Thomas, *Villare Cantianum: or, Kent surveyed and illustrated being an exact description of all the parishes, burroughs, villages and other respective mannors included in the county of Kent* (London, 1659).

Ray, John, *A compleat collection of English proverbs, also the most celebrated proverbs of the Scotch, Italian, French, Spanish and other language* (London, 1737).

Ridley, Lancelot, *A commentary in Englyshe upon Sayncte Paules Epystle to the Ephesyans, for the instruccyon of them that be unlearned in tonges gathered out of the holy scriptures and of the olde catholyke doctors of the churche* (London, 1540).

Risdon, Tristram, *The chorographical description or survey of the county of Devon, with the city and county of Exeter* (London, 1714).

Robartes, Foulke, *The revenue of the gospel is tythes, due to the ministerie of the word, by that word* (Cambridge, 1613).

Sander, Nicholas, *De origine ac progressu schismatis Anglicani*, ed. and trans. David Lewis, *The Rise and Growth of the Anglican Schism* (London, 1877).

Selden, John, *The historie of tithes, that is, the practice of payment of them, the positive laws made for them, the opinions touching the right of them, a review of it* (London, 1618).

Shakespeare's Sonnets, ed. and with an analytic commentary by Stephen Booth (New Haven, CT, and London, 1977).

Smith, Nigel (ed.), *The Poems of Andrew Marvell*, revised ed. (Harlow, 2007).

Smith, Richard, *A bouclier of the catholike fayth of Christes church, conteynyng divers matters now of late called into controuersy, by the newe gospellers* (London, 1554).

Smyth, John, *The Works of John Smyth, Fellow of Christ's College, 1594–8*, with notes and biography by W. T. Whitley (Cambridge, 1915).

South, Robert, *Twelve sermons preached upon several occasions* (London, 1692).

Southouse, Thomas, *Monasticon Favershamiense in Agro Cantiana: or, a surveigh of the monastry of Faversham in the county of Kent* (London, 1671).

Speed, John, *The theatre of the empire of Great Britaine* (London, 1611).

Spelman, Sir Henry, *De non temerandis ecclesiis* (London, 1613).

    The history and fate of sacrilege, discover'd by examples of scripture, of heathens, and of Christians; from the beginning of the world continually to this day (London, 1698).

Standish, John, *The triall of the supremacy wherein is set forouth the unitie of Christes church militant geven to S. Peter and his successoures by Christe: and that there ought to be one head bishop in earth Christes vicar generall ouer all hys churche militant: wyth answeres to the blasphemous objections made agaynste the same in the late miserable yeres now paste* (London, 1556).

The Statutes of the Realm, 11 vols. (London, 1963).

Stow, John, *The annales of England, faithfully collected out of the most authenticall authors, records, and other monuments of antiquitie* (London, 1592).

The annales, or generall chronicle of England (London, 1615).

The survey of London: contayning the originall, increase, modern estate, and government of that city, methodically set downe (London, 1633).

Stukeley, William, *Itinerarium curiosum* (London, 1776).

A supplicacyon of the poore commons (London, 1546).

Taylor, John, *All the works of John Taylor the water poet* (London, 1630).

Toulmin Smith, Lucy (ed.), *The Itinerary of John Leland in or about the Years 1535–1543*, 5 vols. (London, 1907–10).

Tracy, Richard, *A supplycacion to our moste soveraigne lorde Kygne Henry the Eyght* (London, 1544).

Trigge, Francis, *An apologie; or, defence of our dayes, against the vaine murmurings & complaints of manie wherein is plainly proued, that our dayes are more happie & blessed than the dayes of our forefathers* (London, 1589).

Turner, William, *A new booke of spirituall physic for diverse diseases of the nobilitie and gentlemen of Englande* (Rome (i.e. Emden), 1555).

[Turner, William], *The hunting of the fox and the wolfe, because they make havocke of the sheepe of Christ Jesus* (London, 1565).

Udall, Ephraim, *Noli me tangere, is a thinge to be thought on, or vox carnis sacrae clamantis ab Altari ad Aquilam sacrilegam, noli me tangere ne te perdam* (London, 1642).

Weever, John, *Ancient funerall monuments with in the united monarchie of Great Britaine, Ireland, and the ilands adjacent* (London, 1631).

Westcote, Thomas, *A view of Devonshire in MDCXXX, with a Pedigree of Most of Its Gentry, by Thomas Westcote, gent.*, ed. George Oliver and Pitman Jones (Exeter, 1845).

Weston, William, *The Autobiography of an Elizabethan*, ed. Philip Caraman (London and New York, 1955).

Willis, Browne, *An history of the mitred parliamentary abbies, and conventual cathedral churches*, 2 vols. (London, 1718).

Winchester, Angus J. L. (ed.), *John Denton's History of Cumberland*, Surtees Society 213 (Durham, 2010).

Wood, Anthony, *The Life and Times of Anthony Wood, Antiquary, of Oxford, 1632–1695, Described by Himself*, ed. Andrew Clark, 5 vols. (Oxford, 1891–1900).

Wright, Thomas (ed.), *Three Chapters of Letters Relating to the Dissolution of the Monasteries*, Camden Society, old series, 26 (London, 1843).

Wriothesley, Charles, *A Chronicle of England during the Reigns of the Tudors, from A.D. 1485 to 1559*, ed. William Douglas Hamilton, 2 vols., Camden Society, new series, 2 (London, 1875–7).

Secondary Sources

Abrams, Philip, *Historical Sociology* (Shepton Mallet, 1982).

Anderson, Thomas Page and Ryan Netzley (eds.), *Acts of Reading: Interpretation, Reading Practices, and the Idea of the Book in John Foxe's* Actes and Monuments (Newark, DE, 2010).

Archer, Ian W., 'John Stow, citizen and historian', in Gadd and Gillespie (eds.), *John Stow*, pp. 13–26.

'The nostalgia of John Stow', in Smith, Strier, and Bevington (eds.), *The Theatrical City*, pp. 17–34.

Assmann, Jan, 'Collective memory and cultural identity', trans. John Czaplicka, *New German Critique* 65 (1995), pp. 125–33.

Aston, Margaret, *Broken Idols of the English Reformation* (Cambridge, 2015).

England's Iconoclasts: Volume 1: Laws against Images (Oxford, 1988).

'English ruins and English history: the dissolution and the sense of the past', *Journal of the Warburg and Courtauld Institutes* 36 (1973), pp. 231–55.

The King's Bedpost: Reformation and Iconography in a Tudor Group Portrait (Cambridge, 1993).

Lollards and Reformers: Images and Literacy in Late Medieval Religion (London, 1984).

'Public worship and iconoclasm', in Gaimster and Gilchrist (eds.), *Archaeology of the Reformation*, pp. 9–28.

Atherton, Ian, 'Cathedrals', in Anthony Milton (ed.), *The Oxford Handbook of Anglicanism, Volume I: Reformation and Identity, c. 1520–1662* (Oxford, 2017), pp. 228–42.

'Cathedrals, Laudianism, and the British churches', *HJ* 53 (2010), pp. 895–918.

'Viscount Scudamore's "Laudianism": the religious practices of the first Viscount Scudamore', *HJ* 34 (1991), pp. 569–73.

Barrow, Julia, 'Ideas and applications of reform', in Thomas F. X. Noble and Julia M. H. Smith (eds.), *The Cambridge History of Christianity: Early Medieval Christianities, c. 600–c. 1100* (Cambridge, 2014), pp. 345–62.

Bartram, Claire, '"Honoured by posteryte by record of wrytinge": memory, reputation and the role of the book within commemorative practices in late Elizabethan Kent', in Penman (ed.), *Monuments and Monumentality*, pp. 91–104.

Baskerville, Geoffrey, *English Monks and the Suppression of the Monasteries* (New Haven, CT, 1937).

Bates, Lucy, 'The limits of possibility in England's Long Reformation', *HJ* 53 (2010), pp. 1049–70.

Beer, Barrett L., 'John Stow and the English Reformation, 1547–1559', *SCJ* 16 (1985), pp. 257–71.

Tudor England Observed: The World of John Stow (Stroud, 1998).

Benedict, Philip, 'Divided memories? Historical calendars, commemorative processions and the recollection of the Wars of Religion during the Ancien Régime', *French History* 22 (2008), pp. 381–405.

Bernard, G. W., 'The dissolution of the monasteries', *History* 96 (2011), pp. 390–409.

The King's Reformation: Henry VIII and the Remaking of the English Church (New Haven, CT, and London, 2005).

The Late Medieval English Church: Vitality and Vulnerability Before the Break with Rome (New Haven, CT, and London, 2012).

Betteridge, Thomas and Thomas S. Freeman (eds.), *Henry VIII and History* (Farnham, 2012).

Bettey, J. H., *The Suppression of the Monasteries in the West Country* (Gloucester, 1989).

Bigsby, Christopher, *Remembering and Imagining the Holocaust: The Chain of Memory* (Cambridge, 2006).

Blair, Ann, *Too Much to Know: Managing Scholarly Information Before the Modern Age* (Cambridge, MA, 2010).

Blair, John, *The Church in Anglo-Saxon Society* (Oxford, 2005).

Boldrick, Stacy, Leslie Brubaker, and Richard Clay (eds.), *Striking Images, Iconoclasms Past and Present* (Farnham, 2013).

Bossy, John, *The English Catholic Community, 1570–1850* (London, 1975).

Bowden, Caroline and James E. Kelly (eds.), *The English Convents in Exile, 1600–1800* (London, 2013).

Brand, Clinton Allen, '"Upon Appleton House" and the decomposition of Protestant historiography', *English Literary Renaissance* 31 (2001), pp. 477–510.

Briggs, Martin S., *Goths and Vandals: A Study of the Destruction, Neglect, and Preservation of the Historical Buildings in England* (London, 1952).

Broadway, Jan, *'No Historie so Meete': Gentry Culture and the Development of Local History in Elizabethan and Early Stuart England* (Manchester, 2006).

'Symbolic and self-consciously antiquarian: the Elizabethan and early Stuart gentry's use of the past', in Neufeld (ed.), 'Uses of the past in early modern England', pp. 541–58.

William Dugdale: A Life of the Warwickshire Historian and Herald (Gloucester, 2011).

Broomhall, Susan, 'Disturbing memories: narrating experiences and emotions of distressing events in the French Wars of Religion', in Kuijpers et al. (eds.), *Memory Before Modernity*, pp. 253–68.

Brown, Theo, *The Fate of the Dead: A Study in Folk-Eschatology in the West Country after the Reformation* (Cambridge, 1979).

'Some examples of post-Reformation folklore in Devon', *Folklore* 72 (1961), pp. 392–4.

Bush, M. L., *The Pilgrimage of Grace: A Study of the Rebel Armies of October 1536* (Manchester and New York, 1996).

Byford, M. S., 'The price of Protestantism: assessing the impact of religious change on Elizabethan Essex: the cases of Heydon and Colchester, 1558–1594', unpublished DPhil thesis, University of Oxford (1988).

Capp, Bernard, *When Gossips Meet: Women, Family, and Neighbourhood in Early Modern England* (Oxford, 2004).

Carley, James P. 'Monastic collections and their dispersal' in John Barnard and D. F. McKenzie (eds.), with the assistance of Maureen Bell, *The Cambridge History of the Book in Britain: Volume IV, 1577–1695* (Cambridge, 2002), pp. 339–47.

Carruthers, Mary, *The Book of Memory: Studies of Memory in Medieval Culture*, 2nd ed. (Cambridge, 2008).

Carter, Michael, 'Michael Sherbrook, the fall of Roche Abbey and the provenance of Cambridge University Library MS GG.3.33', *Notes & Queries* 63 (2016), pp. 19–22.

Carter, Rodney G. S. , 'Of things said and unsaid: power, archival silences, and power in silence', *Archivaria* 61 (2006), pp. 215–33.

Chedgzoy, Kate, Elspeth Graham, Katharine Hodgkin, and Ramona Wray (eds.), 'Memory and the early modern', *Memory Studies* 11 (2018).

Clark, James G., *The Benedictines in the Middle Ages* (Woodbridge, 2011).

Clark, James G. (ed.), *The Religious Orders in Pre-Reformation England* (Woodbridge, 2002).

Clark, Kenneth, *The Gothic Revival: An Essay in the History of Taste*, 3rd ed. (London, 1962).

Clucas, Stephen, 'Memory in the Renaissance and early modern period', in Dmitri Nikulin (ed.), *Memory: A History* (Oxford, 2015), pp. 131–75.

Collinson, Patrick, *The Birthpangs of Protestant England: Religious and Cultural Change in the Sixteenth and Seventeenth Centuries* (London and New York, 1988).

    From Iconoclasm to Iconophobia: The Cultural Impact of the Second English Reformation, The Stenton Lecture (Reading, 1986).

    'John Stow and nostalgic antiquarianism', in Julia F. Merritt (ed.), *Imagining Early Modern London: Perceptions and Portrayals of the City from Stow to Strype, 1598–1720* (Cambridge, 2001), pp. 27–51.

    'Merry England on the ropes: the contested culture of the early modern English town', in Simon Ditchfield (ed.), *Christianity and Community in the West: Essays for John Bossy* (Aldershot, 2001), pp. 131–47.

    This England: Essays on the English Nation and Commonwealth in the Sixteenth Century (Manchester, 2011).

    'Truth and legend: the veracity of John Foxe's Book of Martyrs', in A. C. Duke and C. A. Tamse (eds.), *Clio's Mirror: Historiography in Britain and the Netherlands* (Zutphen, 1985), pp. 31–54.

    'Truth, lies, and fiction in sixteenth-century Protestant historiography', in Donald R. Kelley and David Harris Sacks (eds.), *The Historical Imagination in Early Modern Britain: History, Rhetoric, and Fiction, 1500–1800* (Cambridge, 1997), pp. 37–68.

Collinson, Patrick and John Craig (eds.), *The Reformation in English Towns, 1500–1640* (Basingstoke, 1998).

Confino, Alan, 'Collective memory and cultural history: problems of method', *American Historical Review* 102 (1997), pp. 1366–403.

Connerton, Paul, *How Societies Remember* (Cambridge, 1989).

'Seven types of forgetting', *Memory Studies* 1 (2008), pp. 59–71.

Cooke, Kathleen, 'The English nuns and the dissolution', in John Blair and Brian Golding (eds.), *The Cloister and the World: Essays in Medieval History in Honour of Barbara Harvey* (Oxford, 1996), pp. 287–301.

Copley, G. J., *English Place-Names and Their Origins* (Newton Abbot, 1971).

Corbett, Margery, 'The title-page and illustrations to the *Monasticon Anglicanum*, 1655–73', *Antiquaries Journal* 67 (1987), pp. 102–10.

Corbett, Margery and David Lightbown (eds.), *The Comely Frontispiece: The Emblematic Title-Page in England, 1550–1650* (London, 1979).

Corens, Liesbeth, Kate Peters, and Alexandra Walsham (eds.), *Archives and Information in the Early Modern World*, Proceedings of the British Academy 212 (Oxford, 2018).

The Social History of the Archive: Record-Keeping in Early Modern Europe, Past & Present Supplement 11 (2016).

Corpis, Duane J., 'Losing one's place: memory, history, and space in post-Reformation Germany', in Lynne Tatlock (ed.), *Enduring Loss in Early Modern Germany: Cross Disciplinary Perspectives* (Boston, MA, and Leiden, 2010), pp. 327–67.

Covington, Sarah, '"The odious demon from across the sea": Oliver Cromwell, memory, and the dislocations of Ireland', in Kuijpers et al. (eds.), *Memory Before Modernity*, pp. 149–64.

Cramsie, John, *British Travellers and the Encounter with Britain, 1450–1700* (Woodbridge, 2015).

Kingship and Crown Finance Under James VI and I, 1603–1625 (Woodbridge, 2002).

Cressy, David, *Bonfires and Bells: National Memory and the Protestant Calendar in Elizabethan and Stuart England* (Princeton, NJ, 1989).

Dangerous Talk: Scandalous, Seditious, and Treasonable Speech in Pre-Modern England (Oxford, 2010).

'National memory in early modern England', in John R. Gillis (ed.), *Commemorations: The Politics of National Identity* (Princeton, NJ, 1994), pp. 61–73.

Cromartie, Alan, 'Harringtonian virtue: Harrington, Machiavelli, and the method of the *Moment*', *HJ* 41 (1998), pp. 987–1009.

Cross, M. Claire, *The End of Medieval Monasticism in the East Riding of Yorkshire* (Beverley, 1993).

'The end of medieval monasticism in the North Riding of Yorkshire', *Yorkshire Archaeological Journal* 78 (2006), pp. 145–57.

Cubitt, Catherine, 'Memory and narrative in the cult of early Anglo-Saxon saints', in Hen and Innes (eds.), *Uses of the Past*, pp. 29–66.

Cubitt, Geoffrey, *History and Memory* (Manchester, 2007).

Cummings, Brian, Ceri Law, Karis Riley, and Alexandra Walsham (eds.), *Remembering the Reformation* (London, 2020).

Cunich, Peter, 'The administration and alienation of ex-monastic lands by the crown, 1536–47', unpublished PhD thesis, University of Cambridge (1990).

'The dissolution of the chantries', in Collinson and Craig (eds.), *Reformation in English Towns*, pp. 159–74.

'The ex-religious in post-dissolution society: symptoms of Post-Traumatic Stress Disorder?', in Clark (ed.), *Religious Orders in Pre-Reformation England*, pp. 227–38.

'The Syon household at Denham, 1539–1550', in John Doran, Charlotte Methuen, and Alexandra Walsham (eds.), *Religion and the Household* (Woodbridge, 2014), pp. 174–87.

Cust, Richard, 'Catholicism, antiquarianism, and gentry honour: the writings of Sir Thomas Shirley', *Midland History* 23 (1998), pp. 40–70.

Davies, Catherine, '"Poor persecuted little flock" or "commonwealth of Christians": Edwardian Protestant concepts of the church', in Peter Lake and Maria Dowling (eds.), *Protestantism and the National Church in Sixteenth-Century England* (London, New York, and Sydney, 1987), pp. 78–102.

Davis, David J., *Seeing Faith, Printing Pictures: Religious Identity during the English Reformation* (Leiden and Boston, MA, 2013).

Dickens, A. G., *The English Reformation*, rev. ed. (London, 1970).

Lollards and Protestants in the Diocese of York, 1509–1558 (Oxford, 1959).

Dillon, Anne, *The Construction of Martyrdom in the English Catholic Community* (Aldershot, 2002).

'John Forest and Derfel Gadarn: a double execution', *Recusant History* [now *British Catholic History*] 28 (2006), pp. 1–21.

Michelangelo and the English Martyrs (Farnham, 2012).

Dixon, C. Scott, 'Luther's Ninety-Five Theses and the origins of the Reformation narrative', *English Historical Review* 132 (2017), pp. 533–69.

Doggett, Nicholas, *Patterns of Re-Use: The Transformation of Former Monastic Buildings in Post-Dissolution Herefordshire* (Oxford, 2002).

Dorson, Richard M., *The British Folklorists: A History* (London, 1968).

Doyle, A. I., 'The library of Sir Thomas Tempest', in G. A. M. Janssens and F. G. A. M. Aarts (eds.), *Studies in Seventeenth-Century Literature, History, and Bibliography* (Amsterdam, 1984), pp. 85–6.

Drabble, John, 'Thomas Fuller, Peter Heylyn and the English Reformation', *Renaissance and Reformation/Renaissance et Réforme*, new series, 3 (1979), pp. 168–88.

Duffy, Eamon, *Fires of Faith: Catholic England Under Mary Tudor* (New Haven, CT, and London, 2009).

Saints, Sacrilege and Sedition: Religion and Conflict in the Tudor Reformations (London, 2012).

The Stripping of the Altars: Traditional Religion in England, 1400–1580, 2nd ed. (New Haven, CT, and London, 2005).

Duffy, Eamon and David Loades (eds.), *The Church of Mary Tudor* (Aldershot, 2006).

Dyer, Christopher and Catherine Richardson (eds.), *William Dugdale, Historian, 1605–1686: His Life, His Writings and His County* (Woodbridge, 2009).

Dzelzainis, Martin, '"Undouted realities": Clarendon on sacrilege', *HJ* 33 (1990), pp. 515–40.

Eekhout, Marianne, 'Celebrating a Trojan horse: memories of the Dutch Revolt in Breda, 1590–1650', in Kuijpers et al. (eds.), *Memory Before Modernity*, pp. 129–48.

Eisenstein, Elizabeth L., *The Printing Press as an Agent of Change*, 2 vols. (Cambridge, 1979).

Elton, G. R., *Policy and Police: The Enforcement of the Reformation in the Age of Thomas Cromwell* (Cambridge, 1972).

Reform and Reformation: England, 1509–1558 (London, 1977).

The Tudor Revolution in Government: Administrative Changes in the Reign of Henry VIII (Cambridge, 1953).

Erler, Mary C., *Reading and Writing During the Dissolution: Monks, Friars, and Nuns, 1530–1558* (Cambridge, 2013).

Erll, Astrid and Ansgar Nünning (eds.), *Cultural Memory Studies: An International and Interdisciplinary Handbook* (Berlin, 2008).

Esser, Raingard M., *The Politics of Memory: The Writing of Partition in the Seventeenth-Century Low Countries* (Leiden and Boston, MA, 2012).

Evenden, Elizabeth and Thomas S. Freeman, *Religion and the Book in Early Modern England: The Making of John Foxe's 'Book of Martyrs'* (Cambridge, 2011).

Fentress, James and Chris Wickham, *Social Memory* (Oxford and Cambridge, MA, 1992).

Ferguson, Arthur B., *Clio Unbound: Perception of the Social and Cultural Past in Renaissance England* (Durham, NC, 1979).

Fincham, Kenneth and Nicholas Tyacke, *Altars Restored: The Changing Face of English Religious Worship, 1547–c. 1700* (Oxford, 2007).

Foot, Sarah, 'Finding the meaning of form: narrative in annals and chronicles', in Nancy Partner (ed.), *Writing Medieval History*, 2nd ed. (London, 2010), pp. 88–108.

Fox, Adam, *Oral and Literate Culture in England, 1500–1700* (Oxford, 2000).

'Friaries: The Carmelites at Taunton', in *A History of the County of Somerset: Volume 2*, ed. William Page (London, 1911), p. 152., *British History Online*, www.british-history.ac.uk/vch/som/vol2/p152.

Fritze, Ronald Harold, '"Truth hath lacked witnesse, tyme wanted light": the dispersal of the English monastic libraries and Protestant efforts at preservation, ca. 1535–1625', *Journal of Library History* 18 (1983), pp. 274–91.

Fulbrook, Mary, *Dissonant Lives: Generations and Violence through the German Dictatorships* (Oxford, 2011).

Fussner, F. Smith, *The Historical Revolution: English Historical Writing and Thought, 1580–1640* (New York, 1962).

Gadd, Ian and Alexandra Gillespie (eds.), *John Stow (1525–1605) and the Making of the English Past* (London, 2004).

Gaimster, David and Roberta Gilchrist (eds.), *The Archaeology of the Reformation, 1480–1580* (Leeds, 2003).

Gaskill, Malcolm, 'Reporting murder: fiction in the archives in early modern England', *Social History* 23 (1998), pp. 1–30.

Gasquet, F. A., *Henry VIII and the Dissolution of the Monasteries*, 2 vols. (London, 1888–9).

Geary, Patrick J., 'Land, language, and memory in Europe, 700–1100', *TRHS* 9 (1999), pp. 169–84.

  Phantoms of Remembrance: Memory and Oblivion at the End of the First Millennium (Princeton, NJ, 1994).

Gedi, Noa and Yigal Elam, 'Collective memory – what is it?', *History and Memory* 8 (1996), pp. 30–50.

Gelling, Margaret, *Signposts to the Past: Place Names and the History of England* (London, 1978).

Gelling, Margaret and Ann Cole, *The Landscape of Place-Names* (Donington, 2000).

Gibbs, Gary G., 'Marking the days: Henry Machyn's manuscript and the mid-Tudor era', in Duffy and Loades (eds.), *The Church of Mary Tudor*, pp. 281–308.

Gillespie, Alexandra, 'Stow's "owlde" manuscripts of London chronicles', in Gadd and Gillespie (eds.), *John Stow*, pp. 57–68.

Gillespie, Alexandra and Oliver Harris, 'Holinshed and the native chronicle tradition', in Kewes et al. (eds.), *Oxford Handbook of Holinshed's Chronicles*, pp. 135–52.

Gillis, John R., 'Memory and identity: the history of a relationship', in John R. Gillis (ed.), *Commemorations: The Politics of National Identity* (Princeton, NJ, 1994), pp. 3–24.

Given-Wilson, Chris, *Chronicles: The Writing of History in Medieval England* (London and New York, 2004).

Gordon, Andrew, *Writing Early Modern London: Memory, Text, and Community* (Basingstoke, 2013).

Gordon, Andrew and Thomas Rist (eds.), *The Arts of Remembrance in Early Modern England: Material Cultures of the Post Reformation* (London, 2013).

Gordon, Bruce, 'History and memory', in Ulinka Rublack (ed.), *The Oxford Handbook of Protestant Reformations* (Oxford, 2016), pp. 765–86.

Gordon, Bruce and Peter Marshall (eds.), *The Place of the Dead: Death and Remembrance in Late Medieval and Early Modern Europe* (Cambridge, 2000).

Gowing, Laura, 'Gender and the language of insult in early modern London', *History Workshop Journal* 35 (1993), pp. 1–21.

Grafton, Anthony, *The Footnote: A Curious History* (Cambridge, MA, 1997).

'Matthew Parker: the book as archive', *History of Humanities* 2 (2017), pp. 15–50.

What Was History? The Art of History in Early Modern Europe (Cambridge, 2007).

Graham, Timothy, 'Matthew Parker's manuscripts: an Elizabethan library and its uses', in Leedham-Green and Webber (eds.), *Cambridge History of Libraries*, pp. 322–42.

Graves, C. Pamela, 'Social space in the English medieval parish church', *Economy and Society* 18 (1989), pp. 297–322.

Greene, Patrick J., 'The impact of the dissolution on monasteries in Cheshire: the case of Norton', in Alan Thacker (ed.), *Medieval Archaeology, Art, and Architecture at Chester* (Leeds, 2000), pp. 152–66.

Greengrass, Mark and Matthew Phillpott, 'John Bale, John Foxe, and the reformation of the English past', *Archiv für Reformationgeschichte* 101 (2010), pp. 275–88.

Greenway, Diana E., 'Dates in history: chronology and memory', *Historical Research* 72 (1999), pp. 127–39.

Griffin, Patsy, '"Twas no religious house till now": Marvell's "Upon Appleton House"', *Studies in English Literature, 1500–1900* 28 (1998), pp. 61–7.

Guinn-Chipman, Susan, *Religious Space in Reformation England: Contesting the Past* (London, 2013).

Gunther, Karl, *Reformation Unbound: Protestant Visions of Reform in England, 1525–1590* (Cambridge, 2014).

Gunther, Karl and Ethan H. Shagan, 'Protestant radicalism and political thought in the reign of Henry VIII', *P&P* 194 (2007), pp. 35–74.

Haigh, Christopher, 'The continuity of Catholicism in the English Reformation', *P&P* 93 (1981), pp. 37–69.

English Reformations: Religion, Politics, and Society Under the Tudors (Oxford, 1993).

The Last Days of the Lancashire Monasteries and the Pilgrimage of Grace (Manchester, 1969).

Halbwachs, Maurice, *Les Cadres Sociaux de la Mémoire* (Paris, 1952), ed. and trans. Lewis A. Coser, *On Collective Memory* (Chicago, 1992).

Hamilton, Gary D., 'Marvell, sacrilege, and Protestant historiography: contextualizing "Upon Appleton House"', in Donna B. Hamilton and Richard Stier (eds.), *Religion, Literature, and Politics in Post-Reformation England, 1540–1688* (Cambridge, 1996), pp. 161–86.

Hamilton, Sarah and Andrew Spicer, 'Defining the holy: the delineation of sacred space', in Sarah Hamilton and Andrew Spicer (eds.), *Defining the Holy: Sacred Space in Medieval and Early Modern Europe* (Aldershot, 2005), pp. 1–24.

Hamilton, Tom, 'The procession of the League: remembering the Wars of Religion in visual and literary satire', *French History* 30 (2016), pp. 1–30.

Hamling, Tara and Richard L. Williams, *Art Re-formed: Re-assessing the Impact of the Reformation on the Visual Arts* (Cambridge, 2007).

Handley, Sasha, *Visions of an Unseen World: Ghost Beliefs and Ghost Stories in Eighteenth-Century England* (London, 2007).

Harding, Vanessa, 'Choices and changes: death, burial and the English Reformation', in Gaimster and Gilchrist (eds.), *Archaeology of the Reformation*, pp. 386–98.

'Monastic records and the dissolution: a Tudor revolution in the archives?', *European History Quarterly* 46 (2016), pp. 480–97.

Harris, Oliver, '"The greatest blow to antiquities that ever England had": the Reformation and the antiquarian resistance', in Jan Frans van Dijkhuizen and Richard Todd (eds.), *The Reformation Unsettled: British Literature and the Question of Religious Identity, 1560–1660* (Turnhout, 2008), pp. 225–42.

Heal, Felicity, 'Appropriating history: Catholic and Protestant polemics and the national past', in Kewes (ed.), *Uses of History*, pp. 105–28.

Hospitality in Early Modern England (Oxford, 1990).

Reformation in Britain and Ireland (Oxford, 2003).

Heal, Felicity and Clive Holmes, *The Gentry in England and Wales, 1500–1700* (Basingstoke and London, 1994).

Heal, Felicity and Henry Summerson, 'The genesis of the two editions', in Kewes, Archer, and Heal (eds.), *Handbook of Holinshed's* Chronicles, pp. 3–20.

Heale, Martin, *Monasticism in Late Medieval England, c. 1300–1535* (Manchester, 2009).

'Training in superstition? Monasteries and popular religion in late medieval and Reformation England', *JEH* 58 (2007), pp. 417–39.

Healy, Tom, '"Making it true": John Foxe's art of remembrance', in Gordon and Rist (eds.), *Arts of Remembrance*, pp. 125–40.

Hen, Yitzhak and Matthew Innes (eds.), *The Uses of the Past in the Early Middle Ages* (Cambridge, 2000).

Hicks, Michael, 'English monasteries as repositories of dynastic memory', in Penman (ed.), *Monuments and Monumentality*, pp. 224–38.

Highley, Christopher, *Catholics Writing the Nation in Early Modern Britain and Ireland* (Oxford, 2008).

'"A pestilent and seditious book": Nicholas Sander's *Schismatis anglicani* and Catholic histories of the Reformation', in Kewes (ed.), *Uses of History*, pp. 153–60.

Hill, Christopher, *Economic Problems of the Church from Archbishop Whitgift to the Long Parliament* (Oxford, 1956).

Hindle, Steve, 'Beating the bounds of the parish: order, memory, and identity in the English local community, c. 1500–1700', in Michael Halvorson and Karen Spierling (eds.), *Defining Community in Early Modern Europe* (Aldershot, 2008), pp. 205–27.

Hiscock, Andrew, *Reading Memory in Early Modern Literature* (Cambridge, 2011).

Hobsbawm, Eric and Terence Ranger (eds.), *The Invention of Tradition*, 2nd ed. (Cambridge).

Howard, Maurice, 'Recycling the monastic fabric: beyond the act of dissolution', in Gaimster and Gilchrist (eds.), *Archaeology of the Reformation*, pp. 221–34.

Hoyle, R. W., 'The origins of the dissolution of the monasteries', *HJ* 38 (1995), pp. 275–305.

The Pilgrimage of Grace and the Politics of the 1530s (Oxford, 2001).

Hui, Andrew, *The Poetics of Ruins in Renaissance Literature* (Oxford, 2017).

Hunt, Arnold, *The Art of Hearing: English Preachers and Their Audiences, 1590–1640* (Cambridge, 2010).

'Laurence Chaderton and the Hampton Court Conference', in Susan Wabuda and Caroline Litzenberger (eds.), *Belief and Practice in Reformation England* (Aldershot, 1998), pp. 207–28.

'Recovering speech acts', in Andrew Hadfield, Matthew Dimmock, and Abigail Shinn (eds.), *The Ashgate Research Companion to Popular Culture in Early Modern England* (Farnham, 2014), pp. 13–30.

Hunter, Michael (ed.), *Printed Images in Early Modern Britain: Essays in Interpretation* (Farnham, 2010).

Hutton, Ronald, 'The English Reformation and the evidence of folklore', *P&P* 148 (1995), pp. 89–116.

The Rise and Fall of Merry England: The Ritual Year, 1400–1700 (Oxford, 1994).

Innes, Matthew, 'Using the past, interpreting the present, influencing the future', in Hen and Innes (eds.), *Uses of the Past*, pp. 1–8.

Jamroziak, Emilia and Janet Burton (eds.), *Religious and Laity in Western Europe, 1000–1400: Interaction, Negotiation, and Power* (Turnhout, 2006).

Janes, Dominic and Gary Waller (eds.), *Walsingham in Literature and Culture from the Middle Ages to Modernity* (Farnham, 2010).

Johanson, Kristine (ed.), 'Approaches to early modern nostalgia', special issue of *Parergon* 33 (2016).

Jones, Andrew, *Memory and Material Culture* (Cambridge, 2007).

Jones, Malcolm, *The Print in Early Modern England: An Historical Oversight* (New Haven, CT, and London, 2010).

Jones, Norman L., *The English Reformation: Religion and Cultural Adaptation* (Oxford, 2002).

'Empowering the earl of Leicester', *Verso: The Blog of the Huntington Library, Art Collections, and Botanical Gardens*, 26 May 2016; www.huntington.org/verso/2018/08/empowering-earl-leicester.

'Living the reformations: generational experience and political perception in early modern England', *Huntington Library Quarterly* 60 (1997), pp. 273–88.

'Matthew Parker, John Bale, and the Magdeburg Centuriators', *SCJ* 12 (1981), pp. 35–49.

Kansteiner, Wulf, 'Finding meaning in memory: a methodological critique of collective memory studies', *History and Theory* 41 (2002), pp. 179–97.

Kastan, David Scott, 'Opening gates and stopping hedges: Grafton, Stow, and the politics of Elizabethan history writing', in Elizabeth Fowler and Roland Greene (eds.), *The Project of Prose in Early Modern Europe and the New World* (Cambridge, 1997), pp. 66–79.

Kaufman, Lucy M., 'Ecclesiastical improvements, lay impropriations, and the building of a post-Reformation church in England, 1560–1600', *HJ* 58 (2015), pp. 1–23.

Kelley, Donald R., *Faces of History: Historical Enquiry from Herodotus to Herder* (New Haven, CT, and London, 1998).

Kelly, Michael Butler, 'The invasion of things sacred: church, property, and sacrilege in early modern England', unpublished PhD thesis, University of Notre Dame (2013).

Ker, Neil R. *Medieval Libraries of Great Britain: A List of Surviving Books* (London, 1941).

Ketelaar, Eric, 'Muniments and monuments: the dawn of archives as cultural patrimony', *Archival Science* 7 (2007), pp. 343–57.

Kewes, Paulina, 'History and its uses', in Kewes (ed.), *Uses of History*, pp. 1–30.

Kewes, Paulina (ed.), *The Uses of History in Early Modern England* (San Marino, CA, 2006).

Kewes, Paulina, Ian Archer, and Felicity Heal (eds.), *The Oxford Handbook of Holinshed's* Chronicles (Oxford, 2013).

Kilroy, Gerard, 'A tangled chronicle: the struggle over the memory of Edmund Campion', in Gordon and Rist (eds.), *Arts of Remembrance*, pp. 141–59.

Klein, Kerwin Lee, 'On the emergence of "memory" in historical discourse', *Representations* 69 (2000), pp. 127–50.

Knapp, James A., *Illustrating the Past in Early Modern England: The Representation of History in Printed Books* (Aldershot, 2003).

Knighton, C. S., 'Westminster Abbey restored', in Duffy and Loades (eds.), *The Church of Mary Tudor*, pp. 77–123.

Knowles, David, *Bare Ruined Choirs: The Dissolution of the English Monasteries* (Cambridge, 1976).

The Religious Orders in England, 3 vols. (Cambridge, 1948–59).

Kuijpers, Erika, 'Between storytelling and patriotic sculpture: the memory brokers of the Dutch Revolt', in Kuijpers et al. (eds.), *Memory Before Modernity*, pp. 183–202.

Kuijpers, Erika, Judith Pollmann, Johannes Müller, and Jasper van der Steen (eds.), *Memory Before Modernity: Practices of Memory in Early Modern Europe* (Leiden and Boston, MA, 2013).

LaGuardia, David P. and Cathy Yandell (eds.), *Memory and Community in Sixteenth-Century France* (Farnham, 2015).

Lake, Peter, *Bad Queen Bess: Libels, Secret Histories, and the Politics of Publicity in the Reign of Queen Elizabeth I* (Oxford, 2016).

'The King (the Queen) and the Jesuit: James Stuart's *True Law of Free Monarchies* in context/s', *TRHS* 14 (2004), pp. 243–60.

'Lancelot Andrewes, John Buckeridge and avant-garde conformity at the court of James I', in Linda Levy Peck (ed.), *The Mental World of the Jacobean Court* (Cambridge, 1991), pp. 113–33.

'The Laudian style: order, uniformity, and the pursuit of the beauty of holiness in the 1630s', in Kenneth Fincham (ed.), *The Early Stuart Church, 1603–1642* (Basingstoke, 1993), pp. 161–85.

Moderate Puritans and the Elizabethan Church (Cambridge, 1982).

Lander, Jesse M., 'The monkish Middle Ages: periodisation and polemic in Foxe's *Acts and monuments*', in Sarah A. Kelen (ed.), *Renaissance Retrospections: Tudor Views of the Middle Ages* (Kalamazoo, MI, 2013), pp. 93–110.

Law, Ceri, *Contested Reformations in the University of Cambridge, 1535–1584* (London, 2018).

Leedham-Green, Elisabeth and Teresa Webber (eds.), *The Cambridge History of Libraries in Britain and Ireland: Volume 1, to 1640* (Cambridge, 2006).

Legon, Edward J., *Revolution Remembered: Seditious Memories after the British Civil Wars* (Manchester, 2019).

Lehmberg, Stanford E., *The Reformation of Cathedrals: Cathedrals in English Society* (Princeton, NJ, 2014).

Levelt, Sjoerd, *Jan van Naaldwijk's Chronicles of Holland: Continuity and Transformation in the Historical Tradition of Holland during the Early Sixteenth Century* (Hilversum, 2011).

Levy, F. J., *Tudor Historical Thought* (San Marino, CA, 1967).

Lindley, Phillip G., '"Pickpurse" purgatory, the dissolution of the chantries, and the suppression of intercession for the dead', *Journal of the British Archaeological Association* 164 (2011), pp. 277–304.

Loades, David, 'The personal religion of Mary I', in Duffy and Loades (eds.), *The Church of Mary Tudor*, pp. 1–30.

Lowenthal, David, *The Past Is a Foreign Country* (Cambridge, 1985).

Lundin, Matthew, Hans Medick, Mitchell Merback, Judith Pollmann, and Susanne Rau, 'Forum: memory before modernity: cultures and practices in early modern Germany', *German History* 33 (2015), pp. 100–22.

Lyon, Harriet, '"A pitiful thing"? The dissolution of the English monasteries in early modern chronicles, c. 1540–c. 1640', *SCJ* 49 (2018), pp. 1037–56.

    'Remembering the dissolution of the monasteries: events, chronology, and memory in Charles Wriothesley's chronicle', in Walsham et al. (eds.), *Memory and the English Reformation*, pp. 64–79.

    '"Superstition remains at this hour": *The Friers Chronicle* (1623) and England's long Reformation', *Reformation* 24 (2019), pp. 107–21.

MacCulloch, Diarmaid, 'The myth of the English Reformation', *Journal of British Studies* 30 (1991), pp. 1–19.

    Tudor Church Militant: Edward VI and the Protestant Reformation (London, 1999).

    'Worcester: a cathedral city in the Reformation', in Collinson and Craig (eds.), *The Reformation in English Towns*, pp. 94–112.

Macaulay, Rose, *Pleasure of Ruins* (New York, 1953).

Macek, Ellen A., 'Advice manuals and the formation of English Protestant and Catholic identities, 1560–1660', in Wim Janse and Barbara Pitkin (eds.), *The Formation of Clerical and Confessional Identities in Early Modern Europe* (Leiden and Boston, MA, 2006), pp. 315–31.

Manley, Lawrence, 'Of sites and rites: ceremony, theatre, and John Stow's *Survey of London*', in Smith, Strier, and Bevington (eds.), *The Theatrical City*, pp. 35–54.

Marshall, Peter, *1517: Martin Luther and the Invention of the Reformation* (Oxford, 2017).

Beliefs and the Dead in Reformation England (Oxford, 2002).

'The debate over "unwritten verities" in early Reformation England', in Bruce Gordon (ed.), *Protestant History and Identity in Sixteenth-Century Europe: Volume 1, The Medieval Inheritance* (Aldershot, 1996), pp. 60–77.

'Forgery and miracles in the reign of Henry VIII', *P&P* 178 (2003), pp. 58–62.

'Is the pope Catholic? Henry VIII and the semantics of schism', in Shagan (ed.), *Catholics and the 'Protestant Nation'*, pp. 22–48.

'Nailing the Reformation: Luther and the Wittenberg door in English historical memory', in Walsham et al. (eds.), *Memory and the English Reformation*, pp. 49–63.

'The naming of Protestant England', *P&P* 214 (2012), pp. 87–128.

'Papist as heretic: the burning of John Forest, 1538', *HJ* 41 (1998), pp. 351–74.

Religious Identities in Henry VIII's England (Aldershot, 2006).

'The Rood of Boxley, the Blood of Hailes and the defence of the Henrician church', *JEH* 46 (1995), pp. 689–96.

Marshall, Peter and Alec Ryrie (eds.), *The Beginnings of English Protestantism* (Cambridge, 2002).

Matsuda, Matt K., *The Memory of the Modern* (Oxford, 1996).

Mayer, Robert, 'The rhetoric of historical truth: Heylyn *contra* Fuller on *The Church-History of Britain*', *Prose Studies* 20 (1997), pp. 1–20.

McBride, Kari, *Country House Discourse in Early Modern England: A Cultural Study of Landscape and Legitimacy* (Aldershot, 2001).

McCall, Fiona, 'Children of Baal: clergy families and their memories of sequestration during the English Civil War', in Neufeld (ed.), 'Uses of the past', pp. 617–38.

McKitterick, Rosamond, *History and Memory in the Carolingian World* (Cambridge, 2004).

McMullan, Gordon and David Matthews (eds.), *Reading the Medieval in Early Modern England* (Cambridge, 2007).

Mendyk, Stan A. E., *'Speculum Britanniae': Regional Study, Antiquarianism, and Science in Britain to 1700* (Toronto and London, 1989).

Merritt, J. F., 'The cradle of Laudianism? Westminster Abbey, 1558–1630', *JEH* 52 (2001), pp. 623–46.

'Puritans, Laudians, and the phenomenon of church-building in Jacobean London', *HJ* 41 (1998), pp. 935–60.

Milton, Anthony, *Catholic and Reformed: The Roman and Protestant Churches in English Protestant Thought, 1600–1640* (Cambridge, 1995).

Laudian and Royalist Polemic in Seventeenth-Century England: The Career and Writings of Peter Heylyn (Manchester, 2007).

Misztal, Barbara A., *Theories of Social Remembering* (Maidenhead, PA, 2003).

'Monks in Motion', Durham University, www.dur.ac.uk/mim/.

Morrill, John, 'William Dowsing, the bureaucratic puritan', in John Morrill, Paul Slack, and Daniel Woolf (eds.), *Public Duty and Private Conscience in Seventeenth-Century England* (Oxford, 1993), pp. 173–204, revised as 'William Dowsing and the administration of iconoclasm', in Cooper (ed.), *Journal of William Dowsing*, pp. 1–28.

Mortimer, Ian, 'Tudor chronicler or sixteenth-century diarist? Henry Machyn and the nature of his manuscript', *SCJ* 33 (2002), pp. 981–98.

Morton, Adam, 'Coming of age? The image in early modern England', *Journal of Early Modern History* 15 (2011), pp. 435–57.

Mottram, Stewart, *Ruin and Reformation in Spenser, Shakespeare, and Marvell* (Oxford, 2019).

Murray, Sophie, 'Dissolving into laughter: anti-monastic satire in the reign of Henry VIII', in Mark Knights and Adam Morton (eds.), *The Power of Laughter and Satire in Early Modern Britain: Political and Religious Culture, 1500–1820* (Woodbridge, 2017), pp. 27–47.

Nockles, Peter and Vivienne Westbrook (eds.), 'Reinventing the Reformation in the nineteenth century: a cultural history', special issue of *Bulletin of the John Rylands Library* 90 (2014).

Neufeld, Matthew, *The Civil Wars After 1660: Public Remembering in Late Stuart England* (Woodbridge, 2013).

Neufeld, Matthew (ed.), 'Uses of the past in early modern England', *Huntington Library Quarterly* 76 (2013).

Nora, Pierre, 'Between memory and history: *les lieux de mémoire*', *Representations* 26 (1989), pp. 7–24.

    Les lieux de mémoire, 3 vols. (Paris, 1984–92), ed. Pierra Nora and Lawrence D. Kritzman, trans. Arthur Goldhammer, *Realms of Memory*, 3 vols. (New York, 1996–8).

Ó Siochrú, Micháel and Jane Ohlmeyer (eds.), *Ireland, 1641: Contexts and Reactions* (Manchester, 2013).

O'Sullivan, Deirdre, 'The "little dissolution" of the 1520s', *Post-Medieval Archaeology* 40 (2006), pp. 227–58.

Olick, Jeffrey K. and Joyce Robbins, 'Social memory studies: from "collective memory" to the historical sociology of mnemonic practices', *Annual Review of Sociology* 24 (1998), pp. 105–40.

Page, R. I., *Matthew Parker and His Books* (Kalamazoo, MI, 1993).

Parish, Helen L., *Monks, Miracles and Magic: Reformation Representations of the Medieval Church* (London and New York, 2005).

'Parishes: Hound with Netley', in *A History of the County of Hampshire: Volume 3*, ed. William Page (London, 1908), pp. 472–478, British History Online, w ww.british-history.ac.uk/vch/hants/vol3/pp472-478.

Parry, Graham, *The Trophies of Time: English Antiquarians of the Seventeenth Century* (Oxford, 1995).

Partner, Jane, '"The swelling hall": Andrew Marvell and the politics of architecture at Nun Appleton House', *Seventeenth Century* 23 (2008), pp. 225–43.

Patterson, Annabel, *Reading Holinshed's Chronicles* (Chicago and London, 1994).

Patton, Brian, 'Preserving property: history, genealogy, and inheritance in "Upon Appleton House"', *Renaissance Quarterly* 49 (1996), pp. 824–39.

Peck, Imogen, *Recollection in the Republics: Memories of the British Civil Wars in England, 1649–1660* (Oxford, 2021).

Penman, Michael (ed.), *Monuments and Monumentality Across Medieval and Early Modern Europe* (Donington, 2013).

Peters, Erin, *Commemoration and Oblivion in Royalist Print Culture, 1658–1667* (Basingstoke, 2017).

Phillpotts, Christopher, 'The houses of Henry VIII's courtiers in London', in Gaimster and Gilchrist (eds.), *Archaeology of the Reformation*, pp. 299–309.

Pocock, J. G. A., 'Machiavelli, Harrington, and English political ideologies in the eighteenth century', *William and Mary Quarterly* 22 (1965), pp. 549–83.

Pollmann, Judith, 'Archiving the present and chronicling for the future in early modern Europe', in Corens, Peters, and Walsham (eds.), *Social History of the Archive*, pp. 231–52.

'Iconoclasts anonymous: why did it take historians so long to identify the image-breakers of 1566?', *Low Countries Historical Review* 131 (2016), pp. 155–76.

Memory in Early Modern Europe, 1500–1800 (Oxford, 2017).

Pollmann, Judith and Erika Kuijpers, 'On the early modernity of modern memory', in Kuijpers et al., *Memory Before Modernity*, pp. 1–23.

Popper, Nicholas, 'From abbey to archive: managing texts and records in early modern England', *Archival Science* 10 (2010), pp. 249–66.

Porter, Roy, 'Seeing the past', *P&P* 118 (1988), pp. 186–205.

Ramsay, Nigel, '"The manuscripts flew about like butterflies": the break-up of English libraries in the sixteenth century', in James Raven (ed.), *Lost Libraries: The Destruction of Great Book Collections since Antiquity* (London, 2004), pp. 125–44.

Rankin, Mark, 'The literary afterlife of Henry VIII, 1558–1625', in Rankin, Highley, and King (eds.), *Henry VIII and His Afterlives*, pp. 94–114.

Rankin, Mark, Christopher Highley, and John N. King (eds.), *Henry VIII and His Afterlives: Literature, Politics, and Art* (Cambridge, 2009).

Reaney, P. H., *The Origin of English Place-Names* (London, 1969).

'Remembering the Reformation', University of Cambridge and University of York, https://internal.hist.cam.ac.uk/rememberingthereformation/index.html.

Rex, Richard, 'The friars in the English Reformation', in Marshall and Ryrie (eds.), *Beginnings of English Protestantism*, pp. 38–59.

Henry VIII and the English Reformation, 2nd ed. (Basingstoke, 2006).

'The religion of Henry VIII', *HJ* 57 (2014), pp. 1–32.

Richards, Thomas, *The Imperial Archive: Knowledge and Fantasy of Empire* (London, 1993).

Richardson, W. C., *History of the Court of Augmentations, 1536–1554* (Baton Rouge, LA, 1961).

Rivett, Gary, 'Peacemaking, parliament, and the politics of the recent past in the English Civil Wars', in Neufeld (ed.), 'Uses of the past', pp. 589–615.

Roberts, Marion, *Dugdale and Hollar: History Illustrated* (Newark, DE, 2002).

Robinson, Benedict Scott, '"Darke speech": Matthew Parker and the reforming of history', *SCJ* 29 (1998), pp. 1061–83.

Ross, Trevor, 'Dissolution and the making of the English literary canon: the catalogues of Leland and Bale', *Renaissance and Reformation/Renaissance et Réforme*, new series, 15 (1991), pp. 57a–80.

Royal, Susan, 'Historian or prophet? John Bale's perception of the past', *Studies in Church History* 49 (2013), pp. 156–67.

Ryrie, Alec, 'Counting sheep, counting shepherds: the problem of allegiance in the English Reformation', in Marshall and Ryrie (eds.), *Beginnings of English Protestantism*, pp. 84–110.

The Gospel and Henry VIII: Evangelicals in the Early English Reformation (Cambridge, 2003).

'The liturgical commemoration of the English Reformation, 1534–1625', in Walsham et al. (eds.), *Memory and the English Reformation*, pp. 422–38.

Sanford, Rhonda Lemke, *Maps and Memory in Early Modern England: A Sense of Place* (London, 2002).

Schama, Simon, *Landscape and Memory* (New York, 1995).

Schwyzer, Philip, *Archaeologies of English Renaissance Literature* (Oxford, 2007).

'The beauties of the land: Bale's books, Aske's abbeys, and the aesthetics of nationhood', *Renaissance Quarterly* 57 (2004), pp. 99–125.

'John Leland and his heirs: the topography of England', in Mike Pincombe and Cathy Shrank (eds.), *The Oxford Handbook of Tudor Literature, 1548–1603* (Oxford, 2009), pp. 238–53.

'"Late" losses and the temporality of early modern nostalgia', *Parergon* 33 (2016), pp. 97–113.

Literature, Nationalism, and Memory in Early Modern England and Wales (Cambridge, 2004).

Scutts, Sarah, '"Truth never needed the protection of forgery": sainthood and miracles in Robert Hegge's "History of St Cuthbert's churches at Lindisfarne, Cuncacestre, and Dunholme" (1625)', in Peter Clarke and Tony Claydon (eds.), *Saints and Sanctity*, Studies in Church History 47 (Woodbridge, 2011), pp. 270–83.

Shagan, Ethan H., *Popular Politics and the English Reformation* (Cambridge, 2003).

Shagan, Ethan H. (ed.), *Catholics and the 'Protestant Nation': Religious Politics and Identity in Early Modern England* (Manchester, 2005).

Shalev, Zur, *Sacred Words and Worlds: Geography, Religion, and Scholarship, 1550–1700* (Leiden and Boston, MA, 2012).

Sharpe, Kevin, *Selling the Tudor Monarchy: Authority and Image in Sixteenth-Century England* (New Haven, CT, and London, 2009).

Sir Robert Cotton, 1586–1681: History and Politics in Early Modern England (Oxford, 1979).

Shell, Alison, *Oral Culture and Catholicism in Early Modern England* (Cambridge, 2007).

Sherlock, Peter, *Monuments and Memory in Early Modern England* (Aldershot, 2008).

'The reformation of memory in early modern Europe', in Susannah Radstone and Bill Schwarz (eds.), *Memory: Histories, Theories, Debates* (New York, 2010), pp. 30–40.

Sherman, William H., *John Dee: The Politics of Reading and Writing in the English Renaissance* (Amherst, MA, 1995).

Shrank, Cathy, 'John Bale and reconfiguring the "medieval" in Reformation England', in McMullan and Matthews (eds.), *Reading the Medieval*, pp. 179–92.

Writing the Nation in Reformation England, 1530–1580 (Oxford, 2004).

Simpson, James, 'Ageism: Leland, Bale, and the laborious start of English literary history, 1350–1550', in Wendy Scase, Rita Copeland, and David Lawton (eds.), *New Medieval Literatures* I (Oxford, 1997), pp. 213–35.

Under the Hammer: Iconoclasm in the Anglo-American Tradition (Oxford, 2010).

Slack, Paul, *The Invention of Improvement: Information and Material Progress in Seventeenth-Century England* (Oxford, 2015).

Smith, Alan, 'The image of Cromwell in folklore and tradition', *Folklore* 79 (1968), pp. 17–39.

Smith, David L., Richard Strier, and David Bevington (eds.), *The Theatrical City: Culture, Theatre and Politics in London, 1576–1649* (Cambridge, 1995).

Smith, Frederick E., 'Religious mobility and the development of English Catholicism, 1534–1558', unpublished PhD thesis, University of Cambridge (2019).

Smyth, Adam, *Autobiography in Early Modern England* (Cambridge, 2010).

Soden, Iain, 'Buildings analysis at Coombe Abbey, Warwickshire, 1993–94', *Post-Medieval Archaeology* 40 (2006), pp. 129–59.

Sommerville, C. John, *The Secularization of Early Modern England: From Religious Culture to Religious Faith* (Oxford, 1992).

Sommerville, Johann, 'Ideology, property, and the constitution', in Richard Cust and Ann Hughes (eds.), *Conflict in Early Stuart England: Studies in Religion and Politics, 1603–1642* (London, 1989), pp. 47–71.

Soulieux-Evans, Alice, 'Cathedrals and the Church of England, c.1660–1714', unpublished PhD thesis, University of Cambridge (2018).

Spence, Jonathan D., *The Memory Palace of Matteo Ricci* (New York, 1984).

Spiegel, Gabrielle M., 'Genealogy: form and function in medieval historical narrative', *History and Theory* 22 (1983), pp. 43–53.

Sponholz, Jesse, *The Convent of Wesel: The Event That Never Was and the Invention of Tradition* (Cambridge, 2017).

Spraggon, Julie, *Puritan Iconoclasm during the English Civil War* (Woodbridge, 2003).

Spufford, Margaret, *Small Books and Pleasant Histories: Popular Fiction and Its Readership in Seventeenth-Century England* (London, 1981).

Starkie, Andrew, 'Henry VIII in history: Gilbert Burnet's History of the Reformation (v. 1), 1679', in Betteridge and Freeman (eds.), *Henry VIII and History* (Farnham, 2012), pp. 151–63.

Starobinksi, Jean, 'The idea of nostalgia', trans. William S. Kemp, *Diogenes* 54 (1966), pp. 84–103.

Stoler, Ann Laura, *Along the Archival Grain: Epistemic Anxieties and Colonial Common Sense* (Princeton, NJ, 2010).

Stoyle, Mark, 'Remembering the English Civil Wars', in Peter Gray and Kendrick Oliver (eds.), *The Memory of Catastrophe* (Manchester, 2004), pp. 19–30.

Strauss, Gerald, 'Ideas of *Reformatio* and *Renovatio* from the Middle Ages to the Reformation', in Thomas A. Brady, Jr., Heiko A. Oberman, and James D. Tracy (eds.), *Handbook of European History, 1400–1600: Late Middle Ages, Renaissance and Reformation*, 2 vols. (Leiden, New York, and Cologne, 1995), i, pp. 1–30.

Summit, Jennifer, 'Leland's "Itinerary" and the remains of the medieval past', in McMullan and Matthews (eds.), *Reading the Medieval*, pp. 159–76.

  Memory's Library: Medieval Books in Early Modern England (Chicago, 2008).

Summit, Jennifer and David Wallace (eds.), 'Medieval/Renaissance: after periodisation', special issue of the *Journal of Medieval and Early Modern Studies* 37 (2007).

Sutermeister, Helen, 'Excavations on the site of the Tudor manor house at Micheldever, Hampshire', *Post-Medieval Archaeology* 9 (1975), pp. 117–36.

Sweet, Rosemary, *Antiquaries: The Discovery of the Past in Eighteenth-Century Britain* (London and New York, 2004).

Tarlow, Sarah, 'Reformation and transformation: what happened to Catholic things in a Protestant world?', in Gaimster and Gaines (eds.), *Archaeology of the Reformation*, pp. 108–21.

Thomas, Keith, 'Age and Authority in Early Modern England', The Raleigh Lecture, *Proceedings of the British Academy* 62 (1976), pp. 205–48.

  'Art and iconoclasm in early modern England', in Kenneth Fincham and Peter Lake (eds.), *Religious Politics in Post-Reformation England: Essays in Honour of Nicholas Tyacke* (Woodbridge, 2006), pp. 16–40.

  The Perception of the Past in Early Modern England, The Creighton Trust Lecture (London, 1983).

  Religion and the Decline of Magic: Studies in Popular Beliefs in Sixteenth- and Seventeenth-Century England, 4th ed. (London, 1997).

Thompson, Benjamin, 'Monasteries, society, and reform in late medieval England', in Clark (ed.), *Religious Orders in Pre-Reformation England*, pp. 165–96.

  'The polemic of reform in the later medieval English church', in Almut Suerbaum, George Southcombe, and Benjamin Thompson (eds.), *Polemic: Language as Violence in Medieval and Early Modern Discourse* (Farnham, 2015), pp. 183–222.

Till, Karen E., 'Memory studies', *History Workshop Journal* 62 (2006), pp. 325–41.

Tite, Colin G. C., *The Early Records of Sir Robert Cotton's Library: Formation, Cataloguing, Use* (London, 2003).

The Manuscript Library of Sir Robert Cotton (London, 1994).

Trevelyan, G. M., *History of England* (London, 1926).

Tumblety, Joan (ed.), *Memory and History: Understanding Memory as Source and Subject* (London, 2013).

Tyacke, Nicholas (ed.), *England's Long Reformation, 1500–1800* (London, 1998).

van der Steen, Jasper, *Memory Wars in the Low Countries, 1566–1750* (Leiden and Boston, MA, 2015).

van Liere, Katherine, Simon Ditchfield, and Harold Louthan (eds.), *Sacred History: Uses of the Christian Past in the Renaissance World* (Oxford, 2012).

Vine, Angus, *In Defiance of Time: Antiquarian Writing in Early Modern England* (Oxford, 2010).

Wabuda, Susan, *Preaching during the English Reformation* (Cambridge, 2002).

Walker, Claire, *Gender and Politics in Early Modern Europe: English Convents in France and the Low Countries* (Basingstoke, 2003).

Walker, Greg, '"To speak before the king, it is no child's play": Godly Queen Hester in 1529', *Theta* 10 (2013), pp. 69–96.

Writing Under Tyranny: English Literature and the Henrician Reformation (Oxford, 2005).

Waller, Gary, *Walsingham and the English Imagination* (Farnham, 2011).

Walsham, Alexandra, 'The art of iconoclasm and the afterlife of the English Reformation', in Antoinina Bevan-Zlatar and Olga Timofeeva (eds.), *What was an Image in Medieval and Early Modern England?*, Swiss Papers in English Language and Literature 34 (Tübingen, 2017), pp. 478–81.

'Chronicles, memory, and autobiography in Reformation England', *Memory Studies* 11 (2018), pp. 36–50.

'History, memory, and the English Reformation', *HJ* 55 (2012), pp. 899–938.

'Idols in the frontispiece? Illustrating religious books in the age of iconoclasm', in Feike Dietz, Adam Morton, Lien Roggen, Els Stronks, and Marc van Vaeck (eds.), *Illustrated Religious Texts in the North of Europe, 1500–1800* (Farnham, 2014), pp. 21–52.

'"Like fragments of a shipwreck": printed images and religious antiquarianism in early modern England', in Michael Hunter (ed.), *Printed Images*, pp. 87–109.

'Matthew Parker, sacred geography, and the British past', unpublished paper, 'Matthew Parker: Archbishop, Scholar, and Collector', Centre for Research in the Arts, Humanities, and Social Sciences and Corpus Christi College, Cambridge, 17 March 2016.

Providence in Early Modern England (Oxford, 1999).

'Providentialism', in Kewes, Archer, and Heal (eds.), *Oxford Handbook of Holinshed's* Chronicles, pp. 427–42.

'The Reformation and "the Disenchantment of the World" reassessed', *HJ* 51 (2008), pp. 497–528.

'The reformation of the generations: youth, age, and religious change in England, *c.* 1500–1700', *TRHS* 21 (2011), pp. 93–121.

The Reformation of the Landscape: Religion, Identity, and Memory in Early Modern Britain and Ireland (Oxford, 2011).

'Reformed folklore? Cautionary tales and oral tradition in early modern England', in Adam Fox and Daniel Woolf (eds.), *The Spoken Word: Oral Culture in Britain, 1500–1800* (Manchester, 2002), pp. 173–95.

'Richard Carew and English topography' in Richard Carew, *The survey of Cornwall*, ed. John Chynoweth, Nicholas Orme, and Alexandra Walsham, Devon and Cornwall Record Society, new series, 47 (Exeter, 2004), pp. 17–41.

Walsham, Alexandra, Bronwyn Wallace, Ceri Law, and Brian Cummings (eds.), *Memory and the English Reformation* (Cambridge, 2020).

Ward, John O., '"Chronicle" and "History": the medieval origins of postmodern historiographical practice?', *Parergon* 14 (1997), pp. 101–28.

Warnicke, Retha M., *William Lambarde: Elizabethan Antiquary, 1536–1601* (London and Chichester, 1973).

Watt, Diane, *Secretaries of God: Women Prophets in Late Medieval and Early Modern England* (Cambridge, 1997).

Watt, Tessa, *Cheap Print and Popular Piety, 1550–1640* (Cambridge, 1991).

West, William N., '"No endlesse moniment": artificial memory and memorial artefact in early modern England', in Susannah Radstone and Katharine Hodgkin (eds.), *Regimes of Memory* (London, 2003), pp. 61–75.

'Who were the nuns?', Queen Mary University of London, https://wwtn.history .qmul.ac.uk.

Whyte, Nicola, *Inhabiting the Landscape: Place, Custom and Memory, 1500–1800* (Oxford, 2009).

Williams, Kelsey Jackson, *The Antiquary: John Aubrey's Historical Scholarship* (Oxford, 2016).

Willmott, Hugh, *The Dissolution of the Monasteries in England and Wales* (Sheffield, 2020).

Willmott, Hugh and Alan Bryson, 'Changing to suit the times: a post-dissolution history of Monk Bretton Priory, South Yorkshire', *Post-Medieval Archaeology* 47 (2013), pp. 136–63.

Wilson, Janet, 'A catalogue of the "unlawful" books found in John Stow's study on 21 February 1568/9', *Recusant History* 20 (1990), pp. 1–30.

Winter, Jay, *Remembering War: The Great War and Historical Memory in the Twentieth Century* (New Haven, CT, 2006).

Sites of Memory, Sites of Mourning (Cambridge, 1995).

Womersley, David, 'Against the teleology of technique', in Kewes et al., *Uses of History*, pp. 91–104.

Wood, Andy, *The 1549 Rebellions and the Making of Early Modern England* (Cambridge, 2007).

'History, time and social memory', in Keith Wrightson (ed.), *A Social History of England 1500–1750* (Cambridge, 2017), pp. 373–91.

The Memory of the People: Custom and Popular Senses of the Past in Early Modern England (Oxford, 2013).

Riot, Rebellion, and Popular Politics in Early Modern England (Basingstoke, 2001).

Wooding, Lucy, *Henry VIII*, 2nd ed. (London, 2015).

'Remembrance in the Eucharist', in Gordon and Rist (eds.), *The Arts of Remembrance*, pp. 19–36.

Rethinking Catholicism in Reformation England (Oxford, 2000).

Woodward, G. W. O., *The Dissolution of the Monasteries* (London, 1966).

Woolf, D. R., 'The "common voice": history, folklore, and oral tradition in early modern England', *P&P* 120 (1988), pp. 26–52.

'Genre into artifact: the decline of the English chronicle in the sixteenth century', *SCJ* 19 (1988), pp. 321–45.

The Idea of History in Early Stuart England: Erudition, Ideology, and the 'Light of Truth' from the Accession of James I to the Civil War (Toronto, 1990).

Reading History in Early Modern England (Cambridge, 2000).

The Social Circulation of the Past: English Historical Culture, 1500–1730 (Oxford, 2003).

Worden, Blair, 'Oliver Cromwell and the sin of Achan' in Derek Beales and Geoffrey Best (eds.), *History, Society, and the Churches: Essays in Honour of Owen Chadwick* (Cambridge, 1985), pp. 125–46.

Roundhead Reputations: The English Civil Wars and the Passions of Posterity (London, 2001).

Wright, C. E., 'The dispersal of the libraries in the sixteenth century', in Francis Wormald and C. E. Wright (eds.), *The English Library before 1700: Studies in Its History* (London, 1958), pp. 148–75.

Yale, Elizabeth, *Sociable Knowledge: Natural History and the Nation in Early Modern Britain* (Philadelphia, 2015).

'With slips and scraps: how early modern naturalists invented the archive', *Book History* 12 (2009), pp. 1–36.

Yates, Frances A., *The Art of Memory* (Chicago, 1966).

Yorke, Peter David, 'Iconoclasm, ecclesiology, and the "beauty of holiness": concepts of sacrilege and the peril of idolatry in early modern England', unpublished PhD thesis, University of Kent (1997).

Youings, Joyce, *The Dissolution of the Monasteries* (London, 1971).

Zemon Davis, Natalie, *Fiction in the Archives: Pardon Tales and Their Tellers in Sixteenth-Century France* (Stanford, CA, 1987).

Index

Brutus of Troy, 112
Buckfast Abbey, Devon, 161, 166
Burgh, Christiana, prioress of Nunkeeling, 44
Burnet, Gilbert, 118–19, 174, 246
Bury St Edmunds Abbey, Suffolk, 27, 136
Butley Priory, Kent, 210
Byford, Mark, 45
Byland Abbey, North Yorkshire, *177*
Byng, John, 212

Caesar, Julius, 112
Calwich Priory, Staffordshire, 165
Cambridge, University of, 61, *see also* Christ's
    College, Cambridge; Corpus Christi
    College, Cambridge; Peterhouse,
    Cambridge; St John's College, Cambridge
Camden Society, 74
Camden, William, 136, 138, 148, 150, 157, 159, 161,
    162, 167
Campion, Edmund, SJ, 134
Canterbury Cathedral, Kent, 153, 210
Carew, Richard, 132, 164, 189
Carthusian martyrs, 47–8, 53, 97, 105
cartography, 180, 185
Catesby Priory, Northamptonshire, 31
Catholicism and monastic reform, 28, 105–6
Cecil, William, lord Burghley, 69–70, 100
Chaderton, Laurence, 108–9
chantries, dissolution of, 86, 95, 117
Chapuys, Eustace, 43–4, 51
charity, decline of, 62, 108, 109, 110, 213, *see also*
    gentry; religious orders
Charles I, king of England and Scotland, 226,
    227
Charles II, king of England and Scotland, 229
Charles V, Holy Roman Emperor, 44
Charterhouse, London, 30, 47
Chatteris Abbey, Cambridgeshire, 167
Chauncy, Maurice, prior of Sheen, 54
Christ Church College [Cardinal College],
    Oxford, 29
Christ Church Greyfriars, London, 145, 148
Christ's College, Cambridge, 29
Christchurch Priory, Dorset, 38–9
Civil Wars, 13, 19, 77, 139, 176, 196, 211, 227
Clark, James G., 7, 50
Claxton, William, 137
Clifford Priory, Hertfordshire, 42
Cogges Abbey, Oxfordshire, 212
Colchester Abbey, Essex, 170
Collaton, Agnes, 204
Collinson, Patrick, 107, 173
Connerton, Paul, 97
conversion of monastic property, 127, 143, 146,
    150, 153, 163, 189

into parish churches, 147, 149–50, 152, 155, 156,
    157, 218
into private houses, 144, 158–69
into schools, 58
into secular cathedrals, 151
Cooke, Kathleen, 44
Cooper, Thomas, 103
Corpus Christi College, Cambridge. *See* Parker
    Library
Cosin, John, bishop of Durham, 109, 226
Cotton Library, 16–17, 67–8, 69, 140, 243
Cotton, Sir John, 140
Cotton, Sir Robert, 16, 67, 243
Court of Augmentations, 4, 5, 66
Cowper, Thomas, 199
Coxford Priory, Norfolk, 225
Cramsie, John, 128
Cranmer, Margaret, 94
Cranmer, Thomas, archbishop of Canterbury,
    15, 55
Crayford, John, 218
Creake Abbey, Norfolk, 29
Cressy, David, 14, 121
Cromwell, Oliver, 211, 227, 234
Cromwell, Sir Henry, 168, 234
Cromwell, Sir Richard, 234
Cromwell, Thomas, 3, 15, 25, 58, 60, 66, 68, 73, 81,
    211, 227, 234, 243
    correspondence with commissioners for the
        dissolution, 27, 30–1, 32, 35, 38, 59, 65, 67,
        68, 74, 243
    correspondence with heads of house, 48
    reputation and the dissolution, 53
Cross, Claire, 44
Crossed Friars, London, 30, 148
Crossing, Richard, 203, 205
Crouchback, Edmund, earl of Lancaster,
    Leicester, and Darby, 145
Crowland Abbey, Lincolnshire, 156, 183, *184*
Cudworth, Ralph, 222
Culmer, Richard, 150–1
Cunich, Peter, 5
Cust, Richard, 164

Darcy, Thomas, Lord Darcy, 51
Dartford Priory, Kent, 159
Daventry Priory, Northamptonshire, 167
Davies, Catherine, 64
Dee, John, 242
Degge, Sir Simon, 228
Denton, John, 157n
Denton, Thomas, 157, 162, 189
Denys, Sir Thomas, 86
Dickens, A. G., 98, 245
Dillon, Anne, 47, 53

For EU product safety concerns, contact us at Calle de José Abascal, 56–1°, 28003 Madrid, Spain or eugpsr@cambridge.org.

www.ingramcontent.com/pod-product-compliance
Ingram Content Group UK Ltd.
Pitfield, Milton Keynes, MK11 3LW, UK
UKHW020357140625
459647UK00020B/2523